The concept of sovereignty is central to international relations theory and theories of state formation, and provides the foundation of the conventional separation of modern politics into domestic and international spheres. In this book Jens Bartelson provides a critical analysis and conceptual history of sovereignty, dealing with this separation as reflected in philosophical and political texts during three periods: the Renaissance, the Classical Age, and Modernity. He argues that the concept of sovereignty and its place within political discourse are conditioned by philosophical and historiographical discontinuities between the periods, and that sovereignty should be regarded as a concept contingent upon, rather than fundamental to, political science and its history.

T0382479

CAMBRIDGE STUDIES IN INTERNATIONAL RELATIONS: 39

A genealogy of sovereignty

Cambridge Studies in International Relations is a joint initiative of Cambridge University Press and the British International Studies Association (BISA). The series will include a wide range of material, from undergraduate textbooks and surveys to research-based monographs and collaborative volumes. The aim of the series is to publish the best new scholarship in International Studies from Europe, North America and the rest of the world.

CAMBRIDGE STUDIES IN INTERNATIONAL RELATIONS

Series list continues after index.

A genealogy of sovereignty

Jens Bartelson
University of Stockholm

CAMBRIDGE
UNIVERSITY PRESS

Published by the Press Syndicate of the University of Cambridge
The Pitt Building, Trumpington Street, Cambridge CB2 1RP
40 West 20th Street, New York, NY 10011–4211, USA
10 Stamford Road, Oakleigh, Melbourne 3166, Australia

First published 1995
Reprinted 1996

A catalogue record for this book is available from the British Library

Library of Congress cataloguing in publication data
Bartelson, Jens.
A genealogy of sovereignty / Jens Bartelson.
  p.   cm. – (Cambridge studies in international relations: 39)
ISBN 0 521 47308 X (hardback). – ISBN 0 521 47888 X (pbk.)
1. Sovereignty.   I. Title.   II. Series.
JC327.B245   1995
320.1\5 – dc20   94–30053   CIP

ISBN 0 521 47308 X hardback
ISBN 0 521 47888 X paperback

Transferred to digital printing 2001

CE

Contents

Preface

This book is a treatise on political knowledge. It is a book about the concept of sovereignty and its relationship to truth, and tries to chronicle some of the major changes this relationship has undergone from the Renaissance to the present.

If this book proves to be hard reading, it is partly because the nature of its subject matter made it hard to write. In order to cover a large territory without merely iterating commonplaces, I had to phrase my questions in an abstract idiom. In order to answer these questions without merely reflecting present prejudices, I had to circumvent the trappings of an old vocabulary. In order to circumvent these trappings without becoming utterly incomprehensible, I had to impute new meaning to old terms and use new terms to convey old meanings.

This book nourishes itself on the possibility of such recontextualization and reinterpretation of terms and concepts, and implicitly argues that this is what political philosophy is all about. This insight is far from original, nor are many of the philosophical arguments presented in this book; its contribution is intended to be more specific, and concerns the consequences of such assumptions for the concept of sovereignty and its history.

As such, this book has grown out of the suspicion that the relationship between questions of authority and questions of truth are more closely interlinked than modern political philosophy and modern history of political ideas have been capable or willing to admit, and that the very divide within modern political science between political questions and the apolitical ones itself is the result of a specific politics of truth. In short, this book seeks to amend this situation by, as it were, *rephilosophizing* politics and *repoliticizing* philosophy.

Some people unintentionally encouraged me to pursue this suspicion. Others intentionally encouraged me to pursue my work
regardless of my suspicions (or theirs). Kjell Goldmann, who has had
the dubious pleasure of supervising my work, has done so with
remarkable patience and critical skill. Erik Ringmar, with whom dialogue has been precious throughout, has contributed generously with
his time and erudition in all phases of my work. Tomas Tranæus has
bothered to read drafts of most chapters with an eye to style; Donald
Lavery read all of them with meticulous attention to grammar. Bo
Lindensjö, Rune Premfors, Cecilia Sjöholm, Erik Tängerstad and Björn
Wittrock all intervened at the final stage of my work and contributed
with many helpful suggestions.

1 Introduction: Sovereignty and fire

What is sovereignty? If there are questions political science ought to be able to answer, this is certainly one. Yet modern political science often testifies to its own inability when it tries to come to terms with the concept and reality of sovereignty; it is as if we cannot do to our contemporaneity what Bodin, Hobbes and Rousseau did to theirs.

Thus posed, the question of sovereignty can be brushed aside as irrelevant to modern political science. One could argue that the discipline has outgrown the need to wrestle with general concepts, and should devote itself exclusively to their concrete instantiations in empirical reality. Today, when empirical reality furnishes us with a great many sovereignty struggles, we should step down from the ivory tower and concentrate on less abstract problems, perhaps to the benefit of their very concrete victims.

Still, the general question of sovereignty is likely to enter through the back door. With some simplification, one could say that the question of sovereignty is to political science what the question of substance is to philosophy; a question tacitly implied in the very practice of questioning. However much we want to get down to earth, few would deny that modern political reality has the state as one of its constituent parts, however intangible and porous it seems at closer inspection, whether this closer inspection purports to deal with questions about 'autonomy', 'integration', 'democracy', or 'justice'.

Typically, when the political scientist stumbles upon the state as a unit of analysis, and is forced to define it as an object of investigation, he will once again become entangled in a discourse on sovereignty as its defining property; for what makes a state a state? Simply put, and as I hope to make clear, to the extent that modern political science deals with political phenomena that are conditioned by the presence of states, it will necessarily presuppose *some* answer to the question of sovereignty in its attempt to classify and investigate those phenomena. Thus, our will to political knowledge is intertwined with the notion of sovereignty right from the start.

Now this book is not an attempt to answer the question of what sovereignty *is*; rather, it is a study of what happens today as well as what has happened in the past when others have tried to answer this essentially essentialist question. It is an attempt to investigate the relationship between sovereignty and truth. Doing this, the overall objective of this study is to provide a conceptual history of sovereignty in its relationship to the conditions of knowledge. Given the nature of the subject matter, what would such a history look like?

As I will argue throughout this book, a history of basic political concepts such as sovereignty necessitates a change in methodological orientation from what is established practice within the study of political ideas. Contrary to the convictions of the conceptual analyst, I will insist that the relationship between the very term sovereignty, the concept of sovereignty and the reality of sovereignty is historically open, contingent and unstable. Contrary to the convictions of the contextualist historian of political thought, I will insist that the history of sovereignty is more a matter of swift and partly covert epistemic discontinuity than of a ceaseless battle of overt opinions taking place within delimited and successive contexts. Nevertheless, and now contrary to the convictions of the conceptual historian, I will insist that the history of sovereignty ought to be studied not in isolation or within a narrow temporal frame of inferential and rhetorical connections, but in terms of its multiple relations with other concepts within larger discursive wholes, these not being necessarily confined to political ones. Finally, contrary to the convictions of the structuralist historian of ideas, I will, however, insist that these conceptual systems or discourses are open-ended and subject to constant modification by means of rhetoric – a battle over truth which moves discourse forward in unexpected directions more by its unintended consequences than by its intended ones.

But why embark upon such a study, which is most likely to be both abstract and laborious? Let us for a moment dwell upon the relationship between sovereignty and knowledge; is not the connection between them already fairly clear to the political scientist? Sovereignty, either as a general concept or as a property of individual states, is already a *given* to experience, semantically or empirically. All that needs to be done is to disentangle the concept from the ambiguities of its everyday use, and give it a sufficiently precise operational definition as a defining characteristic of the modern state. If this were done, sovereignty would be a ready-made object of inquiry for political science, and all further questions of sovereignty would then be empirical ones; under what conditions are we entitled to speak of a state as being sovereign? Exactly where in this or that particular state is sovereignty located?

To this it is of course possible to reply that sovereignty ultimately is something man-made, and also deserves to be studied as such in its reflexive relationship to knowledge and political reality. Not only is hermeneutics able to mark out a territory of his own: it is likewise possible to reply critically that this fight against ambiguity itself is a peculiarity of the sovereign state, and that empiricism is integral to this strategy.[1] But let us for a brief moment stay empiricist, and suppose that sovereignty, like a natural phenomenon, is, at least potentially, a given to experience as an objective reality, and that it is open to investigation as such.

In speaking of something as an object, we are generally inclined to think that we are objective about it, but because we chose it in the first place, there is a possibility that the object of our choice reveals more about us than we do about it. Take fire: since prehistory, fire has been available to human experience as a *datum*. Still, despite the apparent uniformity of the objective phenomenon of fire, it is close to impossible to discern a corresponding uniformity in the accounts of fire since antiquity. From ancient teachings on the elements, through medieval alchemy to early-modern phlogiston theory, fire is an object of knowledge, yet the accounts of it vary to the point of incommensurability. More puzzling, when the question of fire is raised today, one is likely to discover that fire no longer is a reality for science; there is a theory of combustion, but whenever the original question is posed, answers are likely to repeat the most ancient and most fanciful explanations. In modern textbooks in physics, it is as if fire did not exist.[2]

Yet if fire does not exist, we still speak and act as if it did. The same goes for sovereignty. For all that we know, most human societies have confronted problems of power and authority, and where they should be located. Yet recipes differ from one another, in form and content as well as through space and time; within the regional context of European political thought, we can discern how the source and locus of authority is distributed downwards in a slow chronological series, ranging from God to king, and then from king to people. Yet our textbooks in political science have become increasingly silent on the topic of sovereignty; since the latest upsurge in the decades immediately before and after the Second World War, the question of sovereignty is seldom raised, and when it occasionally has been, answers tend uncritically to repeat premodern or early-modern formulæ, or to sociologize it away as reminiscent of a bygone age.

So perhaps we should do to sovereignty what Gaston Bachelard, a physicist who turned to literary criticism, did to fire; we should avoid the direct question of what sovereignty is, and instead ask *how* it has been spoken of and known throughout a period of time, and connect the answer to this question with the question of *why* it seems so difficult to speak of and to know sovereignty today. Posed in this way, the question of sovereignty instead becomes a question of the unthought foundations of our political knowledge and how they relate to the concept of sovereignty, when stripped of all predetermined content and opened to definitional change over time.[3]

This strategy provokes yet another why. Who is going to benefit from such an inquiry? Certainly not our politicians; the outcome will surely not add to the rhetorical resources of someone involved in a struggle over sovereignty, who instead risks being exposed to laughter. Perhaps the mainstream political scientist; hopefully the outcome will prove edifying to him. But also perhaps a bit disturbing. For every inquiry must depart from somewhere, from a point that is self-evident or at least held to be unproblematic, and since the present inquiry has for its object precisely such points of agreement, it will consequently set these points in motion, expose them to contingency, and deprive them of their unproblematic status. As such, it is likely to have an effect on the mainstream political scientist which is analogous to the effects of *his* inquiry upon the ideological protagonist.

If the perspective of the mainstream political scientist is the one of a detached spectator who tries to understand clashes between different versions of the political good, the perspective of this book is the one of the detached spectator who tries to understand clashes between different versions of political truth. Thus, if it is accepted as true that every inquiry must start from somewhere, from where do you start if the object of inquiry is starting points? How can one claim to be a detached spectator, if the position of the detached spectator itself is held to be contingent, quite Protestant and sometimes rather illusionary? Is it

4

possible to study truth-games without becoming involved in them *or* being altogether arbitrary in relation to them?

As we shall see in chapter 3, my response to these problems is that of a spectator who not only tries to be detached from his subject matter, but also *incredulous* towards it by stripping it of some of its pretence. By approaching political science and history as modes of writing rather than as modes of being, we can situate ourselves as detached spectators *within* history, and can avoid making our detachment dependent on something *outside* it. As I shall argue, this is possible by starting out from a problematicization of what appears as evident in the present. Doing this, we can disclaim the Platonic concept of truth, and instead look into the effective formation of *truths*, including the truth of our own story, which would then be arbitrary only to the extent that it is undetermined, and false only to the extent that it claims to be itself timeless, and thus self-refuting.[4]

As a consequence, perhaps the addressees who will reap most benefit from this study are the political philosopher and the historian of political ideas, and among them especially the ones who deal with thought on international relations. As we shall see in chapter 2, we recently have witnessed a renewed interest in the concept of sovereignty among a tiny fraction of scholars devoted to the philosophy of international relations. The upshot of this reappropriation of the concept of sovereignty has been largely critical, and, to my knowledge, no systematic study of sovereignty has yet been undertaken within this field. To the extent that political philosophy merits the label of a science, this fact furnishes another rationale for studying sovereignty. There are few up-to-date studies on sovereignty, and those which do exist tend to take for granted precisely that which is profoundly problematic about sovereignty, or to reconfirm those very distinctions and concepts they set out to analyse.[5]

Simply stated, the main thesis of this book is that sovereignty and knowledge implicate each other logically and produce each other historically. This thesis is based on the more general assumption that knowledge is political, and politics is based on knowledge. If this thesis is circular, it remains for me to explicate this circularity as a healthy one, which better helps us to understand both sovereignty and knowledge as well as their actual historical relationships. Since this book is devoted to such an explication, a few formal and introductory remarks will suffice here.

First, this circle is not closed at the level of definition, since both concepts are held open as to their definitional content, which must remain a historical question. Second, this circle is not closed logically, as in a tautology, since this would indicate a stable inferential connection between concepts, and leave nothing for us to investigate. Third, this circle is not closed from a position outside it, from which we safely could observe the interplay between ready-made and well-defined concepts. If the thesis displays circularity, it is because this circularity is repeated in the topic under investigation as well as in the structure of the study itself. If history is a mode of writing rather than a mode of being, a study of history as narrative must itself be a historical narrative, and follow a narrative course which to an extent reflects the structure of the investigated narratives.[6]

Let us now turn to the *a priori* warrant of the thesis. What makes knowledge political, and what makes politics knowable? Formally, any decision about what is political and what is not political is in itself a political decision.[7] As such, any decision upon the political is a decision based on knowledge, since it either must be taken within a specific body of knowledge or must be legitimized from a vantage point which renders the distinction itself clear-cut or fruitful.

If knowledge is understood as a system for the formation of valid statements, all knowledge is knowledge by differentiation, and this differentiation is a political activity. First, in order to constitute itself as such, some given knowledge must demarcate itself from what is external to it, from what is not knowledge, be it opinion, ideology or superstition. Second, knowledge reproduces itself by internal differentiation, by discriminating between the clear and the opaque, the relevant and the irrelevant, the valid and the invalid, the true and the false. Thus, knowledge implies a set of *ontological* decisions; what does exist, and what does not exist; what is present as an object, and what is absent? From these decisions, two other decisions follow. One is *ethical*, and tells us who *we* are, who is a friend, who is an enemy and who is a stranger. In short, the ethical decision is one of deciding who is Same and who is Other. The other decision is *metahistorical*, and tells us where *we* came from, how *we* became friends, how *we* got here, where *we* are, and where *we* are heading. In short, knowledge, being political to the extent that it differentiates, is indissolubly intertwined with identity and history.

Now knowledge does not differentiate itself wholly by itself; differentiation invariably involves the objects, subjects and concepts that occupy the spaces and positions defined by knowledge. It is here that the problem of sovereignty enters; it is here that the concept of sovereignty is filled with a historically variable content. As such, sovereignty does not stand in a predetermined and internal relation to knowledge, nor in an undetermined and external relation to it. Rather, the relation between sovereignty and knowledge is undetermined *and* internal, and is therefore also a historically open and productive circuit. This productive relationship can be broken down into three distinct types.

First, there is a relation of *supplementation*, by which sovereignty sustains and reinforces the decisions on differentiation within a given knowledge, and by which a given concept of sovereignty is sustained by a specific differentiation within a given knowledge. Second, there is a relation of *articulation*, by which sovereignty is articulated and legitimized within a given knowledge, and by which a given knowledge is articulated and legitimized through a given concept of sovereignty. Third, there is a relation of *duplication*, by which the positions of objects, subjects and concepts constituted by a given knowledge are doubled by the position allotted to objects, subjects and concepts by a given concept of sovereignty.

The primary objective of this book is to describe these conceptual relations within three different periods – the Renaissance, the Classical Age, and Modernity – each of them representing a specific arrangement of knowledge, a specific mode of differentiation and a specific arrangement of sovereignty. A secondary objective is to account for the effective transition between these epistemic arrangements in terms of the internal and undetermined relation between knowledge and the concept of sovereignty. A tertiary but no less important objective is to comment upon and to criticize existing philosophical and historical accounts of sovereignty.

The general approach of this study is genealogical, a notion that will be developed more fully in chapter 3. To say that a study is genealogical is to say three things. First, in so far as genealogy is a historical method, it attempts to be effective history. A genealogy is not a history of the past. Histories of the past can be written either in terms of a present, or in terms of a hypothetical and perhaps idealized future, whereas genealogy is a history of the present in terms of its past. Being effective, it is not a history of causal connections between opinions or precursive relationships between ideological positions, but a history of logical spaces and their succession in time. In order to be effective, a genealogy must start from an analysis of the present, and explain the formation of this present in terms of its past; a genealogy has not as its task to tell what actually happened in the past, but to describe how the present became logically possible. Doing this, I will start out by an analysis of the relationship between sovereignty and empirical knowledge within contemporary political science, and then seek to account for the formation of this configuration in time. Second, and in order to be effective history, genealogy must be episodical. It does not aim to describe or explain past ages or past world-views in their entirety, but focuses only on those episodes of the past which are crucial to our understanding of what was singled out as problematic in the present. Third, in order to be episodical, genealogy must also be *exemplary*. The historical argument of genealogy proceeds by means of examples, and these examples grouped together constitute episodes. An example is not cut out of a corpus of evidence on the basis of its representativeness in relation to a preconstituted field, since what is to be represented is a matter of what is exemplified. Rather, and as with Aristotle, an example is selected on the basis of its multiplicity and excess within a hypothetically determined field; an example is chosen on the basis of a hypothetical rule which governs the formation of examples within this field, and then used to support the hypothesis of such general rule.[8] An example is a good example to the extent that it can be multiplied, and a series of examples is a good series if the series displays a regularity beyond the individuality of each particular example. In short, an exemplary history is based on the possibility of finding general rules for particular cases, and particular cases for general rules.[9]

In this study, the primary object of analysis is *text*. As I shall argue at length in chapter 3, text ought to be treated as autonomous, and as something logically prior to the objects with which it deals and the author which it implicates; texts explain the world, rather than conversely.

The texts used in this book fall into two broad and ideal-typical categories. First, there is what I would call traditionary texts. In this category we find the canon of Western thought, texts that are read and reread as containers of meaning and truth, as *Leviathan* or *Kritik der reinen Vernuft*. Traditionary texts are those that become classics by being constantly interpreted and reinterpreted over a span of time. At the moment of their emergence, traditionary texts are read or intended to be read as *ratio scripta*, the meaning and truth contained in them being the meaning and truth of the world of which they speak. At some fluid moment in time, however, their meaning and truth become documentary, and the texts themselves become part of a historical legacy, either because the world of which they speak has withered away, or, because the world of which they speak has become all too real to the reader, who has become its inhabitant. From this point on, they speak of a world which is no longer simultaneous to the world in which they emerged, but to a world which in its turn has emerged out of it.

Second, and as a silent murmur surrounding the history of canonized texts, we find what I call manuals. If traditionary texts furnish blueprints for reality, manuals help to translate their meaning and truth into reality and action, to animate the world of which the former speak, to disseminate their ideas and turn them into folklore. They are guidebooks to a reality which they simultaneously help constitute. In this category we find works like Rohan's *d'Interest* and Descartes' *Regulae*; works that exercise a strong influence in their own time, but, having performed their function as manuals for thought and action, fall into relative obscurity and partial oblivion.

Like all ideal-types, these categories are not fully mutually exclusive. It is not difficult to find texts that have become traditionary due to their impact as manuals. Nor is it difficult to find writers who have written both traditionary texts and manuals. *Il Principe* is perhaps the most obvious example of a manual which has become traditionary; Bodin and Descartes are good examples of writers who wrote both traditionary texts and manuals.

In this book, both categories of texts are used as examples as well as sources of examples, which means that the texts singled out for exemplification and interpretation are not always those commonly identified as the major ones of an age. Then too, when traditionary texts are used, the reader will perhaps sometimes be surprised to find that the passages utilized for exemplification are those which traditionally have been regarded as peripheral, cryptic or too commonplace to merit any serious attention. My selection of texts, and my selection of passages from individual texts, are both idiosyncratic and self-conscious; throughout, I have tried to avoid the trivial by reversing the relationship between what has been regarded as central, and what has been regarded as peripheral. This reversal, however, is not a reversal for its own rebellious sake, but has been undertaken with a view to what is central and what is peripheral to *my* problem. Thus, if I happen to pay more attention to Rousset and Mably than to Montesquieu, or to

9

read Rousseau's *État de guerre* closer than his *Jugement*, it is not out of disrespect for Montesquieu or out of negligence of the *Jugement*, but out of the conviction that it is effective history that counts, and that the rest is conversation.

Consequently, the specific questions and presuppositions guiding each chapter have also been allowed to guide the sampling and treatment of textual material. For example, one may well wonder why I in chapter 4 chose to read three writers (Machiavelli, More and Vitoria) closely, while in other chapters I use the technique of thematic grouping and exemplification. The answer is fairly simple; it depends on what I want to demonstrate. Specifically, since what is at stake in chapter 4 is to demonstrate rather than merely discourse upon the peculiar relationship between the Renaissance text and extra-textual reality, I must get down to textual detail. This demand becomes less severe with classical and modern texts, since they, although with different emphasis, draw upon and are conditioned by a representational relation between text and reality with which we are much more familiar.

When I have picked editions and translations, I have done so with an eye to authenticity and availability. Whenever a translation has been available, I have used it instead of the original text for quotation and reference, but cross checked the translation of crucial terms whenever a suspicion of anachronism or undue simplification or popularization has arisen. When I have used original texts, I have tried as far as possible to use standard editions. When I have quoted passages in my own translation, I have supplied the untranslated passage in a note.

When I have confronted individual texts with a view to their place in the genealogical framework of analysis, I have done so not in a search for their hidden meaning or their buried truth. As I shall venture to explain in chapter 3, I have tried to stay on their surface, and focused on individual texts as both statements in themselves as well as containers of statements. I have approached them as a felicitous positivist, but not under the illusion that the act of interpretation can be avoided or suspended. As with the choice of texts, interpretation should stay away from the trivial, yet simultaneously it ought to be guided by and relevant in relation to an overall problematic. This double demand always runs the risk of doing violence to the text; throughout this book, I have consistently sought to undo this violence by supplementing the demand of non-triviality and relevance with a demand for coherence and surplus. Thus, I have treated an interpretation of a singular passage as warranted, if and only if the interpretive matrix superimposed on to this passage is consistent with the rest of the text, and hypothetically would help us to make sense of *more* singular passages than is actually needed, given the demand on relevance for the overall problematic.

The rest of this book is organized as follows. In chapter 2, I shall first pose the question of the meaning of the term sovereignty, and briefly describe what is implied in this practice of semantic questioning, and the kind of problems confronted by it. Second, I shall analyse the function of the concept of sovereignty within two regions of contemporary political science *as if* sovereignty signified an objective reality of modern political life. In chapter 3, I shall describe those problems which arise when we try to study the history of the concept of sovereignty within political discourse, and respond to these problems by outlining a genealogical approach to conceptual history. In chapter 4, I shall describe the prehistory of the concept of sovereignty during the later Middle Ages and the Renaissance, arguing that most features we hold to be integral to the modern concept of sovereignty are absent from political knowledge during this period. In chapter 5, I shall focus on the discourse on sovereignty and its relationship to classical knowledge, arguing that while this configuration contains a rudiment of what we mean by sovereignty today, it nevertheless excludes certain features of sovereignty which are judged to be transhistorically present by modern historical and theoretical accounts of sovereignty. In chapter 6, an account will be given for the transformation which the discourse on sovereignty undergoes during the early modern age in close conjunction with epistemic changes during the same period, resulting in the modern notions of a sovereign state and an international system as both opposed and mutually implicating domains of political reality. Chapter 7 is devoted to conclusions.

2   The problem: deconstructing sovereignty

> External/internal, image/reality, representation/presence, such is the
> old grid to which is given the task of outlining a domain of science.
> And of what science? Of a science that can no longer answer to the
> classical concept of the epistémè because the originality of its field ...
> is that the opening of the 'image' within it appears as the condition of
> 'reality'.
>
> Derrida, *Of Grammatology*

What does the term sovereignty mean? In this chapter, I shall focus on
the troubled attempts by modern political science to provide an
answer to this question, directly as well as indirectly. First, I shall argue
that the vain attempts of conceptual analysis have less to do with the
inherent ambiguities of the concept, and more to do with the philosophical tools utilized to this purpose. Second, and as a response, I
shall turn the question of *meaning* into one of *function*, and investigate
how the concept of sovereignty silently informs and takes on meaning
within the empirical discourses of international political theory and
macrosociology. Third, I shall analyse the recent effort by structuration
theory to make sense of sovereignty by turning it into a constitutive
rule of both domestic and international politics.

Making sense of sovereignty: centrality and ambiguity

Passing through the hands of politicians and philosophers during
centuries, the concept of sovereignty has been not only constitutive of
what modern politics *is*, and what modern political science is all *about*,[1]
but also a perennial source of theoretical confusion.[2] Despite the wide

agreement about its central place in our political vocabulary and understanding, the concept has eluded almost every attempt of rigorous definition and conceptual analysis. To take two influential remarks on the concept of sovereignty:

> It [sovereignty] was never more than a convenient label; and when distinctions began to be made between political, legal and economic sovereignty or between internal and external sovereignty, it was clear that the label had ceased to perform its proper function as a distinguishing mark for a single category of phenomena ... The concept of sovereignty is likely to become in the future even more blurred and indistinct than it is at present.[3]

> In the light of this analysis it would appear a mistake to treat 'sovereignty' as denoting a genus of which the species can be distinguished by suitable adjectives, and there would seem to be a strong case for giving up so protean a word.[4]

It is interesting to note that these death blows to the scientific usage of the concept of sovereignty were written before and after the most violent manifestation of sovereign statehood in modernity, and as such they are typical of the standard operating procedure for handling conceptual ambiguity and opacity in empirical political science. Whenever the semantic analysis fails, the recalcitrant concept is banished from empirical discourse, as if the empiricist quest for clarity itself were sovereign.

Now this chapter is a critical prelude to a genealogy of sovereignty, and not another exercise in definition. As Nietzsche once noted, only that which has no history can be defined;[5] to start a history of sovereignty with a definition of the term sovereignty would be to subject its historicity to the sovereignty of the present, and hence to narrow the scope of investigation.[6] Instead, and before embarking on a history of sovereignty, we must pay some attention to the relationship between the centrality and ambiguity of the concept of sovereignty.

In political discourse, centrality and ambiguity usually condition each other over time. A concept becomes central to the extent that other concepts are defined in terms of it, or depend on it for their coherent meaning and use within discourse. These linkages – whether inferential or rhetorical – saturate the concept in question with multiple meanings that derive from these linkages, which make it ambiguous; an ambiguity that is open to further logical and rhetorical exploitation.

The concept of sovereignty is an emblematic example of this; by being essentially uncontested as the foundation of modern political discourse, it is essentially contested as to its meaning within the same discourse. We can note how the centrality of the concept of sovereignty in modern political discourse has enabled it to soak up a multitude of meanings through its various functions, this gradual saturation going hand in hand with rhetorical and metaphorical capitalizing on the resulting ambiguity, so that it has 'crystallized into a kind of unity that is hard to disentangle and analyse'.[7]

Nor does this chapter aspire to outline any comprehensive theory of sovereignty; instead, it is devoted to the problems that arise when a scientific understanding of sovereignty is attempted. As I intend to demonstrate in this chapter, what makes the concept of sovereignty philosophically problematic is not any inherent opacity resulting from the multiplicity of its usages across the history of political ideas, nor any intrinsic ambiguity in the portions of political reality to which it is supposed to refer. My contention is that the problems confronted by conceptual analysis are intrinsic to the meta-language guiding this analysis, and that sovereignty represents a crucial case in this respect. Rather than dismissing the concept of sovereignty because of its ambiguity, we should take a suspicious glance into the practices of definition.

As it is a central assumption in this book that the problem of sovereignty is both logically and historically connected to the possibility of knowledge in general, a critical look at the practices of definition behind the frustrated attempts quoted above may prove instructive, both since the methods adopted when defining a concept often nicely reflect underlying assumptions – whether made explicit or taken for granted as part of the philosophical folklore – about the relation between language and world in general, and since these practices themselves are to be subjected to historical investigation in later chapters.

Conceptual analysis typically begins by closing the concept, while opening up its field of application to divergent interpretations. One begins by isolating ideal instances of the concept to be defined, in order to make it a 'distinguishing mark' or to discover 'a genus of which the species can be distinguished'. When it comes to the case of sovereignty, this is done by identifying a class of properties as 'essential' to statehood, thus demarcating 'sovereignty' from deviant cases and eliminating obnoxious borderline cases by searching for ever more finegrained qualitative differences. The desired outcome is a clarified concept, evident in its logical purity and by the empirical givenness of its referent.

Now this attitude towards concepts is heavily indebted to the codes of semantic conduct drawn up by post-Kantian empiricists, and which have gradually become part of scientific common sense. The underlying assumptions necessary to render this definitory practice defensible go something as follows: since language ought to be a transparent medium for representing what takes place in the world outside the knowing subject, the proper *a priori* meaning of a concept must be fixed through an analysis and determination of its referent. Meaning and reference are interdependent, insofar as their mutual determination is necessary if the concept is to be used in a phrase aspiring to *a posteriori* truth-value. Without the possibility of empirical reference, there is no clear-cut meaning. Without clear-cut meaning, there is no possibility of settling a dispute over truth rationally. Without this possibility, science is lost, rhetoric bursts in and the civil society of political scientists is plunged into civil war.[8]

Applied to sponge concepts such as sovereignty, procedures based upon this essentially *representative* view of language and the world run into considerable difficulties. Conflicting conceptual pressures inherent in the very metavocabulary of conceptual analysis beg the question: does sovereignty refer to the empirical reality of political science, or does it denote a set of juridical rules, such as 'the presupposed assumption of a system of norms whose validity is not to be derived from a superior order',[9] and whose reality therefore is wholly at the level of intersubjectivity? Since there is a strong temptation to get the best out of the two conceptual worlds in order to cover the various usages of sovereignty in modern political and legal discourse, definitions and theories of sovereignty are inclined to reproduce this inherited ambiguity by splitting the difference between the conceptual worlds of empirical political science and normative jurisprudence.[10]

One way to get around those obstacles is to approach sovereignty as an essentially contested concept, by opening it up to divergent interpretations while closing its field of application.[11] Behind this strategy is the assumption of an expressive relation between language and world common to Kant and the romantics. Within this view, language is still ideally transparent, but as a medium for *expressing* the identity and will of a prior subject, rather than for representing what is outside him. Instead of attempting a decontextualized analysis of sovereignty, one analyses the discourse of sovereignty as an expression of the underlying identity of states, and decodes the latter by means of the former, and conversely. Departing from its role in international rhetoric and in the justification of foreign policy, James subsequently strips the concept of sovereignty of a host of 'surface connotations' in order to arrive at a minimal consensus behind its divergent uses by political actors in an international context. What is at stake in this analysis is 'how, nowadays, sovereign states give meaning to the word when they refer to that which makes them eligible for international life'.[12] According to James, sovereignty ultimately refers to a condition of constitutional independence, which is the secret behind all other practices, domestic and international alike.

The implicitly transcendental method employed by James permits an easy leap from 'objective' political reality to the realm of intersubjectivity. Sovereignty is nothing but a set of rules and resources embedded in a collectively held legal understanding in the state system. While sensitizing us to the rhetorical functions of the concept, this quasi-phenomenology of sovereignty suffers from genesis amnesia. The historical question of how this politico-legal intersubjectivity came into being and became constitutive of international and domestic life is simply impossible to answer within James's framework. Making a legal rule foundational begs the question of how it was founded in political practice, and with political practice defined in terms of the same rule, the circle is closed; a history of either except in the terms of the other would have been impossible, had it been James's intention to write one, which it fortunately is not.

Apart from the more or less unsuccessful attempts to furnish a clear-cut and theoretically and empirically fruitful definition of sovereignty, we have in recent years witnessed an increasing emphasis on its constitutive role in modern political reality as well as in our understanding of it. This upsurge of interest in sovereignty ranges from macrosociology to international political theory.

This effort at reproblematization has focused on the fact that the concept seems to connote two contradictory ideas simultaneously, something which has been almost self-evident to historians, but simultaneously philosophically enigmatic:

> [I]n the context of the internal structure of a political society, the concept of sovereignty has involved the belief that there is an absolute political power within the community. Applied to problems which arise in the relations between political communities, its function has been to express the antithesis of this argument – the principle

that internationally, over and above the collection of communities, no supreme authority exists ... these two assertions are complementary. They are inward and outward expressions ... of the same idea.[13]

In political sociology and in empirical international political theory, these efforts have had many implications, one being the reification of sovereignty into an organizing principle or a constitutive rule, endowed with powers of its own. As Giddens has pointed out, 'sovereignty simultaneously provides an ordering principle for what is "internal" to states and what is "external" to them'.[14] This double and constitutive character of sovereignty has been touched upon by Ruggie, to whom sovereignty is a principle of legitimacy peculiar to the post-medieval international system.[15] Similarly, Kratochwil emphasizes the impact of territorial sovereignty in the formation of the modern state as the constitutive unit in the modern state system.[16]

Also, the push towards the reification of sovereignty has been fuelled by the 'agent-structure debate' in international relations theory and structurationist macrosociology. Moving the concept of sovereignty away from its merely descriptive connotations, both Wendt and Dessler turn sovereignty into a basic constitutive rule of the international system, upon which the surface practices of statehood, such as security dilemmas and war, depend.[17]

This dual and constitutive character of sovereignty points in an important direction, and partly explains why it has been so difficult to grasp analytically. At a minimum, sovereignty seems to connote a unified political condition, but turns out to be extremely recalcitrant when thought to refer to something 'internal' or 'external' to states. Sovereignty as a concept seems to float free of its instances in the 'domestic' and 'international' spheres. Instead, it cuts across these levels of analysis, and seems to be the condition behind their separation and interdependence; it forms the crucial link between anarchy and hierarchy.

But, as will be argued later on in this chapter, while structuration theorists in both disciplinary camps have turned sovereignty into an organizing principle or a constitutive rule, they have also simultaneously withdrawn sovereignty itself from study; the more sovereignty is thought to explain, the more it itself is withdrawn from explanation. The theoretical sovereignty of sovereignty leaves sovereignty itself essentially unquestioned; the more constitutive sovereignty appears to be, the less unconstituted it becomes.

The duality of sovereignty has also spurred a critical inquiry into the discourse on sovereignty in international political theory. To Ashley, this duality entails an ethical paradox. Through its function in the discourse of power politics, it effectively separates the domestic from the international sphere by defining the margins of a political community spatially as well as temporally; thus, international theory and practice are rendered immune to criticism.[18] As such, the concept of sovereignty has provided international political theory with a cachet of chic dissidence:

> What is at stake is nothing less than the *question* of sovereignty: whether or not this most paradoxical question, alive in all the widening margins of a culture, can be taken seriously in international studies today. More pointedly, the issue is whether and to what extent the discipline of international studies will be able to exercise its critical resources to engage and analyze the problem of and resistance to sovereignty as it unfolds in all the multiplying deterritorialized zones of a culture in crisis – including that extraterritorial zone called international politics.[19]

Thus, and quite automatically, the question of sovereignty spills over into a questioning of disciplinary identity and cohesion. But while critical theorists have contributed many valuable insights into the logic of sovereignty and its ethical and cultural significance in the present, they cannot be said to have studied sovereignty – whether as a concept or a discursive practice – rigorously.[20] They have limited their investigation to critical reflection upon its present consequences, but without asking how we got into this present, derelict as it appears to them.

It is my contention that the duality of sovereignty has hitherto escaped attention in modern political science and in the history of ideas, and that the main reason for this has to do with what it means to be 'scientific' in political science and 'historical' in the history of ideas. Throughout this book, I shall argue that the problem of sovereignty is inexorably intertwined with the possibility of knowledge; in this chapter, I shall demonstrate that the incapacity of contemporary research practices to make sense of sovereignty has to do with their unanimous acceptance of the modernist assumption that theoretical vocabularies are more or less transparent mediums for representing a ready-made reality outside themselves.

Within the view expounded in this book, discourse is not primarily a medium for representing the world more or less accurately, or to express the unthought habits of a subject. Instead, discourse – whether political or scientific – is actively involved in the construction of reality through – as Nietzsche put it – the mobile army of metaphors. In this chapter, this means that the problems confronted by conceptual analysis give us a strong case for shifting philosophical strategy, if we later are to make sense of sovereignty in its full historicity.

Thus, before embarking on the task of writing a genealogy of sovereignty, a critical inquiry into the contemporary empirical discourse on sovereignty is necessary.

Deconstructing sovereignty

Far from being homogeneous, the contemporary empirical discourse on sovereignty flows from two distinct but complementary fields of knowledge, their separation to an extent reflecting the divide between the external and internal aspects of sovereignty inherent in the concept. Thus, while concern with the former aspect is the traditional privilege of international political theory, macrosociology of state formation aims to explain the latter.

As I shall argue in the following sections, these explanatory priorities put international political theory and macrosociology in an inverse but symmetrical relationship to each other; each discourse takes for granted exactly that which the other takes to be problematic. Sampling from the exemplars[21] in each field, the following sections aim to provide a brief sketch of what is presupposed in the current empiricist understanding of sovereignty in both fields, and to explore the possibility of a more integrated conceptualization of sovereignty as proposed by structuration theory.

The choice of these two discourses also reflects two secondary objectives of this chapter. Since they both are empiricist in outlook, the critical inquiry permits us to judge the impact of this empiricism on the conceptualization of sovereignty. The second reason pertains to their complementary yet opposed character. The theoretical and empirical integration *across* these fields of knowledge is a promise held out by structuration theorists and scientific realists within both fields; the present chapter also aims to evaluate this promise, and to explore the reconceptualization of sovereignty it implies.

The general approach of this chapter is deconstructive. As a philosophical strategy, deconstruction addresses itself precisely to that which is taken for granted or regarded as unproblematic by a scientific analysis. In the present context, deconstruction is a way of exposing the possibility of reference and meaning of concepts to internal criticism. Instead of taking the possibility of reference and meaning for granted, deconstruction asks questions about their relation to *presence*, thus turning semantic problems into ontological ones: what must be regarded as real, basic or original, and what must be considered as absent, derivative or supplementary when making sense of sovereignty in empirical discourse?

Above all, assumptions of simple and firm ontological foundations – a minimum starting point for every discourse that aspires to scientific status – are always targets for deconstructive criticism, which recognizes every ontological foundation as something contingent. This habit of presupposing underlying essences is intimately related to the conceptual zero-sum games that organize and govern all theoretical vocabularies. Typically, a scientific or philosophical language is organized and made possible by a set of binary oppositions, conceptual categories defined as mutually exclusive. It is in and through the play of these categories that theoretical meaning is constructed; the upshot of deconstruction is that the terms involved in each such opposition are hierarchically arranged, so that the term which enjoys logical, ontological, or ethical privilege signifies what is present or foundational, while the other, inferior term, marks off its negation or supplement.[22]

As an antidote to uncritical conceptual analysis, deconstruction involves a demonstration of the metaphysical or ideological character of the presuppositions relied on, and the determination of their place in a wider system of metaphysical or ideological values. Furthermore, deconstruction implies a reversal of the conceptual oppositions discovered in a text, rather than an attempt to criticize them from an allegedly external or neutral perspective.[23] In the words of Derrida, to deconstruct a theory does not consist of 'moving from one concept to another but of reversing and displacing a conceptual order as well as the nonconceptual order with which it is articulated ... It is on this condition alone that deconstruction will provide the means of intervening in the field of oppositions it criticizes.'[24] That is, deconstruction is an immanent form of critique: it borrows its resources from the same theory it deconstructs, and the oppositions and concepts criticized are simultaneously maintained and employed in the deconstructive argument, but reinstated with a different status and meaning in the actual context.[25]

What lies ahead is a deconstructive tour through a vast theoretical territory which of course cannot be covered completely; instead, I will go for the milestones along the road to scientification followed by international political theory and macrosociology respectively.[26] In so doing, I shall limit my inquiry to three related questions concerning the status of the concept of sovereignty in these texts. All of them are key questions to classical political philosophy which take on a different sense when posed within a deconstructivist framework; their formulation is not expected to yield final answers, but to unmask the conceptual problems which a scientific discourse runs into when trying to answer them.

The first and most basic question in this triad concerns the *source* of sovereignty: what kind of origin or foundation is invoked when explaining or justifying the existence of the sovereign state by international political theory and macrosociology respectively? Second, what is the *locus* attributed to sovereignty by these theories? Where, and with whom, does sovereignty reside inside the state? Third, what is the *scope* of sovereignty; exactly what is encompassed and brought under its sway? While the first question concerns the philosophical legitimacy of the state, the second concerns its status as an acting subject, while the third concerns the objective conditions of its unity.

Perhaps partly because of its ambiguity, the theme of sovereignty is marked by its relative absence in contemporary scientific texts, and a reading of them must pay attention to elements rendered marginal by the interpretations encouraged or authorized by the texts themselves, and sometimes ask how this silencing and marginalization take place. A deconstructive reading cannot give the author any interpretative privilege on the basis of what his text tells us to do with it or on the basis of any intentions ascribed to him or declared by him; authorized readings and stated intentions are part of the text, and have to be interpreted as such. Hence, the author is never sovereign within and over the text: he writes in a language and in a logic which he cannot dominate, using them only by letting himself, up to a point, be governed by the system of statements he sets in motion.[27]

International political theory and the givenness of sovereignty

During the last decades, it has been commonplace to note two things about international political theory. While being 'state-centric', it lacks an accurate understanding of its basic unit of analysis. That is, explicit and falsifiable theories of the state as a political actor are nowhere articulated in the literature on international politics.[28]

To be sure, this line of criticism is valid but in a sense trivial. The very term 'international', taken as a mark of disciplinary identity, makes up both for the centrality and unproblematic character of the state in international political theory. Thus Raymond Aron was anxiously guarding his intellectual territory, when stating that 'a complete science or philosophy of politics would include international relations as one of its chapters, but this chapter would retain its originality since it would deal with the relations between political units'.[29] International relations theory is thus 'entitled to take for granted ... the political units'.[30]

No one criticizes chemistry for taking the existence of atoms for granted, lower or higher levels of complexity are simply left to physicists and biologists respectively. Therefore, we should better view criticism along the above lines not as an ontological dispute going on within a preconstituted and homogeneous field of knowledge, but as a contest over a problematic disciplinary identity. For example, during the period when the interdependence of states was emphasized in international relations theory, it became commonplace to insist that the distinction between domestic society and international system was blurred or about to be dissolved. But interdependence theorists could not have it both ways; either they were right in their talk about blurring, with the inevitable consequence that their theories ceased to be theories of international politics, or, as was more often the case, talk about blurring was mere lip-service, this being so since talk about blurring and dissolution always presupposes that that which is blurred *essentially* is distinct; in the end one was tacitly reaffirming the same distinction which one so valiantly criticized.[31]

Every scientific practice has to start somewhere, and international political theory happens to take the existence of the state as foundational for its intellectual enterprise. Nevertheless, even if the state is taken to be ontologically primitive, and its primitiveness is integral to the field of knowledge as such, questions about the state as a political actor have not been avoided by international political theory, even if they occupy a somewhat marginal position.

For what makes a state a state? What is the crucial property behind its capacity for unitary action? What distinguishes it from other forms of political organization?

22

Facing these questions, sovereignty is introduced both as the defining property of the state and in explaining the presence of an international system. For since the state is regarded as historically and ontologically prior to the system of states in the discourse on international politics, the essence of statehood appears to be the necessary condition also of the larger whole, the international system.[32]

In the more traditional exemplars of international political theory, this foundational character of sovereignty is grasped historically, as a result of the fall from a primordial political unity. According to Wight, 'international politics ... came into existence when medieval Christendom dissolved and the modern sovereign state was born'.[33] A similar historical origin is invoked by Morgenthau, to whom 'supreme power over a certain territory' is the very source of legal decentralization, so that without the sovereign state a 'state system based on it could not exist'.[34] To Aron, sovereignty is 'historically incontestable' as the 'original fact' of the international system, the very 'basis of inter-state order and intrastate order'.[35] To Bull, the presence of international relations is conditioned – logically as well as historically – by sovereignty:

> The starting point of international relations is the existence of *states*, or independent political communities, each of which possesses a government and asserts sovereignty in relation to a particular portion of the earth's surface and a particular segment of the human population. On the one hand, states assert, in relation to this territory and population, what may be called internal sovereignty, which means supremacy over all other authorities within that territory and population. On the other hand, they assert what may be called external sovereignty, by which is meant not supremacy but independence of outside authorities.[36]

This traditionalist awareness of the historical roots of sovereignty is replaced by abstraction in the course of scientification. In Waltz's seminal *Theory of International Politics*, sovereignty is stripped of its historical origin and reinstated ahistorically as an organizing principle. What appeared to traditionalists as the outcome of political fragmentation and alienation within Christianity, now carries the burden of explaining 'the striking sameness in the quality of international life through the millennia'.[37]

While 'systemic' in its epistemic priorities, Waltz's theory turns out to be 'reductionist' at the level of ontology. The existence of the international system is ultimately dependent on and explained with reference to sovereignty, which is the most basic and essential unit attribute in Waltz's theory. International anarchy emerges out of the 'the coaction of like units',[38] and 'to call states "like units" is to say that each state is like all other states in being an autonomous political unit. It is another way of saying that states are sovereign.'[39] Thus, we could expect sovereignty to be as immutable as anarchy in Waltz's model: 'so long as anarchy endures, states remain like units'.[40]

Here, sovereignty and anarchy are tied together ontologically at the level of definition, the former term being logically privileged, since it signifies that which is foundational to international politics. The state is conceptualized as an individual, in the sense of being indivisible. Further, by giving epistemic priority to the systemic level of analysis, Waltz creates a watertight circular connection between anarchy and sovereignty; their logical interdependence is conditioned by a gesture outside history but inside the theory itself, by splitting the difference between ontological and epistemic priorities. All this is done in order to extend the explanatory scope to cover everything that looks international from the dawn of history up to the present; Waltz has furnished us with a recipe for explaining the past in terms of the present, in which 'anarchy' and 'sovereignty' seem to be two sides of the same coin, but one cannot, from within this perspective, ever hope to explain how this connection was forged; coming from nowhere, consolidated in the deep structure of international politics, sovereignty is here to stay.

To sum up, the ontological primacy accorded to the state in international political theory implies the *givenness of sovereignty* as its defining property; sovereignty signifies what is inside the state, either constituted by the fall from a primordial unity, or simply taken for granted at the level of definition. In either case, sovereignty is constituted as a primitive presence from which all theorizing necessarily must depart, if it is to remain international political theorizing.

However foundational in itself and with respect to international political theory, sovereignty is not devoid of normative justification. In the discourse on international politics, the source of sovereignty is to be found at the philosophical level, in the logic of conflict inherited from contractual theories.

Within this logic, order grows out of disorder, harmony out of conflict, and it does so by means of a sublimation of otherness. In a historical and dialectical series, conflicting forces of human nature and human societies reach reconciliation by transposing their conflict to a higher level of complexity or to a different stage of history. Briefly put, this logic starts out from an anterior origin – human nature or the nature of the social bond – and then ventures to explain and justify the transition from this anterior and primitive origin as a gradual over-coming of otherness and estrangement; as such, the transition is mediated by culture, and each move marks a step on the ladder of civilization; it marks the triumph of rational and civilized man over the dark forces of nature, but with the undesired yet inevitable side-effect that these forces return at a higher level, and then partly out of man's reach. In international political theory, this regressive progression or progressive regression is that which explains the essential difference between domestic and international politics:

> The state of nature among men is a monstrous impossibility … governments establish the conditions for peace [and are] at the same time the precondition of society. The state of nature that continues to prevail among states often produces monstrous behavior but so far has not made life itself impossible.[41]

> [H]ostility is natural among men; it accepts regulation only within the political unit which is based on opposition and defines itself in its turn by hostilities. In other words, the historical dialectic never sup-presses the recourse to force, but transposes it to a higher level.[42]

Hence, the 'starting point of any valid theory of international rela-tions',[43] that is, the divide between domestic and international politics, comes naturally: 'so long as humanity has not achieved unification into a universal state, an *essential* difference will exist between internal politics and foreign politics. The former tends to reserve the monopoly of violence to those wielding legitimate authority, the latter accepts the plurality of centers of armed force.'[44]

What is portrayed as historically prior to and the moving force behind the transition of the sovereign state becomes externalized through the transition, whether in the shape of an unrestrained urge for power on behalf of individual states, or manifested in new social bond, the international anarchy. The point of departure does not really matter to the logic of sublimation; the universal value of sovereignty is affirmed by its negation, its other. Internal sovereignty is legitimized with reference to what is externalized at the moment of birth, without ever being abolished wholesale; either 'the struggle for power is uni-versal in time and space',[45] and thus beyond remedy, or the state of nature becomes immutable when transposed to the interstate level.[46] In any case, whether departing from man's sinful nature or the corruption of the social bond, the logic of sublimation moves in the same direction and creates the same difference and ethical hierarchy between the domestic and the international. Thus, the ontological priority given to sovereignty is supported by its ethical privilege: '[i]f might does not make right, whether among people or states, then some institution or agency has intervened to lift them out of nature's realm'.[47]

Moreover, the givenness of sovereignty implies that its locus must be treated as a constant rather than as a variable in international political theory; most theories of international politics presuppose a solution to the inherently normative problem of the proper locus of sovereign authority inside the state; a solution which then is turned into a necessary condition of outward agency. The question of the locus of sovereignty is a question of what lurks behind the metonym of the state, and what constitutes it as a political subject in international political theory.

When it comes to the question of the locus, international political theory has difficulty in remaining consistent in its discontinuities. The impetus behind this question comes from two different points. On the one hand, the inherited contractual vocabulary was invented in order to solve the problem of the locus in the domestic context, treating its external aspect as supplementary. In this case, the push towards a solution comes from the genealogy of concepts employed in the logic of sublimation. On the other, international political theory must present an operational solution to the problem of the locus in order to be susceptible to empirical test.

The answers given hover between two legal fictions; either sovereignty is indivisible and concentrated in the hands of one man, or, sovereignty is dispersed in the social body, finding its expression in an indivisible general will or in the consent of a majority.

Morgenthau comes close to the first extreme above. To him, a concentration of power in the hands of one or a few men is necessary for unitary state agency. Since sovereignty is 'the result of the actual distribution of power in the state',[48] 'it stands to reason that two or more entities – persons, groups of persons or agencies – cannot be sovereign within the same time and space'.[49] From this necessary indivisibility of sovereignty follows that 'if the location of sovereignty is held in abeyance ... a struggle, political or military, between the pretenders to supreme authority will decide the question one way or another'.[50] Pushed by his metaphysics of power and his logic of conflict, Morgenthau's indebtedness to Carl Schmitt[51] becomes clear:

[I]n any state, democratic or otherwise, there must be a man or a group of men ultimately responsible for the exercise of political authority. Since in a democracy that responsibility lies dormant in normal times, barely visible through the network of constitutional arrangements and legal rules, it is widely believed that it does not exist, and that supreme lawgiving and law-enforcing authority, which was formerly the responsibility of one man, the monarch, is now distributed among the different co-ordinate agencies of the government, and that, in consequence no one of them is supreme. Or else that authority is supposed to be vested in the people as a whole, who, of course, as such cannot act. Yet in times of crisis and war that ultimate responsibility asserts itself ... and leaves to constitutional theories the arduous task of arguing it away after the event.[52]

In the other, pluralist solution, the being of the state is dependent on an original concentration of power, but its capacity for unified outward agency is not. Instead, as in the case of popular sovereignty, unified agency flows from the collective will of the community, itself an organic unity by virtue of social cohesion and national loyalty. Within this view, 'there can be no presumption that the interest of the state and the action of the sovereign coincide',[53] since the interest of the state no longer is defined as the will of a personalized sovereign. Ideally, foreign policy should be an expression of the general will of the community, and in the 'ultimate case the agreement of the citizens with the government's foreign policy is complete'.[54] However, in the final analysis, this depersonalized and decentralized sovereignty turns out to be a derivative case, since a sufficient condition of unity, without which the state 'could no longer be considered a unit for purposes of international political analysis ... is simply the naked power of the *de facto* sovereign'.[55]

A similar ambiguity is displayed by Aron, but with the difference that organic metaphor is substituted for vague democratic allegiances. Whereas modern states have 'discovered the secret of the ... union of culture and politics, history and reason',[56] we are entitled to conceive of the state as a 'collective personality' being capable of 'thought and choice', but only in virtue of persons acting as 'interpreters or guides of the collectivity'.[57] Finally, to Bull, this tension between princely and popular sovereignty marks the difference between a system of states and a society of states, the latter being the outcome of the recognition of national and popular sovereignty as principles of international legitimacy.[58]

From an operational point of view, the question of the locus of sovereignty is important; at the same time, explicitness on this point seems to block nomothetic aspirations. Thus in Waltz's *Theory*, all possible specific loci are lumped together under the organizing principle of hierarchy, with no further elaboration.[59] This move of course extends the explanatory scope by making a bigger portion of political time-space – past as well as future – look like the present, but to the effect that the question of locus becomes difficult to answer with reference to the present, since sovereignty floats free of location at the domestic level. It is the logical condition of an abstract state and the secret of its unity.

What is more important, however, is what is taken for granted in the practice of identifying or defining the locus of sovereignty. Quite irrespective of whether sovereignty is held to be concentrated or dispersed in the social body, or turned into a property of the state as a whole by means of abstraction, the entire locus problem rests on the assumption that sovereignty is one and indivisible within the political order.[60]

Since Bodin, indivisibility has been integral to the concept of sovereignty itself. In international political theory, this means that whenever sovereignty is used in a theoretical context to confer unity upon the state as an acting subject, all that it conveys is that this entity is an individual by virtue of its indivisibility, which is tautological indeed. What follows from this search for the locus of sovereignty in international political theory, however necessary to its empirical testability, is thus nothing more than a logical sideshow; the essential step towards unity is already taken whenever sovereignty figures in the definition of a political order. Whether thought to be upheld by an individual or a collective, or embodied in the state as a whole, sovereignty entails self-presence and self-sufficiency; that which is sovereign is immediately given to itself, conscious of itself and thus acting for itself. That is, as it figures in international political theory, sovereignty is not an attribute of something whose existence is prior to or independent of sovereignty; rather, it is the concept of sovereignty itself which supplies this indivisibility and unity.

At a less abstract level, the self-presence of sovereignty has two important implications. First, and consistent with the logic of sublimation, it places the metaphysical unity of the state in opposition to its outside, its ethical negation. The international system is marked by the absence of unity right from the start; it is pure plurality. From this opposition, everything else follows: what is listed as essential to statehood is absent in the international realm, and vice versa. The whole range of dichotomies employed in international political theory to demarcate the domestic from the international gains logical and rhetorical impact from this single ontological gesture and the systematic play of identity and difference it brings into being. What makes a state a state and thus identical with itself is its difference from what is different from identity: difference.

Second, the self-presence of sovereignty is the prime source of the perennial tension between democracy and foreign policy. Rather than being the result of mere ideological inclinations, the 'conservative' bias in international political theory flows directly from its ontology; or, more precisely, from the ontological incommensurability between external and internal sovereignty. To say that a state is externally sovereign is in the context of international political theory another way of saying that it is a unity, whose indivisibility hinges on the presence of a monopoly of legitimate violence, and which thus ideally speaks with one voice to its neighbours. To say that a state is internally democratic is in the context of classical political theory another way of saying that it is a divisible manifold, in which a plurality of voices should be listened to.

As a consequence, attempts to bridge this ontological gap are bound to be detrimental to the metaphysical unity of the state, and thus to the coherence of any empirical theory departing from it. Conversely, if we dare to approach this problem at the ontological core level, we shall find ourselves criticizing the inherited divide between the domestic and the international, and all that goes with it.

Moving on to the scope of sovereignty, this aspect of statehood is what is treated as unproblematic when the word state is used metaphorically. In international political theory, the givenness of sovereignty implies the relative constancy of its scope. What is encompassed by sovereignty is from the vantage point of its locus a domain of objects, more or less essential components of a state by being integral to its objective unity as well as to its outward power and recognition.

In the standard solution to this problem, endlessly repeated or simply taken for granted in the discourse on international politics, sovereignty is taken to be a political or legal fact *within* an already given and demarcated territory, simultaneously signifying sovereignty *over* the same territory, and everything that happens to be inside this portion of space. In Bull's phrase, the state asserts sovereignty 'in relation to a particular portion of the earth's surface and a particular segment of the human population'.[61]

Thus, sovereignty and space are conceptualized in logical inter-dependence with one another right from the start, but this conceptua-lization can follow two different routes. Either one takes the compart-mentalization of space into territorial portions to be a necessary feature of sovereignty,[62] or, conversely, the modern state is a 'centralized area unit whose sovereignty, independence and power all resulted from its territoriality'.[63]

The implication of the first route leading from the fact of sovereignty to the fact of spatiality, is that sovereignty then signifies sovereignty *over* a territory, which means that sovereignty has to exist prior to boundaries, and is that which demarcates territory through the drawing of boundaries. In this case, to be sovereign over a territory seems to implicate self-containment and self-demarcation from an environment of other, self-contained and self-demarcating units.

If one follows the second route, leading from the fact of territoriality to the fact of sovereignty, sovereignty then signifies something that exists *within* a *given* territory. In this case, sovereignty must be demar-cated by boundaries, and therefore also logically and historically pos-terior to them, be they analytical or geographical. In sum, a bounded territory can either be interpreted as a necessary condition of sover-eignty, or conversely, sovereignty can be interpreted as a necessary condition of a bounded territory.

However far back we push this chicken-or-egg series in search of a firm theoretical foundation, we will end up in a particular conceptual hierarchy between sovereignty and territory, a hierarchy which in turn will be reflected in solutions to less abstract political and legal problems. If, for example, territoriality is taken to be essential to sovereignty, we are likely to side with Morgenthau and Herz in regarding the territorial impenetrability as the mark of sovereignty, and equate the loss of territory with the loss of sovereignty.[64] Conver-sely, if sovereignty conceptually gains the upper hand, territory will figure as a derivative aspect of relative political and legal sovereignty, and all further questions are bound to concern the locus of sovereignty and the causal conditions of its agency, such as its degree of depend-ence on other political orders, as implied by Waltz and James.[65]

What is more important in this context is how this logical and metaphorical link between sovereignty and space is forged. On this point, Aron is most explicit and lists a series of significations attributed to space in international political theory. First, space is a *physical fact*, since it seems undeniable that any human configuration must occupy a piece of it, irrespective of political organization. Second, space is an *environment*, since it seems likewise undeniable that any human configuration there finds the resources essential to its subsistence. Third, space is a *theatre*, since every human activity requires a spatial framework to exist. Fourth, space is a *stake*, since in every human rivalry, the possession of space is involved, either directly or indirectly. Fifth, space is a *geopolitical fact or a metaphysical essence*, since the sense attributed to space is determined by a particular configuration of all man/space relations listed above.[66]

What is interesting in this analysis is the subdued genealogy it represents; interpreted historically, all these determinations of space constitute a story of its politicization; it moves from the allegedly simple and indubitable to the philosophically and politically contestable. It is precisely in the course of this stepwise transition from the indubitably given to the physical presence of space to its metaphysical reification that the link between sovereignty and territoriality is forged, and opened to infinite reversal. If the crucial move comes when political content is attributed to this physical presence, in order to become naturalized as territory, this linking does not take place in the three last steps in the series, as Aron wants us to believe, but already in the first. When space is acknowledged as a physical fact, it is acknowledged by a subject; already here a man/space relation enters political knowledge as something indubitable, and space takes on political meaning as a clue to the sovereignty of a state; territory is naturalized right from the start, and without this essential conjunction of space, man and politics, sovereignty would lose its meaning as a defining property of that space. The politicization of space does not come when it is turned into a stage or *Lebensraum*, but is present as soon as space becomes an object of political knowledge.

Apart from its territorial base and the inanimate resources it contains, sovereignty also encompasses the social and institutional reality of statehood. At this point, the theoretical impetus towards conceptualizing the state as an empirical and transcendental unity, also pushes international political theory in a vaguely nationalist direction. Most notably in traditionalists like Wight, Morgenthau and Bull, nationalism is not merely a historical episode in the consolidation of European states. Instead, national allegiance is portrayed as a baseline fact of international politics, as an immutable outcome of an irreversible process.

Nationalism came to stay, since the social and cultural homogeneity of a population subjected to sovereignty, along with harmony among its social and political institutions, are conditions of its objective and empirical unity as well as an element of its power. Thus Wight: '[M]odern man in general has shown a stronger loyalty to the state than to church or class or any other international bond ... A power is a modern sovereign state in its external aspect, and it might almost be defined as the ultimate loyalty for which men today will fight.'[67] This view is repeated, though with less eloquence, by Morgenthau: '[T]he nation-state is to a higher degree than ever before the predominant source of the individual's moral and legal valuations and the ultimate point of reference for his secular loyalties. Consequently, its power among other nations and the preservation of its sovereignty are the individual's foremost political concern in international affairs.'[68] And again, now bluntly, by Waltz: '[I]t has been increasingly true in recent centuries, however, that most people feel a loyalty to the state that overrides their loyalty to almost any other group ... the centripetal force of nationalism may itself explain why states can be thought of as units.'[69]

When it comes to the relation between nation and state, Aron the sociologist is better equipped and less uncritical than many of his insular companions, who to him are 'unconsciously putting the seal of eternity upon the historical philosophy of the European nineteenth century'.[70] Instead, Aron brings into discussion the conceptual and causal links between nationalism, citizenship and sovereignty:

> The nation, as the ideal type of the political unit, has a triple char-
> acteristic: the participation of all those governed in the state under
> the double form of conscription and universal suffrage, the coinci-
> dence of this political will and of a community of culture, and the
> total independence of the national state with regard to the external
> world. A nation is always a result of history, a work of centuries. It is
> born through trials, starting from the sentiments of men but not
> without the action of force, the force of the political unit which
> destroys the pre-existing units, or the force of the state which brings
> into subjection regions or provinces.[71]

Ideally, in this masterpiece of history, the locus and the scope of sovereignty coincide to the extent that they become two sides of one and the same coin, which is indivisible sovereignty itself. This ideal union between 'political will' and a 'community of culture', however, merely transposes the difference between state and nation to the

32

depths of history. The underlying tension between subject and object is not resolved, nor mediated; the happy coexistence of state and nation is dependent on a pre-established harmony between 'the sentiments of men' and 'the action of force', the latter collaborating with the former in its desire for unity. Thus, Aron eventually brings us back to square one; the force and the sentiment invoked are the force and the sentiment of unities whose unity was to be accounted for in the first place. Pushing the problem down into the depths of history, Aron himself quite unconsciously puts the seal of nineteenth-century philosophy of history upon his story.

In the abstract and void state of the later Waltz, the social scope of sovereignty drops out as irrelevant together with all other unit attributes except sovereignty itself.[72] Instead, a forever undefined minimum level of differentiation and functional specification among the constituent parts of a political unit is all that is required for it to be ranked as a hierarchy in Waltz's dichotomy of political order,[73] provided that this mode of organization is carried out from some mysterious sovereign point above the social order.[74]

However, the basis of this differentiation and the extent of the functional specification necessary to qualify as a political unit are both held in abeyance by Waltz. As has been pointed out by some of his critics,[75] the unit level is logically amorphous to the extent that the relation between state and society cannot even be problematized within Waltz's analytical framework. The principles according to which social and institutional differentiation takes place are left out, and together with them, all questions of social and cultural cohesion. Their relations to sovereignty are defined away, which is halfway taking their smoothness for granted.

Thus, the question of the social scope of sovereignty, whenever posed within international political theory, is likely to render nationalist, romantic or eurocentric answers. There seems to be no choice but to abstract from one's own position within political time-space, an experience which for international political theorists is a predominantly European and American experience of statehood, and to encompass all the ideological answers given to these questions by eighteenth- and nineteenth-century political thought.

Finding a catchword to describe the mutations that the concept of sovereignty has gone through in the brief conceptual history that can be read off from post-war international political theory, silencing would seem an appropriate term. From being conceptualized as the outcome of a profound historical change by traditionalists such as Wight and Morgenthau, sovereignty takes on a more abstract meaning in the quest for scientific rigor; from being historically foundational to the discipline's identity and the reality this discipline seeks to comprehend, it gradually becomes ontologically and epistemically foundational with respect to both reality and understanding. Its own historicity is silenced as it takes on the task of explaining past and present: it becomes a metaphysical condition of the unity of the modern state.

By the same token, and as a result of its gradual naturalization and deproblematicization, questions regarding the locus and scope of sovereignty have become redundant in international political theory. As best exemplified by Aron and Waltz, the whole array of epistemic and ideological questions which arise in connection with locus and scope are either silenced, or abolished by means of abstraction and a simultaneous fostering of an ethical incommensurability between 'external' and 'internal' sovereignty, between the domestic and the international.

The givenness of sovereignty, which I take to be integral to the possibility of a scientific study of international politics, need not necessarily entail the metaphysical assumption that sovereignty is given outside time-space, contemplating its own indivisibility and immutability. If sovereignty in the present context seems at a minimum to signify the existence of final authority within as well as over a slice of political time-space, there is a tendency – less marked among traditionalists – in international political theory to regard this condition as something situated at and simultaneously being the end of history, beyond which no further change can be imagined. How is this possible?

At its core, international political theory seems to have retained the princely perspective upon which it once was founded. It is the perspective of the sovereign himself, or of the statesman representing him, standing on ground whose solidity he depends upon and must confirm through affirmative outwardly glances, at the Other, the international system. In order to fulfil the task of the international political theorist, says Morgenthau, 'we put ourselves in the position of a statesman who must meet a certain problem of foreign policy ... and we ask ourselves what the rational alternatives are ... and which of these rational alternatives this particular statesman ... is likely to choose.'[76] It is to this perspective the reading of international political theory is encouraged to conform. At the textual level, the givenness of sovereignty is warranted by its coincidence with the position of the authorized reader of international political theory, and the docile spectator of international events. Ultimately, the truth purveyed by international political theory hinges on the possibility of *representation*, on a juxtaposition of the knowing subject with a representable reality, the former creatively animating the latter from his sovereign position:

> The difference between international politics as it actually is and a rational theory derived from it is like the difference between a photograph and a painted portrait. The photograph shows everything that can been seen by the naked eye; the painted portrait does not show everything that can be seen by the naked eye, but it shows, or at least seeks to show, one thing that the naked eye cannot see: the human essence of the person portrayed.[77]

To be sure, this sovereign is a rational and impartial spectator when it comes to the relations of particular states, but since he himself is situated within the system of representation, he is blind to its conditions of possibility, to the unthought premises of his own enterprise; and perhaps must remain so, in order to remain sovereign within and over the corresponding field of empirical knowledge called international political theory.

Macrosociology and the empiricity of sovereignty

Moving the deconstructive inquiry into the multicausal terrain of contemporary macrosociology, we are bound to discover two things: the lack of overall theoretical coherence in the field, and the recent effort to 'bring the state back in' as a unit of analysis after some decades of behaviouralist neglect.[78]

Perhaps this renewed interest in the state as an autonomous yet problematic political actor can be viewed as a simultaneous quest for theoretical and subdisciplinary integration; this possibility is partly to be explored in this section. More importantly, however, this reproblematization of the state implies to some extent a reversal of the conception of sovereignty fostered by international political theory; macrosociology purports to explain precisely that which is taken for granted by the latter. The sovereign state is no longer present as an ontologically unproblematic and primitive entity; it demands a conceptual elucidation and an empirical account of its actual formation in time, of its consolidation and transformation in the European context as well as globally.

Thus, sovereignty is no longer something empirically or transcendentally given, but something contingent upon historical forces; those very aspects of sovereignty whose constancy is taken for granted by international political theory are now dependent variables. Simply stated, by virtue of its conceptual and empirical task, macrosociology displaces the conceptual order of international political theory by turning it outside-in. Chronologically, we find ourselves moving from a past to a present, rather than conversely. Geographically, we witness the global expansion of the state system, and do not regard it as an ahistorical presence.

Starting at the most basic ontological level, most macrosociological accounts of state formation subvert the hierarchy between the domestic and the international which is implicit in international political theory. In the latter, the domestic realm is treated as prior to and constitutive of the international sphere. A prior concentration of power – a monopoly on the legitimate use of violence – is a defining property of the sovereign state, is present right from the start and gives rise to the other, in which this essential condition of order is absent. In international political theory, the external corollary of sovereignty – international anarchy – is defined in terms of *absence* resulting from the prior *presence* of the sovereign state; ethically, the positivity of the state is negativity to the international; everything which is dear to man resides inside states, while the outside is marked by the lack of the same traits, and thus rendered inferior in relation to its origin.

The problem confronted by macrosociologists when explaining the source of sovereignty is analogous to the problem confronted by international political theorists when supplying the baseline fact of sovereignty with ideological justification: that which is defined as absence must be turned into presence. That is, instead of conceptualizing the international as something derivative of the sovereign state, and as a structure that is merely a constraint upon the actions of preconstituted states, macrosociologists are tempted to account for the presence of the sovereign state in terms of generative structural features of a sphere of social action that is thought to exist prior to the state.

The necessity of this conceptual reversal brings us right into the core of 'the conflict tradition' in macrosociology,[79] in which the formation and consolidation of states ultimately are explained with reference to exogenous dynamics and their external relations with each other. When accounting for the origins of the empirical features of sovereignty, this means giving logical and chronological priority to the notion of society as a kind of anarchical condition, out of which the state emerges as a gradual concentration of power.

To Engels, the clash between conflicting economic interests in the absence of overarching authority is the source of power concentration in the social body:

> [I]n order that these antagonisms, classes with conflicting economic interests, shall not consume themselves and society in fruitless struggle, a power, apparently standing above society, has become necessary to moderate the conflict and keep it within the bounds of 'order'; and this power arisen out of society, but placing itself above it and increasingly alienating itself from it, is the state.[80]

Less deterministic in his account of the formation of political communities, Weber regards the very differentiation between outside and inside as something contingent upon the forces of history, but cannot do away with this distinction at the level of definition; what is to be explained has to be presupposed. To Weber, even if '[v]iolent social action is something absolutely primordial', 'the monopolization of legitimate violence by the political-territorial association and its rational consociation into an institutional order' is not.[81] At its first and most primitive stage, the 'forcible maintenance of orderly dominion over a territory and its inhabitants' is not necessarily the function of one and the same community, but 'external' violence and 'internal' domination are distributed among various powers. In the maintenance of dominion over a territory, the action of the community is intermittent, and 'flares up in response to external threat or to an internal sudden impulse to violence'.[82] Consequently, at this stage, what is 'inside' and what is 'outside' is in the eyes of the beholder, not in the understanding of the agents themselves.

The crucial step towards legitimization of violence comes when it is both fitted into a permanent structure, gradually monopolized and concentrated to a single locus of authority, and simultaneously functions as a continuous means of differentiation between insiders and outsiders; in short, when this distinction becomes a living reality, and consequently, stripped of quotation marks in Weber's text:

> If the idea of a specific legitimacy of violence is connected with any type of consensual action, it is with that of the kinship group in the fulfilment of the obligation of blood vengeance. This connection is weak ... with regard to organizational action of a military type, directed against an external enemy, or of a policy type, directed

against the disturbers of internal order. It becomes more clearly perceptible, when a territorial association is attacked by an external enemy in its traditional domain, and arms are taken up by the members in the manner of a home guard. Increasing rational precautions against such eventualities may engender a political organization enjoying a particular legitimacy.[83]

A similar dialectic of conflict is invoked by Elias, who – more than Engels and Weber – is inclined to regard political factors as autonomous when explaining the sociogenesis of the state:

> A human figuration in which a relatively large number of units, by virtue of the power at their disposal, are in competition tends to deviate from this state of equilibrium (many balanced by many; relatively free competition) and to approach a different state in which fewer and fewer units are able to compete; in other words it approaches a situation in which one social unit attains through accumulation a monopoly of the contended power chances.[84]

These themes are repeated by modern macrosociologists. If the state was formed out of a prior state of conflict and war, subsequent state consolidation is also explained with explicit or implicit reference to this anarchy or order void, and with its concomitant sublimation to the international level; bringing the state back in means carving this anarchy out as a given and irreducible structural context, which in some guise or another is present from the alleged historical origin of the state onwards. With the more recent words of Hintze:

> [T]he state is not merely a government internally but a sovereign power externally. Throughout history power has been the main goal of the activities of the state; hence its structure depends at least as much on the conditions of its external power position as on the social-structural conditions of its internal governing activity.[85]

When it comes to actual historical accounts, the standard assumption of a state of nature helps to explain not only why states were formed, but also why a return to the lost primordial unity became impossible, and how this anarchy is reproduced and transposed in the process of state consolidation:

> [T]he very presence of multiple contenders for power, mutually aware and relatively equal in strength, promoted a process of consolidation by means of shifting coalitions among geographically concentrated elites, made it likely that more than one such process would be

going on at a time, and hampered any effort either to impose an authority without contiguous territory or to subordinate a large part of Europe to a single authority.[86]

Once brought into being by the fragmentation of Christian unity, the decentralized political structure in Europe enabled a condensation of otherness in the shape of the sovereign state. Following this logic, order springs out of disorder, presence out of absence; the consolidation of states coincides with the emergence of an international sphere, which then takes on explanatory priority. Thus, explanations of change in modern states must give 'primacy to international dynamics',[87] by conceptualizing the state as 'part of a system of competing and mutually involved states'.[88]

When it comes to the locus problem, we can discern how the state grows out of anarchy, and establishes itself as a relatively autonomous agent, but whose ultimate locus is contingent upon the forces of historical development, taking us from kings to people. However structuralist the explanation of this process, the assumption of some prior agency – however mute or embryonic – is ontologically necessary, be it 'small groups of power-hungry men'[89] or 'warrior families'.[90]

Whether resulting from the activities of megalomaniacs or from the gradual socialization of structural dopes, the story of state formation is the story of how power concentration and personalized sovereignty result from the victorious competition of this logical ancestor of the sovereign; his conquest of land and wealth and his subjugation of populations within the primordial condition of anarchy are essential steps in the formative process. As we reach modernity, however, power concentration gives way to power dispersion; the transfer of sovereignty from kings to people, whether carried out by gradual reform or by social revolution, is portrayed as a gradual consolidation of states, to a large extent dependent on forces in the emergent international system.[91]

Furthermore, and irrespective of the degree of structuralist bias, every theory of state formation 'must refer consistently to a particular kind of unit',[92] in order to qualify as an empirical theory. That is, an acting subject must be present in order to constitute itself and the state as an 'inside' that remains identical with itself throughout the formative process, no matter how it is conditioned by 'outside' forces in the course of its historical development from embryo to full-blown state. Hence, the particular kind of unit which makes empirical reference possible is a more or less rational will, individual or collective; according to the stories of the transfer of sovereignty from kings to people, both the king and the people have a fair share in this common essence of the state, which is also the essence of Man. Ultimately, from the formation of the state to its consolidation, it is the presence of Man within it which makes the state intelligible as an agent.

If the locus of sovereignty cannot be accounted for without reference to a primordial subject, neither can its scope be explained without reference to something more basic and primitive. The scope of sovereignty, representing the objective aspect of the state, is not sociologically intelligible without reference to something that allegedly exists prior to sovereignty, for it would otherwise remain empty; to macrosociology, the questions of locus and scope are logically indissoluble.

When it comes to defining the object of inquiry, macrosociologists in general seem to agree that the state ultimately consists of military control over a territory.[93] This agreement brings us back to the chicken-and-egg relation between sovereignty and space stumbled upon earlier in the context of international political theory, but with the important difference that this radical inconclusiveness now is transposed from the conceptual to the empirical level.

Since it is imperative for macrosociology to elaborate empirically the relationship between the locus of sovereignty and its spatial scope in actual accounts of state formation, we could hopefully expect this elaboration to yield general assumptions about the spatialization of politics and the politicization of space, whereas this relationship is not logically closed as in international political theory. That is, the cumulative chain of possible man-space configurations outlined in the previous section, beginning with space as a physical fact and ending with geopolitical ideology, enters macrosociology as a historically mutable series of relationships in conjunction with the actual formation and gradual consolidation of states, rather than as a series of connotations ahistorically attributed to the concept of territory, whose prior politicization then is tacitly taken for granted.

Moreover, since macrosociologists frequently seek to demonstrate that war made the state (in the anarchical condition thought to precede it) and the state made war (in the international system emerging out of it), macrosociology must be able to explain how space became politicized. Such an explanation ought to take us from the fact that any human configuration occupies a portion of space, to the historical and political coincidence that space became the stage where the politics of state formation took place as a struggle for space itself. Revealing this secret of territoriality is a necessary task, since 'the concept of territory seems to cover something more than just a piece of land on which people live', and since it seems generally valid that 'the state and its subdivisions are organized as territories'.[94]

In the European context, the crucial leap from space as a physical prerequisite to territoriality as *the* principle of the sovereign state is often explained as the result of a prehistorical cultural transition. It is the prevalence of peasantry or the absence of nomadism in some rather arbitrary 'beginning of history' that ultimately conditions the possibility of states organized as territories.[95] The modes of production and the forms of life that come with the predominance of agriculture pave the way for the firm empirical connection between territory, wealth and power that is essential to state formation. Though a recurrent theme in historical materialism,[96] this essential connection was also captured by Elias:

> The house that rules a territory politically is at the same time by far the richest house in this territory, with the largest area of land; and its political power diminishes if its military power, stemming from the size of its domanial revenues and the number of bondsmen or retainers, does not exceed that of all other warrior families within its territory.[97]

Once staged, this materialist drama of mutual reinforcement between territory and power, between the spatialization of politics and the politicization of space, leads to the rise of the state as a territorially organized unit. But what comes first in this rather elliptical chain of development seems theoretically undecidable, unless we quite uncritically assume some exogenous shock in the dawn of statehood, lifting European man up from some primitive form of life to a more developed stage of spatial politics. There seems to be no space for nomads in macrosociology, neither literally, nor metaphorically.

An analogous inconclusiveness arises in macrosociological accounts of the conceptual and empirical relationship between the locus of sovereignty and its *social* scope; the division of the drama of state formation into stages presupposes a conceptual reversibility between 'state' and 'society', which is reflected in the theoretical text. As noted above, most accounts of state formation start from the assumption that society is chronologically and ontologically prior to the state apparatus; this is necessarily the case when the genesis of the latter is explained in terms of the internal relations holding in the former.

Thus, since any reconstruction of the formative process must be guided by a generative logic in order to remain coherent and non-circular, the prior presence of some kind of society is ontologically necessary. Up to this point, macrosociology must remain at least implicitly structuralist in order to furnish a continuation of contractual myth by empirical means.

Beyond this arbitrary point of birth, the emergent state apparatus takes on 'autonomy' in relation to society, and simultaneously gains the upper hand according to macrosociological accounts of its subsequent development. What it means when the mode of reconstruction ceases to be guided by a generative logic and shifts to the reproductive or transformative modes, is that the explanatory privilege is redistributed to the state from the structure out of which it emerged. At the moment when 'formation' gives way to 'consolidation', sovereignty is constituted as 'inside' and the state becomes an agent; from here on, consolidation takes on meaning as a process of domestication carried out by an autonomous agent, turning society from a generative anarchical structure into a docile social body.

Above all, accounts of state consolidation in terms of social transformation are stories of how the power of the state apparatus is secured and legitimacy gradually created through the ethnic, religious, linguistic and cultural homogenization of a subject population, thus lifting society out of anarchic plurality and into orderly cohesion. Furthermore, this mutual reinforcement between hegemonization and homogenization is considered to originate in the state apparatus itself; it is the cumulative result of an autonomous state responding to the dual pressures of popular resistance from within and security struggles from without.[98]

This staging of the state drama into phases of 'formation' and 'consolidation' seems to be theoretically inevitable if the macrosociological plot is to remain coherent. At the imagined end point of the formative process, when the state eventually is constituted as self-identical inside thanks to outside forces, the theoretical vantage point is transferred to this inside. All further changes in the state, including the step towards popular sovereignty once a strategically acceptable level of homogeneity has been attained in the social body, will necessarily be reconstructed from the point of view of an autonomous state: a rational inside coping with problems on the outside, coming from the international system or from pockets of resistance within the territory to be domesticated.

42

It is as if the undecidability between the concepts of state and society is made possible by a necessary tension between agency and structure, a tension which is reproduced by the explanation itself; we cannot 'refer consistently' to both state and society without switching reconstructive mode from formation to consolidation. Bringing the state back in means that the underlying ontological tension between subject and structure is resolved by being distributed in a chronology of stages.

In this section, I have consistently sought to reach beyond epistemic discord and lack of overall coherence within the field, and focused on the troubled logical and ontological relationship between what is to be explained and what is assumed in order to explain; it seems as if the discourse of empirical macrosociology destabilizes itself as a result of its quest for a foundation and its need to refer consistently to an ambiguous and changing object: the state. It is as if the empiricity of this object betrays its own promise; one must begin by assuming the essential identity of precisely that which the discourse itself has to explain as to its essence, and simultaneously never decide definitively the essence of that which one invests with explanatory power: the mytho-anarchic and societal backdrop against which the state is formed. Bringing the state back in as something scientifically problematic necessarily entails that this outside takes on unproblematic presence in the explanatory scheme: the price has somewhere to be paid for a disciplinary identity centred on the theoretical identity of the object to be investigated.

This incommensurability should not be interpreted as a sign of intellectual immaturity. Rather, it is the aim of empirical science itself that gives rise to conceptual indecisiveness and ontological tension; as soon as one decides to investigate something, one has to take other things for granted. The peculiarity of macrosociology resides in the fact that what is at one moment regarded as basic turns out to be problematic in the next; it may well suffer a certain structural inconsistency in its ontological and methodological decisions, but need not be hampered by this in its quest for valid propositions about the empirical realities of the sovereign state. When all is said and done, it is not the task of deconstruction to block this ambition.

When it comes to the empirical nature of the sovereign state, the perspective provided by macrosociology is the reverse of that offered by international political theory, and, as long as an empirical understanding of both the state and the international system is wanted, a necessary complement to it. Textually, the perspective of macro-sociology is less that of the statesman, but more that of the citizen accounting for his own existence within the state as the legitimate heir to royal and personalized sovereignty. As a rational subject, he partici-pates in the subjective and indivisible will of the state, but at the same time he is estranged from it, looking into it and its conflict-filled prehistory from a point outside it, from the mytho-anarchic outside out of which he himself has emerged or escaped. This perspective invites dreams of transcendence or emancipation: the state is the result of crime organized on a huge scale, propelled by massive violence. But so is the citizen-spectator himself, since he is a modality of the same historically determined subjectivity; his estrangement is only partial, and he cannot be emancipated completely from this iron cage of modern sovereignty, without, as it were, simultaneously losing know-ledge of himself.

What was a dependent variable to international political theory was an independent variable to macrosociology, and conversely, what if we let everything vary by attempting a synthesis of these two approaches to modern sovereignty? Doing this will require a prior resolution of the incommensurability between international political theory and macrosociology, which amounts to a settling of the conflict between agency and structure which animates it. In the next section, I shall evaluate this promise of a synthesis between these fields and concepts in order to see how it affects the concept of sovereignty.

Structuration theory and the mystery of sovereignty

As I have tried to demonstrate, the incommensurability between the two concepts of sovereignty contrasted above is parasitic upon an essential ontological tension, which also is reproduced at the empirical level within each field of knowledge. Either sovereignty is taken to be a given and essential property of the state that constitutes its unitary and indivisible character; in this case, the inside takes on ontological priority in relation to the outside; the existence of the international proper is dependent on the internal sovereignty of states. Or, conver-sely, internal sovereignty is contingent upon something structurally prior to it, something which is transposed to a higher level in the course of state consolidation. Here sovereignty grows out of absence, and the inside is constituted from the outside.

A third, essentially dual view of sovereignty can be derived from attempts to cope with the ontological lacuna between agency and structure in both international political theory and macrosociology.[99] In the attempt to graft structuration theory or scientific realism onto the field of international political theory, theorists have typically departed from what they take to be an undisputed truth about all political and social life, irrespective of the level of complexity where it takes place: political or social reality is composed of two kinds of stuff – human agency and social structure – which should be kept ontologically and epistemically distinct, yet conceptualized as interdependent categories, each susceptible to different but complementary forms of explanation.[100]

What has been at stake in this debate is the possibility of mingling an account of the sovereign state as an agent with an account of the international system and its structure, thus bridging the gap between international political theory and macrosociology. Bringing these levels of analysis closer together requires that they are conceptualized as mutually conditioning right from the start, thus splitting the ontological difference between them. Contrary to the ontological individualism of international political theory, a structurationist theory of international politics cannot treat the presence of the sovereign state as something unproblematic; the state, along with all its defining properties, is generated by structural forces or constituted out of a set of internal relations holding in the system as a whole, which both enable and constrain all further state action. Contrary to structuralist macrosociology, however, this generative structure cannot be conceptualized as a mysterious presence existing independently of state agency.

This is not the place to probe deeply into the solutions to this problem resorted to by structuration theory and scientific realism. Suffice it to note here that their reconceptualization of structure amounts to defining it as a set of rules which serves as both medium and outcome of state agency. Thus, the international system is conceptualized in terms of constitutive and regulative rules, which condition the possibility of state action and are reproduced or transformed as a combined result of the intended and unintended consequences of state practices. The existence of the international system is thus dependent on the actual practices of states, and these practices are made possible by the system itself.[101]

Not surprisingly, this effort at a theoretical synthesis has had profound impact on the conceptualization of sovereignty. As a consequence of the rejection of ontological individualism, it is evident that sovereignty can no longer be understood as the timeless essence of the state, since it is precisely the capacity for unified agency and the homogeneous interior presumed by its use in international political theory that are rendered problematic by structurationism and scientific realism. In the words of Giddens: 'The sovereignty of the nation-state ... does not precede the development of the European state system, or the transferral of the nation-state to a global plane ... the development of the sovereignty of the modern state from its beginnings depends upon reflexively monitored sets of relations between states.'[102] From this two claims follow:

> 'International relations' are not connections set up between pre-established states, which could maintain their sovereign power without them: they are the basis upon which the nation-state exists at all.[103]

> [T]he 'actor-like' qualities of modern states have to be understood in terms of the specific characteristics of the nation-state rather than being taken as a pre-given baseline for the study of international relations.[104]

Interpreted in isolation, the above statements seem to point in macrosociological-structuralist direction. But this is not the whole story. As a consequence of this reconceptualization of structure, sovereignty can no longer be understood as a factual condition emerging *ex nihilo* from an anterior absence, from a political void lying there waiting to be populated by sovereign entities. To Giddens, a structure is a set of historically contingent and mutable rules, whose genesis and reproduction in turn are dependent on agency. Thus, 'the very term "international" only has full meaning with the emergence of nation-states which, because of their strictly demarcated character, give a very particular shape to "internal" versus "external" relations'.[105]

Therefore, and as an essential step in the structurationist endeavour to split the ontological difference between the state and the international system, sovereignty is taken to be constitutive of both spheres, hovering somewhere between them, but residing in neither. Turned into the most basic constitutive rule of modern politics, sovereignty now carries the double burden of constituting two realms of politics simultaneously. As Giddens has remarked, 'the juxtaposition of 'order' and 'anarchy' ... is intrinsic to the conception of sovereignty', this being 'one of the most important elements binding the 'internal' development of the state with the 'external' solidifying of the state system'.[106]

Thus, viewed as an organizing principle situated in the very deep structure of modern politics, sovereignty takes on a life of its own in order to connect the emergence of a reflexively monitored state system with the formation of the nation-state as the dominant political form of life in the modern world. Sovereignty is ontologically disconnected from the spheres it constitutes as separate, but it also serves as the crucial link between them: without 'external' sovereignty, no 'internal' sovereignty, and conversely. As such, sovereignty furnishes the domestic and the international with a common historical origin and fixed chronological limits, which conditions their interdependent existence dialectically; they are constituted as separate by their interdependence, and interdependent only by virtue of their separation. Within this view, 'a state cannot become sovereign except within a system of other sovereign states, its sovereignty being acknowledged by them'.[107] Perhaps we could add as a matter of clarification: a system of sovereign states cannot exist without being intersubjectively acknowledged as such by its constituent parts. Sovereignty, taken as a constitutive rule, is both medium and outcome of the internal as well as the external practices of states; it furnishes the very divide between what is internal and what is external with meaning, and thus with political reality for the agents themselves, whose identity in turn hinges on this division.

The synthesis advocated by structurationists and scientific realists not only holds out the hope of resolving conceptual conflicts within existing fields of knowledge. It also makes the breaching of disciplinary boundaries look virtuous, since it promises to settle the ontological differences underlying their compartmentalization into distinct fields. What makes this promise look attractive is the quite naive assumption that the way a problem in political philosophy is formulated is *independent* of the way in which solutions to it are presented. The general incommensurability between agency and structure, first elevated into a problem of imperial proportions by structurationists, is then opened to a glorious peace-by-interdependence between conflicting concepts and estranged fields of knowledge. From a deconstructive viewpoint, however, it is the 'undisputed truth' underlying the 'agent-structure problem' that is the real problem, since it is the former which makes the latter look like a chicken-and-egg debate. To say that all social and political life is ultimately composed of two kinds of stuff is simply to presuppose that essence is essential to social and political theory. Ontological questions invariably yield ontological answers, since they drag the political philosopher into a quest for firm foundations and proper origins. Starting with the assumption that agency and structure are radically different in essence, which it is necessary to do in order to depict all prior theoretical efforts to wrestle with this conceptual zero-sum game as vain, the structurationist then solves his problem by pointing to the fact that what is different always shares one thing in common, namely, the fact of being different.

At this point, the 'agent-structure' debate seems to deconstruct itself; being centred on the quest for essence, it pushes us back in an infinite series of reversals. Whenever a structure is identified, its existence is conditioned by a prior agency, which in turn is made possible by yet another structure, and so forth. However far back we push in this series in search of a foundation, what appears as essential will always prove to be supplementary, in a way that deprives it of the authority of ontological simplicity. The attempted synthesis tries to overcome the same ontological difference that nourishes it: if the problem could be solved, the solution must also indicate that there was no problem in the first place.

The reconceptualization of sovereignty that comes with the structurationist effort to relate the domestic inside and the international outside can be regarded as symptomatic of the quest for essence that governs it. The very problem that the conceptualization of sovereignty in relational terms hopes to solve, merely crops up again at a more certain depth, but now beyond the reach of critical concepts. To say that sovereignty is constitutive with respect to both the domestic and the international by being that which makes the internal internal and the external external, is either to turn sovereignty into an agency that structures or a structure that acts; in both cases the original problem is restored.

Ironically, the structurationist and scientific realist promise to put an end to reification in the social sciences by abolishing talk of ghostly structures and preconstituted agents ends up in the reification of sovereignty itself, without any possibility of explaining how sovereignty entered into the mysterious deep structure of modern politics. Sovereignty ends up being dialectically foundational both to the existence of a domestic inside and an international outside, and yet itself unfounded; it is the condition of possibility of itself.

As I shall conclude in the next section, sovereignty has no essence; if we want to take its relational character seriously, we must abandon the quest for timeless foundations and essences in political philosophy, and instead venture to explain how this talk of forces, origins and foundations made its way into political knowledge together with the modern concept of sovereignty, and became stuck in logical interdependence with it. If we are to understand the concept of sovereignty historically, the problem is not so much a matter of what *sovereignty* is, as it is a matter of what this *is* has come to mean to the modern political scientist.

The parergonality of sovereignty

The primary objective of this chapter was to deconstruct the concept of sovereignty by determining its place in two wider conceptual contexts; this was done by identifying the ontological, epistemic and ideological assumptions that governed its intelligibility in those contexts.

This deconstructive analysis was undertaken as a means of approaching the problem of its meaning and reference from another angle than conceptual analysis. Scientific meaning and empirical reference presuppose the presence of something outside language, whose investigation in turn demands a language purified from ambiguity; definition becomes worthwhile only if we presuppose an order of things separate from signs, whether axiomatic or empirical.

Empirical science hinges on the presence of an object; it has to be about something whose presence it thereby asserts. Typically, a deconstructive strategy yields answers uncomfortable to those who need this solid ground under their feet; asking what a given discourse is inclined to regard as essential, original and foundational, and what this discourse regards as derivative and supplementary does not contribute to the science itself. But it contributes to the analysis of the unthought parts of this knowledge; to an analysis of that which 'goes without saying' within a theoretical or empirical field of study.

When one moves back in the structured order of concept that a science employs when bestowing identity upon its object of study, one follows a genealogical path immanent in this science itself; any science which aspires to be empirical invariably involves silent presuppositions about the reality which it depicts, assumptions resulting from a history of incremental methodological decisions.

Posing the questions of the source, locus and scope of sovereignty within the fields of international political theory and macrosociology, we were able to witness how these discourses yield answers which are both ontologically unstable and sometimes also ideologically saturated; at the same time, these two fields of knowledge stand as mirror-images to each other. What the one takes for granted, the other renders problematic; what was conceptually undecidable within the one, was empirically undecidable within the other. What they share in common, however, are two interrelated things whose emergence and interrelationship are to be explored in chapter 6: they both presuppose the *possibility of representation* and the *sovereignty of Man* as the subject of this representation, whether in the shape of the detached, statesman-like spectator of international politics, or the more entangled, king-like citizen of macrosociology.

In either case, the sense given to sovereignty in the conceptual order was intertwined with the ontological starting point, and the same incommensurability which separates these fields from one another, also draws them together as instances of empirical science. They both have to confront the problems of subject and structure, genesis and transformation; they both, together with the structurationist attempt to mediate between their basic viewpoints, must presuppose 'a line in water'[108] separating the domestic inside from the international outside, a prior demarcation which conditions the possibility of their dialectical interdependence.

As Aron has argued, 'statesmen, citizens, philosophers have always recognized a difference in nature between the internal order of states and the order between states'.[109] The examples from international political theory and macrosociology seem to corroborate this view; the line in water is always drawn at the level of definition, aided by an array of metaphors and ideological presuppositions; this is what Wight once called the intellectual prejudice of the sovereign state.[110] How, then, is the line in water drawn, whenever it manifests itself in theoretical discourse or political practice?

In the present chapter, the answer is fairly obvious; the line in water is drawn in and by the quest for ontological presence which is the condition of possibility of empirical knowledge. As soon as a field of knowledge is to be demarcated, conceptual oppositions are there to do the job by marking off what is present and foundational from what is supplementary or derivative; it is in this role that the concept of sovereignty becomes crucial both to the organization of political reality and to the organization of knowledge of this reality.

Central yet ambiguous, the concept of sovereignty not only assures a continuity between inside and outside, but a simultaneous continuity between knowledge and reality. The concept of sovereignty is both empirical and transcendental; it tells us how to differentiate between different domains of study, while at the same time being the condition of possibility of these domains.

As such, sovereignty has no essence, since it is what makes different spheres of politics empirically representable and intelligible; as soon as we start to demand that the concept of sovereignty should refer to something present in the world of empirical beings, our understanding of the concept itself must presuppose the same line in water which is drawn in and through its meaningful use in political discourse.

Thus, if we want to make sense of sovereignty – logically as well as historically – and then as something which lies between the domestic and the international spheres of politics without itself being a mysterious prior essence, we should pay attention to the internal connections between sovereignty and knowledge. Since contemporary political knowledge seems to take for granted that we more or less rigorously can distinguish what is inside the state from what is outside the state, the agenda of research perhaps ought to be expanded to cover this very discourse of demarcation.

As I have tried to demonstrate in this chapter, the line in water that separates inside from outside is drawn by a series of decisions about what is *a priori* undecidable. These decisions are decisions on sovereignty in both the epistemic and political senses of the word. The discourse on sovereignty – whether empirical or transcendental – has as its prime function to frame objects of inquiry by telling us what they are not. In this sense, the problem of sovereignty resembles the problem of the *parergon* in aesthetic discourse. Present in ancient writings on art, the concept of *parergon* was reintroduced by Kant when discussing a problem analogous to that of sovereignty; what is the relation of a frame or an ornament to the work of art itself and its background?[111]

The solution goes as follows: a frame, a line of demarcation, an ontological divide, or a geographical or chronological boundary all assert and manifest class membership of phenomena, but the frame or line itself cannot be a member of either class. It is neither inside, nor outside, yet it is the condition of possibility of both. A *parergon* does not exist in the same sense as that which it helps to constitute; there is a ceaseless activity of *framing*, but the frame itself is never present, since it is itself unframed.[112]

As such, a frame is a composite of inside and outside, it is 'an outside which is called inside the inside to constitute it as inside'.[113] And conversely: it is an inside which is called outside the outside to constitute it as outside. Once brought into being, a parergonal frame 'detaches itself from two backgrounds, but in relation to each it backs into the other'.[114]

In our present context, this notion of parergonality provides a clue to the problems that arise as soon as we start to attribute fixed reference to the concept of sovereignty, or, by the same token, assume the ontological presence of sovereignty. There is a discursive practice of sovereignty, but sovereignty itself is not amenable to empirical political research, however much essentialist conviction we retain about its power to organize political reality. Yet we speak and theorize as if it did: its function in political discourse can only be properly understood if we detach the concept of sovereignty from the implicit ontological concern of contemporary knowledge, and, so to speak, move it to a non-place. If we succeed in this, our analysis of sovereignty will no longer presuppose that the line in water between the domestic and the international has already been drawn, but will instead help us to explain how it is *drawn* and perpetually *redrawn* inside knowledge, and how, subsequently, the domestic and the international are discursively constituted as self-evident.[115]

Interpreted as a *parergon*, the concept of sovereignty will no longer expend its dual energy erasing the line in water without making it intelligible; it will help to explain the formation of the very body of knowledge which makes this division as evident as it makes the concept of sovereignty difficult to understand.

As I shall argue in the rest of this book, the discourse on sovereignty functions according to the same logic as the *parergon*, but what is constituted as inside and outside respectively, varies dramatically throughout the history of political ideas, and does so in strict interdependence with changes in knowledge. As I shall attempt to show, the juxtaposition of the domestic and the international as we know it today is a fairly recent and essentially modern construct, following from a specific parergonal function attributed to the concept of sovereignty by a likewise specific arrangement of modern knowledge.

3   Beyond subject and structure: towards a genealogy of sovereignty

> [A]s long as we continue to contrast history directly with structure, we persist in believing that the subject can gather, build up and unify matter. But this no longer holds true if we think of 'epochs' or historical formations as multiplicities. The latter escape from both the reign of the subject and the empire of structure.
>
> Deleuze, *Foucault*

The previous chapter started out from a Nietzschean observation: only that which has no history can be defined. But how can we write a history of that which cannot be defined, lacks stable meaning and reference, and which does not exist except by being known, and then within a knowledge which presupposes the sovereignty of the knowing subject?

As I shall argue in this chapter, to write a history of sovereignty is to write a political history of the knowledges that makes sovereignty intelligible, a history of the unthought parts of our political understanding. Strictly speaking, the object of study is therefore held in suspense; as with histories of other central and ambiguous concepts, a history of sovereignty must be a history without fixed referent, since it is precisely a history of this referent and its formation in time. A history of sovereignty cannot be written from the initial assumption of a timeless ontology and unchanging epistemology; precisely as the history of space cannot be anything but a history of geometries and the history of Being cannot be anything but a history of Western metaphysics,[1] so a history of sovereignty cannot be but a history of the epistemic discontinuities, conceptual reversals and changing metaphors that breathe life into political philosophy, and animate the discourse on sovereignty.

Consequently, a history of sovereignty cannot begin by separating the sovereign state from its international outside, for it must be capable of accounting for the formation of the domestic and the international as *imposed interpretations* which organize modern political reality as well as our understanding of that reality as empirically given or analytically evident. Thus, a history of sovereignty must be a history of how and by what means this kind of differentiation into inside and outside, into sameness and otherness, is carried out. It must be a history of how sovereignty, in its modern guise, becomes both an empirical and a transcendental concept.

In chapter 1, I said that this book was intended as a genealogy of sovereignty, and elaborated some of the core assumptions behind a genealogical approach to the history of political ideas. In this chapter, I shall spell out these assumptions more fully, and argue that genealogy is crucial if we are going to answer the basic questions about sovereignty raised in chapters 1 and 2.

Histories of the past as outside stories

In his *Untimely Meditations*,[2] Nietzsche raises an important question: what is the use of history? In the particular context in which this question was posed, its point was directed at the dominant – yet superficially opposed – trends in German historiography of that time: Hegelian idealism and Rankean source criticism;[3] against history as the gradual unfolding of Reason and history as something capable of attaining the status of objective science. His answer was that the historian's history always has more to do with the present than with the past. The young Nietzsche identified three distinct modes of historical reconstruction, all of them reflecting specific present needs and hopes for the future; writing a history of the past is a way of rendering the present meaningful as well as a strategy for making the future look more promising or more gloomy.

Today similar concerns are reflected in what looks like an emergent orthodoxy in the history of ideas, most notably by writers such as Dunn,[4] Pocock[5] and Skinner[6] – the methodology of the latter I shall consider at length below – and sociologists of knowledge such as Barnes, Bloor, Manicas and Rosenberg.[7] The main issue has been how to avoid the twin fallacies of *finalism* and *presentism* respectively without lapsing into what they fear to be complete arbitrariness.[8] Bearing in mind that we are here dealing with philosophical and historiographical paradigms rather than with manifestations in concrete historical research, it is possible to simplify the difference between presentism and finalism. If both hold out the possibility of a *terra firma* from which to study and write history, they differ about where to locate it. Typically, a finalist history is a history of the past in terms of an imagined future; a presentist history is a history of the past in terms of the present. A finalist history treats the present as a projection of the past, by projecting a version of that past onto the present, whereas a presentist history regards the past as a projection of the present, by projecting a version of this present onto the past.[9]

Underlying this problem is a metahistorical conflict. On the one hand, historians of ideas or sociologists of knowledge are in want of a suprahistorical vantage point from which history can be written, validated, judged and criticized with a claim to truth or verisimilitude. On the other, no one would deny that human beings are historical beings, and ultimately the only agents in history, which makes them indissoluble parts of it. But being determined and conditioned by history, how can we ever hope to reconstruct and evaluate it from a point outside it? Man seems to occupy the ambiguous position of being within history, yet he simultaneously stands outside it and contemplates its unfolding.

What is at stake here is the question of man's sovereignty over his past. Both finalist and presentist history can be interpreted as two paradigmatic forms of this quest for sovereignty over the past; both finalism and presentism affirm the possibility of writing history from a point over and above it, while making man the hero within it. In their joint affirmation of a suprahistorical vantage point, presentism and finalism are arguably two sides of the same eighteenth-century coin, however great their differences may seem in terms of their way of grasping the relation between past, present and future and their respective judgement on the possibility of historical truth.

In finalist historiography, it is only possible to write the history of an age when it has reached maturity or is about to fade; finalism typically identifies present truths in embryonic form in a distant past, and then goes on to show the necessity of its progressive development from that point up to the present. Thus Hegel, in a famous passage on the role of philosophy in history:

> As the *thought* of the world, it [philosophy] appears only at a time when actuality has gone through its formative process and attained its complete stage. This lesson of the concept is necessarily also apparent from history, that it is only when actuality has reached

> maturity that the ideal appears as opposite the real and reconstructs this world, which it has grasped in its substance, in the shape of an intellectual realm. When philosophy paints its grey in grey, a shape of life has grown old, and it cannot be rejuvenated, but only recognized, by the grey in grey of philosophy; the owl of Minerva begins its flight only with the onset of dusk.[10]

History is a march forward, undertaken by a transhistorical subject, starting from a primitive origin and continuing towards the realization of some end state; what takes place between these points is either soaked up by the historical spirit, or brushed aside – history itself continuously differentiates what is central from what is peripheral to its own development. Everything – including other histories – is put in its proper place according to the final goal history will attain. Finalist history is history narrated as a coherent plot and a meaningful attainment of such a goal; if finalist history is rewritten, it is the logical outcome of the march of history itself, since it has to digest its own movement infinitely.[11]

The ultimate purpose of finalist history is the justification of some ideal, present or future; its Archimedean foothold is in the transcendental. The flight of the owl is coordinated and directed from a point outside history, or better, from the *end* of history itself. Since long a favourite target of empiricist criticism,[12] this view of history seems to be about to regain at least some of its former academic legitimacy, most notably through superficial readings of Hegel.[13]

Now the historiography resulting from attempts to rid us of finalism has arguably fallen prey to the presentist fallacy. Presentism comes naturally with an insistence on timeless criteria of reconstruction and validity in history. As soon as such criteria are introduced, as rules of source criticism or as principles for the subsumption of historical facts under objective laws, one will inevitably be writing the history of the past in terms of the present. Since these criteria themselves necessarily are presumed to be without history, past events and ideas, whenever they appear to be true or rational to the historian, are explained or made intelligible with reference to this very rationality or truth, whereas that which appears to be false or irrational must be accounted for in causal terms as deviances from the timeless and objective standards laid down or uncritically accepted by the historian.

Thus, if finalist history uses the past for justificatory purposes, it does so more or less self-consciously and without being more unjust to the past than it is to the present. Presentism, on the other hand, finds its justification and foundation outside history in absolute criteria, but is systematically unjust in its treatment of the past while implicitly treating the most cherished or seemingly self-evident traits in the present as timeless. Beliefs and events which cannot be celebrated as harbingers of this present are seen as the results of human folly and superstition, while the ideas and practices most dear to the present are held to be results of rational progress. This present itself has no end point, and cannot wane or come to a conclusion without a simultaneous end to all objectivity and a return to a dark age; the present is here to stay in the future.

Whiggish history is the characteristic genre of presentist historiography.[14] It characteristically begins by taking an institution or an idea from the present together with the contemporary role, function or purpose presently used to justify that institution or idea, and then describes its historical development *as if* this purpose or role had governed its emergence and transformation right from its origin onwards. Or, if whiggish history deals with something absent in or remote from the present, it does so by accounting for that institution or practice in categories totally foreign to it, *as if* these understandings ideally *should* have been available to the past, were it not for the 'limits of that age', while neglecting the categories used by the agents in that past to describe themselves and their own practices and institutions. Whiggish history hinges on this possibility of re-educating the dead into Enlightenment dopes, and then engages in a conversation with these re-educated dead on presumably timeless matters, forcing them to provide answers to questions that are ours.[15] That is, presentism finds its Archimedean foothold *above* history; the owl – allegedly shot down – is now instead firmly fixed in the celestial ceiling, scornfully contemplating past mistakes in view of present standards blown into timeless truths; if presentist history happens to be rewritten, then this is done in the light of new and better historical evidence.[16]

Now much contemporary philosophy teaches us to be equally suspicious about finalist and presentist modes of history.[17] They both narrate history with the aid of a metanarrative, or so a die-hard post-positivist nominalist sceptic would have it. In response, contemporary philosophy has tried to do to presentism what presentism once did to finalism: to demonstrate that its initial assumptions are themselves time-bound and therefore contingent. The main outcome of this anti-foundationalist critique has been an epistemic or conceptual relativism, and the subsequent historiographical debate has been one of degrees: how much relativism can the history of ideas afford without dissolving itself into pure fiction?[18]

For the sake of criticism and contrast, and in the context of this historiographical debate, I shall dwell briefly on an influential attempt to avoid the twin pitfalls of finalism and presentism, and, hence to write *the history of the past in terms of the past*. This done, I shall argue that the very premise of suprahistoricity is a misguided one, and that it would be better to write a conceptual history of sovereignty from within history, and then as a *history of the present in terms of its past*. I shall use the term genealogy to denote such a historiography.

The hermeneutics of conflict

Why should one ever bother to study the history of political thought? Reflecting the anxiety of the traditional political theorist and the intellectual historian in an era when Anglo-Saxon political thought was at pains to cross the threshold of empirical science, it became important to answer this question to those in the endangered species who began to look like odd antiquarians.[19]

If the question itself seems blunt, so was the standard reply. As Skinner's own history of this episode relates, the study of political thought had to narrow its scope and adjust to then-present concerns in order to reap institutional benefit from scientific legitimacy. The standard motive for studying classical political texts was that they purportedly contained timeless ideas, and by studying past answers to these perennial questions, we should be able to learn equally timeless wisdom from them.[20] This motive was invariably linked to what was thought to be the proper focus of the history of political thought: the 'great' texts themselves, and nothing outside them. To suggest that any knowledge of the context in which they were written would be necessary for an understanding of them would have been tantamount to denying that they do contain any timeless elements.[21]

It is against this backdrop that the hermeneutics of conflict was introduced.[22] Skinner – on this point following Gadamer and Collingwood – starts out by assuming that we are in a predicament of prejudgement in relation to the past. Our view of history will inevitably be contaminated by the unconscious application of paradigms, which dispose us to reconstruct and evaluate the past in terms of the present:

> [The] models and preconceptions in terms of which we unavoidably organize and adjust our perceptions and thoughts will themselves

tend to act as determinants of what we think or perceive. We must classify in order to understand, and we can only classify the unfamiliar in terms of the familiar.[23]

This poses a dilemma for the historian; the predicament of prejudgement is as undesirable as it is inescapable. He cannot simply hope to arrive at a 'pure' understanding of the past, and he is in the 'perpetual danger of lapsing into historical absurdity' as a result of this application of paradigms which 'disguises an essential inapplicability to the past'.[24]

On the finalist side of this predicament we find the propensity to hypostatize political and philosophical doctrines into ghostly entities with a corresponding narrative written 'as if the fully developed doctrine was always in some sense immanent in history'. This reification of doctrines leads to history in terms of anticipation; a writer is said to have 'anticipated' some later doctrine or development, which he arguably could not have intended to do.[25] Another finalist fallacy results from the conflation of past meaning and present significance, and arises when the retrospective significance of a concept or an idea is turned into a historical fact of that age. A strange teleology lies at the core of such narratives: the concept or the idea has to await the future to acquire its full and proper meaning.[26]

The presentist historian is disposed to discern conceptual continuity, and thus to be anachronistic when making sense of past ideas, by starting out from the expectation that a writer holds a doctrine at present regarded as constitutive of the matter under investigation, despite the fact that this doctrine is formulated in terms unavailable to the writer himself. One is 'reading in' a doctrine which a given writer could have had no intention to convey. The typical finding of this type of intellectual history is that the writer under investigation only succeeded in articulating a given doctrine vaguely, a fact which then is turned into a matter of reproach. Such history 'is a means to fix one's own prejudices on to the most charismatic names [and] becomes a pack of tricks we play on the dead'.[27] Another presentist fallacy is to impute coherence to a given text, reflected in the common desire of arriving at a unified interpretation by resolving apparent contradictions or discounting entire works which impair the overall coherence of what is thought to be the author's 'system'.[28] The last presentist vice is the worst, and perhaps also the root cause of the others: the historian may be misguided by his own preconceptions so as to fail to describe the reference and sense of past statements correctly. There is always a danger that the historian will misuse his vantage point, by conceptualizing arguments in such a way that its alien elements are dissolved into an apparent but unwarranted familiarity, thereby masking some essential inapplicability to the historical material.

All these vices can be found in abundance in histories of the concept and reality of sovereignty. We have already noted in chapter 3, how analyses of sovereignty – whether conceptual or empirical – tend to take for granted the dividing line between internal and external sovereignty and treat it as a timeless feature of political reality. This is repeated by historians of ideas who deal directly or indirectly with the concept of sovereignty over a span of time.

Hinsley, although very sensitive to the flux and details of history, starts his history of sovereignty with an arguably late-modern definition of the concept, and then transposes the divide between the domestic and the international back into the past by organizing his narrative and its subheadings according to it.[29] Onuf, who is partly excused by the fact that he intends to purvey nothing more than an 'outline of a conceptual history', nevertheless falls prey to the temptation of definition, and then goes on to list the historical antecedents of the modern definition without the slightest attention to other contexts than a factual-historical one.[30] Worse still, in the histories exclusively devoted to the external theory and practice of sovereignty in international relations the fact that political philosophers before the modern age had very little to say about international relations is often lamented.[31] Puzzled by this fact, one continues with an analysis of this silence, instead of reaching the more obvious if not unproblematic conclusion that there was no 'international' until this concept entered political discourse towards the end of the eighteenth century. To Williams[32] and Knutsen, who both are under self-imposed pedagogical constraints, the assumption that there existed something international in antiquity or in the Middle Ages may be forgiven, even if the more clever Knutsen admits that to 'trace the history of a subject-matter which constantly undergoes mutations and transformations ... is much like hunting chameleons,'[33] and that, not surprisingly, '[w]hen Aquinas moves from domestic relations within states [sic!] to relations among states, his arguments become more unclear'.[34] But this absolution cannot be granted as easily to Holzgrefe, who, despite his vast legal erudition, claims that 'the conflation of foreign and domestic politics in Medieval Europe' had as a consequence that sovereign states were not the only entities that exercised the right to treaty,[35] instead of interpreting this fact as an indication that there was nothing there to 'conflate' in the first place. By the same token, Holzgrefe ends up in wonder at the marked disjunction between theory and practice in international politics.[36]

According to Skinner, if we want to avoid these fallacies and give up mythologizing the past, two things must be done. We must rid ourselves of the Fregean assumption that the meaning and reference of words are constant and unchanging through the ages, and consequently extend the scope of historical investigation to recover the context in which the various works were written in order to understand them:

> [W]e must study all the various situations, which may change in complex ways, in which the given form of words can logically be used – all the functions the words can serve, all the various things that can be done with them. The great mistake lies not merely in looking for the 'essential meaning' of the 'idea' as something which must necessarily 'remain the same', but even in thinking of any 'essential' meaning ... at all ... [W]e should study not the meanings of words, but their use. For the given idea cannot ultimately be said in this sense to *have* any meaning that can take the form of a set of words which can be excogitated and traced out over time. Rather the meaning of the idea must be its uses to refer in various ways.[37]

Following Wittgenstein, Austin and Searle, Skinner argues that we should regard words as deeds. The key to a proper understanding of a text lies in what the author intended to do *in and by* writing it; what sort of society was he writing for and trying to persuade; what set of ideological conventions constrained or enabled this enterprise, and how was he trying to use or manipulate them?[38] We should use the particular social, political, cultural and linguistic context, not in order to *explain causally why* that which was written indeed was written, but in order to recover and *understand* the *intentions* or *point* embodied in the act of writing it. To explain causally would be to invite presentism, since that which is supposed to explain need not be present in the beliefs to be explained. To Skinner, therefore, comments on the concept of sovereignty which merely reduce it to an expression of underlying social realities, such as 'absolutism' and therefore as something equivalent to it,[39] a process of 'social atomisation',[40] or 'an instrument for protecting a given system of productive relations',[41] do not put us in touch with the meaning of the concept, no more than with the point embodied in its articulation at a given time and place.[42]

If texts are acts, to understand them we need to get a grasp of the intentions with which they were written. But acts are also texts: they contain intersubjective meanings that can be read off from the context of their occurrence.[43] It follows that the history of ideas should be a history of statements or speech-acts, and of the conditions in which they occurred or were performed; also, and integral to the hermeneutics of conflict, primacy should be given to political and ideological conflict when explaining ideological change.[44] Thus, and as an essential step in any historical reconstruction which aspires to be proper history and not merely a projection of present concerns, we must start out by assuming that:

> [N]o agent can eventually be said to have meant or done something which he could never be brought to accept as a correct description of what he had meant or done. This special authority of an agent over his intentions does not exclude, of course, the possibility that an observer might be in a position to give a fuller or more convincing account of the agent's behaviour than he could give himself. But it does exclude the possibility that an acceptable account of an agent's behaviour could ever survive the demonstration that it was itself dependent on the use of criteria of description and classification not available to the agent himself. For if a given statement or other action has been performed by an agent at will, and has meaning for him, it follows that any plausible account of what the agent meant must necessarily fall under, and make use of, the range of descriptions which the agent himself could at least in principle have applied to describe and classify what he was doing.[45]

Charity is the foremost interpretative virtue, lest we commit the whiggish sin of projecting our own local prejudices upon the past. But, then, how far can we extend our sympathy without simultaneously giving up the possibility of criticism or dissolving our enterprise into literary criticism? A crucial case in this respect is how to explain beliefs that strike us as untrue or absurd.

Skinner tries to solve these problems by separating rationality and truth, and insists on a contingent relationship between them. Following Davidson, he assumes that the holding of true beliefs constitutes the norm among the people we are studying (otherwise we should find ourselves unable to identify what they believe), and that we should not equate the holding of beliefs we judge to be false with a lapse in rationality. Rationality does not necessarily imply truth; a corollary to his theory of language, the rationality of a proposition or belief is dependent on its overall coherence with other propositions or beliefs,[46] and the rationality of such a system of propositions or beliefs is in turn to be evaluated in pragmatic terms:

> When I speak of agents holding rational beliefs, I mean only that their beliefs (what they hold to be true) should be suitable beliefs for them to hold true in the circumstances in which they find themselves. A rational belief will thus be one that an agent has attained by some accredited process of reasoning. Such a process will in turn be one that, according to the prevailing norms of epistemic rationality, may be said to give the agent good grounds for supposing (as opposed to merely desiring or hoping) that the belief in question is true.[47]

> From this another methodological precept follows. However strange the beliefs we are studying may seem to be, we must try to make the agents who held them appear as rational as possible. We should begin our interpretative effort by recreating the inner connections among the beliefs we are studying, and try to identify what was accepted as a good reason for believing something to be true among the people we are studying.[48]

This piece of hermeneutic advice comes close to the impartiality requirement advocated by some sociologists of knowledge, and is the death blow to the possibility of rational evaluation this criterion is said to entail.[49] The impartiality requirement states that we should approach and explain beliefs in the same causal terms, irrespective of the truth-value we are willing to ascribe to them. But here Skinner pulls the emergency brake:

> It is simply that the kinds of explanations we offer for beliefs we judge to be rationally held are of a different order from the kinds of explanations we feel obliged to offer if we once come to doubt whether a given belief is held in a rational way ... [E]ven if we assume that our explanations will in each case be causal in form, the causes of someone's following what are taken to be the relevant norms of reasoning will nevertheless be of a different order from the causes of their violating them.[50]

The upshot of this argument is that we should split the difference between our explanatory priorities, but without insisting on full symmetry between the available modes of explanation. Instead of following the conventional path of taking rational beliefs to be their own explanation, and accounting for lapses in rationality in causal terms, we should devote as much effort to explaining rationally held beliefs. Then attainment of rationality is a considerable achievement, and an inquiry into the conditions that enable agents to attain rationality will be as legitimate as an inquiry into the conditions that prevent agents from attaining it, although the causes in each case will be of a different kind. We should take whatever is said at face value – even if absurd – as a fully valid expression of a belief, and as long as possible resist the temptation to suggest – as anthropologists frequently do – that the given statement is expressive of something other than a belief, and hence treat the speech-act symbolically. The only available criterion for determining when to shift explanatory mode would in this case be 'our own cognitive discomfort'.[51]

Political rationalities are particular and local, and how well any given statement fits into that framework of rationality must be judged by two criteria that reflect its duality in relation to the context. We must ask not only to what extent the actual statement was the outcome of a rational policy on the part of the agent, but also whether it was consistent with the prevailing sense of epistemic rationality. To answer these questions, we must recover the particular context of both ideological conventions and epistemic presuppositions.[52]

Skinner's methodological principles rest on the assumption that the elucidation of the meaning of statements and the concomitant identification of beliefs are logically anterior to the task of explaining them. We need to know exactly what we are going to explain, before we can furnish our explanations. Indeed, what will be the appropriate mode of explanation can only be decided with reference to the recovered historical identity of a given statement or belief. When we have succeeded in doing this, it is legitimate to go beyond the vocabulary in which the beliefs under investigation were stated, and start to explain or comment on them in our own vocabulary, which will be quite certain to include concepts that would have been incomprehensible to the people to whom we apply them.

As we have seen, Skinner recommends that we stay on the hermeneutic surface as long as possible by taking statements at face value, and postpone any suspicions about discursive abnormality, irrationality and falsity until our rationalist account fails completely, and our dialogue with the dead breaks down. We must thus allow for a hard core of emphatic whiggishness, by assuming that our ancestors shared at least some of our beliefs about the importance of consistency and coherence, and regard abnormality and contradictions as parasitic on or derivative from these norms. We should start by assuming that we must in some way have misunderstood or mistranslated some of the propositions by which they are expressed. Hence, and if this procedure happens to fail, these special cases of rationality gone astray are not directly susceptible to illocutionary redescription, since they cannot be identified as literal expressions of belief.

To rephrase the initial question, what can we hope to learn from the history of political thought? Even if we are in an important sense prisoners of the present, Skinner's approach teaches us to question the distinction between historical reconstruction and rational criticism, since it 'enables us to recognize that our own descriptions and conceptualizations are in no way uniquely privileged'.[53] With this insight, we can eventually hope to 'acquire a perspective from which to view our own form of life in a more self-critical way, enlarging our present horizons instead of fortifying local prejudices'.[54] We cannot demand, however, that the history of thought should supply us with solutions to our own problems: 'we must learn to do our own thinking for ourselves'.[55] In doing this, however, we must learn from the past: the alien character of past beliefs is what constitutes their relevance to our present, since our own concepts nevertheless evolved out of them.[56]

The conflict of hermeneutics

Though Skinner's approach has been subjected to extensive criticism, most of his critics have avoided digging into the epistemic and ontological underpinnings of his work. Among the epistemological problems, the first is to be found in the conflict between the ambition to avoid the finalist and presentist fallacies, while retaining a suprahistorical vantage point.

As a result, rationality is relativized into manifold historically specific 'rationalities', each with its own inner coherence and pragmatic justification, whereas the concept of truth is relegated to a place outside time. Says Skinner: 'I have merely observed that the question of what it may be rational to hold true can vary with the totality of one's beliefs. I have never put forward the reckless and completely different thesis that truth itself can vary in the same way.'[57]

Now the history Skinner himself is writing itself aspires to be a true story, or at least he assumes that the question of its truth can be settled in a rational way in the present; at a minimum, truth is the regulative idea of his enterprise.[58] Why Skinner necessarily must raise such absolutist claims, and why he feels such discomfort at the prospect of being surpassed in the same fashion as he himself surpasses the likewise valiant truth-claims of others, is enigmatic.

His prime mechanism of validation, however, is not. The context carries this burden; in principle, it is not only possible to recover and frame, but also possible to saturate it with ever more fine-grained historical facts until it reaches a stage where every conflict between alternative interpretations of a given work or statement finally can be settled or ruled out.[59] While the historical reconstruction and interpretation is allowed to be undertaken with a coherence theory of rational acceptability as the bottom line, the truth of the outcome seems to be warranted by an algorithmic procedure; the notion of saturability clearly points in this direction. Hence, at the same time as Skinner wants to suspend the concept of truth in favour of historicized rationality in the account of past beliefs, he clings to much less mutable a standard when it comes to justifying his own beliefs, and consequently, to side-stepping the hermeneutic circle in order to comment on beliefs which strike him as absurd. Two different conceptual pressures are at work here: on the one hand, Skinner seeks to avoid the presentist fallacy, on the other, he wants to avoid being accused of the arbitrariness said to follow from full conceptual relativism, although there are strong Occamite reasons for giving in to this latter temptation.

In one of his many examples, Skinner brings up for discussion the fact that Bodin wrote a short treatise on witchcraft. As Skinner finds belief in witches both false and bizarre, he is at pains to explain why it was rational, and not merely psychologically intelligible to speak of witches in the particular context of late-Renaissance thought. Though witches never have existed, it was nevertheless rational for Renaissance writers to discourse upon them as if they were real, since denial of their existence would have presented a challenge to the theological authority of the day. With a sojourn in the dungeons as the ultimate reward for undue scepticism, you better stay ontologically correct.[60]

Now a diehard conceptual relativist would take the frequent occurrence and coexistence of statements about witches, mermaids and demons as an indication that they did exist; that the ontological space opened by Renaissance knowledge gave free access to those entities, while excluding atoms, productive forces and international systems, so what is it besides liberal arrogance that keeps Skinner from admitting the existence of witches?

The answer is to be found in the unquestioned and supposedly timeless metalanguage that furnishes Skinner with his suprahistorical vantage point, and which sustains his own truth-claims. Just as talk of rational belief presupposes a *subject*, so talk about existence presupposes a distinctively modern interpretation of *being* in general, both of which are transposed back into the past, the former as its hero, the latter as its essence. Criteria for distinguishing appearance from reality that are *ours*, not Bodin's, are allowed to guide interpretation as if they themselves were without history.

Another problem of general concern to all interpretation that departs from the subject as the privileged locus of meaning is inherent in the theory of language to which Skinner seems to subscribe. Either the interpreter attributes final explanatory power to the everyday meaning of the statements or acts under investigation, by elucidating what they meant to the agents performing them, or he relegates this authority to a deep meaning or hidden significance in the statements or acts themselves, and continues his inquiry with a suspicious glance into the underlying psychological or sociological motives which supposedly govern the speaking subject. In both cases, however, the practices which make both subjectivity and meaning – and therefore also the hermeneutic practice itself – possible are bound to escape the interpreter, who takes them for granted as part of a background understanding shared by both *interpretans* and *interpretandum*.[61]

Following Austin and Searle in his account of language and its relation to the subject, Skinner regards the performative dimension of language as *essentially* – however not always methodologically – parasitic upon its representative dimension. Within this view, language – primarily a means to communication among speaking subjects – functions as a resource as well as a constraint upon communicative action. It is a resource in so far as it allows for the creative manipulation of linguistic conventions; the act performed by a statement is always an intervention into the context, but it is equally constrained by the meaning and reference of that given statement.[62] The latter is itself an artifice of more or less variable linguistic conventions, while the former is founded on intentionality. In order to do things with words, these words must have acquired a prior meaning in order to gain illocutionary force, a meaning which is not fully constituted or determined by their place in a given context, but which still must be supplemented with an intention on the part of a speaking and acting subject.

To Austin, this supplement is provided through the demand that the speech-acts under investigation must be *serious* ones (not necessarily in uptake, but in intention);[63] to Searle, this supplement is provided by a quasi-materialist account of human intentionality,[64] and a set of criteria defining a 'total speech act situation'. The details of these accounts aside, they both – as representatives of an anthropocentric interpretation of the later Wittgenstein – assume that the speaking subject is present on the scene *before* any meaning whatsoever, and that the subject consequently is the ultimate source and locus of all meaning; a meaning which he is then free to manipulate within the bounds of contextual constraints.

The assumptions of fixed being and fixed subjectivity silently inform Skinner's interpretation of political texts, and together constitute the sovereign vantage point from which the history of political philosophy can be reconstructed, but this vantage point is itself withdrawn from the flow of history. As a consequence, Skinner's history of political thought is essentially a doxographical one, a *history of opinions* which moves forward as a result of the ceaseless battle between them. Throughout, however, the epistemic and ontological conditions behind these opinions escape attention, since they are presumed to be an immutable backdrop against which all opinion is formed, articulated and disseminated.

In general methodological terms, this means that any actual historical reconstruction is likely to proceed by *marginalization*; that which looks obscure, absurd or patently false from the viewpoint of our present is systematically subdued, and only that which chimes well with modern knowledge is admitted into the narrative core.

More specifically, in his history of the term state and its terminological predecessors, Skinner seems to demand that an amount of 'self-consciousness' is necessary on the part of a given writer, if we are to be entitled to speak of him as *expressing* a specific concept of the state by using the very term or one of its equivalents.[65] This requisite is of course useful if we want to investigate arguments and debates over this concept as soon as it has surfaced in political discourse and therefore can be expressed by subjects, but if we want to answer the more intriguing question of how the notion of the state as an abstract entity, detached both from ruler and ruled became a logical and ontological possibility, it is difficult to see why the self-consciousness of an author should be vested with this privilege.

No one would put this demand upon a history of geometry or upon a history of poetry, and insist that a given geometrical figure or a specific trope only existed by virtue of being self-consciously expressed, whatever that might mean. Why should the history of political thought and the history of its core concepts be confined to a history of divergent opinions, leaving out or simply taking for granted the background understandings which makes these clashes of opinions possible in the first place? Aside from the difficulties in making inferences about self-consciousness from a text, this methodological requisite entails that one assumes the author–subject to be transhistorically present, and thus beyond the scope of historical investigation; once this is assumed, however, the historical constitution of the self-conscious subject and its interconnection with the concept of the modern state cannot be told, or is doomed to be superficial.

Histories of the present as inside stories

In chapter 2, we saw how the quest for empirical science made the foundations of this science inaccessible to inquiry. In the above section, we saw how this gesture was repeated by Skinnerian hermeneutics. In its quest for validity, the sovereign vantage point itself was withdrawn from history, and inscribed into a timeless stratum; objects, subjects and concepts were all ascribed a position there. In this section, I shall argue that our understanding of the relationship between sovereignty and knowledge gains from a suspension of such a suprahistorical vantage point, and that we should try to situate ourselves within history rather than at the end of it or above it.

Since the problems encountered in the previous section were partly rooted in the theory of language to which the hermeneutics of conflict subscribes, we should begin there, by, so to speak, turning this theory of language inside out. What if we release language from its necessary ties to objects and subjects, and treat it as autonomous and its ties to what is outside it as contingent upon its autonomous functioning as *discourse*? Statements would then no longer be regarded as representative or expressive, but systematically involved in the formation of both the speaker and the objects of which he speaks. In what follows, I shall argue that this step is necessary albeit not sufficient, if we are going to understand the historical relationship between sovereignty and knowledge.

The autonomy and primacy of discourse

Following Foucault, we could begin by carefully distinguishing statements from propositions and utterances, something which Skinner does not do. Statements are not like propositions; they are not logical entities with a fixed and intrinsic meaning and reference: the same proposition with the same meaning can figure as different statements depending on the epistemic conditions under which it occurs. Statements are not utterances: whereas Skinner tends to equate statements with utterances, different utterances can be repetitions of one identical statement.[66]

Thus, statements cannot be defined according to the same logical criteria used in the definition of propositions and utterances respectively: 'one finds statements lacking in legitimate propositional structure; one finds statements where one cannot recognize a sentence; one finds more statements than one can isolate speech acts'.[67] Ultimately, statements are neither words nor things and in analysing them, we 'must suspend not only the point of view of the signified, but also that of the signifier'.[68] The statement is not a structure, nor a primitive unit; it is a 'function that cuts across a domain of structures and possible unities, and which reveals them, with concrete contents in time and space'.[69]

Statements cannot be studied in isolation. They form *discourses* which are held together by regularities exhibited by the relations between different statements; a discourse is a system for the formation of statements.[70] Hence, the analysis of discourse presupposes exactly the step that Skinner tried to avoid. The historian must not only remain neutral as to the truth-claims of the statements under investigation; he must also bracket their claim to meaning and intelligibility, and explain meaning and intelligibility as a function of the text, rather than conversely. Also, the necessity of a suprahistorical vantage point is abandoned, since being and truth now are objects of inquiry rather than points of departure; the analysis of discourse is based on 'a pure description of discursive events',[71] and the analysis of statements, then, is a historical analysis, but one that avoids all interpretation: it does not question things said as to what they are hiding, what they were 'really' saying, in spite of themselves, the unspoken element they contain, the proliferation of thoughts, images and fantasies that inhabit them; but, on the contrary, it questions them as to their mode of existence, what it means to them to have come into existence, to have left traces, and perhaps to remain there, awaiting the moment when they might be of use once more; what it means for them to have appeared when and where they did.[72]

Consequently, the notion of context drops out as a category explaining the meaning of what has been said and done with words. What counts as the relevant context is itself circularly determined as the particular discourse or family of statements in which a specific statement is being used.[73] As Culler has remarked, 'meaning is context-bound, but context is boundless'.[74] Instead, the notion of context is replaced by the concept of *logical spaces* in which the unfolding and transformation of discourse occurs. It is also in this logical space that the correlation of statements and the effective formation of discourse takes place, and in which the positions constituted by it are formed. According to Deleuze:

> If statements can be distinguished from words, phrases or propositions, it is because they contain their own functions of subject, object and concept in the form of derivatives. To be precise, subject, object and concept are merely functions derived from the statement. As a result, the correlative space is the discursive order of places or positions occupied by subjects, objects and concepts in a family of statements.[75]

In the beginning was the word; discourse is autonomous and has primacy, but is not itself foundational; its autonomy and primacy does not reside in any magical or metaphysical ability to produce physical reality, but in its ability to organize knowledge systematically, so that some things become intelligible, and others not. Knowledge presupposes discourse; statements imply and are correlated with subjects, objects and concepts, but maintain no necessary causal or logical relations with them. Insofar as statements are constitutive of subjects, objects and concepts, it is through relations of coexistence and correlation, which makes certain objects possible as objects of knowledge, and certain propositions possible to deny or affirm by a knowing subject, while other objects and other propositions are excluded from the actual domain of knowledge.[76] Thus, what exists is a function of what is knowable, and not conversely. What is possible to say is a function of what is knowable, and not conversely. What is possible for an author to mean or intend, is a function of the text and its relations with other texts, rather than conversely.[77]

Thus, a description of statements and the relations they maintain with themselves is a description of logical spaces, a description of the conditions of intelligibility and knowledgeability.[78] While autonomous and primary, discourse is caught up in a web of practices; its primacy in relation to them depends on its ability to organize them systematically as being essentially *discursive practices*, that is, systems of statements for the organization of practices.[79]

This autonomy and primacy of discourse leads to two interrelated problems. First, since discourses and discursive practices are statements held together by regularities, the problem of how to identify and describe these regularities is bound to arise. If discourses are defined in terms of regularity, their formation and individuation must be governed by rules, but are these rules themselves part of the discourse under investigation, or are these rules situated outside it? On this point, Foucault himself is not very clear. On the one hand, these rules can be regarded as merely descriptive laws of what is going on inside a given discourse, and how statements are tied together into regular unities. In this case, the rules need not be instantiated in the consciousness of authors and agents; they need not *follow* them in order to be formed and governed by them. Consequently, these rules are situated inside discourse, at the same level as statements themselves, and are to be read off inductively from the discourse under investigation. On the other hand, and as Foucault sometimes unfortunately implies, the rules that govern the formation of discourses do so causally and prescriptively, and they operate directly on the level of phenomena, and so govern the formation not only of statements, but also of their derivative functions, such as subjects, objects and concepts. In this case, the rules of formation turn out to be as much constitutive as regulative, much as grammatical rules are thought to function in structural linguistics.[80]

Second, if we choose, which seems the reasonable thing to do, the first and quite positivist interpretation of discursive rules, another problem arises, namely how a given discourse can be transformed. If we had opted for the second interpretation, this problem would have had an imaginary solution awaiting it in the realm of thought its formulation was designed to escape; that of subject and structure. But if the rules of formation are immanent in discourse itself, there is no external point from which to explain discontinuity; we can arrive at thick descriptions of incommensurable discourses, but we will face a serious problem if we want to explain the transition from one glass bowl to another.[81]

Since this book has as its primary aim to describe the relationship between sovereignty and knowledge as it occurs within three chronologically distinct logical spaces, the assumptions of the autonomy and primacy of discourse will guide these descriptions; but since its secondary aim is to relate these three discourses to each other, we must envisage a way of accounting for the interrelationship and the succession of logical spaces in time. As I shall argue in the next section, genealogy provides us with the last clue to the historical relation between sovereignty and knowledge.[82]

Genealogy

Given this inverted relationship between language and world, what would a history of sovereignty and knowledge look like? In chapter 1, I said that genealogy was *effective*, by virtue of being *episodical* and *exemplary*. It is effective in so far as it must start from an analysis of the present, and identify something as problematic in that present in order to write a history of it. As such, genealogy is strategically aimed at that which looks unproblematic and is held to be timeless; its task is to explain how these present traits, in all their vigour and truth, were formed out of the past. Further, genealogy is episodical insofar as it does not aim to supply a history of the past as it actually was, or to recover a past age in its full density or significance. Instead, genealogy deals with those episodes which are involved in the effective formation of that which was identified as problematic in the present. Finally, genealogy is exemplary, but not in the Renaissance sense of exemplary history. It relies on examples, but it does not assume these examples to be transhistorically valid, since this necessarily would presuppose a cyclical recurrence of historical events or a cyclical concept of time, or both. However, genealogy does presuppose cyclical recurrence at the level of narrative time, so that it can account for the formation of its own point of view, and hence justify itself and its choice of examples as a coherent and locally true narrative. In this section, I shall explain these relationships more fully, while leaving out the much-disputed critical and normative implications of genealogical history.[83]

In chapter 2 above, I attempted an analysis of the present, by demonstrating that the problem of sovereignty, as it looks at present, is rigorously intertwined with the possibilities of political knowledge. Sovereignty is the unthought foundation of that knowledge, and vice versa. As such, the historical problem is to explain how these links were formed, and how the concept of sovereignty acquired its present parergonal qualities. Thus formulated, the problem is a Nietzschean one: *how did we get here?*

Now if – as Nietzsche thought – our understanding of the past inevitably is determined by present concerns, it is perhaps another modern folly to try to escape this present. Perhaps we should accept the fact that we cannot hope to get a fully detached view of our past.

Perhaps we should instead situate ourselves self-consciously in the present, not in order to write the history of the past, but in order to write the history of how this very present was formed.[84]

As we saw above, finalism and presentism invariably resulted from the attempt to situate ourselves outside history: as a consequence, we should perhaps abandon the quest for a suprahistorical perspective, and instead try to write history from *within*. If there is no true past from which to lay tracks to the present, we cannot hope to recover true stories of this past without the aid of a metastory telling us what to count as a true story, this metastory itself being a historical artifice.

However, there must be a connection between past and present, lest the writing of history be an impossible or entirely meaningless enterprise. From a genealogical point of view, the present is all history, in the sense that everything in it has a history, including that which is thought to be timeless, unchanging, given or original, and has been elevated into metanarrative. Thus, genealogy is not a history of opinions, but a history of the knowledges and the metastories which furnish other stories with validity and coherence.[85] It does not presuppose objects, subjects and concepts, but aims to explain their emergence. Foucault writes:

> One has to dispense with the constituent subject, to get rid of the subject itself, that's to say to arrive at an analysis which can account for the constitution of the subject within a historical framework. And this is what I would call genealogy, that is, a form of history which can account for the constitution of knowledges, discourses and domains of objects etc., without having to make reference to a subject which is either transcendental in relation to the field of events or runs in its empty sameness throughout the course of history.[86]

> The genealogical side of discourse ... deals with series of effective formation of discourse: it attempts to grasp it in its power of affirmation, by which I do not mean a power opposed to that of negation, but the power of constituting domains of objects, in relation to which one can affirm or deny true or false propositions.[87]

Therefore, if genealogy is effective history, it is because it is deployed strategically to explain those very traits in the present which we feel are without history, and which serve as starting points for other histories and our present sense of identity: it seeks to put everything evident at present in historical motion. As such, it approaches political thought *as if* its history were one of pure necessity and pure contingency simultaneously; as if it were a history of mathematics *and* a history of poetry. Further, to genealogy, there are no fixed identities or fixed truths to be uncovered by the historian: historical knowledge itself is an object of inquiry rather than a ready possibility, and must be explained as the outcome of past and present concerns. The genealogist turns one of Montaigne's laments into his foremost virtue, and devotes his energies less to the interpretation of things, than to the interpretation of interpretations.[88] According to Nietzsche, there is never a pure historical origin and hence no unbroken continuities or successions in history:

> [T]here is for historiography of any kind no more important proposition than the one it took such effort to establish but which really *ought to be* established now: the cause of the origin of a thing and its eventual utility, its actual employment and place in a system of purposes, lie worlds apart; whatever exists, having somehow come into being, is again and again reinterpreted to new ends, taken over, transformed, and redirected by some power superior to it ... for one had always believed that to understand the demonstrable purposes, the utility of a thing, a form, or an institution, was also to understand why it originated.[89]

Where a hermeneutic interpretation would seek to uncover past realities behind past appearances, genealogy seeks to account for the historical mobility of appearances and realities; behind the veil of appearance, a genealogical history does not find reality, but only another interpretation of the difference between appearance and reality. To genealogy, what happens to exist is a matter of how this divide is arranged and rearranged throughout history. In short, it does not deal with realities, but with troubled efforts at naturalization and the realization of logical and rhetorical possibilities. Thus, genealogy is effective insofar as it is capable of historicizing the present, and of demonstrating that its identity and history themselves have a history of their own, a history which in part is a metahistory of other histories and their active involvement in the constitution of present identities.

Also, genealogy is episodical; it does not go back in time in order to restore an unbroken continuity; it does not seek to demonstrate that the past actively exists in the present;[90] instead, it attempts to show how the past exists only by virtue of being reconstructed from a present, and how this present itself is contingent upon that very past. Whereas a history of the past seeks to recover the past as it actually was, without being sensitive to the fact that how things actually were is a function of how things stand in the present, genealogy focuses on the episodes that help to explain the formation of those traits of the present singled out as problematic. It does not aim to depict an age, an event or a culture in its entirety as does conventional history, but only those historical accidents and details which serve to make the present more intelligible.

Therefore, genealogy cannot concern itself exclusively with the great texts or the great events of an age, since the greatness of a text or an event is a function of the significance given to them by a present which is problematic precisely because it has evolved out of these texts and events; instead, it must continuously question the relationship between interpretive centre and interpretive periphery, whether in singular texts or in entire discourses. Also, genealogy is necessarily episodical because it systematically focuses on and differentiates itself from earlier interpretations, and interprets these interpretations as part of the same problem these interpretations themselves sought to solve.

Since genealogy is not a history of essences, but a history of the battles between different interpretations, it seeks to describe how these battles clear the logical space where objects of knowledge, subjects and concepts can emerge within discourse. The emergence and transformation of discourse and its derivatives result not from continuous growth or succession, but from episodical substitutions, transpositions, sublimations and reversals within discourse itself.[91] Consequently, genealogy can never pretend to discover the proper origin of subjects, objects and concepts, since such a search would assume the existence of immobile forms that precede all accident and all interpretation: 'What is found at the historical beginning of things is not the inviolable identity of their origin; it is the dissension of other things. It is disparity.'[92] Nor can genealogy assume an end towards which everything evolves, because this would be to assume that this end already is manifest in the present or in the future, and, consequently, that interpretation itself can ever come to an end. It is episodical because it treats the present as an episode among others, and not as a final episode of a long drama, or as a non-episode from which all other episodes can be comprehended.

Finally, genealogy is exemplary. It is based on examples which are taken from episodes which are invoked to explain the effective formation of the present. As we learn from Aristotle's *Rhetorics*, arguments from examples 'are the result of induction from one or more singular cases, and when one assumes the general and then concludes the particular by an example'.[93] Of course, an argument from examples may be refuted, 'if we have a single fact that contradicts the opponent's example the argument is refuted as not being necessary, even though examples, more in number and of more common occurrence, are otherwise'.[94] That is, an exemplary history uses general assumptions of the nature of an episode in order to choose its examples from a body of evidence, and uses the resulting examples to exemplify the general assumptions of the nature of an episode, this procedure being warranted by the frequency of examples found in the body of textual evidence.

Now the standard objection to such a view of history and the way of writing it is of course that it is arbitrary in outlook, and this to the point that the very distinction between past and present vanishes before our eyes. To the extent that genealogy denies the necessity of a suprahistorical point of view, it must lapse into fiction. To the extent that genealogy does not deal with fixed identities, its object of study is fluid. To the extent that genealogy is episodical, the choice and definition of the episodes to be investigated are never undertaken from a stable set of criteria. To the extent that genealogy is exemplary, its sampling of examples is never representative and does not cover the wealth of sources.

To counter this objection, one may point out that genealogy must start from an analysis of the present, which serves as the point of departure for the historical inquiry. If the task of genealogy is to write the history of the present from within this very present, it must therefore recognize that its own vantage point, its own perspective, is the outcome of the history reconstructed on the basis of it. That is, in order to justify its definition of episodes, its choice of examples and ultimately itself as a coherent and locally true narrative, it must write the history of its own vantage point simultaneously. Thus, genealogy therefore becomes deliberately elliptical in its mode of emplotment and in its narrative structure. Genealogy does not only recognize that what we call the past is dependent on the present, but that the point from which the past is apprehended itself has a past which coincides with our comprehension of the present. If genealogy is elliptical, it is not because history repeats itself or because time is cyclical, but because one simultaneously has to write the history of the concept of history in order to make sense of the present as something contingent upon a specific historical process. It is thus based on a double reflexivity between the historical modalities of past and present and between historical fact and historical narrative. Logically, genealogy is not only a recipe for writing history from within, but also a recipe for writing the inside story of present truths. As Foucault has noted, 'one 'fictions' history on the basis of a political reality that makes it true, one 'fictions' a politics not yet in existence on the basis of a historical truth'.[95]

In short, what genealogy purports to teach us from history is that we are historical beings all the way down; we are but interpretations of earlier interpretations – but also that it is we and only we who do the interpretation. If genealogical history happens to be rewritten, it is because the present changes. If the present changes, it is partly because history is rewritten.

So far the metahistorical outlook of genealogy. In the next section, it remains to elaborate some of the core assumptions of genealogy and the problems associated with them. As I shall argue, these problems invariably arise when one takes genealogy too seriously, either by raising claims about universal truth or by construing it as a critical theory.

Sovereignty and knowledge

To genealogy, all knowledge is a socially and historically conditioned practice: 'truth is a thing of this world, and each society has its *régime* of truth'.[96] Hence, it must be prepared to answer the question of how this knowledge is related to other parts of political discourse. As I shall argue in this section, Foucault's own response to this problem is unsatisfactory, and is open to metaphysical interpretations. Instead, I shall elaborate an alternative interpretation, and spell out its implications for our understanding of knowledge and sovereignty.

As is well known, Foucault's response to the problem posed by genealogy has been to conceptualize knowledge in strict inter-dependence with power, and treat power and knowledge as mutually generative throughout history, within discourse as well as in the realm of non-discursive practices. In order to understand this peculiar relationship between power and knowledge, it must be contrasted with more conventional accounts of this relationship. In modern political thought, two versions of this relationship have been pre-dominant.

First, and then most often as a presentist apprehension of the ideological upshot of the scientific revolution, the relationship between knowledge and power has been understood in pragmatic terms. Knowledge became the key to the subordination of nature to culture, and of man's mastery of his conditions of existence in nature and society alike. With Bacon, knowledge and power are linked together as a means to an end and as a cause to an effect. Knowledge, erected on firm foundations, is the source of human progress; the forces of nature can be brought under control, and society can be rendered susceptible to rational reform. Truth becomes a condition of legitimate power rightly exercised.

Second, and intimately tied to the late-modern interpretations of the political aspirations of the Enlightenment, the relationship between power and knowledge has been understood critically. Illegitimate power is a constraint upon knowledge, insofar as it excludes or represses the use and production of knowledge. The negative and constraining face of power operates by suspending knowledge in favour of ideology, which serves to mask power's ugly face and make its hegemony acceptable. In the liberal and marxist critique of ideology alike, knowledge becomes a strategically important antidote to dominance and repression, and consequently a source of human emancipation, whether by gradual reform or total revolution. Truth becomes the antithesis of illegitimate power wrongly exercised.

These two figures are often accepted as part of the background understanding in the human and social sciences, and the making of modern political theory is in part a matter of striking the right balance between them. As we shall see in chapters 5 and 6, these figures themselves are drawn within two distinct discourses, both of which conceptualize power in terms of causality, and relate power and knowledge at the level of subjectivity.[97] It is this causal interpretation of power, and the linkage of power and knowledge within a founding subject, which has rendered the latter as the centrepiece of modern political theory, while at the same time its formation and emergence within discourse has been all the more difficult to account for, since the subject constitutes the unquestioned foundation of the very discourse which has attempted to account for it. Further, without the founding subject as the locus of both power and knowledge, it has seemed impossible to make sense of these concepts and their possible logical and empirical relationships.[98]

It is against this backdrop we must try to grasp Foucault's theory, since his analysis is addressed precisely to the unthought assumptions underlying both figures. The subject, the object and the concepts of modern political knowledge are subjected to analysis within his framework. To Foucault, power is essentially productive: it must produce reality before it can act as a constraint upon it; it must equally produce truth before it can suppress or conceal it:[99]

> If power were never anything but repressive, if it never did anything but to say no, do you really think one would be brought to obey it? What makes power hold good, what makes it accepted, is simply the fact that it doesn't only weigh on us as a force that says no, but that it traverses and produces things, it induces pleasure, forms knowledge, produces discourse. It needs to be considered as a productive network which runs through the whole social body, much more than as a negative instance whose function is repression.[100]

Thus, whenever and wherever there is knowledge, there is power, and vice versa:

> Perhaps, too, we should abandon a whole tradition that allows us to imagine that knowledge can exist only where the power relations are suspended and that knowledge can develop only outside its injunctions, its demands and interests. Perhaps we should abandon the belief that power makes mad and that, by the same token, the renunciation of power is one of the conditions of knowledge. We should admit rather that power produces knowledge (and not simply by encouraging it because it serves power or by applying it because it is useful); that power and knowledge directly imply one another; that there is no power relation without the correlative constitution of a field of knowledge, nor any knowledge that does not presuppose at the same time power relations.[101]

This is not to say that power and knowledge are identical, or that they stand in a determinate or historically closed relationship to each other.[102] Foucault's analysis of power and knowledge is precisely focused on the contingent articulation and conversion that takes place between them in history. At every point, power both presupposes and produces knowledge, and for this reason, there is no spot itself uncontaminated by power from where to reflect on its interplay with power. Power and knowledge are linked together on the basis of their difference, but the former has a certain primacy over the latter. Power relations would fade or remain embryonic without the operations of knowledge, which integrate and disperse them. Conversely, if there were no differential power relations, knowledge would have nothing to integrate, actualize and redistribute.[103] Hence, power and knowledge presuppose each other, but the one is not reducible to the other. Their mutual articulation excludes full identity and coincidence, but their difference is made possible only through this articulation. There is no 'outside' to power/knowledge: each is the other's inside.[104]

One of the standard lines of criticism directed against this and other forms of perspectivism is that they are self-refuting;[105] if there is no exteriority, and hence no spot uncontaminated by power from where to reflect and judge, *all* knowledge must be ideology. And since this of course must pertain to the perspectivist claim itself, the perspectivist has sawed off the branch he is sitting on, and cannot himself raise any legitimate claims to validity. Worse, if he intends to criticize the discourses he is investigating, his perspectivism extends the critical distance *ad infinitum*, which makes criticism utterly pointless.[106]

To counter this Socratean move, the perspectivist can turn his back on universal logic and go sophist. That is, genealogy cannot raise any claims to universal truth for itself; its truth must remain local and particular, and it cannot validate its own standpoint with reference to a hypothetic future where all power relations are suspended, or a final truth is acquired.[107] Nor does the interdependence between power and knowledge imply that they are mutually reducible: *all* knowledge is not necessarily ideology. Sometimes, as in the natural sciences, knowledge takes off from the practices that got it started, whereas the efforts of modernity to recast political problems in the neutral language of science do not pass the same test.[108]

So far so good. But as soon as we start to question the ontological status of Foucauldian power, we are bound to be disappointed. Foucault never defines power, but invests it with creative powers of its own; it lacks definite locus, since the concept of power has been given the burden of explaining the formation of all logically possible subjectivities; it is not a commodity or a structure, since it is likewise supposed to explain its own commodification as well as the genesis of all logically possible structures. Ultimately, he seems to imply, power is a relation or a set of possible correlations between forces,[109] 'a total structure of actions brought to bear upon possible actions',[110] but at the same time it is supposed to explain the formation of correlations, since as such they cannot reside elsewhere except within knowledge. If 'power is everywhere, not because it embraces everything, but because it comes from everywhere',[111] it consequently either embraces nothing or comes from nowhere.

If power explains everything, it cannot itself be anything. Either it is reified and turned into an essence informing the course of history from above, or it is merely a narrative helper invoked to transcend the *a priori* limits of discourse, and to engage in an analysis of what is outside discourse as if it were inside it. If power really is omnipresent and explains the formation and transformation of discourse, how do we explain the discourse on power and its own conceptual mutations? Either it is explained in terms of its correlations with concepts within the same logical space in which it occurs, or, as seems to be the case in the later writings of Foucault, the discourse on power is bracketed, and explained as a strategy for concealing real power relations, which, as it were, carry the condition of their own invisibility within themselves. To take some of Foucault's own remarks on sovereignty:

> When we say that sovereignty is the central problem of right in Western societies, what we mean basically is that the essential function of the discourse and techniques of right has been to efface the domination intrinsic to power in order to present the latter at the level of appearance under two different aspects: on the one hand, as the legitimate rights of sovereignty, and on the other, as the legal obligation to obey it.[112]

Founded on and tied to the practices of absolutism, sovereignty has since then functioned as a veil of real power: 'Sovereign, law and prohibition formed a system of representation of power which was extended during the subsequent era by the theories of right: political theory has never ceased to be obsessed with the person of the sovereign. Such theories still continue today to busy themselves with the problem of sovereignty.'[113]

Implied in these remarks is a point similar to Maritain's. Sovereignty is but an expression of an outdated political reality, and helps to conceal present practices of power and domination; the political theorist who discusses sovereignty is guilty by association. It seems that either a genealogy of sovereignty would be confined within the logical limits of discourse, and then cannot and should not aspire to be critical, since it has no external foothold from which to criticize the discourse it analyses: it would remain positivist. Or, taking the above statements seriously, a genealogy of sovereignty would transcend the logical limits of discourse, and try to be critical by claiming access to a new reality of power, formerly inarticulable within discourse except as a moment of concealment, which, like all theories nourished by the idea of conspiracies, itself amounts to a truth-claim superseding all other truth-claims, and therefore equally is a claim to power. Thus, if we take genealogy to be regulated by a notion of universal truth, it becomes both self-refuting and without critical point. If we take gene-alogy to be critical, it becomes both essentialist and hypocritical.[114]

If an analysis of political knowledge ever is to succeed, we should perhaps stay within discourse, and do away with conspiracies. If genealogy is critical, it is not because it permits us to judge the present from a point outside history, but because it permits us to cut the present down to size within it. Therefore, and *pace* Ashley, we should suspend critical activity, since the only warrant of this criticism would be a rather chimerical idea of a transhistorical and therefore uni-versally valid communitarian backdrop from which to criticize the theory and practice of sovereignty; as I shall argue later in this book, the effective formation of such a cosmopolitan or transcendental back-drop is itself a major episode of modernity.[115]

Above all, the discourse on sovereignty is a discourse on power, but that does not imply that we ought to reduce it to an expression of factual power relations or to a practice of concealment. Doing this would merely bring us back into the presentism of a sociology of knowledge which the hermeneutics of conflict helped us escape. What we could retain, however, is the insight that power and know-ledge are mutually productive, but within the confines of discourse. The discourse on sovereignty is a discourse on the varying attributes and changing locations of power within political discourse, but power is not its essence or the source of its truth; rather, it is the discourse on sovereignty, as it takes place within different logical spaces and in different historical episodes, that tells us what power *is* within each, and how it should be interpreted, known and measured. Without a proper mode of knowledge to render it intelligible, sover-eignty cannot exist, and loses its capacity to organize political reality through a demarcation of inside from outside, of Same from Other. Without a proper form of sovereignty, knowledge loses its power to organize reality, and to constitute objects and fields of inquiry as well as criteria of validity and truth. If truth is power, and power is truth, this is so because of the different metaphorical relationships they entertain within different forms of knowledge, within different logical spaces, within different discourses; if these forms of know-ledge, these logical spaces and these discourses are different, they are so because of the specific juxtaposition of truth and power they implicate. If we can observe transitions between them, it is because of the battles going on within them; battles over sovereignty within knowledge, and battles of different knowledges within the discourse on sovereignty. This leads to the next problem; how to periodize history from within?

Periodization and the present

As I said in chapter 1, knowledge is knowledge by differentiation. First, a given knowledge constitutes itself as such by demarcating itself from what is not knowledge, be it opinion or superstition. Second, it constitutes itself by an internal differentiation by means of algorithm, which permits us to discriminate between the clear and the opaque, the valid and the invalid, the relevant and the irrelevant, the true and the false. Doing this, a given knowledge necessarily implies a decision on ontology: what does and what does not exist? From these decisions, two other decisions follow: one ethical, which tells us who we are, who is a friend, who is an enemy and who is a stranger, the other metahistorical, which tells us where *we* came from, how *we* became friends, and where *we* are heading. In short, knowledge is indissolubly intertwined with decisions on identity and presence, and is thus inherently political since these decisions invariably actualize conflicts over sovereignty.

As I also stated in the introduction, the historical part of this book is broken down into three periods – the Renaissance, the Classical Age and Modernity – with the aim of describing the genealogically crucial episodes within them as well as effective transitions between them. In this section, I shall venture some remarks on this periodization.

The first point is integral to the historical part of my argument: this periodization is founded on the assumption that there are significant epistemic changes between these periods, so that the answers provided to the above decisions on identity, presence and truth are, if not wholly incommensurable across time, at least sufficiently distinct to warrant the periodization as a heuristic device. This may well be disputed, but so is necessarily all periodization. As such, periodization is an activity both inductive and deductive; one abstracts from one's familiarity with a material, and uses this abstraction to comprehend the material itself, and one samples one's material on the basis of an inherited idea of periods and their differentiation; periodization itself always occurs within an episode, however unperiodized this period may appear to the presentist or finalist historian.

The question becomes from whom one inherits the specific notion of periodization, which in turn is a metahistorical or historiographical question. As we shall have ample occasion to notice, each of the periods singled out has its own episodical claim to newness and its own claim to having transcended the past, a claim for which a peculiar type of historiography figures as the ultimate warrant. In the Renaissance, the claim to rebirth is sustained precisely by a reclaiming of an alien past – antiquity – and the subsequent transposition of traits from this alien past in the shape of exempla into the present, effected by a Valla or a Budé.[116] In the Classical Age, the claim to newness rests on its battle with passion, superstition and inherited tradition, fought most vigilantly by Bacon and Descartes.[117] During Modernity, the period out of which we have not yet escaped, the claim to newness resides in its episodical appropriation of history itself as a mode of being, its reinvention and reconstruction of history into distinct ages and the constructive powers attributed to the subject by Vico, Kant and Hegel.[118]

If we take these claims to newness too seriously, history risks becoming a pack of tricks the dead play on us; if we ignore them, we lose the inductive foothold of our periodization. As genealogy tries to give equal importance to its own sight and that of its object, a genealogy must encompass these claims to newness, and take them for what they are: historical events among others. Hence, they must be related to and explained with reference to the particular discourse and the particular knowledge which engender them. To be effective history, genealogy must explain the exemplarity of its own episodes.

Another way of justifying a given periodization is to justify it from without, either by reference to a received canon of history, or in opposition to it. Here I do both. Since it has been disputed among historians when the particular configuration of sovereignty which separates yet relates the sovereign state with an international system did arise, it is a secondary task to provide a commentary upon and a partial historical explanation of these different claims, and how they arose. This is the strategic argument for my periodization. The periodization is itself based on exempla constituted by modern historiography.

First, there is what I will label the *Renaissance hypothesis*. According to nineteenth-century historians such as Heeren and twentieth-century international political theorists such as Wight, the modern international system has its embryonic origin in the politics of the city-states of Renaissance Italy, with the rise of diplomatic communications and the scientification and monopolization of warfare as its chief manifestations.[119]

Second, there is what I will label the *Westphalian hypothesis*, which has had a pervasive impact on the study of international relations. According to Bull and other proponents of this hypothesis, the international system was formed out of the turmoil of the Thirty Years War, propelled by the consolidation of European states and their mutual recognition of sovereignty as the principle of their future intercourse in the treaty of Utrecht.[120]

Third, there is the *Modernity hypothesis*, which by contrast asserts that the modern international system had to await its emergence until the rise of the nation-state as the dominant form of political life in Europe, with the spread of popular sovereignty and fervent nationalism as both cause and effect of the internationalization of these features themselves.[121]

A genealogy of sovereignty is not exclusively concerned with the history of international political theory, which is a rather short one, but with the formation of the necessary constituents of such a discourse, and their relation to its emergence and later scientification. As a consequence, it must delineate its conditions of possibility within knowledge. As I shall argue in chapter 6, the configuration of sovereignty which makes the present distinction of the domestic and the international spheres viable in theory and practice, is of fairly recent and quite unexpected origin. Therefore, the above hypotheses have more to do with the historicization of being which marks the advent of modernity, and less to do with the specific pasts onto which this historicization is superimposed retrospectively.

That is, if history is written from within itself, it is not only because periods contain episodes, and episodes contain examples, but because periodization must occur within an episode which itself is periodized on the basis of exempla, which in turn have their exemplary status determined by their place within an episode, which is an episode only by virtue of being periodized. Thus, in my interpretation, the periods singled out for investigation are two things simultaneously: first, they form an identifiable regularity of statements, which together constitute the logical spaces within which the discourse on sovereignty and the discourse on knowledge are interfoliated; second, they constitute grids of analysis and interpretation which I have constructed in order to be able to analyse and render intelligible the multiple and complex correlations between knowledge and sovereignty which take place within each. Thus, within periods, the perspective of the analysis and the perspective of the object of analysis necessarily converge. Between periods, and as perspectives multiply, periods can be said, at least to a certain extent, to analyse one another; not because of any ghostly subjectivity on their part, but because knowledge has no outside.

In chapter 4, I shall describe the formation of a general theory of the state within Renaissance knowledge, arguing that this general theory of the state, as it gradually came to encompass the genealogical ancestors of the concept of sovereignty, also carved out a differentiation between Christianity and a heterogeneous outside until Renaissance knowledge imploded in the face of it.

In chapter 5, I shall describe the formation of classical sovereignty within the framework of classical knowledge, arguing that this amounted to a massive rearrangement of the divide between inside and outside, but that this rearrangement simultaneously was inherently fragile and unstable.

In chapter 6, I shall describe how this classical differentiation and the knowledge which sustained it were swept away in the wake of modernity, and how it has been profoundly reorganized to obtain its present shape, as was described in chapter 2.

4 Inventing outsides: proto-sovereignty, exempla and the general theory of the state in the Renaissance

> The sea has opened.
>
> Machiavelli

As Carl Schmitt once remarked: 'All significant concepts of the modern theory of the state are secularized theological concepts, not only because of their historical development ... but also because of their systematic structure.'[1]

As I have argued above, a genealogy of sovereignty is not a history of its inferential connections with other political concepts, but a history of its articulation within different knowledges, within different 'systematic structures'. The aim of this chapter is to trace the genealogy of sovereignty from its prehistory within theology to its articulation within Renaissance knowledge. Methodologically, however, this poses problems. The very term sovereignty was not present within political discourse until Beaumanoir introduced it in the thirteenth century,[2] and even after that date, there is no autonomous discourse on sovereignty, if we by autonomous mean a discourse which has a single system for the formation of statements.[3] The same is true of the concept of the state; during the late Middle Ages and the Renaissance, the term *status* is used to denote many things, but never an abstract entity, wholly disconnected from both ruler and ruled.[4]

Therefore, in this chapter, we must pay attention to the conceptual antecedents of sovereignty and state, and their logical conditions of possibility within theological, legal and political writings in the Middle Ages and in the Renaissance.[5] In doing this – and with perhaps undue simplification – I will use the term mytho-sovereignty to cover the mimetic paradigm of rulership in the early and high Middle Ages, when the legitimacy of the ruler is founded on his resemblance with

Christ or God, and the term proto-sovereignty to cover the polity-centred paradigm of rulership in the late Middle Ages, when the legitimacy of the ruler derives from more profane sources.[6]

A secondary and strategic aim of this chapter is to provide a comment upon the *Renaissance hypothesis*, which fixes the chronological origin of the disjunction between the state and the international onto the Renaissance, with the French invasion of *Regnum Italicum* in 1494 as the decisive point of emergence, an event which turned Italy into a battlefield after some decades of relative tranquillity following the Peace of Lodi in 1454.[7]

It should be borne in mind that genealogical history opposes itself directly to the search for origins and fixed limits, understood as the attempt to capture the exact essence of things or their purest identity, an ambition which perpetually nourishes debate and disagreements among historians. Therefore, in aiming to provide a comment upon this hypothesis, I do not mean to propose an alternative origin, only to demonstrate that the talk of origin is problematic; genealogy is concerned with the *fabrication* of identities and essences out of differences, not with their *purification*.

As I shall argue, and then from a genealogical viewpoint, any talk about something international during the Renaissance is unwarranted, if international is taken to mean something – a system or a society – dependent on yet ontologically distinguishable from individual states. This is so for two different reasons. First, the sovereign state was not individuated as an object of an autonomous political discourse at this stage. Second, even if we readily can discern a discourse on political entities, this discourse does not systematically account for the relationship between fully individuated political units, but treats them as instances of a pre-existent universal. To distinguish what was *within* states and what was *between* states was not fully possible, either in theory, or in practice.[8]

What we have – to borrow a term from Meinecke[9] – is a *general theory of the state*; a theory which as such does not presuppose an outside other than a heterogeneous and largely *unknown* outside of a *Respublica Christiana*. What I shall attempt to show, is how this general theory of the state is sustained and articulated within a specific mode of political knowledge, based on resemblance and validated by an excess of exempla. As I shall attempt to make clear in my analysis of the texts of Machiavelli, More and Vitoria, this general theory of the state, together with the mode of knowledge which sustains it, is gradually undermined during the sixteenth century as a result of its troubled attempt to deal with what is outside its scope, an outside which to some extent is positively constituted and defined by this very discourse.

This chapter is subdivided as follows. In the first section, I shall briefly sketch the prehistory of the general theory of the state in terms of its conditions of possibility and conceptual ancestry. In the second section, I shall situate this theory within the space of Renaissance knowledge, and then describe its articulation and crisis in the texts of Machiavelli, More and Vitoria, each of which I shall treat as exemplary of this episode.

The general theory of the state

Discussing the impact of natural law on the Renaissance concept of the state, Otto Gierke notes that 'the State was no longer derived from the divinely ordained harmony of the universal whole; it was no longer explained as a partial whole which was derived from, and preserved by, the existence of the greater: *it was simply explained by itself*'.[10] What does it mean to be explained by itself? First, this image is indicative of a peculiarity of knowledge. In order for some phenomenon to be explainable by itself within a discursive space, the discursive space itself must be, if not closed, then at least folded in upon itself. Knowledge must in a sense be total, and therefore inviolable; it must be infinite within itself, and able to soak up everything and bring it under its inviolable authority. In other words, the explanation itself must share the same reality as that which is to be explained, and must be situated at a level inseparable from its object. As we shall be able to notice, the general theory of the state is a general theory precisely in this respect, since it does not discriminate between statements and their objects, but is built and validated within a knowledge which links words and things together in an infinite series of resemblances of events and episodes. Thus, within the general theory of the state, legendary accounts and direct observation are intertwined within knowledge. As I shall argue below, this aspect of the concept of the state arises out of its troubled relationship to time.

Second, it points to an ontological peculiarity. Much like in Dante's idea of a *humanitas* who crowns and mitres itself over *itself*,[11] it implies a reflexive ontological image, a liturgical and ceremonial space where subject and object can coincide and constitute each other as such.

Evidently something exogenous and mystical is wanting if this space is to be cleared: even if the state is 'no longer derived from the divinely ordained harmony', it must nevertheless rest on a foundation which is not wholly internal to itself, but which makes its reflexivity possible, and permits it to occupy the dual positions of subject and object at one and the same moment. In short, it implies a discursive space, a void or a silence which is no longer a 'whole' but therefore nevertheless necessary as an arena of emergence. As I shall argue below, this aspect of the concept of the state emerges from the battle between universalism and nominalism in medieval ontology.

In this section, the task is to describe how this theory of the state was gradually assembled out of a mass of theological, legal and philosophical mutations within medieval discourse, the result of attempts to settle the interpretive conflict over whom was to be the legitimate heir to the subjectivity of Christ, and therefore, ultimately, to the sovereignty of God. As we shall see, this development culminates in a more or less decisive break with the high medieval order, and the gradual *generalization* of the theory of the state.

Mytho-sovereignty, analogy and allegory

At its most abstract level, high medieval Christian society was a universal society; it was universal insofar as the Church – the *Ecclesia* – understood itself as an indivisible unity covering every aspect of man's political and social being, and the preservation of this essential wholeness was the prime purpose of earthly authority.[12] This society was also universal in the sense that it remained insensitive to all ethnical, regional and linguistic difference; all social forms were subsumed under the Christian norm. Its structural unity and the uniformity of its content were both ontologically associated with the idea of an immutable hierarchical order connecting micro- and macrocosm together in a preordained and harmonious relationship.

Thus, the *Ecclesia* is something more than the aggregate of persons who compose it; it is a mystical body transcending the material existence of its component particulars, which in turn stand in a relation of functional, organic and ontological dependence to the overarching whole, without which they could not be imagined to exist.

This societal whole was conceived of as an earthly expression of a heavenly pattern; the ultimate task of the *Ecclesia* and its ruler was to guide the body of the faithful from its transitory and earthly existence towards salvation and eternal life, thus effecting a final reunion with the transcendent order. The earthly community was a means to a higher end, and its existence wholly subordinated to it.[13]

The ultimate source of medieval authority was laid down in the Petrine commission, according to which Christ had instituted the universal body of the faithful and handed it over to St Peter and his successors, who – according to the doctrine – were designated to rule over as well as to represent and personalize this mystical reality. The source of all authority, whether in terms of papal *plenitudo potestatis* or lay *imperium, gubernaculum* or *majestas*, was divine; all legitimate power descended from God downwards. According to Matthew, 'Thou art Peter and upon this rock I will build my church ... And I will give unto thee the keys of the kingdom of heaven: and whatever thou shalt bind on earth shall be bound in heaven: and whatsoever thou shalt loose on earth shall be loosed in heaven'.[14]

The genealogy of the conceptual antecedents to sovereignty is very complex and conditioned by the perennial contest between ecclesiastical and lay power, between the unresolvable claims to exclusive authority by *sacerdotium* and *imperium* respectively throughout the Middle Ages; the very demarcation between the temporal and the spiritual was itself a spiritual matter, a question of the proper division of authority within one single body with one single head.[15] As Kantorowicz has shown, the question of the proper locus of supreme authority involved a continuous exchange of the concepts, symbols, insignia and legal axioms of authority between the church and secular authority, with the effect that theological elements were gradually transposed to a secular setting.[16] This substitution, duplication and transmission of signs are visible in the genealogy of authority and subjectivity, taking us from God to king.

In the christomimetic paradigm of rulership, the king is a twinned being, half human, half divine, and holds his powers by the grace of God. These powers, along with his dual character, are bestowed upon him by liturgy and sacramental action before the altar, signifying the duplication of these natures in Christ, and symbolizing his link with God and his distinctive position over and above the community of mortals. The sacramental actions – coronation and anointment – were administered by officers of the church, which made lay rulers both *de facto* and *de iure* dependent on papal authority.[17]

Gradually, however, and as the idiom of Roman law began to penetrate theological discourse on authority during the twelfth and thirteenth centuries, the christological and liturgical paradigm was superseded. Law was substituted for the dual subjectivity of Christ as the mimetic principle of and mediating link between God and king. The position, attributes and symbolism of rulership remained intact in the course of this transition; what changed, however, was the principle of transmission from God to king. As a consequence, the king became a hypostasis or an articulation of an immortal, semi-divine idea of law and justice.[18] Witness Aegidius Romanus, in his *De Regimine Principum* (1277–9): 'the king or prince is a kind of Law, and the Law is a kind of king or prince. For the Law is a kind of inanimate prince; the prince, however, a kind of animate Law. And insofar as the animate exceeds the inanimate the king or prince must exceed the law.'[19]

But how was it possible to sustain these models of political subjectivity – of king as Christ or king as *lex animata*? In the Middle Ages, the questions of authority and the questions of ontology were rigorously intertwined, so that a solution to each more or less automatically implied a solution to the other. As Wilks has remarked, 'the failure to find a universally acceptable philosophical system was itself the root cause of the conflicts in medieval political thought. The constitutional theories of the age were no more than an expression in terms of government of all the discordant elements in contemporary philosophy.'[20]

However, if we for a moment suspend the ceaseless disputes over ontology and authority which characterize the high medieval texts, and instead focus on the mode of knowledge which makes them possible, we are bound to notice how this knowledge rests on complex isomorphic relations within the universal whole and between its component parts, paving the way for an endless series of analogies and allegories.

First, knowledge, in the sense of memory and the retrieval of legal documents, was largely monopolized by the church. Papal superiority in the legal disputes which arose during the Investiture Contest was facilitated by a gradual accumulation of archives and registers. The church had a past of its own, consisting of a continuity of texts linked together by a continuity of commentary and interpretation; its opponents possessed no such past. What was outside this body of texts, ranging as it did from the very words of God down to the tiniest legal protocol, was not admitted as knowledge. Thus, in the midst of the Investiture Contest, when the pope was confronted with the protests of the German emperor Henry IV, who held that what he was doing was in perfect consonance with the custom of his predecessors, the pope could quite confidently reply: 'The Lord did not say "I am custom", but the Lord said "I am the Truth".'[21]

Second, knowledge, in a less material sense, rested on analogy, and was dependent on allegory for its dissemination and reproduction. Within a universalist ontology, everything must take on meaning against the backdrop of the transcendent whole. The various isomorphies, ranging from the celestial order of things down to its various earthly instances, were linked together through a logically infinite series of analogies. As Delany has pointed out, analogy establishes reciprocal logical relations between disparate things; it creates an economy of identity and difference between different systems on different levels of complexity. However, both analogy, and its special case, allegory, are circular; they must presuppose the very universalist framework they articulate, disseminate, reproduce and put into operation. Its 'truth' must be present right from the start; analogy and allegory cannot produce new knowledge, only reproduce what already is manifest in its premises. It speaks to the already convinced; it disseminates, distributes and demonstrates, but it does not have the power reserved for God: to *create*.[22]

Within political knowledge, and closely interlinked with the genealogical transition of authority from God to king, is the *corpus-anima* analogy. Originally, within the christomimetic paradigm, it was used to express in neo-platonic terms the relationship between priesthood and laity; the former stood to the latter in a relationship analogous to that between soul and body; the latter marked by the stigma of the corporeal and perishable, the former with its fair share of divinity. When later transferred to the temporal realm as a model of rulership, it took on a slightly different meaning. Just as a natural body necessarily needs to be animated by a soul, so a social body must be infused by the spirit of right and law, embodied in the ruler. In John of Salisbury's *Policraticus* (1159), the soul is symbolized by the prince, who rightly is the *head* of government, and the functions of each inferior part of the body are duly subordinated to that of the whole; the assembly is compared to the heart; governors and judges with eyes and ears; the fisc with the stomach, and so forth.[23]

Third, if knowledge based on analogy and allegory permitted the reproduction and dissemination of the textual justification for the mimetic paradigm of rulership, it had a counterpart in the visual expression of the same relationships. Both coronation ceremonies and court entries closed the gap between the articulable and the visible, and validated the articulable by means of the visible within the same general structure of universalist discourse.

As noted above, the coronation and anointment of emperors and kings were from the ninth century onwards liturgical acts in which image and reality were brought to coincide, and the theocratic character of kingship put into relief. However, the coronation rituals continued long after the liturgical act had lost its constitutive importance and had ceased to be an effective instrument of ecclesiastical power. This is also largely true of court entries, festivals and funeral rites which enjoyed an upsurge during the Renaissance, even when much of their theological underpinnings had lost their theoretical significance in the overall structure of political discourse.[24]

Perhaps some of the continuing significance of these rituals can be explained in terms of the symbolism they contained; both coronation and anointment touched the head of the ruler, thus conveying the importance of the head or 'soul' as the pivotal point on which the influx of divine grace was combined with a concentration of power. Furthermore, both coronation ceremonies and later also court entries and festivals allowed for a dramatic exploitation of spatial metaphors: seated on his throne, the king's position over and above his subjects cannot be doubted even by the illiterate mind. Finally, these rituals, especially as they were subjected to a gradual technical and scenographic development, became more important for the dissemination of specific and more complex political messages. They could fulfil the same set of persuasive and didactic functions as the *speculum princeps* did to the literate audience, the very idea of *specula* itself reliant on a visual and optical metaphorics;[25] the sacred origin of a dynasty, its glorious history and its present virtues could be rhetorically disseminated to an audience which believed that truth resided in and could be apprehended in images and visual statements.[26]

But how, one may ask, is it possible for such a universalist order to change; does it even recognize such a possibility within itself?

Proto-sovereignty, time, continuity and exempla

Posed at the metahistorical level, the question of change invariably involves the question of time. At least since Plato's *Timaeus*, the question of time had proven a perennial enigma to Western philosophy: does time exist, and if it does, how is it possible to know and measure it? It is in and through the varying responses to this question that the emergence of the general theory of the state must be understood.

What, then, is time? During late antiquity this question had provoked sceptical scorn: time *is* not; time has no being since the future is not yet, the past is no longer, and the present does not remain.[27] It is against the backdrop of this scepticism we should understand Augustine's reply to the problem, as it is presented in the eleventh *Confession* (c. 397): yet if time does not exist, we certainly understand time when we speak of it, and we understand it when we hear it spoken of.[28]

Augustine's solution to the problem of time is to relegate the problem itself from the cosmological level to the level of subjectivity and intentionality; if past, present and future do exist, they do so by being located in the soul, and then by its distention into modalities: 'For these three do somehow exist in the soul, and otherwise I see them not: present of things past, *memory*; present of things present, *sight*; present of things future, *expectation*.'[29]

What makes this quite enigmatic solution possible to sustain and to project onto experience is the contrast between time and eternity, which it dramatizes into ethical opposition. To Augustine, *tempus* signifies the createdness and therefore also the transitoriness of the present world; time is as finite as this world, and has been created together with the transitory world, and will coexist with it from creation to the last day.[30]

In contrast to time, and as its ultimate limit as finite, perishable and momentary existence stands *æternitas*, a timeless stratum of uncreated and therefore immutable being, symbolized by the eternity of God, and in which past and future are contained in one single and unmoving present.[31]

To this contrast corresponds a hierarchy of values: finite *tempus* carries the stigma of man's fragile and incomplete existence in the sinister, yet for the time being inescapable, terrestrial condition, whereas eternity signifies the singular legitimate aim of Christian salvation and transcendence; the relation between time and eternity marks the distance between God and his creation, the latter being entrapped in time, and his subjectivity dispersed in it as memory, perception and expectation.[32]

If change does occur, it does so as a transition from time to superior eternity, or from one time to an inferior time. As Ricoeur has remarked: 'Time must be thought of as *transitory* in order to be fully experienced as *transition*.'[33] That is, change is either positive and vertical, and then involves salvation, a transition of the earthly community into a spiritual realm of concord, harmony and happiness, or, it is negative and horizontal, involving dissolution, decay, destruction, dissimilitude and discord; time is inherently corrosive.[34]

With the gradual reception of Aristotelian texts in the twelfth and thirteenth centuries, time underwent profound change, as did the notion of change.[35] To Aristotle, as to a great part of early Greek antiquity, the concept of time was connected to, however not identical with, the movement of physical bodies in space,[36] an argument rejected by Augustine.[37] From this connection, once released from the Platonic doctrine of the createdness of time, the step was short to asserting the uncreatedness of the world and the infinite continuity of time as well. These tenets, when gradually incorporated into scholastic philosophy, emphasized the permanency of the world against its previous transitoriness, and brought with them an ethical transvaluation of time; from being a sign of the ephemeral, time became a sign of endless duration, of immortality.[38]

In an effort to counter this potentially dangerous conceptual transformation, scholastic philosophy tried to split the difference between eternity and time, through the reintroduction of a middle term mentioned yet largely unaccounted for by Augustine; the *aveum*, situated between *æternitas* and *tempus*.[39] Originally the home of angels – and later also of their subterranean counterparts – *aveum* had connoted both infiniteness and duration, but also motion and change. Whatever entities came to reside in this stratum were understood to be immutable, however. Thus, in the *aveum*, continuity and sempiternity were joined together within an ontological stratum which in itself was discontinuous in character.[40]

These mutations in the concept of time had three consequences that together made possible the general theory of the state, and the simultaneous erosion of the mimetic concept of rulership. These sets of consequences followed different chronologies of dissemination, however.

First, the opening of the *aveum* had profound consequences for political ontology, since this idea of sempiternity both presupposed an account of and made it possible to account for the existence of universals other than in purely liturgical and transcendental terms. Above all, this meant that things previously understood as discontinuous or transitory now could be understood as continuous.

Thus, the body politic could be accounted for as something ontologically separate from the existence of the ruler within it, yet as something continuous, transcending the life of the ruler in time and space.

The symbols, concepts and insignia of rulership and authority could be depersonalized, deprived of momentary liturgical backing, and instead vested with sempiternal existence. The realm or body politic stood thus above the corrosive influence of transitory time; at this point, we witness the first steps towards a theory of inalienability, which implies a set of rights well separated from those of the individual king, and, consequently, the notion of an impersonal Crown protected against alienation through prescription.[41]

Within a given realm, it was now possible to act as if the world were infinite. If the state never dies, one can tie the currents of its inner life to a calendar based on the recurrent pattern of movement displayed by heavenly bodies; for example, it is possible to administer permanent annual taxation with reference to a continuous necessity and link it to the calendar, until it finally becomes a recognized right of the sovereign state.[42]

Moreover, if the life and being of the body politic transcends that of its individual inhabitants in time and space, the *regnum* can demand their sacrifice for the sake of the *patria*, by the same token as God could claim sacrifice from the community of faithful; wars could be waged for the defence of the *patria* as they had been waged against the infidel, and the protection of the *patria* became an imperative as important as the protection of the Faith. The immortality of the body politic is contrasted with the mortality of the individuals within it, and the latter fact could be used to substantiate the former myth.[43]

Furthermore, as the concepts, symbols and insignia of rulership took on sempiternal existence as universals, and as the contest between church and lay authorities gradually was resolved in favour of the latter, they also took on spatial connotations. The body politic could be understood as something continuous not only in time, but also as something continuous in space, and became connected with the concept of territory; the conceptual history of *fiscus* and *patria* is a history of emergent spatial connotations.[44]

In a significant episode, the substantial connection between the body politic and territory was forged in the clash between legal discourses that occurred in an effort to resolve the conflict between imperial claims to dominion and royal independence in the second half of the thirteenth century. This resolution was effected by a reversal of the hierarchy between legal interpretations, a reversal of the *de facto* and *de iure* notions of independence. In this legal battle, French publicists and Neapolitan jurists such as Marinus and Andreas de Isernia set out to dismantle the *de iure* imperial overlordship advocated by Emperor Henry VII against the then undeniable *de facto* independence of the French king,[45] and – more fiercely – against Robert of Naples, who was summoned to appear before the emperor in 1312, accused of having committed the *crimen læsae majestatis*. Robert, ignoring the edict, simply could not see the point in this accusation, since he himself recognized no superior within his realm. Finally, this legal dispute was resolved in favour of the royal claims to independence, and the imperial assertion of *de iure* supremacy was brushed aside by pope Clement V, when in the *Pastoralis Cura* (1313) he gave formal expression to the idea of territorial limitations of sovereignty and hence final practical legitimacy to the formula *rex in regno suo est imperator*, where *regno* now had acquired an unequivocal territorial signification.[46] Thus, by the beginning of the fourteenth century, the continuous existence in time and space granted to a body politic makes it possible to speak, albeit not without anachronism, of a *state*, which, for all its apparent secularity, retained 'a whiff of incense from another world'.[47] Witness a passage from Baldus's *Consilia*: 'A realm contains not only the material territory but also the peoples of the realm ... And the totality or commonweal of the realm does not die, because a commonweal continues to exist even after the kings have been driven away. For the commonweal cannot die ... it lives forever.'[48]

Second, apart from the consequences for political ontology, the new concept of time had a profound epistemic import. Within the space carved out inside continuous political beings, time becomes accessible to measurement on the basis of recurrent patterns displayed by the motion of heavenly bodies and the succession of natural phenomena. If Augustinian time was marked by its transitoriness, Aristotelian time is marked by its recurrence, either in unchanging cyclical patterns or in the successions of events within immutable strata.[49] To the cyclical and reversible pattern of planetary movements and annual seasons corresponds the cyclical pattern of constitutional change in Aristotle, which takes us from degeneration and regeneration, and back. To the irreversible succession of natural events such as birth and death correspond the dynastic successions within a continuous state.[50]

For political knowledge, the consequences of this mutation cannot be underestimated; if time recurs, history must also repeat itself infinitely. History is substituted for Augustinian memory as a clue to the past; it becomes possible to learn from the past, even though the knowing subject is alienated from this past as he is from the future, and situated in a present which is no longer continuous with his memory and expectation. If time is continuous, it can contain discontinuities which affect claims to validity and authenticity: as Lorenzo Valla pointed out in 1440, the Donation of Constantine, a document used to boost papal claims to power for almost a millennium, was a forgery since it was based on a series of apparent anachronisms.[51]

If nothing is new under the sun, but nevertheless changes according to recurrent patterns, what happens in the past will only preserve its validity as a guide to present as well as future action if it is carefully selected from the body of past experience and grafted onto an appropriate context that is defined in terms of its resemblance with other contexts. From this point on, historical narrative as well as political argument proceed by means of exempla.[52]

In Aristotle's *Rhetorics*, the use of exempla is described as a means of persuasion, as a means of producing belief in an audience.[53] As such, an exemplum crosses the boundary between past and present, and the distinction between what is represented and what represents; it denotes both that which is *exemplified* and that which *exemplifies*. It is thus bound to disturb any fixed opposition between appearance and reality and set it in rhetorical motion.[54]

In its late medieval and Renaissance context, argument by means of exempla comes to constitute the core of the political knowledge of continuous political beings, but its validity is not circumscribed by these beings and their concrete conditions of existence in time and space. Instead, this political knowledge is projected onto their diverse and alien pasts on the basis of a resemblance between these pasts, often found to be legendary; the founding subjectivity of Christ is exposed to competition from the founding subjectivity of a Lycurgus, a Moses, a King Utopus, or, most dramatically, a Quetzalcoatl.

The validity of these accounts comes through the back door, as it were: the theory of the state, emerging from the mass of theological concepts and inscribed within sempiternity, is *generalized* by the mass of exempla, and has its range of validity defined by them. Hence, what the general theory of the state has to say about political beings is as applicable to the Roman Empire as it is to a tiny diocese or magistracy, but with the important qualification that the episodes, events or beings commented upon must display morphological similarity. To keep political knowledge by means of exempla going, a cosmology centred around the notion of resemblance is necessary. In the next section, I shall elaborate the notion of resemblance and its connection with the rhetoric of exempla.

The third set of consequences pertains to the ethical level, where, now outside the continuity of the body politic, we find the stigma of transitoriness. If the state grows out of sempiternity in order to find its continuity warranted within it, the ethical negativity formerly allotted to Augustinian time now resides outside it, and poses a constant threat to it in the shape of contingency, difference, discord, and war. What is opposed is no longer eternity and time, the word of God and the voice of man, but the continuous state and the presence of contingency on its outside. What is outside the continuous state is also outside the scope of the general theory of the state, and therefore beyond the grasp of political knowledge, since what is outside the state is also outside the steady flow of recurrent time; outside the state, exempla find their validity undermined. As we shall see below, Machiavelli, More and Vitoria all face this otherness, but present different solutions to how it is to be overcome. Before this can be done, there remains one more episode to explore in the genealogy of conceptual antecedents.

Proto-sovereignty, nominalism and the outside

One way to characterize mytho-sovereignty is to say that it was largely a *descending* theory of government. All power and all authority come from a transcendental sphere above, and the social body is a passive recipient of its animating force. By the same token, proto-sovereignty has been characterized as an *ascending* theory of government, with power and authority flowing from the immanent source of an earthly community.[55]

In the standard account of this theoretical transition, great emphasis has been placed on the reception and dissemination of Aristotle's ethical and political writings, most notably his *Politics*.[56] Whereas the swiftness and transformative power of this reception has been recently contested, the overall impact of Aristotelian thought is not.[57] In an age when ontology was a continuation of politics by other means, the translation and revival of Aristotelian texts brought forth conceptual resources foreign to and potentially destructive of the universalist order.

The early medieval period had not known any independent category of human activity called politics; what is anachronistically labelled political during the Middle Ages is what was expressed in terms of law alone.[58] Whether it was William of Moerbeke's translation of

Aristotle's *Politics* that catalysed the transition from the descending to the ascending theory of government or not remains contested; yet with it came the term *politikos*, and its derivatives *polis* and *zoon politikon* inscribed within a coherent discourse.[59]

These concepts themselves referred to ideas alien to the descending theory of government. The term *politikos* carried the connotation of a ruler who was not logically placed above the law and the community, but instead had his authority both enabled and circumscribed by them.[60] The term *polis* conveyed the idea of a political community, not instituted by divine grace or through duplication of a transcendental community, but which grew from below as a result of the historical collaboration between natural forces and human reason.[61] Finally, the term *zoon politikon* carried a death blow to the subjectivity of man as defined by his place in a universal order whose justification lay in the promise of transcendence. Man emerged as a social and political animal, distinguished by his reason, his sociability, and his capacity for deliberate transformation of his political predicament.[62]

The troubled reception of these ideas within scholastic discourse is well known, as is the incommensurability between the orders of nature and grace it fostered; the one human, the other divine; the one based on reason, the other based on faith and revelation.[63]

On the one hand, this incommensurability sharpened the logical divide between *sacerdotium* and *imperium*, but left the question of their proper interrelationship largely unresolved.[64] On the other, the Thomistic mediation sought to reconcile universalism and the nominalism resulting from radical interpretations of Aristotle.[65]

It is against the backdrop of these ontological disputes that we should pose the question of the outside, and its conditions of possibility; how do the reversals and mediations between universalism and nominalism affect the relationship to the outside which was opened up by time? How does political theology respond to the Occamist thesis that 'every whole is nothing other than the sum of its parts taken together',[66] and hence to the claim that universal substances not only are unreal, but violate a law of economy?

In the *Defensor Pacis* (1324), the ascending theory of government, as well as the claims to independence raised by Italian city-states, are systematically backed by nominalism and naturalism, while papal claims to power are systematically refuted. What is of interest here, however, is not the impact of the *Defensor* on the opinionated forces of the day, but the discursive space within which the conflict between universalism and nominalism is staged, and how the line between what is inside the state and what is outside it is drawn.

First, the idea of a divine origin of power and authority is dismissed as an article of faith rather than an idea susceptible to rational proof.[67] The aims of the state are defined teleologically as the preservation of its health as a self-subsistent body and the well-being of its constituent parts.[68] The state is man-made; its purpose is a purely terrestrial one, and its existence disconnected from otherworldly ends. Consequently, all authority flows from the *legislator humanus*, who is the efficient and primary cause of all law, and who conditions the separation of the parts of the state.[69] The state is a particular unity, not because it is universal within itself, but because it subsumes its parts under a law of economy. Unity within the state is numerical unity, since it is 'a unity of order; it is not an absolute unity, but rather a plurality of men who are said to be some one thing in number not because they are one in number formally but rather because they are said to be related to one thing in number'.[70]

Second, the state is now brought down to earth, but it still retains a purpose – albeit now a profane one – in the core of its concept. But Marsiglio was not able – any more than other writers of the period – to escape the ideal of a single universal and unified body politic, constituting the ultimate scope of authority and governed by one single head; the main arguments of the *Defensor* are cast in universal terms, as if the solutions proposed to the problems flowing from a political nominalism themselves are universally applicable whenever the political condition within a universal body is beset by plurality. Marsiglio assumes the possibility of a multitude of communities whose inner and outer life are regulated by the universalist framework elaborated in the *Defensor*, and thereby begs the question of mediation. This constitutes the essential tension of the *Defensor*: for how can a plurality of particular states be imagined within and reconciled with a universal body politic?

Dante had wrestled with the same problem in *Monarchia* (c.1309), and, unable to solve it, had been pushed back in a universalist direction by assuming the necessity of one single ruler for mankind as a whole, itself ultimately subordinated to a divine end.[71]

But now, in the *First Discourse*, in which Marsiglio sets out to prove the necessity of the numerical unity of supreme government in a particular state by means of a razor argument, the argument from economy itself supports its particularity. In one single city or state, there must be only one single supreme authority, because

> if there were several governments in the city or state, and they were not reduced or ordered under one supreme government, then the judgement, command and execution of matters of benefit and justice would fail, and because men's injuries would therefore be unavenged the result would be fighting, separation, and finally the destruction of the city or the state.[72]

To the economy of ontology corresponds an economy of authority; to posit the existence of more entities than necessary in an argument has an outcome analogous to the discord that follows from competition over authority within one single body politic; a body politic is one and single by virtue of a singularity of authority within it; we see here the naked nominalist logic behind the indivisibility thesis later articulated by Bodin. Faced from the outside, the economy of authority yields the same result; singular authority makes it easier for the community as a whole to 'avoid harmful impending dangers such as are presented by external ... enemies who intend to oppress the community and to take away its freedom'.[73] Here, and as a consequence of its teleological and nominalist underpinnings, the state has an outside; it is inscribed within a void together with a plurality of other states,[74] each being in turn composed of lesser parts, with the individual *zoon politikon* as the least of them.

Now what is universal amidst this plurality seems to be plurality itself, whether this plurality pertains to what is inside the state, or whether the same plurality pertains to the multitude of states themselves, which are 'almost necessarily separate from one another in place, and especially for men who use different languages and who differ widely in morals and customs'.[75]

With this line of reasoning in mind, we could expect to find a clear-cut refutation of papal claims to universal dominion. In the *Second Discourse*, Marsiglio stumbles upon the problem of world government:

> [T]he necessity that there be a single head in a single household is not the same as the necessity that there be a single head in a whole state or in several provinces, because those who are not members of the same familial household do not need the numerical unity of a single family head ... our opponent's [papalistic] reasoning would conclude that it is equally necessary that there be a numerically single head in the entire world, which is neither expedient nor true. For in order that men may live together in peace, it is sufficient that there be a numerically single government in each province.[76]

To a modern theorist of international politics, this argument would seem impermissibly naive. What it does indicate, however, is the presuppositional structure of Marsiglio's thesis. The pope is thrown out because it is supposed – in accordance with the law of economy – that he is unnecessary within the political order, not because the universalist framework itself is redundant or unwanted. Rather, it seems to be the other way around; the universalist premise is assumed to be valid right from the start, and this to the extent that it does not need backing from overarching authority; Occam's razor cuts out papal authority as an unwarranted premise of this order, and turns its presence into an outcome of a prior and highly undesirable act of usurpation. Thus, the outside of the state, as it is opened up by Marsiglio, is but another inside within the big inside, the universalist framework of reasoning; the nominalist argument gains cutting edge only within this framework; without it, there would be nothing to *cut out* in the first place.

If we want to find an outside which is not an inside of another inside during the later Middle Ages, we must inquire into the metaphorical limit of the political world, and how this limit is connected to the theory and practice of proto-sovereignty. We have many examples of how Christianity as a whole deals discursively with the external arena during the Crusades; we have very few examples of how such dealings are connected to its inner political fragmentation.

One such example is provided by the discourse on piracy; it is perhaps no coincidence that Bartolus, one of the most ardent defenders of the independence of states from papacy and empire, was among the first to confront the problem of piracy systematically in *Tractatus Represaliarum* (1353), since it represented a test case of the extent of independence.[77]

Of course, piracy itself was nothing new in the early fourteenth century; it had threatened coastal traffic in the Mediterranean since antiquity, and had perhaps contributed to the otherness associated with the oceans before the age of discovery. The seas – except for the Mediterranean – were still largely unexplored and uncharted,[78] and figured metaphorically as barriers to political knowledge and authority; authority did not extend far out to sea, and beyond its scope lurked an unknown and unnavigable outside, a non-territorial element not susceptible to human mastery. Thus, to Dante's monarch, the 'ocean alone is the limit of ... jurisdiction'.[79]

What was new about piracy, however, was the way it was systematically linked to the discursive practices of the early states – notably Genoa, Sicily and Naples – and its gradual 'legalization' with constant reference to the formula of proto-sovereignty, which by the 1330s had become common legal stock.

The fast dissemination and elaboration of the formula of proto-sovereignty soon gave rise to competing claims between states about sovereignty over the seas. On the basis of such theory, each state could – and did – proclaim an inalienable right to jurisdiction over the seas, and attempted to overrule reciprocal claims made by feudal lords as well as other states. These claims were backed by the creation of a new office, the admiralty, which exercised jurisdiction over the seas.

Most of the admirals had been trained for their post in the profession of pirate, and now continued their old business with royal authorization. A practice formerly occupying a judicial borderline zone, since it had been as often an excuse for war as a pretext for juridical action on behalf of feudal lords, began to fit into the legal categories which were derived from the formula of proto-sovereignty, and which brought a certain order and systematic character to the practice of reprisal.

To be sure, the practices of marque and reprisal were not new to the early fourteenth century; these forms of largely private violence were of Roman ancestry. If a man from one city suffered a loss or injury at the hands of a man from another city, he was legally entitled to recoup his loss or avenge his injury by taking the goods of his antagonist's compatriots, or inflicting a corresponding injury upon them. This practice was not only considered excusable and officially sanctioned, but also regarded as inevitable throughout the high Middle Ages.[80]

Now the practices of piracy and reprisal were also potent political weapons, and enjoyed a shadowy existence somewhere between illegality and war; at sea, this distinction was even less clear-cut than on land at this time. What was left to learned jurisprudence was not only the task of legitimizing this practice by explaining how and why the innocent should suffer for crimes of which others were guilty. More importantly, the jurists were forced to refine their argumentation with respect to the legitimate locus of the right of reprisal; without proper control, the practice of reprisal could easily degenerate into continuous violence, with disruptive consequences for trade and revenue. The solution was provided by linking the practice of reprisal to the discourse on just war; precisely as the waging of war demanded authorization by a superior authority, so now did reprisals.[81]

The significance of this episode is that it involves a twofold articulation. First, the inward practice of proto-sovereignty is systematically linked to the outward practice of piracy; inward fragmentation conditions outward articulation, and vice versa. Second, piracy is systematically organized and to some extent domesticated within the discourse on proto-sovereignty, and the discourse on proto-sovereignty, in its turn, is articulated and refined against the backdrop of piracy, which had hitherto been an Other, an element foreign to authority and political knowledge.

In the above episodes, we have seen how a general theory of the state is gradually assembled out of the most disparate elements. Theological concepts and symbols are fused with elements from Roman Law, and given a literally new reality through the ontological mutations that occur once aristotelian writings are absorbed into theological and legal discourse.

The omnipotence of God and the primordial subjectivity of Christ, the objects of a ceaseless clash of interpretations throughout the Middle Ages, gradually yield to the twin pressures of cosmological time and political nominalism; the discourse on the locus and scope of authority is brought down to earth, but so are its teleological and eschatological underpinnings. The promise of harmony and peace becomes this-worldly and inscribed into the essence of political beings. But to this natural kind, which is held to be continuous in time and space, is opposed what is accidental and foreign to it.

Therefore, if the nominal state is inscribed within a field of sempiternity, a new space of estrangement is opened up in the course of this process. Although the terrestrial condition of medieval man alienated him from his creator and from eternity, Augustinian eternity could nevertheless render meaningful both the accidental and the transitory by presenting it as integral to man's lowly terrestrial condition. But Aristotelian time and nominalism render them utterly meaningless, and instead transpose and reinscribe man's alienation onto a new and imagined surface, an outside of contingency and dissimilitude which sets a limit both to authority and to knowledge.[82] In the next section, I shall focus on the discursive construction of this outside, and the simultaneous attempt to cope with it from a precarious position within a political knowledge itself involved in the act of demarcation.

Inventing outsides

One possible way to approach the sixteenth-century Renaissance is to consider it as a crisis of meaning, as an age in which the founding word of God has become increasingly opaque and ambiguous, and therefore open to diverse interpretations. If God had created the world through one single discursive gesture, he had also woven words and things together in a web of perfect significance, reflecting the perfection of his creation and providing unequivocal clues to its decoding. Words are things, things are words; ontologically sign and signified are inseparable, but since they coexist within a preordained harmony, they speak the same language and are accessible within the same knowledge.

But what happens if their fundamental unity is preserved, but their harmonious intersection is disturbed and destabilized? What if the event at Babel comes true in the *new* time?

At the same time, Renaissance Europe is marked by political crisis; the papacy had proved to be increasingly impotent as an arbiter of conflicts between the rising states, and this development coincided with the stepwise expansion of the Ottoman empire, the only agent on the external arena taken seriously by Christianity. While the presence of something so clearly *anti-Christian* posed a very material threat indeed, the discovery of *non-Christian* forms of life in the Americas posed an analogous theoretical threat to the stability of Christian values.

Perhaps the body of Renaissance knowledge, with its strange yet fairly coherent blend of magic, emergent rationality and ancient exempla, is better understood against the backdrop of such disorganizing events; in this case, Renaissance knowledge can be understood as an effort to restore a broken order by making everything speak again with one voice, by bringing together the visibility of things and the articulability of words, so that things can be read and words seen.[83]

At the most general level, and thanks to the neo-platonist revival,[84] Renaissance knowledge is a knowledge of resemblance between entities whose unity has been shattered; of resemblance between things and of their resemblance to signs. Resemblances proliferate throughout the Renaissance universe; they are able to constitute a chain of things on the basis of their spatial proximity in which 'each species always preserves the same course in its motion so that it always proceeds from this place to that place and, in turn, recedes from the latter to the former, in a certain most harmonious manner'.[85] Consequently, what is found at the beginning of a chain of things, is always found in a similar form at its end, since otherwise 'it would not be directed to one determined region, or quality, or substance, rather than to any other whatsoever'.[86] Furthermore, resemblances are able to constitute series of concentric circles containing disparate elements so that 'some elements, because of a certain heaviness, descend to the centre of the universe; while others because of their lightness, ascend to the vault of the superior sphere'.[87] As a consequence, what is found at a lower level of existence always mirrors what is found at a higher level, and conversely. We need only to perceive, by means of axiom or by means of magic,

> the reciprocal affinity of natures, and applying to each single thing the suitable and peculiar inducements [*magus*] brings forth into the open the miracles concealed in the recesses of the world, in the depths of nature, and in the storehouses and mysteries of God, just as if she herself were their maker; and, as the farmer weds his elms to vines, even so does the *magus* wed earth to heaven, that is, he weds lower things to the endowments and powers of higher things.[88]

Representation, as we know it, is not yet an open possibility; words and things are not correlated within a matrix, or ordered in strict intersection with one another. If there is representation, it is modelled on optical metaphors; what we have is ceaseless reflection, which draws words and things together by visualizing the articulable, and articulating the visible; as a consequence, the relation between projection and reality is as unstable as the relation between discourse and the non-discursive in the Renaissance text.[89] Within this knowledge, the forces of sympathy and antipathy are superimposed upon the web of resemblance, and kept in check by being organized into an intelligible and decipherable order, in which 'all things, no matter how diverse, are brought back to unity according to a single determined harmony and rational plan'.[90]

Resemblances themselves are not visible, since they are buried in the depths of nature; they must be unearthed by the deciphering of visible marks and signs which are hidden beneath the surface of things. The world must be read in order to be known; the sign and what it denotes are of the same nature, but their author has ceased to provide authoritative clues to their interpretation. Consequently, reading and observing are not distinct as methods of knowing, but necessarily intertwined.[91]

Within political knowledge, resemblance and exempla go hand in hand, each sustaining the other. Resemblance is always warranted through exempla, and the choice of exempla is always justified with reference to resemblance. In political discourse, this circular connection is carried out in two different, yet interdependent, ways: as a resemblance of the *events* and *episodes* to be exemplified, or as a resemblance between the political beings to which the exempla are thought to apply, and then in terms of their similarity of *form* and *origin*. As we shall see below, the logic of exempla is systematically upheld by the notion of resemblance between events and episodes, by resemblance of form and origin; together, resemblance and exempla furnish the general theory of the state with validity.

Through the resemblance of events and episodes it becomes possible to describe and discuss present affairs by drawing on the almost infinite corpus of political learning recovered from antiquity, without distinguishing between legend and document; it becomes possible to describe the deeds of a Moses or a King Utopus in the same terms as one describes the recent behaviour of Cesare Borgia or Henry VIII, because it is assumed that they share the same very reality, and occupy the same space of possible political experience.

This strategy is employed in discussions of matters of state, such as how a particular political being can be improved or modified, and more importantly, how war is to be conducted, won, tempered or avoided. During the Renaissance, and then in close conjunction with the general theory of the state, a discourse on war emerges, sustained by ancient exempla.[92] War is no longer understood as the outcome of providence or blind fate, but as an object of human knowledge and as an instrument of power, susceptible to human control.[93] As such, it can be explained in terms of human passions; to most writers preoccupied with war in general terms, it is caused by human greed and manifested in zero-sum competition over territory.[94] Conversely, peace gradually loses its transcendent ring and becomes a this-worldly aspiration, attainable by subjecting passion to reasoned self-interest.[95]

Through resemblance of form and origin, it becomes possible to apply the wisdom of statecraft distilled by means of exempla across time and space, since no *essential* discontinuity between past and present is perceived. If there is discontinuity, it is measured nominally as a discontinuity of form and origin: an exemplum can be grafted successfully from one political being onto another, provided either that the political beings in question display, at the episode singled out for exemplification, constitutional similarity, or, a similarity of origin. Hence, a speech of Pericles may prove edifying at a moment when popular government is beset by decay; a quote from Livy will be helpful to a republic torn by internal strife; the ingenuity of Lycurgus can be invoked when a principality is awaiting a fresh start, and so forth.

As I shall argue in the following subsections, this mode of knowledge constitutes the partly unarticulated foundation on which writers such as Machiavelli, More and Vitoria build, despite their disagreement at the level of opinion. While the fact that these three writers do share this mode of knowledge justifies my selecting their works as exempla of Renaissance texts, the dissimilarity of their opinions makes it possible to discern three distinct formulations of and responses to the 'problem of the outside'.

Machiavelli's mirrors

To Augustine, the image reflected in a mirror is a false, inferior and lifeless reality, but one which has the power of seduction, since 'the mother of falsity is the similitude of things which reaches the eye'.[96] In the Renaissance, the mirror image becomes the mother of truth, and the positive unthought of knowledge. The mirror reflects ideal images, and is able to furnish these images with a reality superior to that of the object mirrored. The *speculum* has not only the power to represent or seduce; it has the power to breathe life into reality by mirroring it. As I shall attempt to demonstrate, this positivity of the mirror is reflected in Machiavelli's attempt to cope with the problem of contingency posed by time and particularity through *innovation*. Such an interpretation has been suggested by Pocock (see n. 82 above).

But first, when the author of *Il Principe* (1532) for a brief moment steps out of his text in order to tell the reader the truth of the text itself, we must begin by asking what it takes to tell the truth of the matter, the *verità effetuale della cosa*. What happens when one attempts 'to concentrate on what really happens rather than on theories and speculations'[97] within a knowledge based on resemblance and exempla?

First, what is at stake in the statement is the possibility of reflection itself, and this from a detached viewpoint. By sidestepping his own text, Machiavelli authorizes a reading of it as an accurate mirror image of a political reality. As we shall see, this act of mirroring is likewise an act of innovation and construction; Machiavelli mirrors a political reality whose very reality itself hinges on the rhetorical impact of the truth construed in and by the act of mirroring. This is what makes it effective truth; he mirrors politics and animates it as presence; he constructs a political reality on the basis of an image that makes it present, and constructs an effective truth on the basis of resemblance between image and reality. Hence, reality is understood as discursive, and discourse as inseparable from reality; discourse not only describes reality, but mimics its structures and processes in writing.[98]

Second, to the act of mirroring correspond the acts that are mirrored; to the total structure of actions and relations depicted in *Il Principe* corresponds closely the total structure of statements set in motion through the act of mirroring. Image and reality duplicate each other, since what the text says about actions, it also to a certain extent does within itself by the rhetorical use of exempla. To a modern, he seems to use both present experience and examples from the past in a wholly arbitrary manner.[99] It remains to see how this strategy of exemplification functions rhetorically, and how it is delimited by the forms of government upon which Machiavelli concentrates.

In *Il Principe*, the form of government whose workings are to be exemplified is princely rule. The state (*lo stato*) is an object of action, but the state itself cannot act. As Hexter has pointed out, Machiavelli's use of the term stato differs from the various usages of its Latin antecedent *status* in the late Middle Ages. If *status* signified either the relative permanency of a *condition*, the immobility of an *estate*, or the *capacity* of a ruler, the concept *stato* is consistently tied to the agency of a ruler, yet as something existing independently of him.[100] As such, it stands as an inanimate object to the animating subjectivity of a ruler; the state as such cannot act.[101] The *stato* is passive; the ruler is active; the relative success of the latter is measured by his ability to and his relative success in acquiring or maintaining the state, and hence also his own position within it; sometimes, they seem inseparable.[102] The state is the objective condition of rulership; rulership is the subjective condition of the state, without a state the ruler ceases to be sovereign, without a ruler, the state ceases to be an object of political knowledge. Hence, the exempla sustaining the logic of action in *Il Principe* are derived from resemblant political beings and episodes.

As we learn in the first chapters of *Il Principe*, states are either republics or principalities, and the latter are either hereditary or new, or a mixture of the two.[103] In hereditary principalities, the art of ruling is facilitated by the legitimacy that comes with tradition and custom.[104]

However, to Machiavelli, the real problem of governance is posed by new states. What makes them new is their sudden acquisition by a new prince; their newness flows from an act of innovation undertaken by the ruler; in the ideal case singled out by Machiavelli, the object of political legitimacy is made rather than found.[105]

In his role as innovator, the ruler must begin by destroying existing political institutions within his newly acquired state, and depriving them of their former legitimacy.[106] Innovation necessitates the prior overthrow of an established order and the erection of a new one, but also relentless action in its defence; the act of innovation itself puts the antithesis between old and new into relief. As such, innovation opens the door to contingency in the shape of Fortuna, since

> all those who profit from the old order will be opposed to the innovator, whereas all those who might benefit from the new order are, at best, tepid supporters of him. This lukewarmness arises partly from fear of adversaries, who have the laws on their side, partly from the sceptical temper of men, who do not really believe in new things unless they have been seen to work well.[107]

Since Fortuna is the arbiter of at least half of our actions,[108] the ruler who owes his position merely to the whims of fortune will likewise be vulnerable to its future caprice, and hence find insurmountable difficulties in maintaining his state.[109] Consequently, the relative success of a ruler in a completely new principality 'will depend on how much ability (*virtù*) he possesses'.[110] The act of innovation itself closely resembles that of foundation, as in the exempla of prophets and mythological lawgivers such as Moses, Cyrus and Romulus: 'Such innovators, then, have to confront many difficulties; all the dangers come after they have begun their enterprises, and need to be overcome through their own ability. But once they have succeeded ... they remain powerful, secure, honoured and successful.'[111]

This logic of innovation is mirrored by a similar logic at the textual level. To the newness of a principality and the problems ensuing from the act of innovation corresponds the conflict between old and new facing the author of *Il Principe*; the affirmation of the newness of the principles of action embodied in *Il Principe* is dependent on the authority of the author, who faces a problem analogous to that of the innovating ruler; he must uproot and delegitimize a form of political knowledge in order to inscribe a new truth of the matter onto a present political reality by means of hitherto unseen resemblances and unauthorized exempla; he must delete the parts of memory which threaten to distort or subvert the act of mirroring.[112] He must be prepared to cope with Fortuna in the shape of distortion and falsity in the mirror used; he himself must be an armed prophet, owing nothing to luck except the opportunity to shape the image into reality.[113] As author, he will face as much recalcitrance as does a prince, since

> it has always been no less dangerous to discover new ways and methods than to set off in search of new seas and unknown lands because the generality of mankind are much more ready to belittle than to praise another's actions, none the less, impelled by the natural desire ... I have decided to enter upon a new way, as yet untrodden by anyone else.[114]

When followed by a prince, the clue to success along the route of innovation is to be found in his relative *virtù*. We must therefore turn now to the precise nature of this virtue, in order to see how the clue to the rhetorical success of the author resides in a transvaluation of *virtù* and its relationship to its other, Fortuna.

The senses of the term *virtù* in *Il Principe* and *Discorsi* have been subjected to much debate. On the one hand, it has been discussed whether the concept of *virtù* in its various occurrences is reducible to one or another more specific form of virtue, and, in this case, where this virtue ultimately is located in the body politic.[115] On the other, the problem has been posed whether Machiavellian *virtù* is compatible with or opposed to other moral standards of action, either present to his contemporaries or accessible to the interpreter.[116]

It is this latter problem which has kept Machiavelli alive throughout the centuries, and concerns the question of the basic moral stance of Machiavelli, and to what extent this stance implies a divorce between morals and politics. With varying degrees of hypocrisy, Machiavelli has been identified with immorality and evil; from Pole and Gentillet in the sixteenth century up to Leo Strauss in the twentieth, his writings have been seen to embody a split between Christian ethics and secular statecraft.[117] In its less rabid versions, this argument has been recast as a contest between morals and politics; to Cassirer, Machiavelli is a precursor of the cool and detached social scientist, preoccupied with facts rather than values.[118] In its more sophisticated version, what is held to be fundamental to Machiavelli's position is his 'clear recognition of the necessity and autonomy of politics, of politics which is beyond or, rather below moral good and evil, of politics which has its own laws against which it is useless to rebel'.[119]

The most recent response to this problem has been to opt for its dissolution. According to Berlin, the entire question rests on the dubious assumption that there once existed a peaceful coexistence between the realms of morals and politics until this coexistence was disrupted by Machiavelli.[120] Rather, the originality of Machiavelli consists in the revival and elaboration of an alternative moral-political standard, largely of pagan origin, and in content as well as in effect incommensurable with Christian ethics. There is simply no way of deciding between these two competing standards with the aid of any overarching criteria: Machiavelli uncovered this dilemma by unhesitatingly taking for granted the superiority of Roman polity-centric values over Christian transcendent values, but left an unbridgeable lacuna between them wide open for posterity.[121]

This thesis is accepted by Skinner, who holds that *virtù* is used in *Il Principe* to refer to 'whatever range of qualities the prince may find necessary in order to "maintain his state" and "achieve great things"'. Sometimes princely *virtù* will overlap with conventional virtues, but 'the idea of any necessary or even approximate equivalence between *virtù* and the virtues is a disastrous mistake'.[122] In Pocock's formulation, the question 'whether the prince should obey moral law therefore becomes a discussion of *when* he should obey it'.[123]

What is neglected by Berlin and Skinner is the language and the logic through which this tension between old and new standards of political conduct is put into relief and brought to bear upon the political reality which Machiavelli mirrors. As McCanles has pointed out regarding *Il Principe*, 'it is in discourse, the rules for its formation, its necessary care to avoid its own disruptions and its own contradictions, that we find the seeds of the disintegration of human rationality and therefore of human order'.[124]

Thus, the relationship between Christian virtue and pagan virtue is not only one of incommensurable ethical opposition, but also one of tension and supplementation at the discursive level. The contradiction between the old order and the purportedly new standard of statecraft is only constructable and articulable within the framework of the old one, and then with the aid of rhetorical ruses and conceptual polarizations familiar to it. The act of innovation partly consists in dramatizing this opposition by means of *exempla*; what is new has to be rendered new against the backdrop of something which becomes old through the act of innovation itself. As we shall see, this act of innovation cuts across the divide between projection and reality, and inscribes the ruler and his state within a realm of contingency made up of other states in the same predicament.

The rendering of the disjunction between old and new is dependent on an act of textual dissimulation by the author which closely parallels the acts of tactical dissimulation recommended to the prince facing the problem of innovation. Political reality is thus reflected in the mirror of the text, the author playing the same set of tricks on his reader as the prince is well advised to do on his subjects outside the text.[125] At this point, the virtue of the author consists in controlling the contingent relations which inevitably arise between text and reader, by subjecting the latter to rhetorical stratagems.

The disjunction between moral standards is most clearly articulated in chapters 15 to 19 of *Il Principe*, where Machiavelli begins by stating that 'how men live is so different from how they should live that a ruler who does not do what is generally done, but persists in doing what ought to be done, will undermine his power rather than maintain it'.[126]

What is presupposed here is the presence of a shared communitarian code of conduct, as well as an equally shared practice deviating from it. This tension is instantiated in some pieces of concrete advice a few lines below

> I know that everyone will acknowledge that it would be most praiseworthy for a ruler to have all the ... qualities that are held to be good ... [B]ecause circumstances do not permit living a completely virtuous life, one must be sufficiently prudent to know how to avoid becoming notorious for those vices that would destroy one's power ... Yet one should not be troubled about becoming notorious for those vices without which it is difficult to preserve one's power, because ... doing some things that seem virtuous may result in one's ruin.[127]

> A ruler, then, need not actually possess all the above-mentioned qualities, [e.g those classified as good in ch. 15] *but he must certainly seem to.* Indeed, I shall be so bold as to say that having and always cultivating them is harmful, whereas seeming to have them is useful.[128]

Hence, the actions of the ruler are to some extent constrained by the moral fabric of his society; he must cultivate a virtuous appearance especially when his actions substantially conflict with the old moral imperatives; simultaneously, however, the old fabric is rendered fragile through this exploitation. But it is the received standard that enables the ruler to act as he does; there would be no need for fake in a world devoid of moral standards, since in such a world, the disjunction between real virtue and dissimulated virtue would be meaningless. The distinction between 'being' and 'seeming' points to the presence of a code of values held to be good. As a consequence, dissimulation itself cannot be universalized since it is parasitic on an already universalized code; precisely as innovation must be undertaken against the backdrop of an established order, so the dissimulation of virtue must take place within an already present structure of virtue, which it cannot hope to abolish or transcend completely. The old and the new are opposed in terms of content, but supplementary in terms of form, a supplementarity which animates their opposition.[129]

Turning now to the realities of dissimulation as they are represented in chapter 18, we are informed how the rift in the moral fabric is brought about through the act of dissimulation itself. There are two ways of contending, says Machiavelli: 'one by using laws, the other, force. The first is appropriate for men, the second for animals.'[130] It follows that the ruler must combine human character with a good portion of beastliness if he is going to succeed along the route of innovation, and withstand the challenges of fortune: 'This policy was taught to rulers allegorically by ancient writers: they tell how Achilles and many other ancient rulers were entrusted to Chiron the Centaur, to be raised carefully by him.'[131]

The significance of this exemplum is complex. First, it presupposes resemblance along the episodic axis, but the episode exemplified is in itself an episode of exemplification: Chiron's twinned being is an exemplum to ancient rulers, and this fact itself constitutes an exemplum to contemporary rulers. Second, there is resemblance along the axis of origin, since Chiron is an innovator: in Pindar's sixth *Pythian Ode*, Chiron is the creator of unwritten law, making it out of pure force.[132] Third, and within this exemplum, Machiavelli relies on an allegory in order to establish a perennial truth about political reality. By representing Chiron's germinant nature as fiction, the opposition between law and force which is coexistent with the opposition between man and animal, is made to stand out as a reality. By grafting allegory onto allegory, Machiavelli fictions a fiction, which, through a play of double negation, is rendered as truth.[133] Fourth, the substance of the centaur's advice is concealed from the reader, and perhaps clear to the statesman only; the centaur is presented as an exemplum, but we are not informed about the content of his wisdom. The mysteries of state and rulership must remain secret in order to become operative.[134]

This concealment is also the prudent textual route to follow by the author, since the success of dissimulation rests on the secrecy of the very act of dissimulation; disclosed dissimulation ceases to be dissimulation, and gives way to outright lie. This is all the more evident in the exemplum of the fox; the fox not only conceals, but has the power of concealing the act of concealment: 'foxiness should be well concealed; one must be a great feigner and dissembler. And men are so naive, and so much dominated by immediate needs, that a skilful deceiver always finds plenty of people who will let themselves be deceived.'[135]

Through double concealment, the rhetoric of innovation becomes superior to established truth. This subversion of the hierarchy between old and new cannot be made operative through an overt opposition or contest between them, but only through a clandestine subordination. Dissimulation and concealment constitute the privileges of the innovator, who can exploit the moral and epistemic resources of the old order while creating a new one; the force of traditional truth rests with the established order, but can be bent to the purposes of the innovator, who uses its rhetorical force to construct a new edifice of law and knowledge. Even here, the act of innovation depends on supplementarity between the old and the new, but the privilege is now shifted from the former to the latter.

This pattern of innovation, authority and virtue is repeated in the *Discorsi* (1519),[136] but with the important difference that the form of government now is republican. If *Il Principe* was focused around the problem of security and written from the vantage point of the sovereign subjectivity of a ruler, this perspective is reversed in the *Discorsi*. It is written from the vantage point of the sovereign subjectivity of a people: whereas *Il Principe* busies itself with the virtue of a ruler as a condition of his security and success in a realm of contingency, the *Discorsi* is an analysis of the conditions of liberty and virtue in the entire body politic, which no longer is an inanimate object, but a living reality itself capable of action.[137]

In the *Discorsi*, Machiavelli sets out to explore precisely that which from the vantage point of the exempla provided by princely rule is anomalous: republics, we are told, are difficult if not impossible to subject to princely rule, since 'they do not forget, indeed cannot forget, their lost liberties'.[138] Hence, the strategy of exemplification now shifts away from 'great rulers' to 'great republics', with republican Rome as the paradigm and Livy as the prime source.

The vitality and survival of a republic is dependent on the liberty and virtue of its citizens, rather than on the animating force of an innovating prince.[139] Thus, in the *Discorsi*, the analysis of virtue by means of exempla is no longer confined to the level of the individual, but extended to the republic as a whole. The amount of virtue within a republic determines its ability to withstand corrosive change and external threats. This thesis emerges most clearly in the analysis of the conditions behind the rise of the Roman Empire:

> For if there is nowhere to be found a republic so successful as was Rome, this is because there is nowhere to be found a republic so constituted as to be able to make the conquests Rome made. For it was the *virtù* of her armies that caused Rome to acquire an empire, and it was her constitutional procedure and peculiar customs which she owed to her first legislator that enabled her to maintain what she had acquired.[140]

A republic is dependent both on good laws for its internal order, and on good arms for its defence and expansion. Ideally, and as in *Il Principe*, good laws are laid down by a founding legislator, such as Romulus.[141] When this is the case, the stability and continuity of the republic are partly guaranteed through the initial perfection of its constitution, but the soundness of its political institutions is dependent on the virtue of its citizens, which can be cultivated only through broad participation in political affairs. The flexibility of a republic, and hence its ability to cope with the capricious forces of Fortuna, demands popular sovereignty (*governo largo*), which in turn goes hand in hand with political liberty.[142]

In the *Discorsi*, the virtues necessary for the survival of a republic are both civic and military; they are two sides of the same coin, and tend to reinforce each other. Whereas civil virtue is the condition of internal liberty, military virtue is necessary for external liberty and outward expansion.[143] The ideal citizen is the armed citizen; the ideal warrior is he who identifies himself primarily by his loyalty to the commonwealth and its structure of civic values.[144]

Thus, the ideal republic is able to mobilize and conserve the virtues and liberties of its citizens only through their active participation in its affairs. However, the republic itself is situated in a realm of particularity, time and contingency. It is born, it lives and it dies as an island in an ocean of fortune; an ocean where power relationships rather than law reign as unobstructed in the relations between states as they did between the prince and his possible opponents within the princely state. Confronting this problem, the virtuous republic organizes itself for aggrandizement right from the start.[145]

Both the prince and the republic face contingency, but in different guises. Whereas the prince stood alone against the forces of fortune, and had to engage in ceaseless innovation in order to carve out and domesticate a portion of time in order to become and remain secure within it, the republic must organize itself for external defence within a space populated by similar entities. Whereas the prince must trust his own cunning and virtue in order to succeed along the route of innovation, the republic can rely on a mutual reinforcement between the virtues of the citizens and the soundness of its institutions and practices; it must embody innovation and translate it into flexibility in its external relations. Thus, both prince and republic, as modes of the same political subjectivity, face analogous problems and present analogous solutions. The prince stands in the same relation to his contenders as does the republic to its neighbours; their success depends on their relative *virtù*.

Now this virtue which is called for both reflects and sharpens the disjunction between Christian standards of political conduct and the demands of revived pagan statecraft; in their clash, the concept of virtue cracks open, and distances itself from its old connotations. The resulting statecraft, operative only in a world where traditional legitimacy has begun to erode, now emerges as a force separating the new political subjectivity of a prince or a republic from its outside. The disjunction thus becomes double: to the opposition between old and new corresponds an opposition between inside and outside; by virtue of being new, the state becomes the Same.

Still, there is a limit set on newness and sameness from within political knowledge itself. There is a tension between the use of exempla and the discursive practice of innovation, manifested both at the level of historical reality and the textual level; the *newer* something appears to be, the less useful exempla from the past become as guides to action and as rhetorical devices for legitimizing it. If, as Machiavelli states, all commonwealths pass through a cycle of rise and decay,[146] how can exempla from these furnish us with guidance if the cycle is stabilized or broken by an act of stabilization or innovation?

By the same token, there is a tension between the modes of producing exempla. As Lyons has pointed out, the production of exempla is internal to the historical process itself;[147] simultaneously, however, exempla are created by the innovative author in order to exemplify the same historical process; he supplies exempla from a point outside the process. If exempla are generated by history, they are effective within it; they close history and stabilize the cycle of change, 'since good examples proceed from good education, good education from good laws, and good laws in this case from those very tumults which many so inconsiderately condemn.'[148] But when exempla are used by an author to authorize a new memory in order to create a new present, exemplary knowledge itself furnishes a *counterexample* of its own usefulness:

> Those who study closely the past and compare it with the present will find that for each case that has led to good results there are any number that turned out to be mistakes ... [y]et so great is man's ambition that, in striving to slake his present desire, he gives no thought to the evils that in a short time will follow in its wake. Nor is he stirred by the lessons of the past, as I have shown in regard to this and other matters.[149]

That is, the same political reality which is constructed and mirrored by means of exempla serves to invalidate exemplary knowledge. In Machiavelli's text, so unwilling to fortify its own premises, Renaissance knowledge implodes in the face of the very reality it makes intelligible. Innovation ends up in paradox; it is simultaneously sustained and circumscribed by exemplary knowledge.

More's reports

If the positive logic of the mirror was able to ensure resemblance and continuity between text and reality in the writings of Machiavelli, a similar function is provided by the interplay of characters and their reports in More's *Utopia* (1516); if a mirror reflects an image of a reality which becomes *real* only through being mirrored as such, the report *re-ports*; it re-covers reality into image under the assumption that this reality has been lost. It recovers reality by isolating its exemplary features, and redistributes these features into one exemplum, structured according to a hierarchy of ethical values. The logic of the report is a negative one; it does not lend itself to innovation, only to isolation through a displacement of existing values, and a nostalgic apprehension of what allegedly went before the corruption of those values.

Rhetorically, *Utopia* is organized by ethical transvaluation and demarcation; what is cherished as examples of virtue in More's present is turned into utmost vice in the non-place of Utopia. The act of transvaluation and demarcation is assisted by the metaphoric devices of voyage and spatial distance; one travels from the realm of vice to the Utopian non-place of virtue in and through More's discourse; what is positivity at the point of departure is negativity at the point of arrival. Also, this discourse dramatizes the very relationship between reality and fiction, between truth and authenticity on the one hand, and rhetoric and play on the other.

Utopia is written in the form of a dialogue, in which More appears as one of the minor interlocutors but at the same time as its principal narrator. In the body of the book, More re-reports the reports of another interlocutor, who at the same time figures as the principal character of the work: Raphael Hythlodaeus.

Raphael Hythlodaeus is a dispenser of factual truth as well as an upholder of truth as an ideal that ought to govern discourse; he has acquired detailed knowledge of the conditions obtaining on the island of Utopia through his travels, yet he is a fictional creature. Now sometimes the author-interlocutor More steps out of the narrative, either to intervene from a likewise fictional position outside it, or in order to supply the reader with authoritative interpretations of the positions proposed in it.[150]

One may wonder how anyone can feel tempted to locate the intentions of the author within such a complex text, written in an age which lacked access to a firm divide between fact and fiction. As Greenblatt has noticed, and despite the fact that the book is subdivided in a way that would indicate a separation between the real and the imaginary, its characters speak the same language: 'there are not two forms of language, one referential and the other non-referential, one for truth and the other for fiction'.[151] The problem becomes all the more puzzling, since More – if we still are entitled to speak of him outside the text – is re-reporting reports of his characters while being a character himself. The truth of a report of something is always questionable; the truth of a report of a report is never questionable beyond its relation to the report reported; when the reported report itself is possibly a re-report, it is no longer possible to keep report and re-report epistemically distinct.[152]

Now the problem of truth is taken up by the character Hythlodaeus, who is the mouthpiece of a scholastic preference for truth over rhetoric. Discussing the 'problem of the council' – whether it is advisable for a man of learning to enter royal service or not – Hythlodaeus argues that it is not, since he wants to 'stick to the truth'.[153] As reported in the First Book, Hythlodaeus fears that as a courtier he 'must openly approve the worst counsels and subscribe to the most ruinous decrees',[154] and 'share the madness of others as I tried to cure their lunacy'.[155]

Against this Platonic insistence on truth, the figure of More adopts a more flexible – that is, a more rhetorical position. There is 'another philosophy, more practical for statesmen, which knows its stage [and] adapts itself to the play at hand ... Whatever play is being performed, perform it as best you can, and do not upset it all because you think of another which has more interest.'[156] The problem of truth is also confronted in a letter to Peter Giles, and then put into the mouth of a critic: 'If the facts are reported as true, I see some rather absurd elements in them, but if as fictitious, then I find ... judgement wanting in some matters.'[157] More faces this dilemma by another act of rhetorical playfulness:

> I do not pretend that if I had determined to write about the commonwealth and had remembered such a story as I have recounted, I should have perhaps shrunk from a fiction whereby the truth, as if smeared by honey, might a little more pleasantly slide into men's minds. But I should certainly have tempered the fiction so that, if I wanted to abuse the ignorance of common folk, I should have prefixed some indications at least for the more learned to see through our purpose.[158]

Read as a report on the quite Epimenidean conditions of reporting, this passage should sensitize us to the play at hand, in which play is substituted for truth; a play which is superior to literal truth, because it has the ability of imposing fictions upon the world, thus forming and transforming it; a literal truth would presuppose that such a structure of meaning already has been imposed upon reality, thus separating it from the imaginary and fictitious.

If the vitality of the Machiavellian republic resided in the liberty of its citizens as they are found to be rather than in the perfection of its institutions, this order of priority is turned inside out in *Utopia*. The question is not how the ruler or citizen ought to act, but how the social and political institutions of a commonwealth ought to be arranged for the benefit of society as a whole, and how men ought to be remade in order to fit into these institutions. *Status*, the etymological antecedent of the term state, is here used to signify the condition of political being: what is the optimal state of a commonwealth, and, secondly, what is the optimal state of man within it?

This question is answered in two steps, the first with the aid of a great number of negative exempla, and the other by means of one complex positive exemplum. Starting with the negative side, More begins by an analysis of the present state of affairs. Cast in a satirical mode, More's analysis concentrates on the practice of war in contemporary European society. War, originating in a primordial corruption of man's relationship with nature, is caused by the greed of kings and the idleness of the nobility;[159] it is perpetuated through chivalric codes of honour and glorified by the perverted education of rulers and the aristocracy. War is to the gross disadvantage of the people and to the tranquillity of the realm, since it necessitates extraordinary taxes and causes impoverishment, which in turn inspires rebellion and criminality.[160] But ultimately and above all, injustice and war are caused by the institution of private property.[161]

What is original about this analysis is not so much its specific content: More reiterates here many Christian humanistic commonplaces about the allegedly derelict character of contemporary European society.[162] What is more of interest is the trick employed to stigmatize and satirize prevalent practices. As both Hexter and Skinner have shown, More breaks away from the pattern of the medieval moralist, who castigates the abuses of the actual warrior class by contrasting them with the chivalric ideal. Instead, he rejects this entire system of norms, and transvaluates the meaning of the terms employed in the medieval celebration of warrior virtues; what was laudatory becomes pejorative.[163]

If there ever was a slave revolt in morality, it took place here in *Utopia* by a rhetorical gesture aimed to reverse an entire ethical order and block all future re-evaluation. More's response to the present standards he finds detestable is altogether reactive; the positive step in the analysis is performed through a negation of what has been singled out as the root cause of social evil, which then is turned into a dream of rational reform. Instead of facing contingency and crisis by innovation, More opts for total reversal and isolation as the proper antidotes; one must say yes only to a negation of what is negative; one must say no to all that which cannot be represented as true virtue; what is true virtue is a reversed false virtue.

This pattern becomes clearer as we look into the institutional structure of the island of Utopia itself. Earlier, it had been part of the continent, and was called Abraxa until the original founder and lawgiver King Utopus conquered the territory and cut it off from the continent. Spread across the island are fifty-four city-states, separated by rural districts and identical in laws and customs.[164] The inner life of each such city-state is governed according to reason, and its citizens are brought under strict surveillance.[165] The basic unit of utopian society is the family; families together elect their governing officials, but to take counsel on matters of common interest outside their assembly or senate is considered a capital offence.[166] Labour is enforced; leisure activities compulsory; dress uniform; property collectivized; the size of families regulated; dining public; promiscuity punished; travelling restricted; language transparent to thought; knowledge empiricist; prediction triumphant; conscience clean. Even if this vision is repulsive, we should not let discomfort guide our interpretation, but view Utopia against the backdrop of the negative step in the analysis of the present. It is egalitarian because unequal distribution of property is the root cause of social evil. It is homogeneous because difference among men breeds discord. It is panoptic, because visibility and surveillance reinforce the values and practices of a truly communitarian life. It is empiricist, because the forces of nature set limits to human perfectibility. It is the same, because it has *assimilated* all difference into one sameness.

Utopia is built upon transvaluation, but this transvaluation does not break the chain of resemblance; the normative content of Utopian institutions is the polar opposite of the normative content of the practices singled out as derelict. In this way, Utopia embodies *true* nobility and excellence, as contrasted with the *false* nobility and excellence exemplified by the European nobility.[167] But as soon as we start to look at its form and origin, Utopia is caught within the web of resemblance. First, when it comes to form, it falls back upon and has its range of exemplarity defined by both Plato's Republic and Augustine's City of God. As such, *Utopia* can be read as philosophical nostalgia about the loss of a transcendent universal – a pure Christianity or a pure ideal republic – but which has lost its power to organize present political knowledge and to guide political action. What, one may ask, would the present society look like, if its evolution had been guided by human reason, without having been corroded by time and contingency?[168] The answer to such a question is necessarily Utopian; it would be a perfectly virtuous society based entirely on the dictates of reason, but stripped of all the redundant trappings of Christian religion and abstract philosophy.[169] Second, when it comes to origin, Utopia is dependent on a founding subjectivity; a mythological lawgiver who performs the act of isolation and transvaluation, and whose position corresponds to that of the author in the text of *Utopia*: 'Utopus, my ruler, converted me, formerly not an island, into an island. Alone of all lands, without the aid of abstract philosophy, I have represented for mortals the philosophical city. Ungrudgingly do I share my benefit with others; undemurringly do I adopt whatever is better from others.'[170]

And then, now on the island of Utopia, it is as if some trick was operative, which is as apt as chance to confound high and low: 'I have been marked out by my Utopians to be their king forever ... I was going to continue with this fascinating vision, but the rising Dawn has shattered my dream.'[171]

It remains to ask how Utopia deals with what is outside it, and therefore also inferior to it. Transvaluation was effected through isolation; one isolates what is derelict in the present, inverts its ethical value, and transposes it to an insular form, in its turn isolated from the mainland of the present. As we are told in More's report, the act of founding Utopia, as it was carried out by its first sovereign, King Utopus, coincided with its physical isolation from the continent. Utopus was drawing a line *of* water between his new creation and its impure origin which hence becomes a past and an other in relation to it. This geopolitical separation, we are likewise told, was not so much conditioned by divine power as it was carried through the positivity of labour.[172]

Now its very insularity also gives it a strategic advantage over its enemies, stuck in their present on the mainland. As the rhetorical play of reporting supports the transvaluation of virtues and the fortification of truth in *Utopia*, so the island of Utopia has a distinct geopolitical advantage; the landing-place is so well defended by nature that a few defenders can prevent strong forces from coming ashore.[173]

As the text of *Utopia* is defended from noxious interpretation by hovering in between fiction and truth, Utopia is defended from conquest by its virtue and rationality. Despite the fact that the Utopians strongly resent the practice of war, men and women alike receive military training in order to be able to protect their territory, but also under the pretext of intervention on behalf of threatened friends in the surrounding ocean.[174] However, even when the cause is just, the Utopians do not willingly do the job of fighting themselves; rather, they first rely on mercenaries, whom they hold to be abominable and hence worthy of extermination.[175]

The worst foreign policy problem of Utopia arises out of the conflict between its isolation and the inevitability of its interaction with other states. As a rational society in which the common interest constitutes the sole yardstick for institutional arrangements, Utopia is also by inclination peace loving. But it is also prosperous and efficient, which affects its relationship with nature, and, by consequence, with other states. Since Utopia has domesticated some of the forces of nature, forces which untamed would work to the detriment of humanity, its population increases.[176] As a consequence, they must break their isolation and start to colonize new territories overseas. Thus, the quest for space flows from the very perfectibility of the utopian condition, and lies in the common interest of Utopia. If the territories under colonization happen to be inhabited, and if the inhabitants refuse to live under Utopian law, they drive them from the territory which they carve out for themselves. If they resist, the Utopians wage war on them. This they consider a most just cause of war, when a people deny the possession of a territory to those who by the rule of nature are better suited to be maintained by it.[177]

Thus, the outside must be assimilated and turned into an inside as a consequence of the perfection which reigns within Utopia; Utopia presents an offer which cannot be refused: become Utopian or die.[178] The very same conditions which were made to look profoundly sinister through the creation of Utopia, and were relegated to its outside through a complex act of transvaluation, separation and isolation, but nevertheless constituted the conditions which made it possible and desirable, now figure as the target of assimilation.

In the end, therefore, the logic of transvaluation and isolation subverts itself; either Utopia stays isolated and perishes from overpopulation as a result of its rational perfection, or it must expand and assimilate. If assimilation were to succeed, however, and Utopia to become universal, its motivating force would be lost; its inner perfectibility hinges on the presence of its opposite outside, but when this outside is turned into an inside, the reactive logic implodes.

Vitoria's circles

The *descombrimentos* had their share in the Renaissance crisis in knowledge. The writings of both Machiavelli and More reflect an awareness of a non-Christian outside. For Machiavelli, the charting of new seas and unknown lands was equivalent to his quest for a new political knowledge.[179] To More, the acquaintance with the New World through Vespucci's reports inspired his textual experiment of ethical subversion. The discoveries, however, coincided in time with the process of reciprocal estrangement which took place in Europe, and added yet another dimension to the problem of particularity and contingency posed by nominalism and time.

For Francisco de Vitoria, however, the discovery of the Americas posed a much more serious problem; how could the newly discovered forms of life be reconciled with the universalist framework of legal reason?[180] That is, where Vitoria was predisposed to find universality and sameness, he was confronted with a striking plurality and otherness, arising out of the discoveries as well as the fragmentation within Christianity.[181] The question was not merely epistemic, theological and legal: a fair share of the New World was since the Bull of Donation in 1493 under the dominion of the Spanish Crown, and on top of this constitutionally fragile construct was a king, simultaneously emperor Charles V and guardian of a Christianity beset by discord.

Vitoria is a primitive legal scholar; whenever read retrospectively, he is seen as one of the founders of international law. As Kennedy has pointed out, such a characterization is bound to be misleading, since in the Renaissance, there is no firm divide between the domestic and the international spheres. Instead the problems of legal knowledge are consistently articulated and solved against the backdrop of a presumed universal order.[182] In Vitoria – a neo-thomist – the overarching legal problem is not how to solve a disagreement between competing sovereigns over the foundations of this order, since, as we shall see, such a disagreement is assumed to be impossible, but how to relate the concentric circles of *resemblant* laws, ranging from divine law down to natural and positive law. In his effort to work out a coherent relationship between them, Vitoria relies on a lexicon of legal exempla, in which a wide variety of textual authorities are invoked in order to support his position, and this without regard to the compatibility of these authorities.

The Vitorian response is as complex as the problem itself. At the apex of the legal order we find divine law, which enjoys primacy over natural and positive law. There can be no other ultimate authority or source of binding law, since '[a]ll power ... by which the secular State is governed, is not only just and legitimate, but it is also surely ordained by God, that not even by the consent of the whole world can it be destroyed or annulled'.[183]

If agreement cannot destroy the moral and legal authority of divine law, nor can disagreement. However willed by God, the power of the state is rooted in natural law, since the state is of natural origin. Invoking Aristotle, Vitoria reminds us that man is a social animal and owes his humanity to the social bond, here necessitated by the Fall.[184] As such, and by virtue of its resemblance to the macrocosm of divine law, no society of men can continue to exist without some supreme power governing it, 'For if all were equal, and subject to no power, each individual would draw away from the others in accordance with his own opinions and will; the commonwealth would of necessity be torn apart; and the State would be dis solved.'[185]

Hence, sovereignty is necessary for the protection and survival of man and is therefore natural in origin, but its establishment is nevertheless in accordance with divine law; nature and grace reinforce each other throughout Vitoria's theory.[186] The presence of the sovereign state entails that men must give up their right to defend themselves against injustices, and collectively hand over this power to the sovereign, be it a king or any other governing body.[187] Furthermore, since the state is now internally pacified and self-sufficient within the twin orders of nature and grace, it enjoys a right of self-defence against external injury: 'the State may in nowise be deprived of this power to protect itself and to guard against every injury from its own citizens or from aliens ... if all the citizens should agree to dispense with these powers ... the agreement would be null and void, being contrary to natural law.'[188] Again, as a corollary, 'the temporal State is perfect, and complete in itself; therefore, it is not subject to any outside force, since if it were thus subject, it would not be complete'.[189]

According to Fernandez-Santamaria, there is a certain irony in the fact that Vitoria, commonly celebrated as the father of modern internationalism, prefaces his internationalist scheme by strengthening the institution most inimical to it: the sovereign state.[190] Now this irony perhaps partly resides in the eye of the presentist historian. Anxiously turning Vitoria into the father of modern internationalism, we will be predisposed to think that he was addressing the problem posed by the presence of sovereign states in the absence of a universalist framework, a problem which was simply not accessible to him. In Vitoria's theory, the sovereign has no capacity – in the ontological sense of capacity – to depart from the word of God, or from the moral consensus of the whole world; instead, his peculiar capacity of being sovereign is vested with him *within* the universal order.[191]

To be sure, there is a problem here, but not of a modern kind; for how is the capacity of particular sovereignty reconcilable with the universalist framework from which they derive? Posed differently, it is a matter of how a process of fragmentation is intelligible from within a a presupposed structure of a unified and larger whole. We could read Vitoria's theory not as a strategy for solving this dilemma, but as a strategy for avoiding it. This is most clearly seen in his doctrine of just war. Faced with a plurality of states,

> a doubt may well arise whether, when a number of [states] of this kind ... have one common lord or prince, they can make war of themselves and without the authorization of their superior lord. My answer is that they can do so undoubtedly, just as the kings who are subordinate to the Emperor can make war on one another without waiting for the Emperor's authorization, *for a state ought to be self-sufficient, and this it would not be, if it had not the faculty in question.*[192]

Here, as in Marsiglio, universal authority has a locus that can be stripped off, yet its content and scope remain intact as warrants of particular sovereignty. In this case, the Augustinian order of logical priority between sovereign authority and just war is reversed: it takes war to make a sovereign in the first place, and a sovereign to make a war just in the second place, rather than conversely. The connection between sovereignty, universal order, and war is circularly reinforcing; the distinction between what is sovereign and what is not sovereign corresponds to a distinction between what is legal and what is not; this distinction, in turn, is universal, and cannot be subjected to disagreement among sovereign authorities without a simultaneous loss of their legal title to sovereignty. Witness this statement, which to a modern theorist of international law would appear to contradict the above one:

> International law [*jus gentium*] has not only the force of a pact and agreement among men but also the force of a law for the world as a whole being in a way one single State, and has the power to create laws that are just and fitting for all persons, as are the rules of international law. Consequently, it is clear that they who violate these international rules, whether in peace or in war, commit a mortal sin. Moreover, in the gravest matters, such as the inviolability of ambassadors, it is not permissible for one country to refuse to be bound by international law, for the latter having been established by the authority of the whole world.[193]

Despite the anachronistic translation, it is clear that Vitoria does not discern any distinction, let alone any opposition, between the kind of law that applies within states and the kind of law that prevails between them, since such a distinction or opposition would merely presuppose precisely what is unintelligible to Vitoria: the absence of divine law laid down by grace in all human institutions. The ultimate subject of the *jus gentium* is mankind, a mankind not yet divided into normatively self-contained units.

This brings us to the second source of destabilization in legal thought: the discovery of the American Indians. If the fragmentation of Christianity into legally self-sufficient units threatened the coherence of universalist legal schemes, the discovery of the Indians posed the problem of the proper scope of divine and natural law. The confrontation with something radically different from the Christian way of life raised the question of what kind of relations it is possible to entertain with this Other.[194] First, to what extent is it possible to know the Indian except as something inferior to the Christian civilization? Second, and dependent on the epistemic status granted to the Indian, to what extent is it possible to bring him into the framework of universal law by giving him the status of a legal subject?

If the Indian is knowable, he is knowable on the basis of his resemblance to the familiar; if he is knowable on the basis of his resemblance to the familiar, he is either *assimilated* to the Christian and therefore denied an identity of his own, or, he is *dissimilated* from the Christian, and therefore denied the status of epistemic and legal subjectivity.

At the time when Vitoria is giving his lectures on the American Indians, the conquest of the Americas is a fact, which is left to jurisprudence to justify; contrary to some of his contemporaries, Vitoria does this by opting for the first of the above strategies. As the legal problem was posed, it was a matter of whether the Spaniards could claim *dominium* in the Americas or not. In the contemporary idiom of natural jurisprudence, the term *dominium* did not only connote property rights, but included also a certain right of political overlordship or suzerainty.

In order to justify Spanish dominion, one had to prove that the native inhabitants of the new continent had in one way or another lost their entitlement to dominion, accorded to them by natural law.[195] This might have been fairly easy, since the Indians took delight in a set of practices which from the Christian viewpoint were highly detestable. But to Vitoria, the fact that they were engaged in incestuous intercourse and ritual cannibalism was not sufficient to dispossess them.[196] Not that these practices did not constitute mortal sin; they certainly did. But to say that those in mortal sin do not have *dominium* was not a possibility open to Vitoria; such a one-way recourse to grace would have thrown him right into the arms of the Reformation, a fact that he was fully aware of.[197] Nor could the fact of their infidelity do the job. Drawing heavily on Aquinas, Vitoria makes the simple point that *dominium* is derived either from natural law or from positive law, and is therefore not destroyed by lack of faith.[198]

A further possibility was to declare them insane or non-human. Neither crackpots nor wild beasts are entitled to *dominium* according to natural law, simply because natural law was founded upon natural reason.[199] Clearly, the Indians were strange, but not wholly irrational:

> The Indian aborigines are not barred on this ground from the exercise of true dominion. This is proved from the fact that the true state of the case is that they are not of unsound mind, but have, according to their kind, the use of reason. This is clear, because there is a certain method in their affairs, for they have polities which are orderly arranged and they have definite marriage and magistrates ... all of which call for the use of reason; they also have a kind of religion. Further, they make no error in matters which are self-evident to others; this is witness to their use of reason.[200]

Even if they sometimes appear stupid, dominion cannot be denied the aborigines on this ground. The upshot of this conclusion is that there are *kinds* of reason, *kinds* of societies, *kinds* of religions, *kinds* of human practices, but which nevertheless all are distinctively human; they are expressions of an enlarged and collective reason. Further, the process by which Vitoria arrives at this conclusion is itself interesting, since it reveals an enlargement, both of the sphere of knowledge and of the scope of law: by saying that the Indians do not err in matters which are self-evident to others, Vitoria by implication says that error only can be measured against evidence, and evidence only measured against error.

But above this plurality there is a universal unity of mankind, provided by the unwritten code of *jus gentium*, warranted by both grace and nature. Whereas it is not wholly derived from natural law, 'but was established as inviolable, from agreement among men',[201] it is based on the consensus of mankind as a whole, and thus concerns all nations; it does not determine the possibility of the legal arrangements within each nation, but well their perfection.[202]

Now, where is the clout of the *jus gentium* to be found? How can this legal order encircle lesser legal orders, and cope with the disagreements that arise from inner fragmentation and cultural plurality in a world in which sovereignty is strongly interlinked with the faculty of war?

In order to avoid the possibility of profound disagreement over the content of a universal moral and legal order, Vitoria draws another circle within the holistic order of law; the *jus gentium* is itself warranted by just war.

First, and according to the inherited doctrine, the waging of just war is a privilege of princes, those who have no superiors within a given realm. Second, war, in order to be just, must be undertaken for a just cause only, such as avenging a prior injustice or reclaiming stolen property.[203] In Vitoria's rendering, where the legitimate authority of the ruler is connected to the presence of a state, the right of waging of war rests with public authority, which, 'has complete power to avenge itself, to recover its own property, and punish its enemies. This truth is evident, because, if the state had not this power, there would be disorder in the world, and injury would be suffered at the hands of the wicked.'[204]

As we saw above, it is this warmongering faculty that makes the state self-sufficient and thus externally sovereign; now it is also its capacity to wage *just* war that preserves the *jus gentium* and makes it efficient. Sovereignty flows from the universal moral and legal order, as does the faculty to make war; the justness of war depends on its being undertaken by a sovereign authority; the existence of sovereign authorities depends on just wars; the preservation of the universal moral and legal order of which sovereign authorities are composite parts depends on the institution of just war as a means to settle disputes within it.

Thus, we have come full circle. Every force or entity which is introduced within the universal order operates as both poison and antidote, as evil and as potential remedy. In a world beset by fragment-ation and opened up to the radically foreign, each political being is conditioned by difference, and is thus inherently ambiguous right from the start. Vitoria does not solve the problem of order posed by these beings and forces, but presupposes an order outside of which this ambiguity and difference becomes unintelligible; what is outside knowledge is thus also outside the scope of law; by making these forces and beings known, they are also subjected to law by being encircled by it and assimilated into it.

The state is presented as a solution to the problems posed by the Fall or by the usurpation of a primordial and sacrosanct power structure. Simultaneously, the introduction of the state within the universal order raises new problems resulting from the state's capacity to solve the original problem; war is a condition of the state, and the state is a condition of war; yet war itself poses a threat which has to be encircled and turned into an antidote and a warrant of the universal order. Finally, the *jus gentium* promises a universality beyond all difference, a full realization of the presupposed structure. But since the inner perfectibility of the lesser legal orders represented by states hinges on the *jus gentium*, and the *jus gentium* in turn hinges on the former, it is also a poison. It reintroduces difference at a new level: states have to wage war in order to preserve both their own particularity and the universal order simultaneously.

Outsides invented

In this section, we have seen how Machiavelli, More and Vitoria respond to the problems created by the general theory of the state, and how their responses in turn are conditioned by this theory, and the knowledge which permits its articulation and sustains it.

As I have argued, the general theory of the state arose out of the conceptual pressures posed by time and nominalism. Time gave political knowledge a new turn, and released political beings from the confines of liturgy and mimesis. Time made possible continuous political beings; yet at the same time, it inscribed them into a domain of change and contingency. Simultaneously, nominalism opened up a logical void inside the universal whole of theological knowledge. The significance of the struggle to think plurality pure was not to be found in its success, but in its relative failure; the universalist framework remained its condition of possibility, but the theory of the state was literally brought down to earth, as were its teleological underpinnings. From this arose the problem of particularity.

When later fused with neo-platonist cosmology in the sixteenth century, the theory of the continuous and nominal state could be supported by means of exempla, chosen on the basis of and closely structured around resemblances between historical events and episodes, and between the origin and form of political beings. The recovery of ancient political knowledge coincided with an exemplary historicization of the general theory of the state, whose range of validity was enlarged to cover beings of other than divine origin, and of other forms than one single transcendent one; the number of possible roads to political perfection increases proportionately, as do the sources of imperfection.

With this complex series of ontological and epistemic mutations, many things and forces which had previously been rendered meaningful by Christian myth were deprived of meaning, and at the same time manifested in political crisis. Otherness, in its various guises, demanded a response at the same time as it set a limit to intelligibility.

It is in this context I have read Machiavelli, More and Vitoria, each wrestling with one aspect of this heterogeneous outside, each providing a different solution of how to cope with otherness.

Machiavelli, facing political fragmentation and the eroding legitimacy of traditional authority, responds with a logic of innovation. But as we have seen, this logic nourishes itself on a foundation which it cannot but tacitly subvert. In his attempt to recover ancient political wisdom and reinscribe it as a guide to the future by means of exempla, either innovation is circumscribed by the validity of the exempla, or the validity of the exempla is circumscribed by innovation. Through innovation, Machiavelli subjects the forces of otherness to what we today would call *rationalization*. Eroding legitimacy can be overcome through dissimulation and concealment; war can be brought under control with the aim of winning it.

More, facing ethical dissolution, war and religious reformation, responds with a logic of isolation and transvaluation. As we have seen, this logic leads to a paradox of perfection; the more perfect Utopia becomes, the more necessary it becomes for it to embark upon the same practices whose transvaluation was the impetus behind its isolation. Through isolation, More withdraws from otherness into the no-place of Utopia, but since its sameness is essentially indebted to what it seeks to overcome and to assimilate, More ends up in a paradox of revolution; discord and war can only be overcome by a new set of transvalued standards, but their universalization necessitates yet another war.

Vitoria, facing political fragmentation as well as a new form of political life, responds by encirclement and assimilation of what is foreign. But as we have seen, this encirclement amounts to a continuous reinscription and redescription of an already presupposed universalist framework, but with the inevitable effect that this framework becomes more inclusive, and so to speak, more tolerant. Every possible disagreement is reduced to a prior agreement within this framework; the disruptive impact of fragmentation, war and aborigines on universalist legal discourse is not denied, nor fully accounted for, but instead subdued and tempered.

Thus, we are left with a general theory of the state whose coherence is constantly threatened by its effort to cope with that which is alien and new to it, and with a residue of concepts and phenomena which together constitute the outside of both politics and knowledge. On this outside, we find pagan deities such as Fortuna mingling with Indians and Utopians; we find war and change, greed and passion, particularity and contingency, but nothing which would merit the label of an international system. As we have seen, there is no autonomous discourse on states in their sovereign particularity and individuality; nor is there any firm line of demarcation drawn between what is inside and what is outside a particular state, only what is inside and what is outside the state as a general concept or as a general phenomenon within a general framework of presuppositions; nor is there any unifying and autonomous discourse on what is outside the general theory of the state, since what is outside it, also is beyond the scope of knowledge. In chapter 5, we shall see how this political knowledge is replaced by a new one, one in which the discourse on sovereignty becomes foundational in its own right.

5   How policy became foreign: sovereignty, *mathesis* and interest in the Classical Age

[S]i l'homme est souverainement raisonable il doit souverainement
faire régner la raison ...

Richelieu, *Testament Politique*

In textbooks of international relations theory, it is a common assumption that the international system originated during the seventeenth century, with the Peace of Westphalia as the decisive point of its emergence.[1] As I shall argue in the present chapter, this thesis rests on a presentist apprehension of the terms 'international' and 'system'. As a distinction in the manner of knowing entails a difference in the mode of being, the international system as we know it today did not exist in the Classical Age, no more than it did in the Renaissance. In these periods, there is no object of knowledge called the *international system*. Take Bull's definition of the term system: 'Where states are in regular contact with one another, and where in addition there is interaction between them sufficient to make the behaviour of each a necessary element in the calculations of the other, then we may speak of their forming a system'.[2]

To be sure, if we extend the range of application of the term international to cover everything that takes place between states, we are entitled to speak of something international in the Classical Age, even if the term itself was never used by classical authors. By the same token, we are entitled to speak of a system, since both Grotius and Pufendorf use the term to convey the sense of a fundamental moral or legal unity underlying the accentuated division into particular states.[3] But if we by international system mean a totality which is something more than the sum of its constituent parts, yet something presumably distinct from a universal *Respublica Christiana*, we have to wait another 200 years for its emergence within political knowledge.[4]

137

In the Renaissance, we could discern an awareness of otherness and the emergence of a heterogeneous outside. To this outside corresponds an inside, defined in terms of proto-sovereignty. There is, however, no theory of particular and individual states; what we find during the late Middle Ages and the Renaissance is a general theory of the state, closely structured around the questions of the origin and form of a body politic.

This differentiation was carried out within one and the same knowledge. With words and objects being inseparable, and knowledge being built on an infinite chain of resemblances, the logical space opened up by political nominalism was not only occupied by the general concept of the state, but also filled with countless observations, justifications and legendary accounts of political communities, indiscriminately taken as *exempla*.

During the first decades of the seventeenth century, the general theory of the state is replaced by a new theory of sovereignty, which relegates the questions of the form and origin of political communities to a secondary position within political discourse.

The concept of sovereignty now enters political discourse with a set of functions entirely different from that of its antecedents in the genealogical series. In the late Middle Ages and in the Renaissance, sovereignty is a mark of superiority or a sign of divine origin, known and disseminated by analogy, resemblance and *exempla*. By the beginning of the Classical Age, the concept of sovereignty becomes structurally interlinked with a new mode of knowledge.

First of all, classical sovereignty is a *principle of individuation*. It is not attributed to a political entity on the basis of an already manifest indivisibility; instead, it is sovereignty which has the power of individuation since it is 'it selfe a thing indivisible'.[5] Consequently, sovereignty itself becomes 'sovereign' in political discourse as 'the most necessarie point for the understanding of the nature of a Commonweale'.[6]

Second, and a corollary of the first point, sovereignty is not exclusively linked to the person of the prince. As a principle of individuation, it is also a *principle of identification*. Sovereignty can be attributed as a predicate either to the state taken as a whole, or to its specific locus within the same state. In classical theories of sovereignty, there is a 'great difference betwixt the state, and the government of the state'.[7] On the one hand, classical sovereignty requires the intense divinization and personalization of authority in the hands of a sovereign, on the other, it necessitates an abstract notion of a naturalized state as a symbol of depersonalized authority.[8]

The King becomes a metaphor of the State, and conversely; classical theories of sovereignty can never arrive at a stable differentiation between these poles and only make the locus of sovereignty relative to perspective; what appears as appearance from one perspective realizes itself as reality from the other. Ideological justifications of absolutism are built upon the problematic attempt to identify these two sovereignties, and a concomitant oscillation between the perspectives and metaphors from which this double signification begins to take place.

Third, and most important, classical sovereignty is a *principle of order* since its concept defines the domain of objects of an autonomous discourse, a science of states. Classical sovereignty identifies and individuates states as concrete empirical beings and makes them accessible to classification, ranking and comparison according to a determined set of variables.

As I intend to demonstrate in this chapter, these profound changes in the discourse on sovereignty, while to a great extent caused by the experience of religious and civil wars following upon the Reformation,[9] are simultaneously entwined with and conditioned by the substitution of classical knowledge based on representation and mathematical constructability for Renaissance knowledge built on resemblance and *exempla*.

My claim that there is nothing that merits the label 'international system' in the classical period must be seen against this backdrop. Although there is no international system, there is nevertheless a *tabulated order of states* in the Classical Age. With the advent of the scientific revolution, we can detect the emergence of a new discursive practice, a system for the forming and validation of empirical statements about states and their intercourse. That is, we have states as well as relations between states in the classical period, but these relations do not themselves exist independently of states.

The source of this discursive practice, however, is not to be found in the depths of the textbook canon on the origin of international relations, commonly identified with Hobbes and Grotius.

As I intend to show, the classical order of states has very little to do with a Hobbesian condition of 'perpetuall war'[10] in which 'Persons of Soveraigne authority, because of their Independency, are in continual jealousies, and in the state and posture of Gladiators; having their weapons pointing, and the eyes fixed on one another,'[11] and even less affinity with the Grotian universalist view of a society ruled by laws 'which are of perpetual validity and suited to all times', founded not on 'expediency alone' but on 'the very nature of man', and which even in the absence of sanction are 'not entirely void of effect'.[12]

Rather, and as I shall argue, the classical order of states is to be found on the surface of empirical discourse about concrete states and their interests. The principal aim of this chapter is to describe the emergence and articulation of the analysis of state interest as an autonomous branch of political knowledge in terms of its conditions of possibility within the more general matrix of sovereignty and knowledge in the Classical Age.

The chapter is subdivided as follows. In the first section, I shall briefly describe classical knowledge and its relationship to classical notions of sovereignty. Following Foucault, I shall argue that classical knowledge is not reducible to 'rationalism' or to 'empiricism'; behind these epistemic opinions we are able to distinguish a set of shared rules for the constitution of knowledge and domains of objects.[13] In the second section, I shall analyse the fundamental theoretical options and presuppositions available to and explored by political theorists and historians in their efforts to analyse state interests, an effort that originated in France on the eve of the Thirty Years War as a self-conscious attempt to rationalize foreign policy. In the third section, I shall analyse the impact of the analysis of interest on the practices of sovereign states, as reflected in their manuals and institutional arrangements.

The science of order and the semantics of sovereignty

In chapter 4, we could observe how the general theory of the state was articulated on the basis of the late-medieval and Renaissance knowledge. We also could observe some surface symptoms of its imminent transformation during the Renaissance, since it was unable to cope fully with particularity and contingency.

In the strange but fairly coherent blend of superstition, recovered ancient erudition and emergent rationality which constitutes the body of Renaissance knowledge, we are able to notice local divergencies which permit us to hear a distant echo of our own political rationality, and which therefore are sometimes unduly emphasized by presentist and finalist historians.

During the classical period, however, one of these divergencies seems to gain the upper hand. Whereas More's dream of a Utopian society is taken up and cultivated into a literary genre by Campanella and Comenius, and whereas Vitoria's provisional enlargement of the scope of natural law spills over into the universalism of Grotius and Gentili, secular statecraft, which carries the stigma of disorder in the Renaissance, becomes the foundation of order in the age of absolutism.

Apart from the impact of the Reformation and the religious wars, one clue to this discontinuity is provided by the simultaneous change in the foundations of knowledge which takes place in the beginning of the seventeenth century. The epistemic foundation of the general theory of the state is swept away and replaced by a new epistemic figure, intimately linked to a new theory of sovereignty that focuses on its indivisibility.

The example of Jean Bodin is interesting in this respect, since the first step towards such a theory of sovereignty has been attributed to him, while its epistemic underpinnings are commonly neglected, since they represent disturbing traces of a different age. First, Bodin is indeed among the first to stress the indivisibility of sovereignty and its function as a mark of the individuality of a state in legal terms, as 'the most high, absolute and perpetuall power over the citizens and subjects of a Commonweale'.[14] Sovereignty stands in a relation of mutual implication to the state; to be sovereign is to be sovereign *over* a state, and the state is dependent on a 'powerful sovereignty'[15] as to its existence. In Bodin's theory, the presence of the state both enables and constrains sovereignty, ontologically as well as legally. Second, this dualistic conception is understood in terms of final causes: sovereignty is necessary in order for the state to fulfil its thisworldly purpose, but within a divinely ordained universe, and the presence of the imperfect state is necessary if sovereignty is to bring its immanent *telos* into existence. Later, when stripped of its Aristotelian *causa finalis*, this dual conditioning will be replaced by a problematic identification between king and state in the mature absolutist ideology.

Third, and contrary to the superficial modernity of the Bodinian theory, it is evident from the last pages of *Six Livres de la République* (1576) that it remains firmly rooted within the framework of Renaissance knowledge:

> Wherefore as of Treble and Base voyces is made a most sweet and melodious Harmonie, so also of vices and vertues, of the different qualities of the elements, of the contrarie motions of the celestial

> spheres, and of the Sympathies and Antipathies of things, by indisso-
> luble means bound together, is composed the Harmonie of the whole
> world ... [s]o also a well ordered Commonweale is composed of good
> and bad ... which so by a wonderfull disagreeing concord, ioyne the
> highest with the lowest ... Wherefore what the unitie is in numbers,
> the understanding in the powers of the soule, and the center in a
> circle: so likewise in this world that most mightie king, in unitie
> simple, in nature indivisible, in puritie most holy, exalted farre above
> the Fabrike of the celestiall Spheres, ioyning this elementarie world
> with the celestiall and intelligible heavens ... unto the imitation of
> whome, every good prince which wisheth his Kingdome and Com-
> monweale not in safetie onely, but even good and belessed also, is to
> frame and conforme himselfe.[16]

For all its superficial modernity, the entire logic of Bodin's theory of
sovereignty is dependent on infinite resemblances and exempla which
multiply throughout his discursive universe, and the forces of antipathy and sympathy which connect microcosm and macrocosm together
in a divine and harmonious order; without God at the apex of the
entire construct, there can be no sovereignty.[17] Nor is a systematic
comparison of individual states yet possible, even if Bodin sometimes
is credited with innovations in historiography and legal methodology.[18] Bodin's theory of sovereignty is based upon the premise of
recurrent cycles in historical time, which restricts comparison across
history and between indivisible political beings to one of exempla:

> Yet doubt I not but that some more certaine precepts might be given
> of the chaunges, and ruines of Commonweales, if a man would enter
> into a certaine account of the time past even from the beginning of
> the world ... going backwards, shall of all the eclipses of the Sunne
> and of the Moone ... by most certaine demonstrations comprehend
> the reason of the whole time past: and compare the histories of the
> most true writers amongst themselves, and with the oppositions and
> coniunctions of the celestial starres and bodies, knit and conioyne the
> same with numbers, whose force in all the course of nature is
> greatest.[19]

Bodin's position is therefore utterly problematic; for how can indivisible things be parts of a whole, which itself is indivisible? It seems to
me that the significance of Bodin's theory of sovereignty lies in its
attempt to elaborate a logic of indivisibility within the framework of
the general theory of the state, and so to speak, justify indivisible
sovereignty from within a framework which simultaneously is undermined by its presence.

The epistemic edifice underlying Bodin's reasoning is thoroughly demolished in the early seventeenth century, while the logical core of the theory of sovereignty is retained, articulated and refined during the same century, until it becomes the centrepiece of the new cognitive and political order.[20]

Knowing: analysis and the mathesis

To the classical writers, there can be no knowledge except by intuition or deduction, by pure observation or by valid inference from indubitable premises, but underlying both these strategies of knowing is the necessity of comparison, understood as the systematic detection of identity and difference among objects: 'in every instance of discursive reasoning we know the truth with precision only by way of comparison'.[21] Knowledge ceases to be structured around resemblance and sustained by exempla, and the dominant method of knowing becomes *analysis*: 'If we perfectly are to understand a problem we must abstract from it every superfluous conception, reduce it to the simplest terms, and by means of an enumeration, divide it up into the smallest possible parts.'[22]

Reading, for example, Descartes' *Regulae* (1628), we learn that this analysis must proceed from the detection of identity and difference only between 'those objects of which our minds seem capable of having certain and indubitable cognition'.[23] Further, it must continue by strict comparison of objects, which consists in 'the ordering and arranging of the objects' so that we can distinguish the 'simple things from those that are complicated and set them out in an orderly manner'[24] and reduce 'obscure propositions step by step to simpler ones',[25] so that finally 'every single thing relating to our undertaking' can be surveyed in a continuous and wholly uninterrupted sweep of thought, and be included in a 'sufficient and well-ordered enumeration'.[26] Finally, this uninterrupted enumeration and ordering can take place along two main dimensions. Objects can be arranged either nominally and qualitatively according to their 'absolute' differences, or, they can be arranged ordinally and quantitatively, according to their 'relative' differences.[27] Comparison can then take place along those dimensions, either, as in the former case, as a *comparison of order* or, as in the latter, as a *comparison of measurement*. Ultimately, however, the comparison of measurement is dependent on an already detected and sequential order of objects, since measurement has to be undertaken from a common unit in terms of which the intervals between the

143

ordered objects can be expressed. Order, however, can be detected by the mind without reference to any exterior unit, and furnishes the unit necessary for measurement.[28] In the Classical Age, to know is in essence to be able to classify things according to relations of equality and inequality, and to be able to represent all relationships of identity and difference in a continuous table or taxonomy.

This knowledge built on systematic comparison and simultaneous ordering is what Descartes calls a *mathesis universalis*, or a general science of order based on first principles of order applicable to any domain of objects – or rather being that which constitutes objects as well as domains of knowledge. For objects, to be *knowable* is to be *orderable*, and conversely; to exist becomes a function of being known.

As Lachterman has pointed out, the analytic method not only codifies the rules of procedure necessary to attain knowledge; it defines the objects to which it is applied so that their intelligibility becomes identical with their susceptibility to analysis. The being of objects coincides with their ability to enter into determinate ratios and proportions with other beings.[29] In short, the *mathesis* implies constructability, so that what exists ultimately depends on its ability to display ordered relationships with other things, and these ordered relationships in turn result from their being *representable* as ordered.

As such, the *mathesis* clearly disqualifies the general theory of the state as a branch of knowledge. The general science of order, being – as Descartes says – no more altered by its subject than sunlight is by the variety of things it shines on, not only finds reason to doubt the existence of Chiron the Centaur and many other entities which populated the general theory of the state, but also the loose comparison according to resemblance of origin and form it employs in its exempla. It also throws doubt on the sources of exempla, distilled as they are from a mixture of astrological observation, mythological accounts and rhetorical historiography; it questions the very pattern of historical recurrence that makes exempla edifying and useful as clues to future events.[30] Within the general science of order, we should confine our investigation to what we can rationally intuit or empirically perceive, and 'set aside probable conjectures' and 'assertions on obscure matters'.[31] As a consequence, science is separated from the inherited genre of exemplary history, and observational or introspective accounts become epistemically distinct from documentary or legendary ones: as we shall see, edifying exempla are replaced by problem-solving *analysis* in the knowledgeable practice of statecraft.

Speaking: language, society and representation

Now if we cut deeper into the conditions of the *mathesis*, we find that it stands in a relation of mutual presupposition to a separation of language and world, a systematic disjunction between signs and things, and an analysis of language as a grid of representation. In the late Middle Ages and in the Renaissance, signs are objects and objects are signs; our access to the world goes through the decipherment of the infinite and homogenous stratum of things and words. Language is not an arbitrary system of signs, it is part of the world; the names of things lie hidden in the things they designate. There is no fundamental difference between what is written in a book and what can be read in the examination of an object and through detection of its resemblances to other objects or words.[32] Consequently, there are no distinctions between subject and object, fiction and reality, nor between reason and rhetoric.

This arrangement is profoundly reorganized in the seventeenth century. The first distemper of learning, says Bacon, is 'when men study words and not matter',[33] since knowledge 'is nothing but a representation of truth: for the truth of being and the truth of knowing are one, differing no more than the direct beam and the beam reflected'.[34] But in order for knowledge to constitute itself as such, the beam must be dusted off: 'The mind of man is far from the nature of a clear and equal glass, wherein the beams of things should reflect according to their true incidence; nay, it is rather like an enchanted glass, full of superstition and imposture, if it be not delivered and reduced'.[35]

In order to dust off and disenchant the glass, the referential possibility of language is theorized and elevated to hegemonic position, while its rhetorical possibilities – so important to the Renaissance – are subdued or declared abusive by a set of moves themselves rhetorical in character: it is no coincidence that philosophers such as Hobbes, Locke and Pufendorf devote so much labour to the problem of language in their political works; the systematic rearrangement of the relationship between language and world becomes an essential step towards a new order.

Doing this, they begin by asking how a sign could be linked to what it signifies, and respond by analysing representation, which presupposes and articulates a binary relation between the sign and what is signified. The harmonious relation between words and things are no longer guaranteed by a divine order of the world: what once started in Babel is brought to completion by the end of the sixteenth century:

> man still striveth to reintegrate himself in those benedictions, from by his fault he hath been deprived; and as he hath striven against the first general curse [the Fall] by invention of all other arts, so hath he sought to come forth of the second general curse (which was the confusion of the tongues) by the art of Grammar ...[36]

From here on, the relation between the sign and the signified is to reside inside knowledge, and to this binary relationship effected by grammatical analysis corresponds a simultaneous division of subject and object into 'mind' and 'body'.[37] The relation between language and world is duplicated in the bond between one idea and another on the inner arena of human consciousness, which is, when dusted off, a passive recipient of representations. The use of speech, says Hobbes, consists in signification, in the 'Registering of the Consequences of our thoughts, which being apt to slip out of our memory ... may again be recalled, by such words they were marked by [and] to Register, what by cogitation, wee find to be the cause of any thing, present or past.'[38]

In order to signify something, a sign must *represent* what it signifies, and also make manifest the very relation that connects it with its signification: 'The manner how Speech serveth the remembrances of causes and effects, consisteth in the imposing of Names, and the Connexion of them ... By this imposition of names ... we turn the reckoning of consequences of things imagined in the mind, into a reckoning of the consequences of Appellations.'[39]

Thus, as Foucault has pointed out, the representative link between a sign and what it signifies is dependent upon the fact that an idea can be the sign of another, not only because a bond of representation can be established between them, but also because representation itself can be represented within the idea that is representing: the signifying idea becomes double, since superimposed upon the idea that is replacing another there is also the idea of its representative power.[40] Language, in order to function as a locus or grid of representation, must be built around the notion of duplicated representation: the verbal sign must represent, but that representation, in turn, must be represented within it if language is to become transparent to thought. Ideas, signs and things must be ordered according to the same principles, but on different strata; consciousness, language and reality must be linked together isomorphically and as projections of each other within the same logical space.

As a consequence, language and knowledge both become logically interdependent of – and also *within* – the grid of representation:

> [T]ruth consisteth in the right ordering of names in our affirmations, [and] a man that seeketh precise truth, had need to remember what every name he uses stands for; and to place it accordingly.[41]

> From this we may see what truth is ... it is that our words should fairly represent the sense of our mind.[42]

To the classical writers, this rearrangement poses a dilemma, since language must occupy two positions simultaneously within the *mathesis*. First, language is a grid of analysis. Language is necessary both to bestow order upon the world, and to represent this order as accurately as possible. Second, language itself constitutes an object of analysis, and must be ordered by a simultaneous gesture in order to function as a grid of analysis. Language must analyse, but must also be analysed in order to be able to perform its analysing function. It must be *known* as an object in order to function as a grid, and it must *function* as a grid in order to be known as an object. In short, language must analyse itself by itself.

Another problem created by the demythologization of signs concerns the relationship between language and society. If language is no longer woven into the world by an original and divine gesture at the moment of creation, its signs are either natural or artificial, presented to men by things themselves, just as 'smoke is a sign of fire'[43] or established by convention or agreement. To Hobbes, the names of a language are a system of marks before they are a system of signs; they are individual property before they can be collectively shared and used as a means of communication.[44] A similar view is held by Locke: 'that then which words are marks of are the ideas of the speaker: nor can anyone apply them as marks ... to anything else but the ideas he himself hath'.[45] Here the very fact that the representative relation between ideas manifests itself on the inner surface of consciousness is sufficient to make language private, and also sufficient to make outward reference equally problematic: 'all our names are imposed to signifie our conceptions; and all our affections are but conceptions; when we conceive the same things differently, we can hardly avoyd different naming of them'.[46]

If the collective nature of representative content is problematic, it is so because an agreement on signification is lacking. Without such an agreement on signification, 'the use of a language would become meaningless [since] everyone could give an object any name he wanted'.[47] The possibility of representation thus becomes tied to the social character of language and its use as a means of communication. Hence, without 'an accord on the consistent employment of sounds',[48] there is no 'shadow of society',[49] since speech is necessary 'to make known to others our wills, and purposes, that we may have the mutuall help of one another'.[50]

At the same time, without a common language, there is no possibility of knowledge. As Hobbes reminds us, in the state of nature, there can be 'no knowledge of the face of the earth'.[51] Classical knowledge must therefore confront three problems simultaneously, which are tightly linked together into one single *problématique*: without language, there can be no society and no knowledge, since language is the basis of communication and representation; without society, there can be no language and no knowledge, since society is the basis of agreement on representations and truth; without knowledge, there can be no language and no society, since knowledge is the basis of cognitive order and social peace.

The terms of this problematic are not commensurate, and none of the component problems can be solved without disturbing the solution of another, unless we repeat the divine gesture by resorting to an external event or entity, which takes on the heavy responsibility of solving them all. First, any solution must account for the social nature of artificial languages, and explain generically how artificial languages first emerge, and then, how individual representations in the course of this process become collective ones. Second, this solution must explain and present as *immutable* the relative constancy and stability of the representative links between ideas, signs and things, two features which are necessary if language is to be susceptible to analysis according to the rules of the *mathesis*, and at the same time serve as the grid of any such analysis, irrespective of its domain.

To these problems the classical writers responded according to two main options. The first might be labelled the contractual solution, and is clearly expressed by Pufendorf:

> [W]e must understand, that the ability of those objects which affect our senses, is such, as not only to give us notice of their own presence ... but likewise to afford our Reason an opportunity of attaining the Knowledge of other things, and this, either because there is a Natural Alliance and Connexion between those Objects and Things with which they thus bring us acquainted; or because Beings endued with

> Sense and Understanding have, without this Natural Relation, fix'd such Notions upon them, as to make them capable of representing continually the Images of certain things to the Mind. Hence ariseth the distinction of signs into those which are Natural, and those which owe their force and validity to custom and compact ... By compact, Men have imposed the use and power of signifying, on certain Things, actions and Motions, and above all, on Words.[52]

However, the contractual solution of the classics suffers from a severe logical difficulty, whether it is used to explain the genesis of a language or to justify the presence of a sovereign: the entity to be explained or justified must be presupposed right from the start if the explanation or justification is to hold, but its presence must be kept secret if the presented solution is to have the desired rhetorical impact. It is not clear whether classical writers such as Hobbes and Pufendorf were aware of this difficulty, since what makes us experience it as a difficulty is the distinction – arguably a modern one – between a real and a fictitious contract. On the one hand, if we interpret a contractual agreement as something at least hypothetically real, the tautological implication between starting point and end result will itself look *real*; as Rousseau and Condillac later were to point out, any such compact or contract between men presupposes that the essential step has already been taken. For men to agree on representations necessitates a pre-established communicative bond between them, a shared language in which they can phrase all further agreement.[53] There is a parallel argument for sovereignty: for subjects to agree on a definite and indivisible locus of sovereignty in society, a central authority is necessary. On the other hand, if we interpret a contractual agreement as pure fiction, taking place within a grid of representable relationships between political beings but outside real time, the contractual solution merely renders the relationship between language and society or between subject and sovereign undecidable; the one is the condition of possibility of the other.

The second theoretical option available is to explain the genesis of language and representation as the outcome of agency. In some fictitious beginning, man receives from nature the material preconditions to make signs, and the first primitive signs produced serve as a baseline for further agreement upon which signs, among those it is possible to develop by means of analogy, are to be retained or discarded, until a communicative bond is formed.[54] As we shall see below, both these solutions are tacitly premised on the presence of what they are invoked to justify.

Ruling: sovereignty

While hypotheses of contract and action helped the classical writers to explain the social roots of language or the linguistic roots of society, none of them could account for the necessary constancy and stability of representation and signifying. Rather the opposite: why should we expect signs of any language to cease their development from primitive roots at a given moment, and, so to speak, 'freeze' in an indissoluble union with what they *contingently* happen to designate in the realms of consciousness and reality? This problem becomes all the more crucial in relation to a conception of truth as accurate representation: since classical truth hinges on the perfection of language – on the exactness of naming, on the precise formation of propositions about a classifiable world – no flux in the latter can be permitted without contaminating the former with contingency and indeterminateness. If 'reason ... is nothing but the reckoning ... of the Consequences of generall names agreed upon, for the marking and signifying of our thoughts',[55] this is still not enough to account for the simultaneous *orders* of society, language and knowledge, since

> no mans Reason, nor the Reason of any number of men, makes the certaintie ... and therefore, as when there is a controversy in an account, the parties must by their own accord, set up for right Reason, the Reason of some Arbitrator, or Judge, to whose sentence they will both stand.[56]

> It belongeth therefore to him that hath the Soveraign Power, to be Judge ... of Opinions and Doctrines, as a thing necessary to peace; therby to prevent Discord and Civil Warre.[57]

Now, just as there must be an ultimate source of the distinction between right and wrong if order is to be established in society,[58] someone must be accredited with the right to decide upon representations and truth; someone must monitor and regulate discourse, since language constitutes the baseline of all further order in society. It is here, at this crucial juncture, that the *sovereign* enters the game for the first time: 'a Commonwealth, without Soveraign Power, is but a word, without substance, and cannot stand ... seeing the knowledge of all Law, dependeth on the knowledge of the Soveraign Power ...'[59]

Repeating the Platonic rhetorical stratagem designed to end all rhetoric, the relationship between truth and rhetoric is once more reversed. To Hobbes, the proper use of speech for representation corresponds to a series of abuses, 'which may also be numbered amongst the sorts of Madnesse' such as 'inconstant signification' and metaphorical use of words, 'in other sense that they are ordained for', or when 'put together, have in them no signification at all'.[60] To Locke, even more devoted to the purification of language since 'speech being the great bond that holds society together', the worst abuse of words is to detach them from clear and distinct ideas or to conflate them with things proper.[61] To Thomas Sprat, one of the founders of the Royal Society, 'specious tropes and figures' should be banished 'out of all Civill societies as a thing fatal to peace and good Manners'. In their own activity, the Royal Society should avoid 'myths and uncertainties', and instead its members are recommended to choose a 'close, naked and natural way of speaking … as near mathematical plainness as they can'.[62]

It is in this lacuna the analysis of representation and the theory of sovereignty coincide and mutually reinforce each other: in the absence of preordained order, someone must repeat the divine gesture. To the classical authors, to whom the possibility of internal organic evolution is unknown, there cannot be order without an *orderer*. A contractual theory of sovereignty or of language can never explain the presence of the sovereign or the presence of stable representations, except by making their absence seem impossible *post hoc*.

Further, a classical theory of order can only make order intelligible and desirable in contrast with what went before it, such as the disorder caused by civil war, rhetoric and passion. Against this backdrop of an otherness, which is contained in the prehistory of the state as a state of nature from which it emerges, the sovereign is introduced into knowledge as its condition of possibility through a complex set of rhetorical moves.[63] Being the vanguard of peace and truth and the sworn enemy of rhetoric, he is the source of all representation and the ultimate guarantor of its stability and constancy in time. Just as the value of a coin in the mercantilist economy is ultimately assured by the sovereign, the sovereign must be in charge with the definition of words *before* he can give and enforce laws. The namegiving function of Leviathan thus logically precedes his lawgiving function, and the links between one idea and another and the simultaneous connection between a name and the object it is to designate must be silently regulated and safeguarded as the basis of cognitive order and right reason: without this stability, taxonomic classification is impossible, and without such cognitive order based on continuity and the enumeration of objects, political order and security itself becomes literally *unintelligible* in the absolutist scheme.

Thus, the quest for epistemic certainty and the quest for stable representations are connected to the quest for security, peace and social order, and this in three different ways: first, through supplementation, since epistemic certainty sustains and reinforces the order upheld by the sovereign, and conversely; second, through articulation, since stable representation articulates and legitimizes sovereign power, and conversely; and third, through duplication, since the positions allotted to words and things by a knowledge based on representation are duplicated by the position of the sovereign and the positions which the sovereign allots to subjects, objects and concepts within the political and social order.

These relations are manifest also at the level of opinion. If the tacit presence of the sovereign is what guarantees the continuity between language and world which is integral to both representation and analysis, he himself cannot be represented within the same knowledge, either as part of the political structure, or in its ideological underpinnings. Being the condition of representability, the sovereign escapes representation and disappears in front of our eyes at the moment when analytic reason attempts to reach its secret foundation. Just as no axiomatic proposition can be analysed in terms of its derivatives, so sovereignty, which is 'no more divisible than a point in geometry'[64] can no more be justified or criticized through an analysis of representation than the existence of the point can be demonstrated from within geometry; it must remain closed to analysis in order to be wide open to faith.[65]

Ideologically, this ontological and epistemic arrangement has four important consequences pertaining to the identity of state and sovereign. First, it conditions the structural relation between the sovereign and the state, and defines the continuity between personalized authority and the abstract entity of the state in equal terms, either metaphorically, or, as we shall see in the next section, through the crucial notion of *interest*. Second, it reverses the theory of political representation, and articulates it strictly parallel to the concept of representation within language and knowledge. If a republican theory regarded representation as warranted by the unity of the represented, an absolutist theory of government has it the other way around; if being presupposes representation in knowledge, the being of the state presupposes representation by the sovereign within the political order. Even in the subtle Hobbesian-nominalist case, in which the identity between state and sovereign cannot be accomplished through an easy metaphorical leap, their continuity is guaranteed by political representation.[66] To be sovereign is, in essence, to be *representative*: 'the Common-Wealth is no person, nor has capacity to doe anything, but by representative (that is, the Soveraign)',[67] because 'it is the Unity of the Representer, not the Unity of the Represented, that maketh the Person One'.[68]

Third, the tacit presence of indivisible sovereignty within knowledge helps to account for the ideological deification of sovereign authority. The theory of sovereignty, in its stepwise articulation and unbridling from Bodin onwards, not only placed the sovereign above the law and made him the sole source of right and wrong in the state. As Schmitt has noted, the King is the God of baroque philosophy,[69] accountable to none except God himself, and therefore subject to no human limitation whatsoever, except the undeniable fact of mortality. By taking the place of God, notes Louis XIV in his *Mémoires*, 'we seem to participate in His knowledge as well as in His authority'.[70] The state, however, was permanent and continuous, and independent of the transitory existence of its personification. Now themes from the mimetic paradigm of rulership are brushed off: the intense divinization of the sovereign goes hand in hand with a corresponding mystification of the state, to the effect that both become elevated to a point inaccessible to ordinary reason. King and State are sacred, and demand an ideological silence; this ideological silence is in turn conditioned by the limits of representation in language and knowledge. Thus Priézac was able to observe that

> it seems that the same band which so gloriously encircles the monarch's head also ties our tongues in order to prevent us speaking of it. To discuss it [Royal Majesty] meanly is to injure it; one senses its secret movements much better than one expresses them; and it is not with imperfect speech but with religious silence that we should respect the features the divine hand imprints on the foreheads of those with whom He designs to share his power.[71]

This is not only an explicit ideological denial of any higher reference point that could be used to evaluate and criticize the actions of the ruler; it is also indicative of the logical difficulty of establishing any such reference point. It is not only that the sovereign wants to be immune to criticism; rather, in the absolutist order, criticism, as we have come to know it since the Enlightenment, is not yet an open discursive possibility.[72] As Schmitt has observed, sovereignty continued to be firmly connected to the notion of infallibility even in the nineteenth century.[73]

Third, and most important, sovereignty, being the defining property of both ruler and state as a whole, confers indubitability upon the existence of both; what makes the state a state is the presence of a sovereign; what makes the sovereign sovereign is the presence of a state, which constitutes the absolute limit of his sovereignty in space; what constitutes this space as absolute is the presence of sovereignty within it. The relation between the sovereign and the state is analogous to that between a point and the notion of space in analytical geometry: as a result, the state, in its indivisible formation as a spatial entity, is constituted as an object of knowledge, which is accessible from the position of the detached spectator. The state is no longer explained by itself: one must now speak of the state as if one stood outside it. The classical theory of sovereignty thus opens up a field of empiricity and individuality, in which the state can be inscribed on the basis of its identity as sovereign; states are qualified as objects of knowledge since they all share the minimum requisite of being sovereign, and by enumeration of all further differences which can be detected through comparison, it is possible to create a science of states which obeys the rules of the *mathesis*. It is to this science of states we now must turn.

The analysis of interest

Among historians of ideas, one way to approach the change that occurs in the discourse on politics somewhere between the end of the sixteenth and the beginning of the seventeenth century, is to reconstruct it as a conflict between politics and religion, between the forces of secular statecraft embodied in the ideology of Reason of State and the fundamental principles of Christianity, or, as in Viroli's recent and more sophisticated study, between Reason of State and the 'politics' of civic humanism.[74] Those who choose this path conventionally begin by tracking the dissemination of 'Machiavellian' ideas down in textual detail, and then go on to study their basic manifestations in the formative experiences of actual states, until they can safely detect manifestations of secular statecraft in the practices of mature absolutism.[75]

Such a history will depict the troubled and sometimes violent battle between ideological positions, but it will most likely be insensitive to what it regards as disturbing mutations in the epistemic stratum.[76] The final victory of Reason of State will thus appear as the result of a battle of mere opinions, or worse, as the conscious and progressive discovery of political reality, previously hidden from the West by the veil of Christian myth.

Now even if we generously assume that there exists a loosely structured ideology called Reason of State whose basic propositions at a minimum display a family resemblance through time, the fact that it became so widely disseminated remains something of a mystery if we make it a matter of conflict between opinions. As Meinecke has noted 'It is a peculiar thing, which in history is always cropping up with reference to action prompted by *Raison d'État*, that one is perfectly capable of allowing oneself to be guided by it *involuntarily*, and yet also of turning away in anger from its fundamental propositions.'[77]

To be sure, this statement points to a series of important facts about the troubled reception of secular statecraft. Almost no one accepted its premises wholesale without qualifications, but struggled to elaborate constraints of degree and circumstance on the use of force and dissimulation in state practices.[78] Even those who arduously opposed it in theory nevertheless borrowed from it freely and employed the entire range of stratagems made available by the new ideology, such as secret publication and circulation of manuscripts, rhetorical ruses and textual dissimulation, in order to combat it, so to speak, on its own territory.[79]

These facts become all the more puzzling when introduced into an explanatory account. In a history of political ideas written as a battle of opinions rather than as a battle of knowledges, acceptance and refutation of a given opinion are necessarily opposed; one cannot accept what one refutes without being disqualified as the narrative hero in doxographic history, since it demands a consistent and rational subject at its centre. Hence the term 'involuntarily' is introduced in the above statement by Meinecke; through it, what one does not accept can nevertheless enter consciousness and govern action.

But how, and from where? We can interpret this *involuntariness* in two different ways. Either, as seems to be implicated by Meinecke, the basic propositions of Reason of State must be accessible to consciousness as a bundle of unthought premises, so that which is involuntarily accepted is already present before the fact of its dissemination, which was to be explained in the first place. Or, the political reality that makes the fundamental assumptions of Reason of State both an accurate representation of that reality and a feasible guide to practical conduct in the same reality, is already present to perception and deliberation, leaving the particular opinionated agent with the choice of adapting or perishing, as the ideology to be explained itself prescribes. In the first case, that whose presence is to be explained is assumed to be present by the *explanandum*, whereas in the second case, the explanation is but a continuation of *explanans* with other means, here transposed to the level of opinionated forces. In either case, by virtue of its familiarity, Reason of State is explained by itself.

Perhaps one should abandon the effort to study the ideology of Reason of State as a continuous tradition, and, despite the recurrence of family-resemblant motifs, write its history discontinuously and in terms wholly contemporaneous with its manifestations. As I intend to demonstrate in this section, the dissemination of secular statecraft is not a matter of ideological opinion, but rather a matter of its epistemic transformation. In the course of the seventeenth century, Reason of State – if we are still entitled to use the concept – is disconnected from its problematic foundation in the general theory of the state, which it to an extent also absorbs and renders obsolete: it will not make much sense within classical knowledge to say, for example, that a hereditary king should obey a different political rationality than a usurper, or that an aristocracy should be governed according to different principles than a monarchy: the questions of origin and form are relegated to a secondary position.

Instead, and closely connected to the emergence of the *mathesis*, Reason of State emerges as an autonomous field of knowledge, with its own domain of objects and its own rules for the formation of valid statements. It is this discursive practice, empirical in outlook and problem-solving in its objectives, which I shall label the *analysis of interest*.

Studying this discursive practice, I shall be less occupied with the books that at the time were collecting dust in libraries, but all the more with the ones that travelled in saddlebags.[80] The analysis of interest is not a *theory*: its central assumptions are rarely made explicit, and they have never been condensed into the abstract or codified into *regulae*. Rather, it is a political technology for dealing with concrete problems of foreign policy, often in a distinct historical perspective, but from a shared set of presuppositions. It is these presuppositions, and their relation to the *mathesis*, rather than the practical recommendations that flow from the analysis, which are my chief concern in this section.

The core variable which determines this field of knowledge and its proper object is *interest*. To the modern political scientist, this term is so familiar that its basic connotations are as self-evident as its precise definition is contested.[81] In order to understand this concept in terms contemporaneous with it, we must therefore avoid a retrospective reading which would merely endow the classical analysis of interest with unity and coherence in the light of modern political theory; we must not allow the modern meaning of interest to permeate into its classical sphere of application. Rather, we should ask how the analysis of interest became possible on its own terms, and how, long after it was excommunicated from the territory of the political sciences, its core concepts could be appropriated again and given new meaning by nineteenth-century historiography.

Passions and interests

As has been frequently noted, the term interest, far from being absent in earlier vocabularies, takes on new importance and meaning with the beginning of the seventeenth century, until references to interest become a commonplace or 'a cachet of sophistication'[82] in political philosophy towards the end of the same century.[83]

While the importance of the term interest in classical political litera-ture seems undisputed, the explanations of this phenomenon differ. Gunn argues, for example, that interest provided an essential concep-tual tool for overcoming the difficulties inherent in the late medieval way of conceptualizing the conflict between public and private. After the experience of the English Civil War such a tool was needed that could accommodate and resolve the conflicts it gave rise to in the political and economic spheres.[84]

To Hirschman and Keohane, the swift acceptance of interest as the linchpin of political thought and action is more symptomatic of emer-gent capitalism. In both cases, the concept of interest is seen as a strategic device introduced in order to combat otherness in the shape of passion. Cupidity, avarice and glory, figuring as crucial motivating forces in the self-understanding of the Middle Ages and the Renais-sance, become an anathema to an age struggling to place politics and economy on a rational footing, and must therefore either be repressed, neutralized or canalized into purely rational ends. According to this explanation, interest constitutes a middle ground on which the passionate impulses of the ego and the rational imperatives of the community can coincide to the advantage of both. Interest splits the difference between passion and reason, so that private vices can be translated into public virtues.[85]

Thus, in both these explanations, the concept of interest is analysed in terms of its consequences as a harbinger of capitalism in the domestic arena. While it may be true that 'interest made the journey from the council chambers to the market place very quickly',[86] this functionalist line of reasoning fails to account for two important facts. First, by focusing exclusively on the impact of the term in the domestic context as a function of its victory over the passions in moral discourse, this view has difficulty accounting for the fact that the term was first introduced in the discourse on interstate relations, a sphere which had long since been defined by the absence of morality, or placed outside its range of application.

This move was not so much a result of a conscious effort to 'amoralize' the intercourse between princes, but rather the unintended outcome of the efforts to cope with the most pernicious implications of secular statecraft by subjecting it to the constraints of degree and circumstance, while retaining the moral autonomy of the state. From Montaigne, Lipsius and Charron up to Descartes and Naudé, we can discern a series of practical recommendations that place severe limits on such practices as deceit, dissimulation, disinformation and corruption in the domestic context, but became increasingly permissive about using them in dealings between princes, or against an unspecified and variable 'enemy', or in the face of an unexpected crisis.[87]

Thus, in its interstate figuration, the concept of interest has been seen either as an antidote to the more obnoxious forms of secular statecraft, or as an articulation of it,[88] but not as the core concept of an autonomous discourse.

Second, by focusing on the rhetorical battle between the passions and the interests in moral discourse, the functionalist explanation has perhaps granted too much to the self-understanding of the classical authors by taking their version of this Platonic opposition at face value. Hence, one is led to regard this opposition as a clash between moral opinions, rather than as a surface symptom of a conflict between knowledges.

What makes the reconstructive value of these moral battles suspicious is the fact that they are consistently linked to an assertion of newness. Just as Hobbes understands his effort to create a new rational

self out of the 'feare of death' and a new 'scientific' politics in opposition to rhetorics and dogma,[89] and as Bacon and Descartes understand their new science as a radical break from inherited opinion,[90] so
our political technologists understand their analysis of interest as an
approach opposed to that of exemplary history. Unless we deconstruct
the opposition between passion and reason all the way down, it will
remain an enigma how Rohan and Pufendorf are able to heap scorn on
the use of history as a guide to political action in the prefaces to their
historical works, and then continue to sprinkle their works with
'lessons' for the benefit of statesmen, an enigma that can only be
solved by considering the profound change in metahistorical outlook
which the scientific revolution brings about.

As we may recall from chapter 4, the general theory of the state had
its range of application and validity defined by exemplary history,
such that every political occurrence touching upon 'matters of state'
could be subjected to judgement according to exempla, and that these
exempla, when pertaining to the relations between princes, not
infrequently depicted these relations in terms of cupidity and avarice,
chiefly manifested through territorial aggrandizement.

As we may also recall, the appeal to self-interest as an antidote to
war was among the commonplaces of Christian humanism in the
Renaissance.[91] Ironically enough, self-interest now bursts in, but
without its desired pacific effects. The analysis of interest is opposed
precisely to the politics of passion and to a historical narrative which
has passion as its centrepiece, but also to exempla as the source of
legitimate action and validity. Instead, the analysis of interest ventures
to reconstruct the past and create a present in a mode narrowly
circumscribed by the rules of classical science. Writes Hobbes:

> From the principal parts of Nature, Reason and Passion, have pro-
> ceeded two kinds of learning, *mathematical* and *dogmatical*: the former
> is free from controversy and dispute, because it consisteth in compar-
> ing figure and motion only; in which things, *truth*, and the *interest of
> men*, oppose not each other; but in the other there is nothing undis-
> putable, because it compareth men, and meddleth with their right
> and profit; in which, as oft as reason is against man, so oft will a man
> be against reason.[92]

The *mathesis* links together truth and peace, and places them in
opposition to rhetoric and war. When grafted onto the category of
history, the *mathesis* promises us an archimedean point from which to
write and pass judgements on the past, unaided by exempla and

uncontaminated by the conflicts stirred up by passion and rhetoric. Still, history, in the presentist or finalist modes we know it today, is a possibility not yet open to the seventeenth century. In the analysis of interest, time is not a principle of the internal organic development of societies or of an international context; time is still entirely external to objects, and poses a constant threat to the identity of individual states as well. It remains to see how this identity is safeguarded, and how the Classical Age copes with contingency and particularity.

The duality of interest

Our knowledge of the past is scarce and distorted, says Courtilz de Sandras, since the passion of men 'has been the brush with which they have been painted for us'.[93] Here, as in the rules of the use and abuse of speech in Hobbes or Locke, passion is evil primarily because it subverts the act of representation. What appears to be most problematic to Courtilz is not the fact that men sometimes are guided by passion; rather, the historiographical problem arises out of the impassioned self-description of these men. They cannot think of themselves or their past in terms of accurate representations; the passion governing their deeds will inevitably be duplicated in their accounts of past and present, and distort their truth and usefulness. Their stories will tell us less about political events, and much more about the authors themselves; there is no critical possibility here, no archimedean point from which to judge events, no *scientia*, only *legenda*.

There is at all events no longer any need of historical exempla more than as curiosities since it is not possible to establish any 'immutable rule for the government of states', when 'that which causes transformation in the affairs of their world, also causes change in the basic principles of ruling'.[94] Here, all the precepts that could be distilled from the general theory of the state are found lacking in value: when history no longer repeats itself infinitely, exempla become useless as guides to action; the inherited category of history must be declared null and void.

Thus, the sense of newness and innovation has its beginning at the metahistorical level; it is not simply an awareness of historical change that catalyses this sentiment; it is a matter of controlling time itself, and of freeing oneself from the threat it poses to the stability of a knowledge based on *mathesis* and representation. If a history is to be written, it must be written as an analysis which can subject historicity to the limits of reason: its objects must be defined and remain identical with themselves, so that they can be placed in an ordered series, ranging from the simple to the more complex, or distributed on a scale and measured according to common qualities. A 'history' founded on the rules of general science must assume rational reconstructability of its field, so that one can decide what is a *historical event* and what is not; it must assume an ordering principle which permits the historian to arrange these events in a manner accessible to understanding and analysis. The categories necessary to perform this task must, however, themselves be able to withstand corrosive change when applied across time: ideally, one should be able to use the same categories to explain and understand an event of a distant past as those which one uses to illuminate present affairs. These categories and their representative content must not be allowed to vary according to the differing self-understandings of the agents of different times, but instead must ideally be able to order these self-understandings on a surface wholly simultaneous to and correlative to that of historical events, so that the one can be described and explained in terms of the other; subjective 'belief' and objective 'event' will henceforth be linked to one another as cause to effect and effect to cause, but firmly divided as to their essence, the one being cognizant, the other extended in space.

To be sure, there had been efforts at comparison prior to the analysis of interest. The discovery of America had sensitized Christianity to cultural differences, and given rise to an entire genre of literature devoted to the explanation and understanding of these differences between peoples.[95] Simultaneously, the early seventeenth century witnessed an intense polarization between the Habsburg and the French crowns, and it was left to philosophers to explain this discord within Christianity in terms of accidents of climate and geography.[96] Now what is peculiar to the analysis of interest is that it starts with sovereignty as the ordering and individuating principle that makes states worthy of further comparison: if sovereignty endows the *state* with the essential self-identity needed to qualify it as an object of knowledge, the concept of interest provides the point from which the detection of differences in a plurality of *states* can proceed. For just as 'princes command the people and interest commands princes',[97] so interest defines the field of objectivity of seventeenth-century historiography, since 'there are no princes in the world that do not conduct themselves according to their interest'[98] and since 'knowledge of this interest is as much elevated above that of the actions of princes, as they themselves are above the people'.[99] That is, regarded from a vantage point outside time, the affairs of states are regulated by interest; it appears as the only legitimate principle of historical reconstruction and qualitative and quantitative comparison of states. Consequently, what counts from now on as a 'historical event' is a clash of interests or a reversal of a power relationship.

Parallel to its introduction in the discourse about states, however, the notion of interest was permeating the political folklore of the age, and gradually became reified as the secret condition behind all agency. To La Rochefoucauld, the 'virtues lose themselves in interest as the rivers are lost in the sea'.[100] To Silhon, even more incapable of discerning other motivating forces than interest, 'almost all the actions of our life are excited by some notion of interest of whatever genre [and] to wish to ban interest from our lives would be to take from a machine the springs that make it move, and destroy the part of a compound object that makes it act'.[101] To Cardinal de Retz, 'the truest maxim for judging sanely the intentions of men is to examine their interests, which are the most ordinary rule of all their actions.'[102] To Herle and Nedham, interest is an autonomous social force, whose workings go beyond individual agency in both scope and impact.[103] As a result, agency cannot be understood in terms other than interest, and understanding itself is animated by the notion of interest: despite the passive role allotted to subjectivity by classical philosophy, to understand is just one activity among others.

In the analysis of interest, the concept of interest is as ambiguous and primitive as it is central. Interest is never defined in the abstract, but used to define all other concepts with which it entertains inferential or metaphorical connections. These concepts stand in a dual relationship to the empirical estimate of interest that results from the analysis: first, as determinants of interest in general or as variables in an analysis of actual interests, and second, as prescribed objectives of policy in general and foreign policy in particular. Four such determinants or objectives are pertinent to the classical analysis of interest: *power, wealth, security* and *reputation*.

That is, if one possesses accurate knowledge of the size of a country, its natural resources and the size of the royal revenue, the number of its inhabitants and their natural inclinations, one simultaneously possesses a fair estimate of its military strength and hence of its interests.[104] Power and wealth, in theory as well as in the concrete political practices of the Classical Age, are inseparable: not only in terms of a causal relationship or in a strategic calculus of ends and means, but also at the level of signification. Wealth is a sign of power and power is a sign of wealth; to display wealth is to display power, and conversely.[105]

In relations between states, both power and wealth are conceived of in zero-sum terms. The concept of power, previously interpreted as an ability or disposition inherent in particular substances, is successively released from its logical connections to Aristotelian causality and reinterpreted in terms of mechanistic causality.[106] If the objects of the physical world are inanimate, so are the forces responsible for their movement in space; if the objects of the political and social worlds are animate, this is because the forces responsible for their interaction reside with an agent. Thus Hobbes, anxious to demythologize power, was stripping the concept of power of its previous connotations and reinscribing it within the *mathesis*: 'Power and cause are the same thing. Correspondent to cause and effect, are power and act ... Wherefore the power of an agent and the efficient cause are the same thing.'[107]

As a consequence, power becomes a measurable property rather than a disposition or a relation; like wealth, it can be acquired, alienated, and exchanged and its possession can be communicated and translated from one form to another. Power and wealth can be subjected to calculation in the same fashion as weight or velocity, and since their quantity in the world is constant, a conflict of interest will be discernible whenever their distribution is unequal. Furthermore, intimately tied to the new concept of power, is the concept of the political subject. If power is thought of causally, and if its possession is to be communicated with an eye to a desired effect upon an adversary, subjects must not only be able to communicate their intentions, but also able to gain introspective knowledge of their interests. As we shall see below, this connection between power and the *cogito* is duplicated in the analysis of state interests.

If the analysis of interest were based on the distribution of power and wealth alone, the relations between states would inevitably resemble a zero-sum game,[108] but when it comes to security and reputation, the classical analysis becomes more complex, and its concepts look even less familiar to us. If both power and wealth are constituted, represented and measured as material objects, security and reputation are connected as predicates to the subjective side of the state, to sovereignty itself. The ultimate subject of security is sovereignty, whether personalized in the sovereign, or in the abstract and naturalized sense of the state as a whole, but its precise signification varies with the point of reference. When *securatio* figures as an attribute of personalized sovereignty, it connotes the personal preservation and well-being of the sovereign, but when it is attributed as a property of the state as a whole, it signifies the identity of a particular state and its ability to remain identical with itself. Thus, when security refers to the state, it does not do so primarily in terms of a preconstituted entity that wishes to preserve itself from an identifiable danger; rather, it points to the identity of the state as that which has to be rendered secure in the first place.[109]

This means that security is not primarily an object of foreign policy; before security can be brought to function as such, it requires a prior differentiation of what is alien, other or simply outside the state and therefore threatens it, and what is inside and therefore constitutive of it. In the Classical Age, the discourse of security has as its main task to make intelligible what has to be secured, by a prior differentiation between political order and its opposite, so that this identity can be established in political practice. Security must be defined in terms of fear, friendship in terms of enmity. Writes Hobbes: 'The Multitude sufficient to confide in for our Security, is not determined by any certain number, but *by comparison with the enemy* ... Nor is it enough for the security, which men desire should last all the time of their life, that they be governed, and directed by one judgement, for a limited time.' For in the absence of continuous sovereign power, 'they must ... by the difference of their interests dissolve, and fall again into a Warre amongst themselves'.[110] As in the classical theories of contract, negativity and otherness do not reside primarily in the spatial outside of individual states, but are contained in their traumatic prehistory as a threat of religious and civil war. The sovereign state is an offer you cannot refuse, since enmity and discord can burst in at any time. Thus Spinoza in his *Tractatus Theologico-Politicus* (1670): 'there is no body who doth not desire to live in safety and out of fear ... He that lives where there is continual Enmity, Hatred, Wrath and Deceit, must live always in danger and fear ... if Men will live securely without fear, there is an absolute necessity of uniting themselves and agreeing together....'[111]

By the same token, reputation must not be understood primarily in the superficial sense as the 'prestige' of a ready-made state in relation to its formal equals.[112] To be sure, it carries this signification, but it is then restricted to personalized sovereignty, to the prestige of a king.

When attributed to the state as a whole, reputation is consistently linked to the reflexive and reciprocal construction of state identity. A sovereign state acquires part of its identity from being recognized sovereign by other states: a state without *reputatio* is not a state in the eyes of other states, and hence not qualified to be a political subject. The reputation of a state – its 'stateness' – is in part dependent on the reputation – in the today familiar sense – of its king. As a consequence, reputation must be understood as a baseline component of state identity before it can be understood as an aim of foreign policy. In short, the recognition of a state hinges on the reputation of its king, and the reputation of its king hinges upon the recognition of his state; the reputation of a state hinges on its prior recognition as a state. Richelieu, in his *Testament Politique*, spells out part of this connection clearly:

> Reputation is so very necessary to a prince that he of whom one has a good opinion does more with his mere name than those who are not esteemed do with their armies. They [princes] are obligated to value their reputations more than their own lives, and they should risk their faith and grandeur rather than allow their honor to be compromised, being certain that the first diminuation that occurs to a prince's reputation, however slight, is the most dangerous step that he may take towards his ruin.[113]

If the discursive practice of *securatio* creates identity by a rhetoric of otherness and enmity, the discursive practice of *reputatio* structures a table of identities by means of the fragile sameness and friendship provided by mutual recognition. Interpreted as structural principles, security and reputation together establish state identity from two different directions and by means of a grid of difference: security divides every state ontologically from every other form of political organization by presenting everything that is prior in time or external in space as a threat, while reputation rests on reciprocal recognition from the other in order for the state to become a site of sameness and hence a subject to be rendered secure. Before security and reputation can be understood as *objectives* of foreign policy, they help constitute the agent by defining what is *foreign* to it.

The end product of the analysis of interest is the *maxime*. The interest of each state or prince can be broken down into components and compared with those of other states and princes, and the detected qualitative and quantitative differences can then be reduced to a set of simple principles or *maximes*. Precisely as the determinants of interest were Janus-faced, the *maxime* has both a representative and a norma-tive content. Each specific *maxime* should be interpreted dualistically; historically, it condenses the 'objective' forces and motives behind the present political status and current foreign policy of a state, and, simultaneously, by virtue of its 'truth', each *maxime* contains more or less precise guidelines for the future policy of each state or prince, provided that the state or prince shares the most basic interests in power, wealth, security and reputation, whose validity the historical analysis makes transparent by connecting them to present identity.

Maximes can be derived from a comparison of states and their differences in two different ways, each of which corresponds to one of the two main theoretical options available to the analysis of interest. For want of better terms, I shall borrow the two terms *systemic* and *methodical* analysis from the contemporary discourse on natural history, which obeys analogous rules of formation and validation of statements.[114]

The first option can be labelled the systemic option. The analysis of interest here departs from a predetermined set of variables, which can be subjected to an ever more fine-grained analysis by decomposing them and measuring them on an ordinal scale. Following the systemic option, one begins by selecting a finite or relatively small number of characteristics which together define the domain of knowledge, the table or taxonomy of sovereign states. Variations in these character-istics can be studied in any particular state and then compared with those of other states. To Rohan, the actual interest of states depends on six such elements. However intersected in practice, the military strength of a state, its geopolitical situation, the cohesive force of its religion, its capacity to entertain *intelligence* with other states, the nature of its negotiations with them and its *reputation* in the family of states are the crucial variables which permit us to compare it with other states and represent their reciprocal interests by cross-tabulation in order to determine whether they are opposed or coincide.[115] Hence, in his *Interest* of 1638, the interests of France and Spain are found to be opposed, and their *maximes* are mirror-images of one another: not surprisingly, France is everything that Spain is not; already by means of classification, it becomes possible to make the enemy look inferior, not only morally, but also logically.

To Pufendorf, the interest of any particular state at any particular moment in time can be determined with increased certainty by divi-ding interest into *perpetual* and *temporary*. As Pufendorf has it, the perpetual interest of a state is dependent on the more or less invariable facts of its geographical situation, the size of its natural resources and the natural inclinations of its people, while its temporary interest can best be judged in terms of its power relationships to its neighbours, 'for as those vary, the Interest must also vary'.[116] This more abstract taxonomy of interest permits Pufendorf to cover a larger span of time in his *Introduction* (1682), so that the political history of states from Assyria up to contemporary affairs can be understood as a continuous clash of interests, and the formation and decay of states can also be accounted for in the same terms. The once legendary or mythological history of ancient states is reinscribed into a calculus of opposing interests and forces:

> It is evident out of History; that the deeper you search into the most ancient Times, the more separate small Commonwealths you will meet withal; from the coalition of which great Empires in process of time did arise, some uniting by common consent, and others subdued by the more powerful.[117]

Now the systemic option is by its very nature arbitrary. The number of possible systems of comparison are theoretically infinite, however actually circumscribed by practical considerations arising out of the Thirty Years War: each possible system must simply ignore those differences between states that fall outside the range of comparison initially specified by the variables selected as characteristics in the analytical system, but it does not exclude the possibility that the specified dimensions will prove exhaustive of the field of knowledge, since within the range delimited by the variables, ever more fine-grained differences can be found in the class of empirical states. Furthermore, the arbitrary basis of the systemic option not only makes it possible to imagine many different and perhaps conflicting analytical systems, but permits each of them to constitute its own field, depending on the number of elements and variables it explicitly includes or implicitly excludes. The greater the number of variables or elements, the more intricate and complex the differences of interest between states will appear to be, and conversely: the fewer the variables, the more straightforward and simple the differences.

The second option might be labelled methodical analysis, and employs a reverse logic. Instead of starting with a predetermined and limited set of variables and elements, comparison here begins with a definition of a concrete field of investigation in time and space. Since 'the general affairs of Christianity are of such large extension' that a full and accurate description of them would 'fill entire volumes', it is more 'useful and convenient' to stick to recent and important events, and on the basis of them pass judgements on the future.[118] That is, instead of determining the interest of individual states by measuring their relative differences according to a fixed set of variables, one begins with their relations and interactions, describes the formative events and main reversals of power within the field of investigation as a whole, and distils from them a series of *maximes* pertaining to the past, present and future conduct of each state the other; the actual condition and interests of a state are the outcome of a linear succession of political events and interactions, rather than conversely.

In the methodical analysis of interests, the elements of interest are not determined in advance; they are deduced stage by stage from the juxtaposition of individual states and the political events responsible for their present condition. For example, Ardier begins, albeit from an explicitly French perspective, with a detailed examination of diplomatic history up to a certain point in time, in this case April 1633, and derives the *maximes* to be observed from the prior interplay of interests. The *maximes* appear here as resultants of opposed 'mechanical' forces, either to be kept in equilibrium or reversed. For example, since 'the interest of France is in every respect opposed to that of Spain', it follows that the former ought to desire peace between the Italian princes, since if united they can act as a counterpoise to Spanish power while safeguarding their own liberty and sovereignty.[119] Moreover, the French cannot hope for any restraint or moderation on behalf of the Spanish crown, since it will live forever in envy of the French, and continue to pose obstacles to French designs.[120] In Ardier, as in Rohan, the political ontology itself serves to define and stigmatize the enemy, by making his interest and his *maximes* the inferior term in the opposition: 'France' is positivity to the negativity of 'Spain'.

In another version of methodical analysis, Courtilz begins with a comparison of the contemporary condition of European politics with what purportedly existed before on the European scene: a set of communitarian values, possibly – or hopefully – to be restored in the shape of a *monarchie universelle*. In this first step, qualitative difference is identified across time rather than as variations across individual political entities. To Courtilz, the recurrent feature of European politics is the opposition between France and the Habsburgs, a bipolar tension which structures the relationships between all the lesser powers and serves to explain the existing pattern of alliances in terms of what we today would call jumping on the bandwagon. According to Courtilz, the qualitative difference consists in a change of *maxime* in European politics as a whole: interest had taken precedence over religious affinity or enmity and dynastic pretensions as the motivating force in politics.[121] The 'new' art of politics simply consists in 'knowing how to conduct one's own affairs, while hindering others from conducting theirs'.[122] For individual states 'there does not exist a single *maxime* that may not have to be reversed in accordance with the circumstances. Everything must yield to the interest of the state.'[123] If interest is the overarching principle of interstate policy, no elements of interest can be determined in advance, but must be derived through a methodical comparison of states in their concrete political circumstances. In this sense, Courtilz explicitly opposes himself to the systemic option: if everything varies, every element or characteristic variable in an analytical system will inevitably lose explanatory power by even the slightest reversal of power. Instead, Courtilz pursues an alternative analytical path: he first arranges states on an ordinal scale according to the amount of power they can be said to possess after due empirical investigation of their relative position, that 'in which God has placed them'.[124] Starting with the great powers and then continuing downwards to the tiniest principality, relationships of equality and inequality can gradually be detected and cross-tabulated. He then describes each state and its web of relationships with other states in their entirety – from great powers to small ones – and determines inductively the values of all variables crucial to their specific interest towards one another. In every instance of methodical analysis, the description of a state and its foreign policy aspires to be total and exhaustive, but with the essential difference that nothing that has been said about the first state will be repeated in the description of the second, and so forth. Thus, in the end, we are left with a series of thick empirical descriptions which are mutually exclusive and together exhaustive of what European politics *is* at the initially specified moment in time. Furthermore, these descriptions are to an extent relative to the initial ranking: if the distribution of power changes, the basic interest of states must also change. This explains why Courtilz insists on a divinely ordained ranking between states as the guarantee of analytical stability.

Despite the differences between the systemic and methodical forms of analysis, they are both conditioned by the same basic epistemic principles of the *mathesis*. They both rely on a comparison of complex empirical individuals, whose individuality has been constituted in advance by the concept of sovereignty. If sovereignty defines the general identity of the state from the inside, the analysis of interest constitutes the identity of specific states from an outside by means of a grid of difference in power, wealth, security and reputation. In the analysis of interest, knowledge of states can be acquired from a continuous tabulation of their differences in terms of resources and interests; what is left out, however, is the consideration of the origin and form of states as autonomous variables. If origin and form are analysed, they are analysed as determinants of the crucial variables. The state is describable, and the totality of states orderable: the practical result is a political taxonomy in which the reciprocal relations between states can be represented, and possible lines of action can be evaluated with respect to their expected utility. This epistemic arrangement has three important consequences.

First, and as a consequence of its indebtedness to the *mathesis*, the analysis of interest subordinates the question of being to the question of knowing. Only that which can be tabulated or arranged within a taxonomy of interest does exist, and what is outside the tabulated order is marked by non-being. If Descartes compared objects inaccessible to reason and representation with distant countries like China and Mexico,[125] the analysis of interest confines itself to the European context, and passes few remarks on what lies outside it. This is hardly surprising; what is surprising, however, is the fact that the impact of colonial trade with the New World on the distribution of power between European states most often is presented as something exogenous. In chapter 6, we shall find the New World rediscovered by the Enlightenment; to the classical analysts of interest, it hardly exists.

Second, interest, being crucial to the outward identity of each state, is also that which links together the past, present and future of a given state as a continuous series of political events. This continuity is established by the duality of the *maxime*, a duality which connects past events with future possibilities. The *maxime* not only contains and condenses the lessons of history; it also furnishes each state with a specific past that can be used as a clue to both present identity and its future fate within the table. Consequently, one is permitted to speak of the policy of 'France' during the Italian Wars and the policy of 'France' during the Valteline not only in the same terms (that is, in terms of interest) but also, and more importantly, *as if the acting subject in fact always remains and will remain identical with itself* on the stage of politics.

That is, the basic identity of a state is not affected by its military and economic fate, nor by contractions or extensions of its territory, nor by revolutionary upheaval in its internal structure. When seen from the outside, France is constituted as 'France' long before this identity is ideologized, and this by means logically different to the organic metaphors of nineteenth-century nationalism. The impact of this discursive practice cannot be overemphasized: it works to make the state, whose history is linked to that of the concept of time, immune to the corrosive threat posed by contingency and particularity. As we shall see below, it is this discursive move that makes it possible to speak of a tabulated order separate from and independent of the concrete historical being of states, an order which we today still presuppose and draw on when we use the name of a state in the grammatical position of subject in a phrase.

Third, what is sometimes labelled the great power perspective has its point of emergence in the analysis of interest. To some extent, this perspective reflects the considerations of a bipolar age, but more importantly, it is immanent in the analysis itself, since the ordinal measurement of the distribution of power and wealth is that which defines an entire order as classifiable, and without which there would be no field of empirical entities to investigate.

Truth and interest

The discourse on interest constitutes a domain of knowledge and imposes order and regularity upon it in order to render it analysable; but what makes it function as true? We have seen how it draws on the fundamental rules of classical science: it proceeds by orderly enumeration and the representation of differences between individual objects, whose empirical reality and identity it thereby establishes; it renders them comparable within a taxonomy; it renders their interests calculable by measuring their differences on an ordinal scale.

Still, the analysis of interest, however indebted to the classical epistemic figure, is an autonomous discourse, with its own rules for the formation of valid statements. So when Courtilz solemnly tells us that the reason why he has undertaken to write his *Nouveaux Interets* is that he 'loves very much to tell the truth',[126] we must ask specific questions of this love that excites Courtilz' imagination: how is this truth possible, how is it safeguarded, and how does it perform its validating function?

Like every claim to truth, a truth based on accurate representation of political reality requires a privileged point from which it can be established and justified. In the analysis of interest, this problem becomes all the more puzzling in face of the duality of the concept of interest. On the one hand, the analysis is supposed to represent as accurately as possible various state interests, on the other, it is undertaken in order to prescribe proper lines of action for interested parties. Now, is its representative accuracy warranted by its prescriptive impact, or, is it perhaps the other way around? Is it true because princes and states act as if it were true, or ought states to act in accordance with certain *maximes* because they are true?

To us, this question is analogous to the question of the validity of a grammatical system, and presents us with a dilemma of undecidability between description and prescription. To the classical authors, however, this dilemma was not present; as I shall attempt to show in this section, there is no such divide between knowledge and ideology in the classical period; the term *idéologie*, when it eventually was coined by Destutt de Tracy in the late eighteenth century, referred to the systematic analysis of representations and their formation in the mind, and was thus inseparable from an analysis of the conditions of human knowledge.[127] As I shall argue below, the validation of the analysis of interest is carried out through a duplication of the representation and the represented.

Let us begin with the overt claims to truth made by the analysts of interest, and the epistemic warrants they invoke. The first warrant is a Baconian consideration of practical utility, according to which one should be accustomed to 'judge of the proportion or value of things as they conduce and are material to our particular ends'.[128] Already in the anonymous *Discours* of 1624, we are told that 'the best advice one can give in matters of State ... is based on special knowledge of the State itself'.[129] To Rohan, for a prince to enlarge or preserve his state, he is not in need of any higher viewpoint; it suffices for him to consider the interests of other princes in the present.[130] To Pufendorf, who held the study of history to be 'pleasant and useful for those who design for Employment in the State', knowledge of interest is of paramount importance to the security of the state.[131] To Ardier, this knowledge permits one to judge the future, and thus contribute to the good of the state.[132] That is, one's successful participation in the game of politics requires accurate representations of the interests of other states, and the accuracy of the representation is, in the final analysis, determined by the success it achieves: the analysis of interest is valid because it furthers the interest it analyses. It is useful because of its truth, and true because of its usefulness.

Second, and sometimes linked to this pragmatic self-justification of the analysis, is a claim to impartiality or objectivity. For example, Courtilz tirelessly assures his readers that he is on nobody's payroll, and therefore, he seems to believe, automatically reliable.[133] Although on the Swedish payroll, Pufendorf goes further in his *De rebus sueciis*:

> In this work we have (as is the principal duty of the historian) tried very conscientiously to ensure reliability; we have taken the decisions from the authentic documents and interpolated nothing, and our portrayal of events is based on the reports of army commanders and envoys. In general we have not troubled to present the decisions and actions of the enemy party, except insofar as these entered the field of view (as it were) of our own side. We considered it rash to try and divine or interpret their secrets by conjecture. Altogether, we have given the reader freedom of judgement, without introducing our own opinion unnecessarily. Our intention was to relate the deeds of others, and not to pass judgement on them ... [H]istory does not hesitate on the basis of its right to transmit what it has found for the consideration of posterity ... it is required of the historian that he should say nothing false and should not refrain from saying anything true.[134]

To live in the world as if one stood outside it: the analysis of interest is logically interwoven with the possibility of a detached spectator, and the source criticism it makes possible. The accuracy of historical representation hinges on the presence of an elevated intersubjectivity, a vantage point dependent on the prior alienation of the author from the concerns of any particular state, and situated over and above the play and counterplay of actual state interests which structure and animate the raw historical material into a narrative of events: its truthful character resides in the disinterested detachment of the spectator, and this disinterested detachment in turn requires an amount of self-estrangement of the author from the material under consideration. Says Courtilz: 'we were born in a state, which is not subject to either of the two crowns [France and Spain], but our profession is that of telling the truth'.[135] At the same time, however, this viewpoint necessitates a close identification with the state as an abstract entity, defined in terms of its sovereignty. Hence, the position of the spectator in relation to state interests in their external manifestation is here analogous to that of the king with regard to their internal manifestation in a particular state.

But how, one may ask, is the truth of this disinterestedness in turn to be represented? Is an historical account true because it is disinterested, or is it disinterested because it is true? As such, disinterestedness is a special case of interest: defined either intersubjectively as the point where all other interests happen to coincide and become neutralized, or, in terms of a wholly sovereign position situated above the politics of interest proper, the very term 'disinterestedness' takes on meaning only in relation to 'interest', and then as the inferior term in such an opposition. We cannot make sense of disinterestedness without – however tacitly – invoking the notion of interestedness. In either of the above cases, this justification seems as elliptical as the one centred around utility: disinterestedness is established on the basis of interests that makes it true, and the existence of these interests can only be securely determined from this disinterested point of view.

Turning now to the internal mechanisms of validation, this close relationship between interest, truth and utility in the passages explicitly devoted to justification is also duplicated inside the analysis of interest itself; in fact, it is this duplication that permits the analysis of interest to function as a regime of truth in interstate politics. As we may recall from above, the idea of representation has to be duplicated in every specific act of representation in order for the latter to impose an unbroken relation between words, things and ideas, such that the signs that replace and help analyse representations must also be representations themselves. In the same fashion, the analysis of interest must, so to speak, remain open to and indeed execute an analysis *of itself in its own terms*. It must work back on itself, not reflexively, but constitutively: the analysis represents a political reality, but it is also represented in this political reality; it represents a politics animated by the notion of interest, and thus represents itself as represented in political reality.

As a first step in this duplication, the analysis of interest is rendered *unfalsifiable*. The prince, says Rohan, may well be deceived by corrupt counsel, but interest itself will never fail or betray him. According to whether it is well or badly understood, it preserves or ruins states.[136] Part of this statement was later absorbed in political discourse and turned into the self-evident maxim that 'interest will not lie'.[137] According to Herle, 'if a man state his own interest aright, and keep close to it, it will not lie to him or deceive him'.[138] To us, these statements border on the trivial and the tautological: one's interest cannot lead one astray, since a failure would merely point to the fact that the course of action undertaken had actually not been in one's true interest.

The truth of interest is therefore a necessary truth: if a line of action fails, this is simply because the agent misperceived his true interest, and let himself be deceived by an imaginary or subjective interest, a deviation from rationality resulting from the weakness of his own judgement. Now, if every instance of political success automatically is a corroborating instance of the analysis of interest, we must ask how the analysis accounts for political failure.

Having established the true and objective interest of every Christian prince, Rohan goes on to account for the sources of failure, and finds passion and superstition to be responsible for most cases of misperception:

> [I]n matters of state one must not let oneself be guided by disorderly appetites, which make us often undertake tasks beyond our strength; nor by violent passions, which agitate us in various ways as soon as they possess us ... but by our own interest guided by reason alone, which must be the rule of our actions.[139]

In his *Troisième Discours*, this idea structures the explanation of the negotiations between Paul V and Venice in 1605: the reason why the former fails and the latter succeeds is that Venice 'followed exactly that which was their interest', while the Pope was driven by 'ill-considered zeal' or 'inflamed by the desire to leave his mark on posterity' or simply carried away by the violence of his passions.[140] To Courtilz, to act in accordance with one's interest is to 'use politics', but whenever one fails to do this, one acts 'against politics'.[141]

Pufendorf, asking 'how it oftentimes happens that great Errors are committed in this kind against the Interest of the State', goes on to explain that

> those who have the Supreme Administration of Affairs, are oftentimes not sufficiently acquainted with the Interest both of their own State and of their Neighbours; and yet being fond of their own Sentiments, will not follow the advice of understanding and faithful Ministers. Sometimes they are misguided by their Passions ... or else are led away by a private Interest ... or else, being divided into Factions, they are more concerned to ruin their Rivals, than to follow the Dictates of Reason.[142]

Hence, a political failure can never falsify the analytical truth of interest; instead, every such failure merely indicates that the agent simultaneously has failed in his analysis, and ought to be persuaded as to where his 'true' interest lies by the alternative mode of explanation introduced by the analysis to account for failure. Rhetorically, and much like in the logic of Descartes' *Fourth Mediation* (1641), the verisimilitude of the analysis is increased by the possibility of error and misperception of interest. In the analysis of interest, political 'success' is represented as the normal case, and it does not have to be explained other than tautologically; the fact of political success indicates that a given line of action was in accordance with the true interest of an agent. What has to be explained, and explained in other terms than success, is the failure to attain political rationality in its seventeenth-century form, that is, the failure to perceive, internalize and act upon the concepts of the analysis itself. Hence, the agent must be persuaded by his 'failure' to grasp the truth of the analysis, a truth which, as we noted above, also was a truth about himself and his identity as an actor on the political stage. Every political 'failure' is thus turned into a potential rhetorical success of the analysis, since interest always is 'objective' before it is 'subjective' in the analysis: it must exist in order to be perceived and known, and perceived and known in order to make any talk of 'misperception' possible. Misperception, as all error, is not pure negation, but rather a lack of knowledge that ideally should be present, clear and distinct to the consciousness of the agent.[143] That is, the 'misperception' of interest and the disasters it brings with it helps the 'accurate perception' of interest to constitute itself as the normal and therefore rational form of self-understanding.

As a second step in the duplication, the concept of interest is rendered *indubitable*. As noted earlier, what is other to interest is passion. The stigma attached to passion is not primarily a result of this conceptual opposition in the analysis itself, but to a larger extent the outcome of a clash between different political knowledges. It is passion which continually threatens representation by subverting – or perverting – the binary relationship between words and things.

If the self-understanding of agents were altogether passionate, passionate agency would constitute the normal and therefore rational form of behaviour. But as such, passionate understanding would not be susceptible to the kind of rationalistic persuasion that the analysis of interest insists on; it makes little or no sense to speak of 'true' or 'false' passion, nor is it meaningful to divide passions into 'objective' and 'subjective' ones. In an age when the unconscious had not yet been invented, everyone is correctly supposed to have privileged access to his passions. By the same token, one may well deliberate upon or to an extent choose one's interest, whereas passion is not susceptible to self-conscious deliberation or choice.

In an age such as the Renaissance, which had no logical space for a separation of matter and consciousness, and whose political self-description was centred around passion as its main motivating force, the rhetoric of interest is not yet a strategic possibility in discourse: the concept of interest – along with the differentiation between objectivity and subjectivity which is integral to it – is wholly simultaneous to the Cartesian differentiation of the world into an immaterial and perceiving substance and an extended and material substance whose being known is dependent on being perceived.[144] In order to combat passion at the level of epistemic justification, the analysis operates analogously to and in close interdependence with the systematic reversal of Renaissance scepticism carried out by Descartes,[145] and leads to a political counterpart of the *cogito*. It starts out by doubting the possibility of political knowledge: it is not reducible to principles, and rests merely on inherited opinion, which is distorted by passion, and therefore inherently fallible. What cannot be doubted, however, is interest: it cannot lie or deceive. To doubt the truth of interest is in essence to doubt the existence of oneself as a political actor. What must incessantly be doubted, however, is one's perception of particular objective interests, since in 'many cases the grasp of the senses is very obscure and confused'.[146] Thus, the indubitability of interest is not the result of a prior differentiation between 'subjective' and 'objective' interest that makes us believe that we cannot doubt the reality of the latter; rather it is by rendering a political subjectivity defined in terms of interest indubitable to itself that this differentiation is carried out. What can be doubted is not the fact that one is interested, only one's ability to perceive one's interests, whose objectivity consists precisely in being partly veiled from the interested subject, and transparent only from a semi-divine and sovereign vantage point – a vantage point so indispensable and dear to the Classical Age: I am interested, therefore I *am*.

To recapitulate this double gesture of validation through duplication: first, by rendering itself immune to falsification by presenting its core concept and its inferential connections with other concepts as a necessary truth, it readily absorbs and explains any contrary evidence as a deviation from the norm of a political rationality. This explanatory stratagem legitimizes an act of persuasion, whose force flows from the structure of and the negative terms employed in the mode of explanation reserved for political failures. Through this stratagem, it represents the politics of states as if the analysis of interest itself is *the* knowledgeable practice of their political intercourse. The analysis of interest analyses the interplay of interests as if they were the outcome of a finite series of similar analyses undertaken by the agents themselves, and criticizes these analyses on the basis of their degree of deviation from the final analysis, which, after having been superimposed upon the hypothesized calculations of the agents also explains the relative success or failure of their strategies. Second, by rendering the concept of interest indubitable, the analysis displaces or absorbs all vantage points but its own, and renders all other political knowledges imperfect. The analysis of interest, and the domain of being it singles out as objective, is wholly simultaneous with the genesis of Cartesian consciousness as a mirror of representations.

Once grasped, the concept of interest offers no escape: it gives rise to an infinite series of possible identifications between the position of the spectator and that of an agent in a given analysis. In the dedicatory letter accompanying *Il Principe*, Machiavelli compared his vantage point with that of a cartographer, mirroring the conditions of rulership from a point *below it*.[147] The analysis of interest reverses this perspective, since its position of detachment coincides with the position of the ruler, contemplating the course of political affairs from above. Perhaps it is this duplication that makes the study of history 'pleasant', and not only 'useful' to the classic. To live in the world as if one stood outside it is to live in it as if one were king: both the disinterested analyst and the interested prince are together placed in the epistemic position of subjects, who stand in a determined strategic relation to the object – the state and its interests. Through duplication, 'we seem to participate in His knowledge as well as in His authority'.

The duality of interest, which joins together representative accuracy with prescriptive force in an undecidable relation, is a corollary to this duplication. The analysis of interest is a science of order: it elaborates a set of cognitive rules for the perception of order and its measurement, derived from the analysis of representation. Once order is perceived, it is naturalized and turned into an object of representation inside representation: it becomes a living reality which can be represented more or less accurately, and which can be acted upon strategically more or less successfully by its inhabitants as long as they remain *subjects* to it. Thus, description is not parasitic on prescription, or conversely. Nor is ideology prior to knowledge, nor knowledge prior to ideology: they are simultaneous and impossible to separate analytically in classical knowledge.

The consequences of interest

Thus far, I have described the analysis of interests as an autonomous discursive practice, and analysed it in terms of its conditions of possibility and its relationship to classical knowledge. In this section, I shall describe the analysis of interest in terms of its relationship to practice. How does the understanding of political reality it encourages condition the self-descriptions of agents, and how does it inform and organize the practices in which they engage?

Power and predictability

As we have noted, there is a strong tendency to reify the concept of interest in seventeenth-century moral and political discourse. This tendency results partly – at the macro-level of discourse – from the mutually reinforcing relationship between its centrality and its ambiguity, but is also the outcome – at the micro-level – of its duplication inside the analysis of interest. Thus, the proverb that 'interest rules the world'[148] must for a moment be taken at face value; but how does this world appear to those trying to intervene creatively in it?

First, since the world as one perceives it is the world in which one acts, there is an ordered *separation* between states. What is inside and outside a specific state can be determined with at least empirical certainty, and the divide will appear as natural. The analytical border between states is coexistent with the recognition of their factual and territorial separation. It is not a coincidence that Richelieu in his *Testament* devotes an entire section to the necessity of a well fortified border;[149] semiotically, we can read the theory of sovereignty and the analysis of interests as two mutually reinforcing textual strategies to 'fortify the border' of the state from rhetorical intrusions. The identity of a specific state is assured from two points simultaneously, one universal, the other particular.

The distinction between domestic and foreign policy, which was so opaque and so problematic to the Renaissance and the early classical scholars,[150] can now be drawn analytically as a distinction between the state and what is outside it; the interplay of interests between states has its counterpart in the interplay of interests on the domestic arena, and the paramount strategic problem of absolutism is to subordinate the latter to the former by reduction. It is this analytical divide that permits the discourse on state consolidation to gain impetus: both Rohan and Courtilz find war to be a highly recommendable activity, not only for reasons of immediate external gain, but also to assure the inner stability, order and cohesion needed for further adventures on the outside.[151] It is at this point in political discourse that foreign policy takes on primacy over domestic policy, not as a result of an overt ideological move, but at the very moment of their analytical separation into spheres of action, different in complexity but both governed by interest. The domestic sphere is constituted as a 'part' in a bigger 'whole'; a part whose identity must be carefully monitored and safe-guarded from outside intrusions. Without a 'foreign policy' there can be nothing domestic, since the former has as its task precisely to define the latter by *domesticating* what initially was *foreign* to it, buried in the depths of its violent prehistory and inserted as a state of nature in its contractual justification. That is, foreign policy is to classical analysis of interest and sovereignty as much a policy for dealing with a traumatic past, as it is a policy for dealing with a spatial outside.

Second, and by the same token, there is an ordered *relationship* between states. Not only are states constituted as separate by a grid of identity and difference in the analysis: they can also be ranked accord-ing to the amount of wealth and power they possess. They are sover-eign, but not yet equal even in a formal sense:[152] *securatio* and *reputatio* are still predicates of a problematic statehood, which makes it difficult, not to say impossible, to articulate and uphold a norm of sovereign equality between them. The world of states does not yet form a system in the modern sense of something that is more than the sum of its parts, but rather a continuous *table of states* which permits calculations of power and interest.

Furthermore, a world ruled by interest is at once more predictable and transparent to its inhabitants than a world ruled by passions, which, according to Spinoza, make man 'changeable and incon-stant'.[153] Passions cannot be measured or ordered on a continuous scale, their object cannot be safely determined, but vary according to circumstance. Passion provides no lasting basis for the resolution of conflicts, or for stable cooperation. Whereas, in Herle's formulation, 'if you can apprehend wherein a man's interest to any particular game on foot doth consist, you may surely know, if the man be prudent, whereabout to have him, that is, how to judge of his design'.[154]

Since the tabulation of states makes it possible to calculate interest, the calculation of interest both presupposes and reinforces the structure of the table. If interest both organizes tabulation and agency simultaneously, the order of states takes on predictability. Foreign policy is less prey to the whims of Fortuna: the motives of the other become more transparent, since he is recognized not as a stranger, but as an enemy; as an interested political subject, and therefore, a mirror-image of oneself. Foreign policy can become a dialogue with what is much like oneself, however adversarial, instead of a one-way battle-cry addressed to a stranger – a dialogue in which the desire for knowledge and the struggle for power and security are intertwined.

As a consequence of calculability *balance of power* emerges as a possibility, both as a policy designed to prevent war through the active balancing of forces, and, more importantly, from 1713 onwards, a principle of ordered opposition subscribed to by states acknowledged as sovereign entities in the table.[155] Even if they do not use the concept itself, both Rohan and Courtilz develop a logic of balance-of-power politics. To Rohan, it is evident that other countries tend to gravitate towards either Spain or France, such that alliances form more or less spontaneously from their self-interested activity, since it is necessary to 'oppose force with force'.[156] Half a century later, Courtilz is able to develop a sophisticated explanation of the formation of alliances in balance-of-power terms, while effectively ruling out all religious and dynastic motivations from the account.[157] Even in the anonymous tract of 1666, which mainly consists in a compilation of dynastic pretensions and religious differences, alliances are seen to be forged from and motivated by asymmetrical power relationships.[158]

Diplomacy and discipline

The drive towards predictability and calculability is reflected in contemporary manuals of diplomatic practice. Diplomacy, in its seventeenth- and early eighteenth-century form, derives its main concepts from the analysis of interest. And conversely: the enormous amount of empirical information about the conditions other states needed to analyse interest was obtained chiefly by diplomats. Risking oversimplification, one could say that classical diplomacy is a practical articulation of the analysis of interest, while the analysis of interest is a theoretical articulation of diplomatic practice.

In the first page of his *L'Ambassadeur et ses fonctions* (1681), Wicquefort describes diplomatic activity as 'a science of mathematical principles, or founded on demonstrative reason, on which one can make certain and infallible rules'.[159] Even if this was to remain a vain hope – as Wicquefort himself was to confess later[160] – since practice never can be reduced to rules of mathematical certainty, this statement reflects the beginning of a fusion of classical knowledge and rituals of power into a new political technology. Since the analysis of interest had put an end to exemplary history as the privileged form of political memory, this reorientation is parallelled and reinforced by a corresponding bureaucratic development. By the end of the seventeenth century, the first steps towards creating a *dépôt des affaires étrangères* in France were taken. Diplomatic documents were placed under royal seal, collected, centralized and classified according to year and country;[161] by 1715, the depository contained some 2000 volumes of documents generated by regular diplomacy.[162] The entire project was motivated by the desire to cope with the uncertainties, contingencies and eventualities of interstate relations and to predict the behaviour of France's enemies in an age so 'attentive to interest'.[163] Soon after, a *Projet d'Estudes* for the education of diplomats was initiated, with its curriculum firmly centred on the countrywise extraction and systematization of empirical knowledge of past and present diplomatic negotiations from the collected documents, making tables of contents and summaries revealing 'the form of government and the interests of the court in question'.[164]

At the same time as the diplomatic manuals are stripped of exempla they become less occupied with legal questions and more with the problems of interest, which also govern their sampling and reconstruction of historical precedents. As Keens-Soper would have it, diplomatic literature was released from the dead hand of an alien past.[165] According to Wicquefort, the main task of the ambassador is to 'preserve the reputation as well as the interest of his prince'.[166] One of his foremost duties in this regard is to gather information with 'diligence and exactitude' about the interest of the particular state to which he has been sent as an envoy, and about the sizes of its forces and revenues, its form of government and the pretensions, personal inclinations and particular passions of its sovereign.[167]

The ideal ambassador is an 'honourable spy': he has before him the task of penetrating the secrets of other states,[168] but his task is circumscribed by the unwritten rules distilled from past and present diplomatic practice. He must not lie or be dishonest in order not to risk his reputation for trustworthiness, which is an essential asset in the diplomatic game.[169] He must show moderation and prudence on every occasion, so that he does not betray the designs of his sovereign.[170] Reports and treatises must be made in a lucid language, untainted by passion, in order to avoid any misunderstanding on points of fact or intentions.[171] The community of diplomats (and ultimately also that of states) is not depicted as a society where interest is pitted against interest in unresolvable oppositions. Rather, it is a disciplined society, at once transparent and predictable to its inhabitants, however held together and governed by a consciousness of political necessity:

> The necessity of Embassies establishes the security of Ambassadors by the universal consent of all nations on earth; and it is this general consent that creates what is called the Law of Nations. It occupies a place between Natural Law and Civil Law, and is all the more considerable than the last, since it neither can be changed nor altered with less than the same unanimous consent of all peoples. There is no sovereign who can authorize himself to explain the laws of which this Right is composed, and there is no judge who can extend his jurisdiction over those persons whom this Right protects; because he would thereby upset a commerce, whose freedom is founded on an indispensable necessity, and he would thereby take away from mankind the means of maintaining society, which could not exist without this principle, which is more than mathematic.[172]

> It must be borne in mind that all the States of which Europe is composed, have necessary ties and commercial relations with each other, which makes it possible to regard them as members of one and the same Commonwealth, and [that] there can hardly occur a considerable change in one of them, which is not capable of disturbing the calm of all the others.[173]

This is not the world of either Hobbes or Grotius, even if the influence of both is discernible. Much labour has been devoted to the elaboration and analysis of distinct 'Hobbesian' and 'Grotian' traditions in international politics, but it might be argued that these traditions have more to do with our present than with the seventeenth century, a fact that becomes more evident when the scholar fails to see any explicit continuity between what Hobbes or Grotius in fact said, and what their self-styled followers in the twentieth century say.[174]

Whereas Hobbes says that the 'Law of Nations, and the Law of Nature, is the same thing', and that the sovereign therefore was granted full outward autonomy by the latter,[175] Grotius held that sovereign authority was restricted precisely by the two of them taken together, since 'observance of these is binding upon all kings, even though they have made no promise'.[176] Neither Wicquefort nor Callières does rely on the standard assumptions of natural law to justify their reasoning: there is no need here to invoke human nature and the social bonds and the timeless norms it is said to necessitate. Instead, an ordered and knowledgeable practice arises precisely out of the self-interested activity within the table of states.

Classical diplomatic practice, governed by the notion of interest, is not a crude zero-sum game, but involves relations of articulability between sovereignty and knowledge. First, the pursuit of state interests presupposes communication and exchange, which have to take place against the backdrop of a shared vocabulary in which negotiations can be conducted and described. This means that the discourse of interest itself has to be common property among the interlocutors. It forms the basis for an agreement about what to disagree about, and more importantly, an agreement about *who* is disagreeing: sovereign states. The discourse on interest is as much a discourse on the identity of the interlocutors and its constitution through reciprocal recognition of one another as sovereign and interested parties.

Second, the pursuit of state interests exercises, so to speak, a moderating influence upon itself. This may sound paradoxical, but it is not: the politics of interest presupposes predictability, and predictability is an antidote to myopia. This helps to explain the sometimes tedious emphasis placed on *honnêteté*, *prudence* and *moderation* as guidelines for diplomatic conduct. These values are not merely lip-service to aristocratic ideals of the day,[177] but are more or less singularly justified in terms of long-term state interest, and safeguarded by a diplomatic culture based on reciprocity of action. In classical diplomatic literature, therefore, it is as if the evolution of cooperation already had taken place: in a 'commerce, whose freedom is founded on indispensable necessity', outright lies and deceit do not pay off in the long run, since they undermine one's reputation, and with it, one's identity as an actor on the diplomatic stage.

Thus, classical diplomacy should not be understood as something external to the politics of interest, or as something whose primary function is one of restraint and moderation. Rather, the function of diplomacy is best understood as one of enablement and articulation; without diplomacy, there can be no pursuit of interest, since the practices of diplomacy constitute the communitarian backdrop against which identities can be recognized and interests expressed and communicated. And conversely, without interest as an organizing principle of absolutist politics, there would be no need for a diplomacy focused on its articulation and the gathering of empirical information.

Therefore, order does not come to the politics of interest from without, from the depths of natural law or from the benevolent workings of an invisible hand. Rather, order comes from within the politics of interest; to the extent that the politics of interest is a systematic and coherent practice, it is organized and reinforced by the analysis of state interests. The tabulated and taxonomic order of states does not form an anarchical society, held together by some intangible organizing principle; it comes from the articulation and duplication of the principles of the *mathesis,* and functions as its supplement. Classical political order, therefore, is as cognitive as it is normative; it is but a tiny regional manifestation of the general order bestowed upon the things of the world by knowledge in an age when – in Pope's words – mad *mathesis* alone was unconfined. In chapter 6, I shall describe how this order withers away, and is replaced by a specifically modern juxtaposition of the sovereign state and the international system, each a condition of the other.

6 Reorganizing reality: sovereignty, modernity and the international

> The old philosophy assigned to man an entirely incorrect standpoint in the world by making him into a machine within the world, a machine which as such was meant to be wholly dependent on the world or on external things and circumstances; in this way it made man into an almost passive part in the world. – Now the *Critique of Pure Reason* appeared and allotted man a thoroughly *active* existence in the world. Man himself is the primordial creator of all his representations and concepts and ought to be the unique author of all his deeds.
>
> Kant, *Der Streit der Facultäten*

The word international, writes Bentham in his *Principles* (1789), 'is a new one ... sufficiently analogous and intelligible'.[1] What, we must ask, are the conditions that make it intelligible as an object of knowledge? What makes it possible to speak of something international, and to subject it to theoretical and empirical inquiry?

It has been said by historians that the modern theory and practice of the present international system originated somewhere between the end of the eighteenth century and the Napoleonic wars, with the waning of absolutism and the rise of the nation-state as the main forces behind its development.[2] This may be true, but for reasons which themselves are part of my problem; I have already criticized the ambition to fix chronological and geographical limits upon what is fluid and constituted by its absence, and argued for a genealogical approach. But what about the very discourse of chronological and geographical limits? Is perhaps the quest for origin simultaneous and logically connected to the emergence of the international?

My main argument in this chapter is that the international at the point of its emergence is inseparable from its own essential historicity;

history, as we now it, is as much a precondition of the international as a result of it, since both arise out of a new and distinctively modern arrangement of identity and difference in knowledge. Arguing this, I shall venture to find an alternative starting point for political modernity; those who organize their erudition according to textbook labels will feel tempted to call this starting point either 'romanticism' or 'historicism' or both.[3]

In the Classical Age, the international was a possibility not yet open in knowledge. As argued in chapter 5, the *mathesis* enabled an analysis and tabulation of state interest, but this analysis was doomed to remain profoundly nominalist; the classical state is a space of power and interest, and can be represented and analysed as such; states, looked upon from the outside, can be ordered into a continuous table, which permits comparison and calculations of reciprocal interests. To the extent that states, in their precarious identity, enter into relationships with something other than themselves, it is with the reminiscences of Christian universality and unity, expressed in terms of law.

In the late eighteenth century, this order of states is swept away, and gradually replaced by an international system, or, if you want, a society of states.[4] The main objective of this chapter is to describe genealogically the formative moments of this discursive transformation in terms contemporaneous with itself.

Following the general argument of my thesis, I shall contend that this discontinuity is made possible by a simultaneous epistemic change, which both conditions the discourse on sovereignty and is conditioned by it in a mutually productive relationship.

With the advent of modernity, the *mathesis* is gradually deprived of its power to organize reality. The general area of knowledge ceases to be that of fixed identities and differences, and being itself is no longer uniformly subordinated to the grid of representation. The strict intersection between objects and words is broken, or rather, begins to appear artificial; hence, representation loses its power to provide a foundation for knowledge, and itself becomes questioned as to its possibility.[5]

Instead, the field of empirical entities is populated with organic structures, connected to each other by analogous relations. Both the natural and political world take on depth; empirical beings are related to underlying forces and causes, provided with origins, and posited and studied on the basis of their historicity. History is no longer external to the order of objects or to their sequential order within a table, but becomes the very condition of their existence. Language, from having been a system of representations, takes on reality and becomes expressive of man's being in time and in culture; it is at once turned into an object of study and a medium of scientific knowledge.

With the historicization of all being, constructability takes a new and radical turn. In the Classical Age, representation and language are the loci of knowledge; to know is to receive and to *represent* representations accurately in speech and thought, an act in which the role allotted to the human mind is the purely passive one of *mirroring* what is external to it. In contrast, modernity is marked by epistemic *activity*; from Vico and Kant onwards, man emerges as the sovereign creator of his representations and concepts; in short, of the world he – *the modern subject* – inhabits. At the same time, and as the result of the same epistemic change, man emerges as an object of knowledge, who speaks, acts and lives according to knowable rules. Thus, to attain knowledge of man is to attain knowledge of the possibility of knowledge, since he is the condition of the latter.

As I intend to show, this *reorganization* of knowledge has profound effects upon political discourse.

First, modernity marks the return of analogy into the core of political knowledge, but now as analogy between relations and not as analogy between beings, which was the case in the Middle Ages. The modern state is conceptualized as an organized being made up of internal relations between its components; it is knowable as a totality of analogous relations between its elements. Within this profoundly reconceptualized state, sovereignty retains indivisibility as its defining property, but indivisible sovereignty now is attributed to a totality of relations, themselves constituted by the logic of this indivisibility. The sovereign state is released from the table of interests, and is regarded as the outcome of a dialectical conflict between underlying forces in history. Time, perennial enemy of the state, is now its father.

Second, modern knowledge bestows subjectivity upon the state. The state is no longer a mere object of knowledge, but is conceptualized as being itself able to know and act in analogy with man. The inner identity of the state is no longer secured by a metaphorical relationship between personalized sovereignty and an abstract space; sovereignty, once moved outside representation, can no longer represent king and state as identical. Sovereignty is depersonalized and dispersed within the social body and therefore rendered invisible, whereas the state is constituted as a person in itself; by means of analogy, modern sovereignty focuses on the relation between man and state; the modern subject and the modern state are linked inside knowledge, and the concepts of the nation and community are used to express their unity and cover the problematic character of this unity. Within the state as well as within knowledge, Man becomes King: modernity, as I will characterize it in the present chapter, is marked by the troubled sovereignty of Man.[6]

Third, and perhaps most important, modern knowledge turns sovereignty into a principle organizing our political reality as well as our understanding of it. If classical sovereignty was a principle of identity, modern sovereignty is, above all, a principle of difference. It is simultaneously transcendental and empirical.

On the one hand, sovereignty establishes the transcendental conditions of possibility of the modern state as *subject*, telling us in the abstract what is a state and what is not, and what a state is and what it is not. Sovereignty differentiates the state ontologically and ethically from other forms of political life, and furnishes us simultaneously with the conditions for knowing the state as such. As a consequence, if what was other to the state in the Classical Age was what went before it and constituted its fictitious prehistory – a state of nature – then what is other to the modern state is what is over and above it: a state of war between states.

On the other hand, it renders the state susceptible to empirical knowledge as an *object*; sovereignty is no longer withdrawn from knowledge and reflection, but inserted there as its prime target. Sovereignty not only establishes the transcendental limits of political knowledge, but constitutes its proper objects: the modern state and the international system do not only emerge as the outcome of transcendental reflection and speculative dialectics. Both the sovereign state and the international system are established within the field of empirical beings as logically and historically interdependent, and opened to historical and empirical investigation according to a finite set of methods and procedures.

It is from the vantage point of this duality of sovereignty that the emergence of the international must be seen. In the classical table, states were ordered in a continuous series according to their interests, and were – theoretically as well as practically – well able to entertain relations with one another; but these relations were never themselves representable within the table. With modernity, this set of relations becomes an organized reality, a system of relations analogous to,

interdependent with and yet qualitatively different from those relations which together constitute the modern state as a coherent and
functional totality. This wholly simultaneous organization of two ethically opposed yet ontologically implicating spheres of political being –
the domestic and the international – is both the medium and the
outcome of modern sovereignty.

As was argued in chapter 2, this simultaneous constitution of political understanding and political reality by means of unquestionable
division is what makes modern sovereignty a *parergon*; without this
parergonality of sovereignty, there can be no intelligible talk of the
state or anything international, nor any empirical disciplines devoted
to the analysis of their finitude.

In the present chapter, I shall proceed in three chronologically and
logically overlapping steps. This procedure is based on the fundamental assumption that the crisis of the classical order of states and the
rise of the modern international system are both inextricably linked to
the epistemic change which gains impetus towards the end of the
eighteenth century.

First, I shall briefly analyse the criticism directed towards the
Classical order by the Enlightenment. Second, I will trace genealogically the foundations of this criticism in the largely contemporaneous
epistemic change. Third, I shall attempt to explain the emergence of
the modern state and the international system as conditioned by this
epistemic change.

Criticizing: crisis and revolution

In an important sense, the absolutist state was a paradoxical construct,
since it was at once both cause and effect of its own foundation. To
Hobbes, Spinoza and Pufendorf, the state had its ideal point of origin
in a preordained contract between men. It was of no real importance
whether this origin was a real historical event or merely a hypothesis,
since its 'chronology' resided inside a table. In either case, the contract
ultimately owed its existence to that which was to be explained: the
presence of the sovereign.[7]

In the classical order, the state and the king were metaphors for one
another, and the analytical separation between domestic and foreign
policy was based upon a fragile identity of interests between the king
and his state.

As a result of its analytical separation from domestic policy, external policy had an instrumental privilege: the table of *inter*state interests was of a logically different and higher order than the table of *intra*state interests. Premised upon civil conflict, the classical state transformed inner conflict of interest to external conflict of interest precisely by drawing a firm line between them, making all previous feudal and religious jurisdictions obsolete. The classical state *domesticated* what was *foreign* to it; it assimilated all that was alien to it in its prehistory of religious and civil war. To the theoreticians of state interests, external warfare was as much a royal prerogative as an antidote to the fearful return of internal unrest.

In this section, I shall describe how this order is undermined, how its fundamental distinctions and concepts are subjected to criticism and gradually lose their power to order political experience. As we shall see, this criticism carries over into crisis, and crisis culminates in pleas for revolution.

If we read some of these critics retrospectively, which seems to be common practice, we will be inclined to find in their writings the expression of an internationalism, a set of solutions to problems we – as moderns – have been accustomed to accept as inherent in the international system, but whose own formation within discourse is withdrawn from analysis.[8] If, on the contrary, we reverse this retrospective reading of texts, and instead question the criticism with respect to its conditions of possibility, we are bound to discover that the problem itself is contemporaneous with its solutions, and that the alleged 'solutions' in fact are prior to the 'problem'. The plea for republicanism and democracy as antidotes to war, and the reliance on the spirit of commerce as the vehicle of political progress are the most notable examples of forces subjected to this kind of retrospective interpretation.[9] To resist this reading, we must start at a rather technical level, and question the foundations of criticism and crisis.

To begin with, and towards the second half of the eighteenth century, the concept of interest gradually loses its power to confer unity upon the state, and the analytical techniques for establishing the *maximes* of individual states are modified. The state gradually escapes from the fixity of the table; its interests take on complexity and depth, lose their previous immutability and become subject to revolutionary change, a qualitative change which disrupts the previous order of state interests. Due to 'extraordinary revolutions', writes Rousset, 'one cannot find one single maxime in those authors [Rohan and Courtilz] which could be in use today'.[10] In Rousset, the analysis becomes not only excessively complex, but in some cases even impossible in the eyes of the author: for example, the United Provinces cannot be devoted a chapter of its own, since according to one of its *maximes* matters of religion and government are to be excluded from the discourse of its inhabitants: hence, its *maxime* eludes tabulation.[11]

In Mably's *Principes des Négociations* (1758), the revolution in inter-state relations is produced by colonial trade, and its impact on the nature and distribution of capabilities between states. Wealth, acquired through trade rather than from cultivating the soil, radically alters the zero-sum nature of classical power. As a consequence, state interests are no longer deducible from the specific individual character of each state; rather, their *maximes* are determined solely from their relation to other states; what matters is whether a state is a *puissance dominante* or a *puissance rivale*. States are no longer situated in a position in which God has placed them, but *displaced* into a succession of altering power relations. Thus, the technique employed in establishing *maximes* must be reversed: instead of traversing an uninterrupted sequence of states ordered according to the identity and difference of their interests, Mably starts out from the fact of analogy: what really counts is not individual attributes of states, but their *role and function* within a larger context.[12]

A second, and more ideologically potent source of crisis in the classical order is the fact that the analytical distinction between external and internal policy – coexistent with a subordination of morality to politics – is itself questioned at the analytical level. In the Classical Age, the sovereign power was inaccessible to criticism based on or targeted at knowledge, since the place of the sovereign was duplicated inside the latter as its condition of possibility; to draw a firm line between morals and politics and deny the former any political impact was itself a moral necessity, as was political sovereignty itself. The battle of opinion and ideology, together with all signs of the *guerre civile*, is relegated to the non-place of civil conscience in the absolutist order.[13]

During the Enlightenment, this mutual separation and polarization of morals and politics, of state and society and of the internal sphere from the external, was to become a prime target of criticism, a criticism that silently draws on the conceptual hierarchies it seeks to displace and subvert, but without ever questioning their existence, or its own universalist foundation. Beginning with a concealed subjection of politics to the verdict of a universalist ethic, the particular interests of states are criticized from the vantage point of a general interest of mankind or of human society, which then spills over into a questioning of the analytical and ideological divide between domestic politics and foreign policy. Starting from a universalist foundation, one either criticizes the internal structure of states on the basis of their external effects, or, one criticizes the external practices of states on the basis of their internal effects.

As a condition of this criticism, the origin of the state is moved outside representation and historicized. To the classics, it was of little importance whether the contractual origin of the state was reality or fiction, since it took place within representation and outside real time.[14] From Montesquieu on, the state becomes a container of tradition. The *form of government*, present in the analysis of interest only as a determinant of power, takes on renewed significance in relation to external policy: in his *l'Esprit des loix* (1748), we learn that it is against the nature of a 'democratic republic to conquer towns that could not enter the sphere of democracy', but that offensive wars are to be expected from monarchies and despotisms.[15]

Further, the distinction between a real and a fictitious contract – a distinction which exists only for modernity – begins to make sense with Rousseau. As a result of the analytical method it employs, says Rousseau, the classical theory of the contract transposes back to the state of nature those traits in mankind which result from its actual historical and present social conditions,[16] such as inequality and warfare: there is no war between men in a state of nature, only between societies as the result of their emergence from that state. To the classics, the natural condition antecedent to society was the state of war, which made society necessary. To Rousseau, here following Montesquieu, the formation of societies in real time is a condition of war, making it a social evil:[17]

> bodies politic, remaining thus in a state of nature among themselves, presently experienced the inconveniences which had obliged individuals to forsake it; for this state became still more fatal to these great bodies than it had been to the individuals of whom they were composed. Hence arose national wars, battles, murders, and reprisals, which shock nature and outrage reason.[18]

As a result of the formation of societies, constantly and mutually disposed towards war, the human species finds itself in a manifest contradiction, having traded particular war within for generalized war without:[19]

> Between man and man we live in the condition of the civil state, subjected to laws; between people and people, we enjoy natural liberty... Living at the same time in the social order and in the state of nature, we suffer from the inconveniences of both without finding security in either of them.[20]

What makes this situation look real and inescapable is that the source of these distinctions is unknown. To Rousseau, it is to be found in absolutist sovereignty, and its subjection of law to force: the prince speaks to his citizens in the name of law, and to foreigners in the name of *raison d'état*.[21] 'We should see the multitude oppressed from within, in consequence of the very precautions ... taken to guard against foreign tyranny.'[22] That is, modern man is stuck within a *système mixte*, subjected to tyranny on the inside, and aggravated by the security dilemmas coming from the outside.

As a second step in the criticism of prevalent state practices, there is an effort to temper the social evil of war by subjecting it to the verdict of universal morality.[23] Reading Vattel's *Le Droit des Gens* (1758), we can discern a concealed moment of criticism; the discourse of natural law is reinstated in the rationalist and communitarian context of Enlightenment philosophy, resulting in a subversion of the analytical and ideological hierarchy between the external and the internal spheres. The Law of Nations, says Vattel, is '*necessary*, because Nations are absolutely bound to observe it'[24] and because it flows from 'the universal society of the human race [and] all men of whatever condition are bound to advance its interests and fulfil its duties',[25] which is 'to advance their own perfection and that of their condition'.[26]

The fact that mankind is divided into separate states does not overrule universal duty: each nation 'may be regarded as a moral person, since it has an understanding, a will, and a power peculiar to itself; and it is therefore obliged to live with other societies or States according to the laws of the natural society of the human race'.[27] However, this universal morality is not immediately binding upon the external conduct of states: 'each has the right to decide in its conscience what it must do to fulfil its duties, the effect of this is to produce, before the world at least, a perfect equality of rights among Nations'.[28] Sovereign equality, when translated into concrete practice, has utopian implications; it is able to transform classical interstate politics from a 'confused heap of detached parts' into a

> sort of Republic, whose members – each independent, but all bound together by a common interest – unite for the maintenance of order

and the preservation of liberty. This is what has given rise to the well-known principle of the balance of power, by which is meant an arrangement of affairs so that no State is to have absolute mastery and dominate over the others.[29]

Thus, the sovereign state is conditioned by its place in the universal society of mankind, being as much its foundation as its effect: 'the conduct of a sovereign state should be in keeping with the end of the society which exists among them'.[30] Without sovereignty, the state cannot be understood as a moral person and fulfil its duties; without a wider set of universal values, this moral person cannot be sovereign, while at the same time its right to a 'definite position in this great society' is dependent on its sovereignty.[31]

As a consequence, the ends of the state are subordinated to the *internal* ends of civil society: its end is to procure for its citizens the necessities, the comforts, and the pleasures of life, and in general their happiness. In a secondary position, and then only as a means to these ends, comes the defence against *external* violence:[32] 'Humanity revolts against a sovereign who, without necessity or without pressing reasons, wastes the blood of his most faithful subjects and exposes his people to the calamities of war.'[33]

With Rousseau and Vattel, classical interstate practices and the divide between the internal and the external that silently justify them are, as it were, *denaturalized*, and therefore exposed to moral criticism. As a third step in Enlightenment criticism, this denaturalization is supplemented by a positive view of revolution as a means of transgressing the divide in the name of mankind and universal morality.

As Koselleck has remarked, in the Classical Age, the concept of revolution was both supra-political and reserved for foreign policy.[34] In its supra-political sense, revolution signified change according to cyclical and recurrent patterns; the concept was modelled upon the movement of heavenly bodies. When occasionally applied to the political context, it was connected to the Aristotelian doctrine of constitutional forms, and then signified their cyclical recurrence. Within this view, a limited number of constitutional forms dissolved and replaced each other by revolutionary upheaval, the form of political government being affected by revolution, whereas the cycle itself cannot be transgressed.[35] Even as late as in Montesquieu, revolution signifies pure negativity: 'all our histories are full of civil wars without revolutions; those of despotic states are full of revolutions without civil wars'[36] When applied to foreign policy, as in Mably and Rousset, the term 'revolution' is introduced in the analysis of state interest on an *ad hoc* basis, and then in order to explain an event wholly external to the tabulated order and unpredictable from within it, such as a massive redistribution of capabilities between states resulting from a major war or from a sudden acquisition of wealth resulting from exchange with the colonies.

To classical knowledge in general, revolutions did not bring anything new, only the sudden recurrence of something familiar. However destabilizing this suddenness was to the conditions of knowing – as in the analysis of interest – the semantics and metaphorics of revolution parasitized on the assumption that historical time was uniform, repeatable and without discontinuous breaks. While the form of government might alter through revolution or civil war, the social order itself remained unaffected.[37]

With the Enlightenment, however, the concept of revolution takes on a different meaning and a new function. First, it becomes a metahistorical concept, signifying linear development and transcendence of the existing order; revolution comes to signify progress. Second, it takes on inevitability and positivity as something that can be predicted and bent to the desires of men; the metahistorical concept of revolution places man as the transhistorical subject realizing itself through revolution. Third, revolution is understood as a totalizing historical process, encompassing not only the form of government but culture and society and even mankind as a whole, for whose benefit it is undertaken: man makes history through revolution.[38] Writes d'Argenson: 'Everything is revolution in this world: the states have their time of progress and decay.'[39]

Raynal is not only a good example of this transvaluation of the concept of revolution, but also a good example of the ideological rediscovery of the New World, a process which is logically and temporally simultaneous to Enlightenment criticism. In his *Histoire philosophique et politique* (1770), Raynal begins by asking if revolutions – past and future – are of any benefit to man.[40] His answer is, as the title indicates, as much historical as it is philosophical: covering a continuum of revolutionary development from the state of nature up to the rise of the New World and the prophesied decline of the Old, mankind unfolds as the master of its own political destiny.

From the state of nature, writes Raynal, emerges the 'enormous machines we call societies' which 'act and react with all the violence of their particular energies, creating artificially a veritable state of war'.[41]

Everywhere, order springs from anarchy: every civilized people has been savage; every savage people is destined to become civilized.[42] All nations have oscillated from barbarism to the civil state, and from the civil state back to barbarism:[43] civil government is always momentary, carrying within it the seeds of its own destruction and replacement; revolutions are bound to succeed each other with a speed which one has difficulty to follow.[44]

However, the civilizing process obeys a different chronology with a different pattern of progress and regress in different parts of the world: it is far from uniform, and increased social and legal complexity is not always a sign of moral progress. While European states pride themselves on their internal legislation, their external relations are governed by the same set of uncivilized principles that organize the relations between the savages of the New World, to whom legislation is unknown. Looked upon from a moral perspective, the savages of the New World and the sovereign states of the Old are equals, but looked upon from the vantage point of the civilizing process, the innocence of the savages distinguishes them from the guilt and corruption of European princes.

To Raynal, therefore, a lasting peace between the present European states is an impossibility. In an absolutist state, being no more than the personal property of one single person, sovereign authority is located in the hands of a king, who safeguards internal peace through external warfare. Government is arbitrary, laws are obscure and a military spirit prevails. Balance of power is chimerical since it is founded upon treaties which are made by a sovereign, 'who always sacrifices his subjects to injustice, and his obligation to his ambition'.[45]

Raynal's work is as much prophesy as it is history; in fact, at the time he is writing, the distinction between history and prophesy is difficult to uphold consistently. Like More's *Utopia*, Raynal's *Histoire* projects a moral incommensurability onto a global political space; but unlike More's *Utopia*, Raynal's *Histoire* grafts his revolutionary utopia onto a time, its realization being the inevitable outcome of a globalized history. As Koselleck has remarked, 'overseas and the future were the fictive area of exculpation that indirectly guaranteed the triumph of morality'.[46]

Asking how the discoveries have influenced both those who discover and those who have been 'discovered', Raynal finds in the exchange between the New and the Old World the prime forces of revolution. The discoveries are as much a remaking of Europe as they are a conquest of the outside; they signify the mastery of otherness, but also a loss of sameness. The rise of the New World marks the decline of the Old; trade, founded on natural justice, works to establish reciprocal influence between peoples. With trade, the general interest of mankind gradually comes to prevail over the forces of particularity and decay represented by absolutist sovereignty.[47] With trade, communication establishes social bonds between peoples, while breaching and rearranging the divide between inside and outside; the external practices of states perpetuate oppression within, so liberation must proceed from without, from overseas, from the future.

The denaturalization of the classical state, the criticism of the divide which constitutes it as a space of power and interest with a sovereign at its apex, the emergence of mankind as a privileged and transhistorical subject, the insistence on revolutionary and progressive necessity in history; all these signs of crisis coincide and culminate in the distinction between the *civilized* and the *uncivilized*, as in Paine's *Rights of Man* (1791/2):

> All the European governments ... are constructed not on the principle of universal civilization, but on the reverse of it. So far as these governments relate to each other, they are in the same condition as we conceive of savage and uncivilized life ... Being yet in an uncivilized state, and almost continually at war, they pervert the abundance which civilized life produces to carry on the uncivilized part to a greater extent.[48]

> Revolutions, then, have for their object, a change in the moral condition of governments ... If commerce were permitted to act to the universal extent it is capable, it would extirpate the system of war, and produce a revolution in the uncivilized state of governments.[49]

To Paine, a new system is now opening to the view of the world.[50] The twin forces of popular sovereignty and commerce will eventually gain the upper hand; politics will be subordinated to universal morality, foreign policy to the general interest of society, violence and oppression to reason and liberty. But what, we must now ask, is the unthought foundation of this criticism? What makes its appeal to mankind possible, as something which permits the crossing of all boundaries, and which is to manifest itself through revolution?

Knowing: language, man and nation

'As my subject interests mankind in general', says Rousseau, 'I shall endeavour to make use of a style adapted to all nations, or rather, forgetting time and place, to attend only to men to whom I am speaking.'[51]

In this section, I shall analyse the prehistory of the epistemic change which runs parallel to the emergence of the international, and which contributes to its genesis through a rearrangement of identity and difference. In classical discourse, identity and difference are rigidly polarized, yet they implicate each other in the ordering of empirical individuals. With the advent of modern knowledge, the fact of their mutual implication is turned into a dialectical opposition, an opposition between relations that sets everything it touches into historical motion; therefore, my description must include a genealogy of those identities which in Rousseau are accorded the same status but represented as different: language, man and nation.

Contrary to what has been proposed by Foucault, however, I shall argue that this genealogy has a reverse seriality: language and man does not take on historicity as the result of a prior epistemic change; rather, the epistemic revolution launched by Kant is carried out in response to a prior destabilization of the *mathesis*.[52]

To the classical writers, language was a grid imposed on the world in order to analyse it. Language was posited as the analysis of representation, and it defined the mode of being of the objects brought under its sway, so that a parallelism between things and words – between classification and nomenclature – could serve as the foundation of knowledge. When language itself is investigated, the aim is to perfect its ability to represent. When language is criticized, it is on the grounds that language lacks accuracy in representing. Language could have no history and no reality outside that of its representations; a language could only change in response to changes in the order of empirical individuals, and then in order to be able to represent the modifications things had undergone.[53]

During the second half of the eighteenth century, this power to represent is relegated from language to the speaking subject himself. Language becomes a *medium* of representation, rather than its privileged locus. The strict parallelism between words and things is broken, and instead the power to represent becomes a faculty in the mind of a knowing subject. Words continue to represent, but only in the mind of someone that employs and understands them. Words take on *meaning*, more or less transparent in relation to what they represent, but only by virtue of being spoken and known by a subject, individual or collective. From here on, *conceptual analysis* becomes possible, and later –

as words become saturated with meaning – necessary in order to purify language as a medium of scientific knowledge.

Being rooted in the subject rather than in external objects entails that language becomes expressive of something other than itself. It reflects the experience of an individual, or it manifests the tradition of a collective political being. Language itself takes on historical reality, and shares the same chronology as that of its speaker, whose thoughts and habits can be rendered accessible through interpretation of the written or spoken word. As a result of the expressive function allotted to it, language becomes subject to *interpretation*, designed to unmask what is beneath it.

To the classics, language and society both resided inside the logical space of representation, the facts of their common root and logical interdependence being reducible to a hypothetical contract between men, signed, as it were, outside time, yet in need of the sovereign's ink and seal. From Vico onwards, this common root is grafted onto time and turned into an origin. This leads to an unending quest for the proper chronological and geographical limits of this origin, at which language and society are essentially pure and harmoniously united. It is no longer the possibility of an origin which gives rise to the historicity of man, language and nation, but their very historicity which makes the quest for an origin necessary if their identity in the present is to be unambiguously established. This quest for origin is as much an epistemic drive as it was to become a political one: language and nation not only share the same organic and profoundly historicized mode of being, but being the expressions of one another, they also share the same identity which conditions a mode of knowledge as well as the cohesion of a nation.[54]

To Vico, this pure origin is poetic imagination: 'We find that the principle of these origins both of languages and of letters lies in the fact that the first gentile peoples, by a demonstrated necessity of nature, were poets ...'[55] To trace the particular origin of a society or a nation, one must retrace its source in language; '[b]y such a method, the beginnings of the sciences as well as of the nations are to be discovered.'[56] Language, in its dense reality, is able to 'tell us the histories of the institutions signified by the words, beginning with their original and proper meanings and pursuing the natural progress of their metaphors'.[57] Metaphors, being banished from classical discourse as a threat to civil peace and representative rigour, are now thought of as expressive of an underlying and decodable reality.

From this necessary beginning a universal history can unfold. Uniform ideas originating among entire peoples unknown to each other must have a common ground of truth; this makes it possible to establish a 'mental dictionary for assigning origins to all the diverse articulated languages'.[58] What is true of language is true of natural law as well; they share the same succession in time, and are co-present and consistent with human institutions: 'the order of ideas must follow the order of institutions'.[59] Hence, they share the same diversity of origin: 'the natural law of the gentes had separate origins among the several peoples, each in ignorance of the others, and it was only subsequently, as a result of wars, embassies, alliances, and commerce, that it came to be recognized as common to the entire human race'.[60]

However, beyond this diversity lies the essential unity which is the proper object of Vico's *scienza*, by which the eternal idea of this world of nations can be grasped:[61] 'There must in the nature of human institutions be a mental language common to all nations, which uniformly grasps the substance of things feasible in human social life and expresses it with as many diverse modifications as these same things may have diverse aspects.'[62]

With Vico, a first step is taken towards the replacement of the classical *mathesis* with a new, modern and subject-centred constructability.[63] To Vico, the indisputable truth of mathematical knowledge derives from the fact that it has been made as a *scientia operatrix*. Its deductions and demonstrations are but ways of making truth; the figures of analytical geometry are knowable only by virtue of being constructed by the knower. The criterion of truth, says Vico, is to have made it.[64]

Since man has not made physical nature, it is not susceptible to the same methods of knowing as is the world of geometry. Cartesian 'clear and distinct ideas' may appear self-evident, but nothing assures their validity as soon as we move outside the realm of what is constructed by the mind; even introspectively, the criterion of indubitability does not hold sway, since the mind does not make itself. The world of human institutions, however, is ultimately made by men, and can therefore be known as a mode of self-knowledge. Human institutions invariably reflect human activities and human intentions, and are therefore knowable from the inside, from the historical chain of internal causes that gave rise to them as manifestations of knowledgeable self-transformation: 'the world of civil society has certainly been made by men, and ... its principles are therefore to be found within the modifications of our own human mind ... since men have made it, men could come to know'.[65]

The *certum* – as opposed to true knowledge (*verum*) – attainable of the beings in the external, physical world has its political counterpart in a merely 'probable judgement' of reason of state. What is certain in the laws is not only that which is backed by authority, but also that which is irreducible and particular; *certum* means not only certain, but also particularized or individuated, and is opposed to that which is common:[66] 'since this world of nations has been made by men, let us see in what institutions all men agree and always have agreed. For these institutions will be able to give us the universal and eternal principles on which all nations were founded and still preserve themselves'.[67] The world of nations and the science of that world must therefore be wholly logically simultaneous, since 'the sciences must begin where their subject matters began'.[68] Consequently,

> history cannot be more certain than when he who creates the things also narrates them ... as geometry, when it constructs the world of quantity out of its elements, or contemplates that world, just so does our science create for itself the world of nations, but with a reality greater by just so much as the institutions having to do with human affairs are more real than points, lines, surfaces, and figures are.[69]

Thus, language, man and nation traverse the same field of ideal history, obey the same inner laws of birth and decay, and are knowable according to the same set of rules, which also draws them together in the same space of history. Yet simultaneously, and precisely within this very space of history, they together constitute the conditions of knowledge, and are folded back upon themselves in a ceaseless act of reflexivity, their 'being' and 'knowing' themselves subject to endless modification and undecidable alteration: man *is* because he is known by himself, and is *known* by himself because he *is*.

To Rousseau, the origin of language marks the beginning of its own degeneration, since it follows the same line of development as do man and society.[70] It is not, says Rousseau in his first *Discours*, 'a light undertaking to distinguish properly between what is original and what is artificial in the actual nature of man, or to form a true idea of a state which no longer exists, perhaps never did exist, and probably never will exist; and of which it is, nevertheless, necessary to have true ideas, in order to form proper judgement of our present state'.[71] Thus, the origin of language and society cannot be restored in all its purity and simplicity, but it can serve as a hypothetical point from which present deviation and degradation can be measured. Beginning with a 'cry of nature', a language of sounds and gestures is slowly articulated from inarticulate cries; the savage wanders in the forests without speech, since it would be of little use in the ordinary course of his life; communication requires co-presence, but the mark of man's natural condition is solitude. The closer we come to the dusk of barbarism, the more complex and articulate man's signifying capacity becomes.[72]

But this articulation can only proceed to a certain limit: as long as man remains in his pre-civil state, he cannot develop general propositions and abstract ideas. To every single object, a particular name is attributed, 'without regard to genus or species, which these primitive originators were not in a position to distinguish ... so that, the narrower the limits of their knowledge, the more copious their dictionary must have been'.[73]

To Rousseau, as to the classical writers, the conditions of possibility of language, society and knowledge are rigorously intertwined; to the Classics, their development resided within representation, representation itself being conditioned by their interdependence: the sovereign was introduced in order to stabilize their intersection. To Rousseau, and to many modern theories of meaning, the interdependence of language, society and knowledge is a fact of their development in time; none of them alone could traverse the same succession of events; the fact of their analogical relationship – in, for example, 'a form of life' – is not present at their common prehistorical origin, but is constituted through a vast mutation which draws them together, 'a fortuitous concurrence of many different causes':[74]

> I cannot imagine how [men] would ever be induced to give up their primitive liberty ... to impose upon themselves unnecessarily the labours and the inevitable misery of a social mode of life.
>
> He who willed man to be social, by the touch of a finger shifted the globe's axis into line with the universe. I see such a slight movement changing the face of the earth and deciding the vocation of mankind: in the distance I hear the joyous cries of an insane multitude; I see the building of castles and cities; I see the birth of the arts; I see nations forming, expanding, and dissolving.[75]

Who, then, is responsible for this 'slight movement'; this exogenous rupture which actualizes everything hitherto dormant in human nature? Is it, as has been argued, that man's fall from his original innocence into the wickedness of civility 'certainly concerns God', and that this external event 'remains nonrational as the origin of reason must'?[76] This event is itself irreducible to logic, since it produces its origin from without; from a negativity exterior to the system that is overturned. What this interpretation fails to notice is that the supplementary character of the catastrophic event that produces language, society and knowledge has *man* as both its foundation and effect. In Rousseau, it is as if Dante's poetic vision of a humanity that crowns and mitres itself over itself comes true in time: man was born free; his place of birth is in the lacuna between the natural and the artificial; his date of birth is the very moment when he comes to know of his own historicity, when he situates himself in time and begins to distinguish what went before him from what is simultaneous to himself; at the same time, he is everywhere in chains, in the chains of a time he has forged himself by attaining civility.[77] The limit which separates the barbarous from the civil is crossed at the moment it is pointed out, and the subsequent loss of innocence marks – or rather, announces and performs – the coming of a new era, of modernity, of man.

With modern man, with language, with society, the same evils that once united separated people now tend to separate those who are united. The classics, so anxiously trying to repair the damage created at Babel, now find themselves surpassed by a new disaster; the birth of society is the death of representation, of its naturalness, of its power to organize the world. With modernity, what once happened at Babel was not only the disruption of the divine order forging words and things together, but the diversification of languages:

> Every language has its own form, a difference which may be partly cause and partly effect of difference in national character, this conjecture appears to be confirmed by the fact that in every nation under the sun speech follows the change of manners, and is preserved or altered along with them.[78]

From this point, natural unity is replaced by artificial difference. The primordial harmony and innocence of mankind is broken, and replaced by war between nations and between significations. Only reason is common to all men;[79] from now on, reason constitutes the unquestionable foundation from which it is possible to speak in the name of man, and from which to criticize the duality of man's political condition.

In addition, reason and knowledge are historicized. If language is expressive of deep social identity and hidden political forces, and constantly bears witness to man's creative and constructive powers, it becomes possible to trace the development of reason and knowledge through the genesis of language. The play between reason and language becomes a constant roundabout, says Herder, since, 'Without language, man can have no reason, without reason no language.'[80] Thus the genetic relationship between man, language and reason can be subjected to the perennial question of which came first, an undecidability which leads to the continuous retreat of their origin to a new, always allegedly more primitive and primordial presence. To Herder, and then *pace* Rousseau and Condillac, language first receives a history proper to it, which releases it from all fixed chronologies; a history which then can be superimposed upon man as the knowledgeable creator of language, who is 'one cipher in the cumulative progression of his species'.[81] 'Man, endowed with a mind ... has by his first act of spontaneous reflection invented language.'[82] Further, since language is both the seed of all knowledge as well as an expression of the hidden subjectivity of the speaker, our study of language must be directed beneath the surface of representation:

> we are not concerned with the external sound of a word; we are examining the internal genesis of a word as its essential characteristic which we associate with a clear and distinct *consciousness* ... [I]t is remarkable how this self-created inner sense of the spirit constitutes in its very origin also the means of communication.[83]

The history of the human spirit becomes the history of language, 'a study in the labyrinth of human imagination and passions'.[84] We are beings with a language, an organism designed to create language, living in a space adapted to our capacity for thinking through a medium of which the form and material content are determined by the organization of all senses: 'We may indeed speak of this creature endowed with mind and language, with discerning consciousness and creativity as a *system*.'[85]

To Herder, the diversification of language is a natural corollary of human diversity, and as such the result of a dialectic which proceeds by mutual estrangement and conflict:

> Contempt and enmity cannot but lead to complete separation and estrangement. For who would associate with so contemptible an enemy as a barbarian? Who would like to share with him the family traditions, the memory of a common origin and, above all, language, this very symbol of tribal identity?[86]

To the incommensurability of languages corresponds an analogous incommensurability of cultures,[87] of organic wholes ordered in a succession of time and space; yet beyond their difference, there is a more profound identity. As in Vico and Rousseau, there is a macrocosm of mankind, which forms 'one progressive totality, originating from one common origin within one universal order', and from which the transmission of language and knowledge proceeds: 'This international transmission of social cultures is indeed the *highest form of cultural development.*'[88]

Thus, from Vico to Herder, the triad language-man-nation is both *organized* and *historicized*. Each can be identified in the present on the basis of the individual history of the other, and each can be given a history on the basis of the present identity of the other. They are drawn together by means of analogy, ordered into historical succession as 'ages' that are separated by chronological thresholds, and distributed in space as 'cultures' or 'nations' with geographical limits.

Further, each entity in the triad is a *doublet*. Language is expressive of underlying identities and forces, and figures simultaneously as a more or less neutral medium of knowledge. Man is inserted both as an object of knowledge, and as the condition of knowing in general: man knows and is known in a ceaseless game of mirrors. The nation, finally, is knowable as a manifestation of man and language, but is ultimately also the site in which the collective resources of knowledge are buried.

As a consequence of this development, and from Kant onwards, the problem of knowledge can no longer be formulated and solved against the backdrop of a unifying *mathesis*, but must be directed explicitly at the relation between what is given empirically and that which constitutes the transcendental conditions of knowledge. From this point on, to neglect the duality of subject and object will only lead philosophical inquiry into a dead end or into a dogmatic slumber. Moreover, philosophy must discriminate between *territories* of knowledge, each obeying different rules and duly separated by the strict legislature of pure reason.

Human reason has fallen into perplexity, writes Kant: 'it begins with principles which it has no option save to employ in the course of experience, and which this experience abundantly justifies it in using'.[89] But in its quest for self-knowledge, it must remain incomplete; by overstepping all possible empirical employment, it precipitates itself into darkness and contradictions. If the powers of the mind are limited to passively mirroring what is external to itself, while it is at the same time supposed that our knowledge conforms to objects in themselves, the unconditioned character of our representations cannot be thought without contradiction. But if we, as is the revolutionary upshot of *Kritik der reinen Vernuft* (1781), 'suppose that our representation of things, as they are given to us, does not conform to these things as they are in themselves, but that these objects, as appearances, conform to our mode of representation, *the contradiction vanishes*'.[90]

  If man, as in Vico and Rousseau, is able to create himself together with the social world he inhabits, by repeating a sublime gesture – whether poetic or catastrophic – he is nevertheless not entirely at home in this world; he is at once free and alienated. Nature is both an object of nostalgic reverence and a limit to the constructive powers of his mind, and the classical attempt to enlarge uncritically the scope of constructability through a universal *mathesis* causes what Kant calls a disfiguration of sciences. Allowed to trespass upon one another's territory, each mode of inquiry is in fact prohibited to enter upon the same royal road of science as mathematics and physics.[91]

  The historical success of mathematics depends on a revolutionary liberation of the mind, an event that once and for all reversed the singular subordination of the mind to the object of inquiry. Instead of taking the object as a primitive given, and, so to speak, reading off its properties from its concept, the true method is to bring out what is necessarily implied in the construction that the mind presents to itself.[92]

  In his effort to revolutionize philosophy in the direction of a science, Kant opens up a lacuna which, in its various guises, is regulative of modern knowledge in its entirety. Whereas the creative powers of man implied in mathematical constructability cannot be transposed wholesale to the realm of philosophy, since philosophical inquiry cannot detach itself completely from what is given to it by experience,[93] Kantian philosophy opens a gulf between what is constructable and what is not, between what is *a priori* and what is *a posteriori*; between the powers of speculative reason and the demands of empirical understanding, between moral freedom and natural necessity. This lacuna, which, as we shall see below, structures the international system right from the moment of its birth, has plagued our understanding of it ever since, and spurred ceaseless debates concerning its identity as an object of investigation as well as about how to deal with it methodologically, and how to cope with it morally.

  The *First Critique* deals a death blow to representation as a mode of organizing knowledge; it questions representation, not as to its possibility as such, but as to its fundamental character and its limits. By posing the question of what conditions representation, Kant ventures beyond it and opens up a new metaphysical theme, firmly centred around the transcendental conditions of knowledge.

At the same time, however, the 'empirical' is bracketed, and restored into a territory of *a posteriori* knowledge, founded on and delimited by formal rules of valid experience rather than determined by the essence of its objects, which by definition cannot be known.

From this point on, the scene is also set for the endless controversies of modern knowledge. On the one hand, the notion of a language as a transparent medium of knowledge gives birth to the project of formalizing concrete experience and of constituting pure empirical sciences. On the other, the expressive dimension bestowed upon language gives rise to methods of exegesis, devoted to the investigation of human subjectivity as a locus of meaning. Whether 'positivist' or 'hermeneutic', whether devoted to 'explanation' or 'understanding', man has now once and for all replaced the king as the secret condition of all knowledge; in the former case, the object is the condition of his experience, in the latter, he himself is the condition of the object.[94]

In this section, I have also touched upon the rearrangement of identity and difference that takes place in the discourse of man and language during the latter half of the eighteenth century. First, identity and difference are uncoupled from each other, and moved from the level of *properties* to the level of *relations* in the constitution of objects. Now the individual object is formed out of its analogical relations with other objects, relations that in turn define and are defined by their organic mode of being. The set of relations which defines an object and its structure from *within*, is analogous to the set of relations that hold *between* objects, their only difference being that of hierarchy and complexity, the difference of 'microcosm' and 'macrocosm'. Second, identity and difference, their opposition itself now being thought in relational terms rather than as something to be read off from the order of empirical beings themselves, help constitute uninterrupted successions of objects of the same complexity as well as dialectical relations between objects of different complexity. For example, a specific language and a specific culture go together in succession, making it possible to debate which of them is to be accorded temporal priority, and to explain the genesis of one in terms of the presence of the other. Simultaneously, however, they both can be referred back and related dialectically to a higher level of organic complexity, be it a universal language or a universal man. Behind the diversity of individual forms lies a prior structural identity; anterior to this identity, there is a play of genesis and succession conditioned by yet another universal or another organic structure.

Once knowledge of beings is both *organized* and *historicized*, there can be no indisputable end point to this dialectic; what is different can always be shown to share in common one single property, namely that of being different, which then in fact makes them identical; what is identical can always be shown to suffer from an initial separation (how else could the question of identity ever come to the fore?), which makes it different from itself. In the next section, it remains to explore the consequences of this play between identity and difference for the emergence of the international.

Being: the emergence of the international

What one criticizes, one often simultaneously yet unwittingly restores at a level inaccessible to the mode of thought from which the act of criticism sprang. We have already touched upon the criticism directed against the separation of inside and outside in classical political discourse; it now remains to demonstrate that the emergence of the international is logically connected to this criticism, by drawing upon the same fundamental epistemic premises and utilizing the same set of metaphorical resources. What makes the international intelligible as an object of discourse also serves as the unthought foundation of Enlightenment criticism; what modernity with one hand so eloquently questions from the vantage point of a universalist ethic, it reconstructs, reorganizes, reifies and naturalizes at a new logical and historical depth with the other.

As I shall argue in the present section, the emergence of the international must be understood as logically linked to the emergence of the concept of the modern sovereign state, although it is not reducible to it. The latter is not a necessary condition of or a cause of the former, nor is it the other way around; what is true, however, is that they both emerge in indissoluble union with one another, and supplement each other within modern political knowledge, emerge together with a specific historicity of their own and an explanation of their origin and future.

That is, the modern state and the international system do not only arrive in the same epistemic and ontological package, but enclosed in the package is a manual for how to understand them and how to explain their dialectical-historical-empirical interconnection scientifically, and then in the various senses accorded to the word from Ranke to Waltz. Moreover, the goods within the package are dependent on the manual for their existence; without the empirico-transcendental mode of knowledge accorded privilege in this manual, both the sovereign state and the international system would cease to be intelligible, and the manual would lose its power to construct and to organize modern political reality along its most seemingly self-evident and constitutive dividing line, separating the sovereign state from the international system. We must now turn to the partly neglected prehistory of this manual of modern sovereignty; much energy has been devoted to the internal logic and justification of the modern state, but little attention has been paid to the constitutive relations it entertains with its outside.[95]

The nation-state and the dialectic of conflict

If the classical concept of the state was based on a problematic – and to our eyes highly fictitious – identification of the person of the sovereign with the abstract space of power and interest, one could say with some simplification that the modern state is based on an equally problematic identification of state with nation, concealing its sovereignty by dispersing it at the ideological level. However, the epistemic and ontological resources used in establishing this identity are radically different from the ones employed by the classics.

Instead of approaching this problem through a sociology of modern nationalism,[96] a brief genealogy of the conditions of possibility of both the state as a reified acting subject and the nation as an imagined community will help us to note how the identity of nation and state gradually is secured in the early-modern discourse on the state; the nation, first defined in empirical terms as a deep-seated cultural and linguistic identity, is cross-fertilized with the more abstract and transcendent concept of a territorial state.[97] The outcome is well known: the nation-state, with both state and nation defined in analogous terms as organized beings; it is no coincidence that modernity marks the return of the *body politic* as the paradigmatic metaphor of the state.[98]

By the same token as the superficial unity of king and state was articulated and secured through the analysis of state interest in terms of the identity and the difference between them, the notion of a general interest or will forms the crucial link between nation and state in the modern scheme of sovereignty. As I shall argue in the present section, the precarious identity of state and nation, as well as their mutual reification, is carried out through a dialectic of conflict that is present in political texts as well as in the historical relations between them, and with a *sublimation of otherness* as both the intra- and intertextual outcome. This dialectic of conflict establishes identity out of difference, sameness out of otherness; it does so by a continuous reiteration of a fundamental presupposition of modern knowledge; it treats identity and difference as qualities that implicate each other logically as well as temporally, and distributes their opposition in a succession of historical events and actual relationships between entities simultaneously organized and constituted by the dialectic.

Asking how sovereign authority can be strengthened through popular participation, d'Argenson responds with a theory of general interest. To him, the strength of a whole consists in the union of the parts, and the problem of politics is to discover the true general interest among the mass of particular interests. Between man and man, as between nation and nation, there are conflicting interests, and 'each interest has different principles. The agreement of two particular interests is reached on grounds opposed to those of a third. It is this that makes good general laws so difficult to compose.'[99]

That is, a 'general interest' can only be articulated or realized against the backdrop of an opposed interest; as soon as a general interest is formed or derived out of this conflict, its negation is also formed, thus dissolving its generality into particularity at the next level of conflict. Whenever a conflict of interest yields to a rule at one level, it does so only by virtue of being opposed, thus transposing the conflict to another level of complexity, which in its turn awaits a general rule.

This dialectic of conflict is repeated and further articulated by Rousseau, Kant and Hegel, and lies at the heart of their concepts of the state. Explaining the genesis of the social compact in terms of the clash of particular interests, Rousseau points out that 'men cannot engender new forces, but only unite and direct existing ones, they have no other means of preserving themselves than the formation, by aggregation, of a sum of forces great enough to overcome the resistance'.[100]

The realization of the social compact demands a mutual and total alienation of individual rights to the whole of the community, which then becomes sovereign over itself; as in the classical analysis of sovereignty, its locus and scope are metaphors for one another, yet they are now twin aspects of the same body politic; the general will is general in its *object* as well as in its *essence*. It must 'come from all and apply to all'.[101] Sovereignty is the expression of this general will and a common interest; it must be indivisible because it is general, and it is general because it is indivisible; it is inalienable because the sovereign cannot be represented except by itself; it cannot be represented except by itself because sovereignty encompasses all members of the body politic.[102]

In Rousseau, and now contrary to the classical writers, sovereignty is expressive of an underlying identity of nation and state, rather than a sign of their logical separation into state and society. The general will is both a source of unity and a consequence of it, since 'if the clashing of particular interests made the establishment of societies necessary, the agreement of these very interests made it possible':[103] were there no point of agreement between particular wills, no society could exist in the first place. Hence, the people are absorbed into the state and constituted as a collective, which presupposes a general will in order for it to be intelligible as a unity and as *the* basis of its assimilation within the state, a general will which already presupposes as a condition of its existence a prior unification of the people into a community or nation in order to be manifest in the state. Thus, if the unity of the people flows from the sovereignty of the state, and the unity of the state grows out of the sovereignty of the people, and the identity of state and people derives from the common source of a general will, which is the mark of the sovereignty of each and therefore also of their *difference*, we end up with a paradox:

> For a young people to be able to relish sound principles of political theory and follow the fundamental rules of statecraft, the effect would have to become the cause; the social spirit, which should be created by those institutions, would have to preside over their very foundation; and men would have to be before law what they should become by means of law.[104]

The possibility of a mythological lawgiver, so dear to exemplary knowledge, is no longer open to the early-modern Rousseau; the ultimate source of legitimacy must be sought elsewhere.[105] As a consequence, the identity and indivisibility of the sovereign state cannot be thought simply to emerge from the successions of conflicts that brings us from a state of social corruption and inequality to the civil condition, where man is author of the law, and enjoys equity and liberty under the guidance of a general will. There is an unbridgeable lacuna here: the truth of the general will must be recognized by man in order to become a historical actuality, but the very same set of conditions which makes its recognition desirable, also constrains its realization. The objective truth of the general will must be translated into subjective will before it can be recognized as objective, and it must be recognized as such before being internalized as subjective will: as in the transition from the state of nature to the social condition, the system is incapable of transforming itself from within. One must have 'recourse to an authority of a different order, capable of constraining without violence and persuading without convincing'.[106]

What is attainable in history is unattainable in man, and conversely. *Du Contrat Social* provides no clear solution to this problem of historical finality and human imperfectibility, but responds to it by a logic of sublimation, which diverts conflict to the outside:

> [T]here can be no general will directed to a particular object. Such an object must be either within or outside the State. If outside, a will which is alien to it cannot be, in relation to it general; if within, it is part of the State, and in that case there arises a relation between whole and part which make them two separate beings, of which the part is one, and the whole minus the part the other. But the whole minus a part cannot be the whole, but only two unequal parts; and it follows that the will of one is no longer in any respect general in relation to the other.[107]

The state, being general unto itself, inhabits a realm of particularity. In fact, it is general unto itself only by virtue of being particular in relation to other states. Its self-identity derives from its difference, not from other states in their own particularity, but from the larger whole formed by them together. Here, sovereignty constitutes and incessantly reconstitutes the state through division, through the demarcation of inside from outside, of presence from absence. The sameness of the Rousseauan state can only be articulated and legitimized against the backdrop of a more encompassing social context, now site of what was formerly purged out of the Same through the dialectic of conflict.

In contrast to the classical authors, the early-modern theory of the state defines the Other of the state as something chronologically simultaneous yet spatially exterior to it; the outside, however, is an ontological doublet of the inside; it is intelligible since it subscribes to the same chronology as the state, and is conceptually analogous to it, in as much as the set of relations which holds inside states also holds between them.

This dialectical pattern is repeated and further articulated by

Kant.[108] The state, says Kant, 'is a society of men ... [l]ike a tree it has its own roots, and to graft it onto another state as if it were a shoot is to terminate its existence as a moral personality.'[109] Ideally, such a state should be founded on an original contract, an 'act by which the people constitutes a state for itself';[110] Kant explicitly denies the historical reality of such a contract, but turns the general will into an idea of reason, 'which nonetheless has undoubted practical utility; for it can oblige every legislator to frame his laws in such a way that they could have been produced by the united will of a whole nation'.[111]

Such are the dictates of the moral law. Actual states, however, have grown out of conflict; as we shall see later, history is as much poison as antidote, as much cause of what from Kant onwards comes to constitute the problem of order as the final solution to it. In historical reality, the state has developed out of *antagonism*; to Kant, antagonism is the unsocial sociability of men, their tendency to come together in society coupled with their tendency to break this society up.[112] Antagonism is inherent in the human species as a whole, and manifests itself at every level of social complexity from microcosm to macrocosm. The subjection to laws, however imperfect, has taken place as a result of a clash of forces, conducted by nature. War has driven people into all regions of the earth and compelled them to enter into more or less legal relationships, yet separated them by linguistic and religious differences. The fact of culturally and geographically determined difference between peoples leads us to expect that even if they were not compelled by internal dissent to submit to the coercion of public laws, war would have produced the same result from outside; each people would find itself confronted, thus forcing it to form itself into a state in order to encounter the Other as an armed power.[113] Hence, the same unsociableness which forced men together into states gives rise in turn to a situation in which each state, in its external relations with other states, is in a position of unrestricted freedom, which is a condition of war.[114]

To Kant, the sovereignty of man is a political tragedy. States are formed out of discord and otherness, but with the logically inevitable side-effect that human antagonism merely sublimates to a higher level of social complexity in the course of the civilizing process. What once was prior to the state and prevailed among men in their barbarous freedom is relegated to a higher sphere the very moment the state emerges out of it, and therefore also becomes beyond reach: in his effort to overcome the otherness immanent in himself, man merely reifies it. The price has to be paid for his sameness within the state, yet

214

antagonism is also contained within man as a positivity, a spring of his moral and cultural development; what bears the stigma of moral negativity in the international sphere is simultaneously the condition of its transcendence, and the ultimate emancipation from the evils of war. As we shall see below, sovereign man himself is the battleground between moral autonomy and natural necessity, a battle against his own finiteness.

The dialectic of conflict, and the melting together of state and nation into a whole against the backdrop of an exterior simultaneously produced by the dialectic, has its most decisive moment in Hegel.[115] To him, it is in its external relations that a state becomes an actual state, and it is through external relations that the citizens experience a collective identity within the state as well as an identification with it and its cause.

Already in his *Verfassung Deutschlands* (1802), we learn that, 'A multitude of human beings can only call itself a state if it be united for the common defence of the entirety of its property.'[116] The essential unity of the state does not reside in an anterior cultural, linguistic or religious identity, but in the allegiance to a common authority for common defence. Cultural identity, writes Hegel, has lost its importance as the foundation of unity, and 'is now to be reckoned among the accidents whose character does not hinder a mass from constituting a public authority'.[117] Further, the social and cultural diversity of society 'may not hinder the chief activity of the state, since … this activity must secure itself before all else'.[118] Hence, the sovereign state is sovereign only to the extent that it has the capacity to secure itself in relation to what is external to it, and not in relation to what is merely contingent and therefore absorbable within it: 'dissimilarity in culture and manners is a necessary product as well as a necessary condition of the stability of modern states',[119] since in their external relationship 'States stand to one another in a relation of might … this relation has been universally revealed and made to prevail.'[120]

Later, in the *Rechtsphilosophie* (1820), the assimilation of the concept of the nation to the concept of the state is brought to completion through the mutual implication and opposition between the sovereign state and what is external to it. The state is 'the spirit of the nation … which permeates all relations within it and also the customs and consciousness of the individuals who belong to it'.[121]

For the Hegelian state to reach actuality – which is to constitute itself as a unified acting subject – two interrelated steps, already discernible in Rousseau and Kant, are necessary: it must unite subjectivity and objectivity, and it must resolve the tension between particularity and universality.

Hegel's theory of the state is not a theory of states as empirical beings. The Hegelian state is above all the actuality of an ethical idea, and must as such be present to itself as consciousness and self-knowledge before it can be understood as an empirical reality. It acquires subjective and substantial will as a result of being conscious of itself, and being conscious of itself, it is rational in and for itself. The unity of the state is 'an absolute and unmoved end in itself'.[122] The state must know itself in order to exist, and its self-knowledge is mediated through the self-consciousness of the individual citizen, since in his knowledge of the state and in his identification *with* it, the individual citizen finds the source of his freedom *within* it.

As such, the idea of the state has three different determinations, each necessary and together sufficient for its actuality. First, *internally*, it is related to itself and takes on actual existence only in relation to itself as a self-contained organic being. Second, *externally*, the state stands in a relationship of mutual exclusion to other states, taking on actual existence through outward differentiation of itself. Third, *historically*, it takes on active existence as a subject by virtue of its place in world history.[123]

First, in its internal determination, the universal and the particular are brought to coincide within the state. The actuality of the state as a political being resides in the unity of the particular and the universal within it: without this mutual resolution of particularity and universality the state cannot actualize itself, only subsist in an inferior form.[124]

This means that the state is unable to attain reality without the knowledge and interest of particular forces within it; men do not live within the state merely for the realization of their particular interests, but direct their will to a universal end. Thus, the state exists objectively as well as subjectively, and it is only through his membership in the state that the individual can take on objective reality, truth and ethical life. As such, the individual embodies in himself individuality and universality: he knows and wills for himself, and simultaneously discovers in his self-consciousness a universal element, present in his social and political institutions. Thus, the state is both an expression of universal interest as such and a medium for the conservation of particular interests within the universal interest:

> The principle of modern states has enormous strength and depth because it allows the principle of subjectivity to attain fulfilment in the self-sufficient extreme of personal particularity, while at the same time bringing it back to substantial unity and so preserving this unity in the principle of subjectivity itself.[125]

Second, and externally, the state is an indivisible and therefore exclusive unit, and the relations it entertains with other states constitute a necessary supplement to its internal unity, structure and constitution. Turning its will to differentiation outwards, the state manifests itself as pure inside, since it has 'incorporated the subsistent differences into itself'.[126]

However, in their concrete historical appearance, the external determination of the state takes precedence over its internal determination. The historically primary authority which states possess, writes Hegel, is their external independence, 'even if it is abstract and without inner development'.[127] Ultimately, all relations that the state has to itself have been formed out of its constitutive relation to what is outside itself; its self-identity, rationality and actuality have grown out of prior difference and contingency. In fact, it is in its external determination that the state becomes possible both as an object of consciousness and a historical reality:

> In *existence* this *negative* relation of the state to itself thus appears as the relation of *another* to *another*, as if the negative were something external. The existence of this negative relation therefore assumes the shape of an event, of an involvement with contingent concurrences coming *from without*.
>
> Nevertheless, this negative relation is the state's *own* highest moment – its actual infinity as the ideality of everything finite within it. It is that aspect whereby the substance, as the state's absolute power over everything individual and particular ... and makes it present to the consciousness.[128]

In Hegel's logic of sovereignty, the state is formed by an 'involvement with contingent concurrences coming from without', that is, by war with other states; 'the ideality which makes its appearance in war in the shape of a contingent external relationship is the same as the ideality whereby the internal powers of the state are organic moments of the whole'.[129]

The nature of its external relationship with other states is determined by the sovereign, and decisive power is concentrated in his hand. Sovereignty, which initially is vested in the state as such as an abstract and universal concept, can exist only as a subjectivity which is 'certain of itself'. The sovereignty of the state, in both its outward and its inward determination, must therefore be embodied in a person, which has 'being for itself' and thus is capable of attaining absolute self-knowledge. The concept of the monarch, says Hegel, cannot be derivative from any other concept, but must be posited as 'entirely self-originating', and thought of as possessing immediate individuality.[130]

Even if accorded almost no formal importance in Hegel's theory,[131] the person of the sovereign is introduced at the very theoretical disjunction of the state's external and internal determinations; it is the presence of the immediate will of the sovereign which draws the line in water between the inside and the outside of the state. Formally, internal sovereignty lies with the people, but only if we speak of the state as a whole, for without the monarch and 'that articulation of the whole which is necessarily associated with monarchy, the people is a formless mass'.[132] In short, it ceases to be an internally organized state, and all its determinations lose their applicability; it melts together with the outside, and lapses back into contingency and anarchy. Its ethical life is terminated, and its subjectivity vanishes with the absence of the sovereign. Thus, in a situation of crisis, says Hegel, and then prefiguring Schmitt[133] and Morgenthau: 'whether in external or internal affairs – it is around the simple concept of sovereignty that the organism and all the particular spheres of which it consisted rally, and it is to this sovereignty that the salvation of the state is entrusted, while previously legitimate functions are sacrificed'.[134]

In relation to other states the sovereign state is an individual, and now by virtue of being recognized by them as such. Without relations with other states, the state cannot be an actual individual, any more than an individual can be an actual person without a relationship with other persons. Its internal legitimacy must be supplemented by recognition, but in order to be recognized, the state itself must recognize other states; in this act of recognition, the other state is accredited with self-consciousness.[135] In their mutual relationship, states exist in a condition devoid of right; sovereignty organizes their internal as well as their external relations; the latter is a relationship of independent units which makes mutual stipulations but at the same time stands above those stipulations.[136] Thus, from Hegel's logic of sovereignty follows a state of war between states; both as an anterior and hidden condition of their emergence in reality and in consciousness, and as the inevitable outcome of their actualization as individual subjects. But in the broadest view of these relations, says Hegel, 'the ethical whole itself – the independence of the state – is exposed to contingency'.

Out of the juxtaposition of first and second determinations of the state arises the third, historical one. In its second determination, the state is exposed to contingency, flowing from its reciprocal relationship with other states. Now if the task of philosophical inquiry is 'to eliminate the contingent',[137] the third determination carries the promise of assimilating this contingency to a higher moral purpose; in its particularity, the state is exposed to contingency in its external relations, and these relations are the 'manifest dialectic of [their] finitude'.[138] Thus, the mutual relationships between states give way to their place in *world history*.

In its third determination, the state stands as a particular in relation to a higher universality, which encompasses the totality of states and determines their historical destiny. World history is not an irrational necessity, a force of fate and contingency, but the necessary development of reason to self-consciousness and freedom; as such, it passes verdict over the state and its concrete existence in time and space.[139]

The spirit of a nation or state is the universal spirit in a particular form; the world spirit, whose self-realization animates Hegel's philosophy of history, transcends its particular manifestation in the state, but uses the latter as a means towards the realization of a higher end. Reason cunningly utilizes and exploits the particular interests and passions of individual states in order to 'realize its essence and to obtain the prerogative of freedom'.[140]

States, seen from the vantage point of world history, have their own actuality and are governed according to their own inner principles, but in their preoccupation with their own particular interests, they are at the same time 'the unconscious instruments and organs of that inner activity in which the shapes which they themselves assume pass away, while the spirit ... works its way towards the transition to its next and higher stage'.[141]

That is, the conflict between subjectivity and objectivity which formerly manifested itself within the state and rendered it imperfect, is now transposed to world history; sovereign statehood is posited as the end of history, yet states are the agents of history, acting according to principles which they in their particularity cannot change. States are the authors of history; they make history by drawing upon forces which they cannot affect to a greater extent than these forces affect the course of states themselves.[142]

In Hegel, we have seen how the dialectic of conflict reaches its apex, and how the sublimation of otherness is concluded. Ontologically, the state and its outside are caught in a game of mirrors, warranted and perpetuated by the logic of sovereignty which continuously reinscribes its duality into our political understanding. The logic of sovereignty produces what it asserts, and confirms what it produces; the state, in all its positive determinations, arises out of otherness; otherness, in all its negativity, arises out of the state.

In its mutations from d'Argenson to Hegel, the concept of the sovereign state becomes successively both more abstract and more comprehensive. The problem confronted by d'Argenson and Rousseau was how to interpret a general will or interest in terms of particular interests, and how to reconcile the objective truth of indivisible sovereignty with the subjective will and the deliberations of the citizens. Turning the idea of an original contract and a general will into an idea of reason, Kant reduces the problem of the sovereign state to a conflict between the concepts of freedom and nature, simultaneously inscribed in the cognitive faculties of man, and transposed to the international sphere. Finally, Hegel's theory of the modern state attempts to resolve all these conceptual conflicts, but in doing so, it merely relegates them to a more certain depth and a more comprehensive totality: to a world history governed by reason to an ultimate end of freedom within the state.

Throughout the dialectic of conflict, the state is understood as a profoundly historicized being; it traverses history in a succession of conflicting mutations that lead towards inner perfection and cohesion. As an outcome, the theory of the modern state is inherently *finalist*; the dialectic employed to constitute it as an acting subject is governed by a vision of a final resolution of all its internal conflicts. But history is not only proposed as the solution of the problem of order; history is not only the source from which the sovereign state springs forth in conceptual purity or empirical reality; history is not only invoked to explain the modern state as the outcome of conflict. It is not merely the case that the state *has* a history or *is* history all the way down; rather, and from Hegel onwards, history as a field of study *becomes* essentially a history of nations and states. As we shall see below, it is from within this history the international emerges as an object of knowledge, a knowledge which from its start is historical.

The historiography of the international

With modernity, as we have noted above, historicity begins to permeate all aspects of human existence, and furnishes man and his political and social institutions with chronological and geographical limits and fixed origins. Moreover, history becomes a singular History. If both exemplary knowledge and the analysis of interest dealt with history in the plural, early modernity dissolves these histories into one mode of being, one temporality and one chronology, which then is superimposed upon events.[143] As Savigny remarked, history is 'no longer a collection of examples but rather the sole path to true knowledge of our own condition'.[144] Or, as Mommsen wrote in a commentary upon the aspirations of classical historiography, history is 'instructive solely in that it inspires and instructs independent creative judgement'.[145]

Having become at once singular and the essence of individual beings, history establishes a multiplicity of identities, each of them possible as objects of knowledge. Informed by the dialectic of conflict, history as a field of study constitutes the fertile ground in which the disciplines of social science later can grow; in our case, history establishes the sovereign state as an object of empirical inquiry, and opens it up to investigation from two vantage points simultaneously, points which correspond to the dialectical polarity of its concept; hence, from Weber onwards, we see the formation of a *macrosociology of the state*, and a century later, from Manning, Carr and Morgenthau onwards, the gradual formation of an amorphous and eclectic body of empirical knowledge which I have labelled *international political theory*.

In the previous section, we saw how the modern sovereign state evolved out of dialectical relations with its other, the more comprehensive totality of states, and how this totality itself took on being simultaneously. We also were able to witness how this constitutive separation was carried out by the logic of the concept of sovereignty itself. In this section, it remains to see how the state and the international system themselves are turned into objects of historical investigation, a historical investigation conceptually informed by the philosophy of history, yet aspiring to the status of an empirical science.

In the classical age, we had a history of states and their interests. The *maxime* was not only based on an analysis of present interests and forces, but also used to bestow a particular past upon each individual state, and to delineate a succession of historical events that account for the present identity and future fate of that state. History was analysis; historicity was subject to the immutable rules of classification and comparison. Risking anachronism, we could say that seventeenth-century historiography was nomothetic and explanatory in spirit; its principles of reconstruction were themselves thought to be timeless and independent of the varying self-understandings of the agents. Modern historiography, by contrast, is ideographic and interpretive: in fact, those very distinctions relied on here are inseparable from the epistemic revolution brought about by Vico and Kant.

A history of the international proper cannot be the history of individual states and their modes of interaction. A history of the international system may of course encompass the actions and interactions of particular states among its dependent variables, but it must depart from the principles which organize the international into a whole, into a set of relations that is something more than the sum of its components.

Furthermore, in order for such a history to be empirical, it cannot remain content with speculative dialectics or delimit itself to an elaboration of the teleology of the world spirit. History, says Hegel, 'is concerned with what actually happened', and demands a procedure which is 'at variance with the essentially self-determining activity of conceptual thought'.[146] Historical events, in their full detail and multiplicity, require the assistance of concepts in order to be representable, but they must not be singularly *reduced* to concepts or assimilated into the independent movement of reason. Thus, already in Hegel, the stage is set for a conflict between the demands of an *a posteriori* history, and the demands of an *a priori* philosophy of history: while the former is able to furnish the historian with an indiscriminate collection of events, the latter supplies him with narrative coherence and explanatory concepts. From von Humboldt to Ranke, Heeren and Michelet, this conflict constitutes the core problem of nineteenth-century historiography,[147] and through the different solutions proposed to it from Dilthey to Collingwood, ultimately leads to the late-modern split between history proper and the history of ideas.

First, if the historian's task is to present what actually happened, and if this representation necessitates a conceptual grid in order to be intelligible, the historian is confronted with a problem. For where does he find the appropriate concepts in the absence of the unifying power of a *mathesis*? In his *Considérations générales* (1801) Ancillon had drawn attention to the fact that history had to be created out of a mass of events and deeds, and this by arranging them in a continuous and homogeneous series.[148] Later, not even nature spoke for itself: even a simple depiction of nature, writes von Humboldt in his *Über die Ausgabe des Geschichtschreibers* (1821), 'cannot be merely an enumeration and depiction of parts or the measuring of sides and angles; there is also the breath of life in the whole and an inner character which speaks through it which can be neither measured nor merely described'.[149]

An historical event, being all the more animated by spirit, cannot be apprehended solely in the positivist and *a posteriori* mode, since it 'is only partially visible to the senses; [its] manifestations are scattered, disjointed, isolated; what it is that gives unity to this patchwork, puts the isolated fragment into its proper perspective, and gives shape to the whole, remains removed from direct observation'.[150] Language no longer has the power to organize experience into representations, since 'growing out of the fullness of the soul – it frequently lacks expressions which are free from all connotations'.[151]

The facts of history are little more than the result of a tradition which one has agreed to accept as true, and constitute the necessary basis of history, its raw material. But the historian must not stop his inquiry at this point, sacrificing the inner truth of events; he has to 'become active, even creative ... in giving shape by his own powers to that which by mere intuition he could not have perceived as it really was'.[152] That is, finding himself with a language which is expressive and therefore necessarily opaque as a medium of knowledge, he must supply the representative concepts himself by fusing his inquiring intellect with the object of inquiry. The fabric of events is spread out before the historian, 'in seeming confusion, merely divided up chronologically and geographically'; as a consequence, he must 'separate the necessary from the accidental, uncover its inner structure, and make visible the truly activating forces in order to give his presentation the form on which depends ... its truth and accuracy'.[153]

Second, the historian now stands in the same relation of active subjectivity towards his object as mankind stands towards its historical destiny in the speculative philosophy of history; creativity and constructability is both warranted and circumscribed by history itself; man is subjected to the forces of history, and history is subjected to and enacted by the creativity of man. Modern historiography has depth, it is no longer confined to the surface of representations or present in the revolutionary transition from one taxonomy to the other. An event is only an object of historical investigation insofar as it is a sign of an underlying historical reality; history is no longer a history of mere events and their chronological succession, but a history of the forces and relations causing their occurrence and determining their nature.

It is to these active and productive forces that the historian must turn; he must render a strict account of their inner nexus and recognize their inner trends at a given moment; he must inquire into the relationship of forces to the existing state of affairs and to the changes that have preceded it.[154] Therefore, the understanding of an event must always be guided by concepts and ideas. Ideally, in his activity, the historian must be guided by the same ideas which govern history at the period of inquiry, since 'all these things partake in the nature of thought, which can only be sustained by being thought'.[155] In order to bring form to the multiplicity of events of history, the historian must abstract that form from them, a form which is not projected onto history, but is the essence of history itself.

Hence, from von Humboldt onwards, the task of the historian becomes the reverse of the task of classical historical analysis; the accuracy of historical representation is no longer measured in terms of the explanatory scope and power of a *maxime*, but in terms of a congruence between the self-understanding of the historian and that of his object, since his understanding presupposes 'an analogue of that which will actually be understood later; *an original and antecedent congruity between subject and object*'.[156]

Splitting the difference between the demands of *a posteriori* empiricity and the demands of *a priori* narrative coherence, the historian has to proceed with two tasks simultaneously: 'the investigation of the effective factors in historical events and the understanding of their universal relationship'.[157] As a consequence of the creative powers attributed to the historian to represent the past as it actually was, the field of history itself is turned into a place in which the universal and the particular are joined together in a coherent, stable and yet unfolding scheme. History is a system of relationships which draw together parts and whole, but this system itself remains immutable through history; it has no history of its own, since it is its own timeless essence.

The history of the world is from its conception a history of relations between nations and states, of the hidden forces and principles organizing them into a system and making them intelligible as individual parts of this whole. The original and antecedent congruence of subject and object – justified by and yet justifying the creative and constructive powers given to the subject – turns the historian's concepts into doublets of the reality to be depicted, and reality into a doublet of these concepts. The pattern of world history corresponds to the matrix of concepts used to represent and narrate it. To von Humboldt, 'the affairs of this world ... compose an infinitude which the mind can never press into one single form, but which incites the historian to try ... and gives him the strength to achieve it in part'.[158]

To von Humboldt, the clue to the world historical process lies in the individuality of states: 'in many areas the inner drive is more easily recognized in them than in individuals ... [t]he spiritual principle of individuality therefore remains active in the midst of the history of nations.'[159] This duplication of subject and object in which the concepts organizing political reality also organize historical reality, so essential to a history which aspires to be realistic, is repeated by Ranke: 'The particular bears the general within itself ... no one can escape the urge to survey the whole from a detached viewpoint ... Out of the variety of individual perceptions a vision of their unity involuntarily arises.'[160]

That is, sovereignty not only organizes relations between states by drawing them together into a system of states; it gives the modern state a past proper to its present, and a present proper to its past, and this by drawing them together in a unity. With Ranke, the international is constituted as a genuinely historical mode of being, logically inseparable from the existence of states, but with its own organizing principles that are corollaries to internal sovereignty. Further, Ranke considers the clue to the internal conditions of states to be contained in their external relationships and thereby points to the possibility of a macrosociology of the state.[161] The *full* significance of the state, says Ranke in *Politisches Gespräch* (1836) lies in its being contained in a system: 'these many separate, earthly-spiritual communities called forth by genius and moral energy, growing irresistibly, progressing amidst all turmoil of the world towards the ideal, each in its own way! Behold them, these celestial bodies, in their cycles, their mutual gravitation, their systems!'[162]

With Ranke, what I have labelled the Westphalian hypothesis emerges as something logically inseparable from his conception of an international system. The international system constitutes itself as presence out of the turmoil of the Thirty Years War.[163] Without this sudden establishment of sovereignty as the organizing principle of international relations, history itself becomes close to incomprehensible to him: 'what would have become of our states', asks Ranke towards the end of *Die grossen Mächte* (1833), 'if they had not received life from the national principle upon which they are based?'[164]

> World history does not present such a chaotic tumult, warring, and planless succession of states and peoples as appear at first sight. Nor is the often dubious advancement of civilization its only significance. There are forces and indeed spiritual, life-giving, creative forces, nay life itself, and there are moral energies, whose development we see ... They unfold, capture the world, appear in manifold expressions, dispute with and check and overpower one another. In their interaction and succession, in their life, in their decline and rejuvenation, which then encompasses an even greater fullness, higher importance, and wider extent, lies the secret of world history.[165]

The European state system as envisaged by Ranke is formed and preserved through a balance of power.[166] In the classical analysis of interest, a balance of power existed between two adversary powers or between two adversary alliances, either as a result of a deliberate act of *balancing*, or as a result of a spontaneously established equilibrium of forces; a spontaneously formed balance could be disrupted by an act intended to balance, and an act intended to restore balance could be disruptive of it. Thus, as was indeed argued by Mably,[167] the very notion of balance of power itself could disturb the balance of power; in its name, the weaker part could justify an increase in military strength through arms procurement or realignment and thereby disrupt an imaginary or desired balance. The classical balance of power, parasitic upon a mechanistic and zero-sum interpretation of the concept of power, was therefore out of balance. As Kant ironically remarked, it was like a 'house constructed in such perfect harmony with all the laws of equilibrium that it collapsed as soon as a sparrow alighted on it'.[168]

Now, with the waning of the *mathesis* and the emergence of knowledge of historical and organic beings, the balance of power is gradually established as a property of the larger whole, and then in analogy with the division of powers advocated in the domestic context. From Montesquieu and Vattel on, and most explicitly in Ancillon's *Considérations générales* (1801), von Gentz's *Fragments* (1806) and Clausewitz's *Vom Kriege* (1832),[169] the balance of power is understood against the backdrop of an underlying unity, whose individual and universal parts are interlinked; 'balance' now refers to an equilibrium between the forces of particularism and the forces of universalism in the system of states. As such, the modern concept of the balance of power is Janus-faced; it is the principle organizing the present system as a fusion of particular and universal forces, thus providing a guide for reflexive state action, yet at the same time it is designed to explain the historical transformations of this system, as well as its momentary deviation from the particular balance of forces which the historian judges to be ideal or 'normal' according to his ideological whims: to oppose force with force is to maintain order and harmony. Hence, if sovereignty is constitutive of the system and renders it structurally immutable, the balance of power is regulative, and explains both change and stability within the limits set by sovereignty:

> In great danger one can safely trust in the guardian spirit which always protects Europe from domination by any one-sided and violent tendency, which always meets pressure on one side with resistance on the other, and, through a union of the whole which grows firmer from decade to decade, has happily preserved the freedom and separate existence of each state.[170]

Moreover, the emergence of the international system is also inexorably intertwined with the simultaneous emergence of what I have labelled the Renaissance hypothesis. Being the first to sketch a comprehensive history of the European state system, Heeren projects the reciprocal freedom and independence of states acting together in a system onto the 'prehistory' of this system; he is able to furnish the state system with a past by abstracting from the forces and tendencies of his present, and transpose them backward in time, and thus appropriate what otherwise would be an alien past. A conservative writing in the aftermath of the restoration, he, much like Burke had done before him,[171] sees the revolutionary wars and the hegemonical attempt of the French as a deviation from the ideal equilibrium between particularism and universalism which has characterized the state system from its allegedly rightful chronological origin, but which now happily has been restored back into its proper equilibrium through the reintroduction of monarchy in France; that is, by a change in the internal structure. Witness the opening phrases of Heeren's *Handbuch* (1809/22):

> The history of the European state-system is anything but the history of individual states. On the contrary, it is the history of their relations with one another, especially the great powers, insofar as they evolved out of the essence of particular states, out of the personality of rulers and the ruling ideas of the time. The general condition of change in

227

those relations, and consequently for the general character of the state-system, is its internal freedom; e.g. the autonomy and mutual independence of its members. To show how it was formed, endangered and transformed, becomes the main task of the historian; a task which can be solved only by exposing the entire chain of the internal relations in the system, and the causes, which gave rise to it.[172]

To Heeren, as to Clausewitz, modern history is marked by and inseparable from the gradual genesis of an international system, composed of 'intelligent beings, acting in accordance with simple logical rules'.[173] The Italian wars, the discovery of America, the refined technologies of war in the Renaissance; all these events and the forces they release neatly coincide to establish the chronological origin of both modernity and the international. Burkhardt was not the only, nor the first, to provide modernity with a noble ancestry out of darkness by a swift rupture; both Heeren and Ranke furnish their creations with a past, a past which is the condition of their empiricity; 'to present what actually happened' can only be done from a present in which the universal concepts necessary for the coherent representation of particular events and forces are present.

That is, in its empirical-historical mode, the international system is *presentist* at birth; it emerges out of a knowledge together with a past, out of a knowledge which must deny its own historicity in order to be both historical and empirical at once. As an object of empirico-historical inquiry, the international system is immutable from its conception; it is established together with its geographical and chronological limits; it can undergo ideological mutations, withstand revolutionary redistributions of power, but its basic organizing principles remain the same all the way from its origin to its mature phases and prophesied expansion. It suddenly emerges in the empirical realm as if the notion of a *system* itself had no history, as if it had been manifest in the substratum of timeless and invisible forces, awaiting discovery at the level of events by the historian, romantically attuned to what is universal in history.

Furthermore, from the domain of history, conditioned as it is by the dialectic of conflict, emerge two possible vantage points from which to explain empirically modern sovereignty and the interrelationship between state and system it gives rise to. Like Ranke, one can start from the outside constituted by sovereignty, and from there explain the inner structure of the state and its transformations in terms of its external relations, or, like Heeren, one can start from the inside thus constituted, and explain the international system, its genesis and transformations in terms of the internal relations of the state.

If something is present because it has a past, and has a past because it is present, it also has a future. It is with this future that I shall end my investigation.

Expansion and transcendence: man, the state and peace

In the classical analysis of interest, the future existed merely as a cyclical recurrence or as a constant threat of displacement and upheaval. States could be affected by change, but this simply constituted a quantitative redistribution within the fixity of the table. In the absence of a future radically alien to the present, nothing could be projected onto it or turned into dreams of progress. Hence, in the Classical Age, utopianism is a dead letter; Campanella, Bacon, Harrington, and Comenius were all well able to formulate utopian visions of political harmony, but lacked the resources essential to conceive of their realization in the world, namely a concept of the future, understood as open and linear historical time.[174]

With the advent of modern historicity, the future is opened up to ideological exploitation. In the first section above, we saw how Raynal was able to project the conflict between absolutism and the revolutionary Enlightenment onto time-space, and stage his drama as a historically inevitable confrontation between the Old World and the New. In the second section, we saw how man, nation and knowledge were embodied in a progressive teleology, so that the development of man and community is interlinked with the proliferation and growth of subject-entered knowledge. In the third section, we have seen how the state grows out of a finalist dialectic in its effort to temper and reconcile all conflicts in the earthly community of knowing subjects; as such, and right from the start, the modern state embodies a utopian promise.

This finalist and utopian promise, is continuously compromised by the ponderous presence of the international system, however. The duality of the human political condition – so lamented by Rousseau – is not eased by the profound reorganization of political knowledge; rather, it is realized and reinscribed at a deeper, and seemingly inescapable level of thought. History, in all its organizing power, is not only posited as the source of this duality, but constantly invoked as the means of transcending it. Therefore, we must ask how the sovereign state and the international system are connected to the future.

At their logical juncture, and at their point of emergence in modern political discourse, the state and the international system have, as it were, two futures. One is centred around the prophecy of expansion, while the other is centred around the promise of transcendence.

To the classics, the table of states contained a finite number of political beings, by the same token as the taxonomy of plants and animals contained a fixed number of species. Outside the table of states, there was an external arena to which the analysis of interest could not readily could be applied. Russia and the Ottoman empire are either left out altogether,[175] or, their interests are glossed over in a most superficial manner;[176] it is no coincidence that Descartes compared objects inaccessible to analysis with distant countries like China and Mexico.[177]

At the moment of its emergence, the international system has a future of expansion as much as it has a past of unfolding. In its peculiar blend of universalism and particularism, in its fusion of cognizant subjectivity and objective empiricity, the international system is an identity encompassing prior differences between states; as a universal spirit, it does to European identity what Christianity did in the Renaissance and before, and what a *monarchie universelle* sometimes threatened to do in the Classical Age.

Whether in its transcendental or empirical mode of being, and as a system both competitive and conflictual, cooperative and cohesive, it stands to the non-European arena as Same to Other; the ideal unity of sovereignty and anarchy is historically destined to spread, and sweep away all other, inferior forms of political organization. Individual states, says Hegel, 'recognize one another as independent individuals, and the independence of each is only respected insofar as the independence of others is also recognized'. This mutual recognition forms the foundation of international law, '[b]ut in world history, a higher right comes into play. In fact, this is even recognized in reality in those situations where civilized nations come into contact with barbarian hordes.'[178]

Hegel's eurocentrism becomes clear in his discussion of the geographical basis of world history, and in his elaboration of its phases; the spirit of the world travels from East to West, soaks up that which is cherished in the present and which provides hallmarks of European identity, but brushes aside exactly that which is present in the self-definition of the non-European Other.[179] To Heeren, the happy restoration of hereditary monarchy as the inner guarantee of stability of the state-system coincides in time with the expansion of the European state-system on other continents, bringing forth a *Weltstaatensystem*.[180] To Ranke, the superiority of Europe consists in its ability to resist hegemony in all guises, this being so since '[i]t is not always recognized that the European order of things differs from others that have appeared in the course of world history by virtue of its legal, even juridical nature.'[181]

Whereas the prophecy of expansion projects the presence of the international system onto the future spaces of history, the promise of transcendence projects the finalist dialectic of the state onto the future of a globalized international space. If the presence of an international system poses an antithesis to what is dear to the civil condition, and constitutes a perennial threat to the utopian project of the modern state by generating discord and war, how can it be transformed in a more cosmopolitan direction?

To the classical writers, the problem of peace was not a problem of transcendence in time; it was a problem of substituting a rosier constellation of interests for the existing one. With no epistemic access to a dialectic of conflict or a history of deep forces and origins, the projects of Crucé, Sully, and Bellers were doomed to be either nostalgic about a past unity or sceptical about a present plurality, or both.[182]

As posed by the dialectic of conflict since Saint-Pierre and Rousseau,[183] the problem of transformation invariably involves the problem of finality. War is a social evil, ultimately generated by the international system itself as a result of the absence of central authority; this absence follows as a corollary to the presence of the sovereign state as the prime supplier of internal peace as a social good. Thus, war made the state, and the state made war. Writes Clausewitz: 'if we regard State policy as the intelligence of the personified State, then amongst all the constellations in the political sky whose movements it has to compute, those must be included which arise when *the nature of its relations imposes the necessity of a great War.*'[184]

Simultaneously, however, a transformation of these relations can only be carried out from below, through the sovereign agency of particular states themselves; this means that the very same international anarchy that one promises to transcend, also poses the ultimate obstacle to the fulfilment of this promise. The ethical *contradiction* between man's civil condition within the state and the state of war between states rests on the ontological *implication* between the sovereign state and the international system, and if this duality cannot be overcome by one swift and collective gesture, such as the establishment of a federation or a world government, 'it is not because it is chimerical, but because men are foolish, and to be sane in the midst of madmen is another sort of madness'.[185]

Man, as the hero of modernity, made the state out of conflict, but out of the state inevitably arises a new state of conflict; man, in his quest for sovereignty, has pushed the tragedy of his political predicament out of his hands by making the Other the condition of possibility of his essential sameness within the state. From Rousseau on, early-modern strategies of peace have no option left save to proceed by domestic analogy when it comes to international transformation;[186] at the same time, the dialectic of conflict can only constitute harmony out of conflict by the logic of sublimation; as Hegel remarked on the possibility of a federative solution to the problem of transcendence: 'even if a number of states join together as a family, this league, in its individuality, must generate opposition and create an enemy'.[187]

Thus, it appears as if the modern promise of transcendence is based upon an ontology whose inherent dialectic continuously pours cold water on the hope of its immanent fulfilment. History, as the unilinear and dialectical succession of conflicting forces, is as much poison as it is antidote; it solves the problem of order within the state, but poses a problem of finality outside it. What can be attained and perfected within the state cannot be attained or perfected within history, unless we posit the sovereign state as the end of history, which brings us back to square one. But what if we, so to speak, put unilinear history out of joint, and regard past and future as contained in one 'present' of endless duration?

Above, we saw how the duality between the concept of human freedom and the concept of natural necessity was opened up in Kant's *First Critique*, and how this conflict was as much a conflict between the faculties of reason and understanding in man, as it was a conflict between forces in the political world. In his *Zum Ewigen Frieden* (1795), the realization of perpetual peace was made dependent on a dialectic between these concepts, but every seemingly successful resolution of this conflict merely transposed it to a higher level, where it was to manifest itself conceptually as well as in the phenomenal world of institutions and practices; antagonism reasserts itself at every level, and is present within philosophy as the rule of the game in the contest between man's cognitive faculties.

On the one hand, political institutions are partly rooted in the realm of nature and are hence subject to the blind mechanical forces reigning unobstructed in the world of phenomena. On the other, political institutions, no matter how embryonic or imperfect, are partly rooted in the moral world, revealing the possibility of moral progress and bearing witness to the development of human reason.[188]

These two contrary views flow from the activity of understanding and reason respectively. From the vantage point of understanding, our past and present will look like a chaotic multitude of historical events which at best form an empirically regular series.[189] From the vantage point of reason, however, our past and present will appear to be a gradual accomplishment and a progressive unfolding of human capacities, in which freedom permits the reasoned transformation of the political and social world according to moral ends.

Now the viewpoint of presentist understanding, though epistemically warranted and possible to support with empirical evidence, gives no moral guidance whatsoever. Rather, it serves to justify the political realist in his self-interested pursuit, and therefore ultimately to perpetuate the very reality it represents as *real*. Hence, when the faculty of understanding is in charge, it is impossible to justify any assumption of actual progress taking place in history. Politics will appear as an activity guided by crude necessity alone, and idealistic hope gives way to realistic despair.

By contrast, the finalist viewpoint of reason, while capable of supplying firm and universal rules for moral action, goes beyond the boundaries of possible experience and must nourish itself on speculative thought. It is thus illegitimate both from an empirical and a critical standpoint: politics appear as unrestricted emancipation or as the unconstrained realization of moral ends without any sobering influences from experience.[190]

Now, if we cut somewhat deeper into Kantian philosophy, and ask how the idea of historical progress and transcendence is possible to sustain and project onto the international realm, we find two solutions, both much neglected by Kant's modern commentators, most of whom have taken the duality between freedom and necessity – between 'idealism' and 'realism' – for granted, which arguably itself is a presentist and realist practice.[191]

Turning to Kant's *Third Critique*, the *Kritik der Urteilskraft* (1790), we find that its main task is to bridge 'the immeasurable gulf between the sensible realm of the concept of nature and the supersensible realm of the concept of freedom'.[192] The *Third Critique* is not concerned with a definitive settlement of the contest between reason and understanding, but with the exploitation of their antagonism, a solution which is also vaguely echoed in *Zum Ewigen Frieden*.[193] The mediating link between the two is provided by judgement:

> In the family of supreme cognitive faculties there is a middle term between the understanding and the reason. This is the *judgement*, of which we have cause for supposing according to analogy that it may contain in itself, if not a special legislation, yet a special principle of its own to be sought according to laws, though merely subjective *a priori*. This principle, even if it have no field of objects as its realm, yet may have somewhere a territory with a certain character for which no other principle can be valid.[194]

That is, while we cannot observe any purpose in history or infer it logically from any higher principles, judgement nevertheless permits us to supply such an idea mentally, in order to bring coherence to a multitude of political events which otherwise would seem random and meaningless. We are epistemically entitled to reconstruct our past and regroup its constituent events into a series *as if* they were indicative of progress in history.[195] Judgement here supplies a higher and disinterested viewpoint from which to contemplate the course of history without uncritical resort to speculative reason. Still, judgement is in a sense weak, since the objective reality of a natural purpose is simply not susceptible of proof through reason; the concept of natural purpose is merely a regulative idea.[196] Hence, its predictive – and creative – power is limited; it makes progress in the past look purposive and certain from the vantage point of the present, but its continuation into the future appears less certain, unless we seek to justify it with the quasi-theological idea of an original understanding (*intellectus archetypus*) as the cause of the world and author of its purposiveness.[197]

The second and more decisive step towards a reconciliation between the concepts of determinism and freedom is taken in *Der Streit der Facultäten* (1798), which explicitly addresses the question of how the notion of a moral purpose in history can be reconciled with its empiricity. This short essay deals with the possibility of historical knowledge from a prophetic vantage point. What we are seeking to know, says Kant, 'is not a history of the past ... but a history of future times'.[198] Such a predictive history must necessarily be *a priori*, and this is possible only if the historian himself produces the events he predicts: the historian must become prophet. Here, as in the *Critique of Judgement*, experience or reason alone is insufficient to warrant progress, but prophesy must nevertheless be based on some event which suggests that man is both *cause* and *author* of his own improvement.[199] If we find such an event, it would be one of those rare moments in history when mechanical forces and moral freedom coincide and reinforce each other, but we cannot hope to identify these rare events as proper causes of progress, only as *historical signs*, themselves indicative of progress. We need only to search for a single event, and

> [t]his inference could then be extended to cover history of former times so as to show that mankind has always been progressing, yet in such a way that the event originally chosen would not in itself be regarded as the cause of progress in the past, but only as a rough indication or *historical sign* (*signum rememorativum, demonstrativum, prognosticon*). It might then serve to prove the existence of a tendency within the human race as a whole, considered not as a series of individuals ... but as a body distributed over the earth in states and national groups.[200]

In the *Contest of the Faculties*, the opposition between reason and understanding is finally dissolved. The promise of peace becomes a prophecy of peace. First, the ontology underlying this opposition is displaced. The historical world does not present itself subdivided into subject and object, universal and particular, but as a kind of writing in the broadest of senses: *signs are substituted for events* as the knowable unit of the history. In a political history of signs, there is no essence, no substratum of forces beneath the surface of signs. Second, it follows that man is reintroduced into history in a different shape, and in a new relationship to time. He no longer stands as a subject in relation to the phenomenal reality of historical events, his creative powers circumscribed by the stratification of his consciousness into will and cognition. Instead, his creative task takes on divine proportions in a world devoid of essence and meaning; he alone is the author of historical signs, and he alone is able to decipher them.

His task becomes as much poetic as it is hermeneutic; if meaning is not intrinsic in history, it has to be created through ceaseless decoding and recoding. Third, time is put out of joint, so to speak. A historical sign collapses past, present and future into one moment of duration and presence, since it simultaneously recalls, shows and anticipates progress; it introduces man as the *efficient cause* in all three temporalities simultaneously. Time is no longer a substratum in which history simply occurs, or the canvas against which progress can be projected or prophesied. Time is no longer an external condition of possibility of

235

history, but something internal to it. It shares the same reality as other historical beings, that of being created by man. In the *Contest of the Faculties*, it seems as if Augustine's *Æternitas* has finally been brought down to earth, but now with man as its creator. Unilinear time is replaced by man-made eternity, into which history is assimilated and ceases to be a supplier of change and a source of the finiteness of the beings subject to it.

What, then, characterizes a historical sign? It is not, says Kant, a mere reversal of power. Instead, a historical sign is best provided by a complex historical event, such as a great change or upheaval. What matters is not the event itself, but the *enthusiasm* it gives rise to on behalf of the spectators. Enthusiasm, as presented in the *Critique of Judgement*, is a modality of the sublime. It is 'the idea of the good conjoined with strong affection',[201] and as such it proves that man has a moral character, since its sublimity presupposes susceptibility to moral ideas.[202]

What Kant does is thus to turn the problem of historical transcendence in international politics into a problem of overcoming time itself. A historical sign, where and whenever it occurs, permits us to infer progress in the 'present'; it bestows coherence upon the specific 'past' which led up to the event in question, and contains a 'future' within this *here and now* of endless duration.[203] Perpetual peace is no longer only perpetual in the sense that the quest for it must be perpetual; it is perpetual in the sense that it is only realizable outside the time of the world.

To return to the question initially posed in this chapter: if the international is intelligible, it is because man is the source of all intelligibility and himself intelligible; he is sufficiently analogous with his own construct. With this last step, the genealogical series of modernity is completed; man is not only the author of his own deeds, concepts and representations, and creator of his own history and self-knowledge; his sovereignty is no longer confined to nature and culture, but also encompasses the source of his finiteness and the limit to his creative powers; having usurped Time, man is not only king, but also God. He is released from the duality of his political condition and the alienation fostered by it; he stands not at the end of history, but at its beginning, always ready to remake it. But if God was killed by the king, and the king was killed by man, who is going to kill man, and thus make sovereignty once more unintelligible; who is next to draw a line in water?

7   Conclusion:
the end of sovereignty?

In this book, I started out by turning a question of being into a question of knowing. Instead of asking what sovereignty *is*, I asked what happens when one tries to answer this question; instead of posing a question which would merely invite yet another political metaphysics, I tried to circumvent the question of being by investigating the relationship between sovereignty and knowledge logically as well as historically, as it has manifested itself in political and philosophical discourse since the Renaissance. In this chapter I will summarize the outcome of this investigation.

The contingency of sovereignty

In chapter 1, I started by saying what a history of sovereignty *would not* look like, and the rest of this book has been an attempt to justify these destructive remarks, both through philosophical argument and through historical narrative. As I hope now stands clear from chapter 2, a history of core political concepts based on a prior conceptual analysis must indeed fail, and this for two reasons. First, since conventional conceptual analysis seeks to isolate a stable relationship between the meaning and reference of a given term, it runs into severe problems with sponge concepts such as sovereignty, since their very centrality is conditioned by their ambiguity, and conversely. Second, there is a tension between our definitional practices and our historical ambitions, such that the very semantic identity established by a definition is either violated by the historical analysis, or makes the historical analysis an empty reflection of the content of the definition.

An alleged remedy comes from the contextualist history of political ideas. However well suited to reconstructing debates on the politically good, contextualist history is much less helpful when it comes to the politically true. As I hope to have made clear in chapter 2, the concept of sovereignty is so firmly linked with the epistemic and ontological foundations of political inquiry, that it hardly can be touched upon without simultaneously evoking questions about these foundations. In chapter 3, I tried to demonstrate that contextualist history – as a brand of hermeneutics – itself contains an unquestioned set of presuppositions that makes it difficult to investigate the historical linkage between sovereignty and knowledge without lapsing into either presentism or finalism.

A possible way to avoid the problems posed by the silent suprahistoricity of contextualist history would be traditional conceptual history, an approach to which this study is greatly indebted in the way it formulates historical research problems. However, as should be obvious to the careful reader of my episodical narrative, single concepts are tied up in a web of relationships to other, temporally and logically simultaneous concepts. Whereas a conceptual history is able to make sense of the actual function of each such concept within a larger system, it does not explicitly deal with their conditions of possibility or their multiple relationships within that larger discourse.

Now the study of such systems or discourses has been the prerogative of a structuralist history of ideas, but with the unwelcome side-effect that these discursive wholes risk becoming closed entities, the transition between which it is hard to account for. As I hope to have conveyed both in chapter 3 and in the historical parts of my argument, things are more complex indeed. Whereas we can identify regularities and correlations between statements within a given period, there is always a limit and a battlefront, moments of corrosion and fights over truth. To paraphrase Veyne's metaphor: we do not inhabit glass bowls, but are surrounded by semi-permeable membranes which separate us from our past and our future.

So much for methodological precepts; what has happened to the concept of sovereignty?

In chapter 2, I first attempted to demonstrate that the concept of sovereignty – however opaque it may appear to a conceptual analysis – constitutes the unthought foundation of two empirical discourses: international political theory and macrosociology. Second, as I continued to argue, the position of the concept of sovereignty within each of these discourses is firmly connected to their scientific aspirations, their very separation being conditioned by a corresponding duality inherent in the modern concept of sovereignty, since each science takes one aspect of this duality as foundation of its inquiry. Third, as I have argued, this duality also makes it difficult to speak of sovereignty as something existing outside knowledge, or as something ontologically independent of the political spheres it constitutes as separate within political knowledge. Finding a logical equivalent within aesthetic discourse, I compared the problem of sovereignty with the problem of the parergonal frame; that which constitutes two classes of phenomena as distinct cannot itself be a member of any of these classes.

To deconstruct a concept is to demonstrate that it is contingent upon the text in which it figures. One way to summarize the findings of chapter 2 is to say that sovereignty should be understood as something contingent upon the entire system of concepts which is constitutive of our political reality as well as of our understanding of it, and that this system in its turn is contingent upon the concept of sovereignty. Sovereignty brings order to political reality by dividing it into two distinct spheres of thought and action that nevertheless imply each other, and opens these up to empirical investigation and ethical deliberation. It is constitutive of the very practice of political questioning, and regulative of the methods employed in the practice of answering.

To say that sovereignty is contingent is to say that it is not necessary or essential, but that its central and ambiguous place in modern political discourse is the outcome of prior accidents. To say that sovereignty is neither necessary nor essential is to say that we have to account for its place in modern political discourse in order to explain how and why the concept took on a necessary and essential character within it. However, because sovereignty is rigorously interlinked with the foundations of modern political knowledge, it cannot easily be disentangled and analysed; because sovereignty is so profoundly involved in the naturalization and reification of political reality, it is a difficult object of political knowledge. Indeed, to the extent that sovereignty constitutes the unthought foundation of political knowledge, it is beyond the scope of that knowledge. Thus, a historical investigation has to account for the formation of this linkage by phrasing the question *how did we get here?*

In order to be able to answer this question, I undertook a methodological detour. Finding textual support in Nietzsche and Foucault, my main conclusion was that if one ventures to write a history of sovereignty and knowledge, this history must be genealogical in the sense of being *effective, episodical* and *exemplary*. We must now turn to the outcome of this investigation.

Changing knowledges

First, and as I said in chapter 1, knowledge exists through differentiation. In order to become a system for the formation of valid statements, knowledge must demarcate itself from what it is not, and must furnish criteria which permit one to distinguish the valid from the invalid. The topic of sovereignty is invariably involved in this process through the relations of supplementation, articulation and duplication which it entertains with knowledge in its formative stages.

In the late Middle Ages and the Renaissance, there was no unified and autonomous discourse on sovereignty. Instead, we found an array of conceptual antecedents or paradigms of rulership, which were supplemented, sustained, legitimized and duplicated in an ever-proliferating chain of analogies and allegories running throughout the Christian universe and binding it together. Later, these conceptual antecedents were gradually soaked up and articulated within a general theory of the state. This general theory of the state, formed under the twin pressures of time and nominalism, was systematically sustained by resemblance and validated by exempla. What was outside the scope of the general theory of the state was also outside political knowledge; what was outside the scope of authority was also outside the scope of understanding. Therefore, in the Renaissance, the same set of presuppositions which made the conditions of rulership and statehood knowable also set a limit to political understanding. In their efforts to cope with the forces of particularism and contingency, Machiavelli, More and Vitoria all faced this limit, each of them responding differently but quite unsuccessfully to it.

In chapter 5, we saw how this mode of knowing gradually was brushed aside by the beginning of the Classical Age, and replaced with a political knowledge that reflected the concerns of the scientific revolution. Resemblance and exempla became associated with superstition, rhetoric and war, yet they remained active at the level of pre-understanding. But at the core of political knowledge we were able to witness the emergence of an autonomous discourse on sovereignty, firmly centred on its indivisibility and the particularity of states, and systematically supplemented by and articulated within a knowledge governed by the *mathesis* and the analysis of representations. At the apex of this construct, we found the sovereign, the condition of representation as well as of political order. Within this knowledge, what could not be represented or tabulated did not exist; we found an analysis of interest, analytically differentiating between particular states, and comparing them according to a determined set of variables. This analysis of interest was validated through relations of duplication between what is represented and what represents.

With the coming of modernity, however, this arrangement is profoundly reorganized. As we saw in chapter 6, the political and social worlds acquire a new dimension. Man enters knowledge as its sovereign source, as an active subject vested with constructive powers. The political and social worlds take on depth and become thoroughly historicized; political and social beings become surface manifestations of hidden forces and long chronologies, and are investigated with respect to their historicity and dialectical interrelationships. Sovereignty, retaining its logic of indivisibility, becomes an organizing principle of political reality as well as of our understanding of it, a principle that divides political reality into ethically opposed domains that nevertheless implicate each other. The state becomes conceptualized as a whole, capable of assimilating political and social differences into one form, held together by an array of analogical relationships which mediates between the universal and the particular, and between subject and object. What now is outside knowledge is opinion and ideology; what is inside knowledge is brought under the sway of epistemic foundations.

Changing realities

My second point was that knowledge, understood as differentiation, implies decisions on ontology. What exists and what does not exist must be decided within a knowledge in order for it to be able to discriminate between true and false propositions.

In the late Middle Ages, we saw how the beings once so real to Christian myth are successively drained of reality, and replaced by beings wholly or partly anomalous to it. Politically, this meant that the mimetic paradigm of rulership, in which the legitimacy of a ruler derives from his resemblance to Christ or God, gradually gives way to law-centred or polity-centred versions of rulership. At the same time, however, other theological concepts and insignia are invested with new meaning as continuous and universal beings, and come to signify permanent rulership and statehood as a result of mutations in the concept of time. By the same token, the emergent political nominalism permits the body politic to enjoy an independent existence within the framework of universalist assumptions. Through its particular juxta-position of universalism and particularism, the general theory of the state gives reality to the state as a container of mythical power and virtue, but only insofar as it remains inscribed within and articulated against a universalist backdrop, coexistent with Christianity as a whole. What exists is the state as a general mode of political being. Machiavelli's troubled attempt at innovation, More's utopian revival of Christian ethics and Vitoria's inability to disentangle the state from divine law all bear witness to this. In the Renaissance, particularity resides in the practices of political reflection and deliberation that are made possible by resemblance and exempla.

In the Classical Age, the universalist backdrop remains a living reality to natural law and to Utopian literature, but the emergence of an analysis of particular states and their interests for a moment gives nominalism the upper hand in the discourse on actual states. Thus, what primarily exists in the Classical Age are individual states as containers of calculable resources and predictable interests, their exist-ence being conditioned by the presence of sovereigns within them. If there is an aspect of universality, this aspect is to be found in the shape of a tabulated order, a taxonomy of states whose interrelationships are governed by interest and expressed in the concrete and knowledgea-ble practices of classical diplomacy, practices which themselves are conditioned by the *mathesis* and language as a matrix of represen-tation. In the Classical Age, what is universal are the rules of the new science.

With modernity, this two-dimensional simplicity vanishes. Modern political knowledge is a knowledge of organized and historicized political beings; man, occupying the dual position of active subject and knowable object simultaneously, replaces the king as the source of knowledge as well as the locus of sovereignty. In the process, the state is constituted as whole in and for itself, assimilating all prior social and cultural differences between communities, by, so to speak, nationaliz-ing them. The state becomes doubly abstract, disconnected from ruler as well as from ruled, yet dependent on mediation or the equivalence between them. Thus, the modern sovereign state is composed by an array of self-subsistent analogical relationships, drawing together and mediating between the internal aspects of particularity and universality, between subjectivity and objectivity. But, being constituted out of conflict between the forces of history, the sovereign state can only transpose these conflicts to a new sphere of political reality: the international system.

Changing estrangements

If knowledge differentiates itself from what it is not, and separates the true from the false and the present from the absent, it also differentiates between ethical identities: who is Same, and who is Other?

From the late Middle Ages up to the Renaissance, we are able to discern how this ethical differentiation gradually becomes more complex, as it evolves out of man's estrangement from the Christian God. What is Other to the Middle Ages is the infidel and reminiscences of the pagan culture which went before it; what gradually becomes Other to the Renaissance are the beings and forces, that are released through the recovery of pagan antiquity, that are discovered afresh overseas, or that emerge from within political knowledge itself, such as particularity and contingency, for example. These beings and forces – the American Indian, the elusive paths of Fortuna, or, the process of political fragmentation taking place from within – are not Other to Christianity by virtue of being its enemies, but by virtue of being radically foreign to it, and therefore difficult to comprehend.

During the classical period, the political world suddenly seems to contract. What is Other to the classical writers is above all to be found within the prehistory of civil and religious wars which it appropriates itself and reinscribes as a fictitious state of nature into the justificatory accounts of sovereignty. The paradigmatic form of Otherness is no longer what is strange or beyond comprehension, but what is ever present both as an enemy to, and therefore also as a justification of, the absolutist state, such as civil war and internal discord. Secondarily, however, this threat perception is spatialized and projected outwards as a means of securing the identity of the Same. Thus, between states we can expect mutual estrangement as well as mutual recognition; what is Other to every particular state is a specific state or a variable pattern of alliances between other particular states, which, according to the distribution of wealth and power between them, determine the relative level of enmity and friendship within every specific constellation of states.

With modernity, ethical differentiation takes on a new complexity. Above all, what now is Other to the state is not primarily contained in its own prehistory, but temporally simultaneous yet spatially distinct from it. If the modern state emerges out of a dialectic of historical forces, it also transposes otherness to a place not only outside itself, but to a sphere ontologically over and above itself. First, in the dimension of enmity, the Other of the modern state is to be found in the international system, and in the violent practices it engenders or necessitates. The international system is partly obstructive of efficient reform and transcendence, yet simultaneously it is the condition of possibility of the sameness of the modern state, and the animating force behind its utopian promise and its efforts at transcendence. Second, in the dimension of strangeness, the international system is from its emergence estranged from the external arena of other cultures; modern sovereignty is prophesied to expand and turn all strangers into inherent adversaries within a world-system. Thus, ethically, modern sovereignty is profoundly paradoxical, since it contains both a prophecy of interstate anarchy and a promise of cosmopolitan redemption in which the international itself vanishes in favour of global domestication.

Changing histories

If knowledge implies decisions on ontology and ethical identity, it also furnishes beings with a past, a present and a future, safeguarding them from the corrosive influence of time and contingency.

In the Middle Ages, time signifies the transitoriness of earthly existence. If there is history, this history is laid down in a providential plan, beginning with the creation of the world and ending with Judgement Day. First, Augustinian time is psychological or subjective time, signifying man's separation from divine eternity and the dissimilitude and discord that characterizes his earthly condition. Through the troubled reception and gradual acceptance of Aristotelian and cosmological time, the possibility of historical change is opened up to theological and legal discourse; change becomes modelled on the patterns of cyclical movements displayed by natural phenomena. Change is possible, but brings nothing new under the sun; constitutions dissolve and are replaced, but the pattern of their succession cannot itself be transgressed. Second, and as a consequence, an alien past as well as present identity can be appropriated and textualized by means of exempla. It becomes possible to learn from the past, and use this learning as a guide to future action as if history repeated itself indefinitely; the state and the conditions of ruling are released from the singularity of Christian myth, and are understood as continuous with other political beings – documentary or legendary – on the basis of their formal resemblance with them. Third, within the general theory of the state, all states share a common history precisely by virtue of its being general, and their common history is plural by virtue of the multiplicity of episodes and examples laid down in one vast text of the world.

In the Classical Age, histories constructed on the basis of exempla and resemblance are replaced by histories structured by the demands of the *mathesis*, which is superimposed upon exemplary historiography. First, time retains its basic cyclical character, and if there is linearity, it is in the form of dynastic succession. Second, the past of a particular state is reconstructed on the basis of principles which also provide this particular state with a present identity independent of its place within a more general framework; these principles are themselves immutable and without history, and thus treated as universally and transhistorically valid. Third, within the analysis of interest, each particular state has a history of its own resulting from all its prior interactions with other particular states, and each of these histories serves as a clue to its present identity as well as to its future fate within the table of states; its position within the table can change, but the table itself cannot.

With modernity, history is no longer multiple and external to words and things. It becomes integral to the very being of things, and simultaneously singular; histories *about* beings are replaced by History as a mode of being. First, historical time is no longer cyclical, but opened up to the future, understood as revolutionary progress. Through history, man, language, nation and state take on identity and become intelligible as the outcome of conflicts between historical forces. Second, history constitutes the fertile ground from which the social sciences can emerge, each devoted to a specific empirical domain singled out by history. Third, through modern history, the sovereign state and the international system are constituted to implicate each other as opposed domains of political reality, each knowable from one of the two vantage points that correspond to the dual face of the concept of sovereignty. Through modern history, both the state and the international are constituted together with their past; expansion and transcendence are predicated about their future.

The end of sovereignty

How are we to interpret these developments? Certainly, they do not lend themselves to simple interpretations in terms of progress or decay, since the metahistorical plots of progress and decay themselves are part of this story. Interpreted from the vantage point of nostalgia, the above genealogy would indicate a fall from the primordial beauty of Christian unity, whereas interpreted from the vantage point of a modernized historical process, it would look like a progressive series, in which man becomes the master of his own political destiny by emancipating himself from dogma and superstition.

Interpreted as transformations in the conditions by which knowledge constitutes itself through differentiation, the genealogical series appears as a more or less random succession of discursive and epistemic events, grouped together into incommensurable periods or systems for the formation of statements, that succeed each other as the result of rhetorical battles over truth and being. There would be no hidden eschatology or suprahistorical regularity in this random succession; no meaning, just pure contingency. The question *how did we get here*, in which by *here* is meant our specific late-modern fusion of sovereignty and knowledge within the regional context of empirical political science, would then be given a most prosaic answer, like the questions of how we came to wear the kind of clothes we are wearing, or how we came to eat the kind of food we are eating.

Thus interpreted, the simultaneous rise of the modern sovereign state and the international system within political knowledge would appear quite accidental, as a result of more general and fairly recent mutations in knowledge. There would be no hidden meaning behind their emergence on the surface of empirical objects more than the meaning imputed to these constructs by the specific past and future attached to them when they were invented.

That is, we got stuck with our parergonal notion of sovereignty and the dualities it entails within our political understanding, not as the result of any immanent logical necessity in history or in the development of political thought, but as the result of the cumulate consequences of random mutations in the conditions of knowledge. The modern notion of sovereignty does not result from the fulfilment of Enlightenment promises of revolution and emancipation, nor from the failure to realize these promises. Nor is the modern concept of sovereignty singularly reducible to the organic thought of historicism;

rather, it emerges as the unintended consequence of the clash between the core concepts and forces of modern knowledge, between the *a priori* and the *a posteriori*, between the empirical and the transcendental, between subject and object, between the universal and the particular, between philosophy and history, between finalist dialectic and presentist historiography, between Man and his Other.

When sovereignty and knowledge are interpreted in isolation within the regional discourses and over the span of time investigated in this book, their episodic configuration looks highly discontinuous. But interpreted together, and inscribed within a genealogical series in which the conditions of knowing are productively interlinked with discourses on rulership and sovereignty, their discontinuity is counterbalanced by a certain thematic continuity. Concepts may vary as to their meaning and function, yet their interrelations – for all their indeterminateness and openness – seem to remain intact in their most abstract form. Thus interpreted, the periods exemplified in this study appear as sedimentary in our political understanding, together constituting something – not despite, but rather by virtue of its immanent plurality – which would merit the label of tradition.

Within this tradition, sovereignty does not merely mean different things during different periods, function differently within different epistemic arrangements, or that it *is* something altogether different from time to time; rather, the topic of sovereignty – the concept of sovereignty as opened to definitional change across time – is so rigorously intertwined with the conditions of knowing, that we could inductively expect a change in the former to go hand in hand with a change in the latter even in the future, if indeed there is one.

If this is true, and even if we take due caution against overinterpreting, we could perhaps expect the imminent dissolution of our topic. If the foundations of modern knowledge today appear as shaky as political reality itself, and are questioned from many points simultaneously, we should not expect sovereignty to remain unaffected in its ability to organize modern political reality into the two distinct spheres of the domestic and the international. By the same token, we should not expect modern political science to be able to deal consistently with a political reality in which the parergonal divide between the domestic and the international spheres is increasingly blurred. I say 'deal consistently'; it is not that political science becomes null and void in the absence of a *parergon* which permits it to classify its phenomena according to what is inside and what is outside the state, but the identification of objects of investigation is bound to be less self-evident and more laborious than before, at the same time as broad syntheses within the field are called for.[1] Precisely this loss of parergonality is the destructive upshot of critical international political theory today; the insight that modern knowledge has man as its privileged foundation, and that this foundation is as contingent as the modern subject itself makes the fact of sovereignty less self-evident and all the more fragile, but it does not do what earlier versions of epistemic and ontological criticism did; it does not tell us where to go from here, neither as political scientists nor as citizens. It proclaims modernity an absurd dream from which we are about to escape, but it does not tell us what to do with those who never started to dream of progress and transcendence, but who have nourished themselves on the exported positivity of revolution and war, and now are knocking on the door of what to some appears as the post-historical world. Critical theory rephrases universalist questions and reclaims epistemic sovereignty, but cannot answer the questions of where to locate it, who *we* are, who is Other to *us*, and where *we* are heading.

So where do we go from here? I began this book by stating that knowledge is political, and that politics is based on knowledge. I should end it by observing that if epistemic change is essentially political, it also involves the political responsibility of deciding upon sovereignty, a decision which we for the moment seem unfit to make.

Notes

1 Introduction: sovereignty and fire

1 Zygmunt Baumann, 'Modernity and Ambivalence', *Theory, Culture & Society*, vol. 7, 1990 (SAGE Publications, London), *passim*.

2 Gaston Bachelard, *The Psychoanalysis of Fire* (1938) trans. by A.C.M. Ross (London, 1987: Quartet Books).

3 A similar procedure lies at the heart of *Begriffsgeschichte*, see Reinhart Koselleck, 'Begriffsgeschichte and Social History', in *Futures Past: On the Semantics of Historical Time*, (Boston, 1985: MIT Press) pp. 73–91.

4 Cf. John Keane, 'More Theses on the Philosophy of History', in J. Tully, ed: *Meaning and Context: Quentin Skinner and His Critics* (Cambridge, 1988: Polity Press) p. 214.

5 Cf. Francis H. Hinsley, *Sovereignty* (Cambridge, 1986: Cambridge University Press), Robert A. Klein, *Sovereign Equality Among States: The History of an Idea* (Toronto, 1974: University of Toronto Press). Older full-scale studies include Charles E. Merriam, *History of the Theory of Sovereignty Since Rousseau* (New York, 1900: Columbia University Press).

6 Paul Ricoeur, *Time and Narrative*, vol. 3, (Chicago, 1988: University of Chicago Press), pp. 241ff.

7 Cf. Carl Schmitt, *Political Theology: Four Chapters on the Concept of Sovereignty*, (Boston, 1985: MIT Press) p. 2.

8 Aristotle, *Rhetorics*, (London, 1947: Heinemann), book II, xxv. 8.

9 Cf. Immanuel Kant, *Critique of Judgment*, Bernard (New York, 1951: Hafner), p. 16 where he develops the idea of reflective judgement.

2 The problem: deconstructing sovereignty

1 For the centrality of the concept of sovereignty in modern political science, see for example: Anthony Giddens, *The Constitution of Society* (Cambridge, 1984: Polity Press), p. xxxiii; A. Giddens, *The Nation-State and Violence* (Cambridge, 1985: Polity Press), pp. 198f, 281f; R.B.J. Walker, 'Sovereignty, Identity, Community: Reflections on the Horizons of Contemporary

Political Practice' in R.B.J. Walker & S. Mendlovitz, eds., *Contending Sovereignties: Redefining Political Community* (Boulder, 1990: Lynne) pp. 159–60; Robert H. Jackson, 'Quasi-States, Dual regimes, and Neoclassical Theory: International Jurisprudence and the Third World', *International Organization*, vol. 41, Fall 1987, p. 519; R.B.J. Walker, *Inside/Outside: International Relations as Political Theory* (Cambridge, 1993: Cambridge University Press), esp. pp. 1–25.

2 See for example W.J. Stankiewicz, 'In Defence of Sovereignty: A Critique and an Interpretation', in W.J. Stankiewicz, ed., *In Defence of Sovereignty* (London, 1969: Oxford University Press), pp. 1–38; Christopher Brewin, 'Sovereignty', in James Mayall, ed., *The Community of States: A Study in International Political Theory* (London, 1982: Allen & Unwin), Nicolas Greenwood Onuf, 'Sovereignty: Outline of a Conceptual History', *Alternatives*, vol. 16, 1990; James Rosenau, 'Sovereignty in a Turbulent World', paper presented at the conference on sovereignty and collective intervention, Hanover, N.H., May 1992, pp. 1–4.

3 E.H. Carr, *The Twenty Years Crisis 1919–1939* (London, 1978: Macmillan) pp. 230–1.

4 Stanley I. Benn, 'The Uses of Sovereignty', *Political Studies*, vol. 3, 1955, no. 2.

5 F. Nietzsche, '"Guilt", "Bad Conscience" and the Like' in *On the Genealogy of Morals*, (New York, 1969: Vintage), p. 80.

6 Hinsley, attempting a history of sovereignty, nevertheless starts out from a definition of it, see F.H. Hinsley, *Sovereignty* (Cambridge, 1986: Cambridge University Press) p. 26.

7 Nietzsche, '"Guilt", "Bad Conscience" and the Like', p. 80.

8 For a critical analysis, see Richard Rorty, *Philosophy and the Mirror of Nature* (Oxford, 1980: Basil Blackwell), chs. 3–4.

9 Hans Kelsen, 'Sovereignty and International Law', in Stankiewicz, ed., *In Defence of Sovereignty*, p. 119.

10 See for example the analysis by Carl Schmitt, *Political Theology: Four Chapters on the Concept of Sovereignty* (Boston, 1985. MIT Press), ch. 1 in which this problematic distinction between a legal and a sociological understanding of sovereignty is discussed.

11 See W.B. Gallie, 'Essentially Contested Concepts', in Max Black, ed., *The Importance of Language* (Englewood Cliffs, NJ, 1962: Prentice-Hall); William O. Connolly, *The Terms of Political Discourse* (Oxford, 1983: Martin Robertson).

12 Alan James, *Sovereign Statehood* (London, 1986: Allen & Unwin) p. 83.

13 Hinsley, *Sovereignty* p. 158.

14 Giddens, *The Nation-State and Violence*, p. 281.

15 John Gerard Ruggie, 'Continuity and Transformation in the World Polity', in Robert O. Keohane, ed., *Neorealism and its Critics* (New York, 1986: Columbia University Press), p. 144.

16 Friedrich Kratochwil, 'Of Systems, Boundaries, and Territoriality: An Inquiry into the Formation of the State System', *World Politics*, vol. 39, 1986, no. 1.

17 Alexander Wendt, 'The Agent-Structure Problem in International Relations Theory', *International Organization*, vol. 41, 1987, no. 3, p. 357; David Dessler,

'What's at Stake in the Agent-Structure Debate?', *International Organization*, vol. 43, 1989, no. 3, p. 469.

18 Richard K. Ashley, 'The Geopolitics of Geopolitical Space: Toward a Critical Social Theory of International Politics', *Alternatives*, vol. 12, 1987, pp. 412–15; Cynthia Weber, 'Reconsidering Statehood: Examining the Sovereignty/ Intervention Boundary', *Review of International Studies*, vol. 18, 1992.

19 Richard K. Ashley, & R.B.J. Walker, 'Speaking the Language of Exile: Dissident Thought in International Relations', *International Studies Quarterly*, vol. 34, 1990, p. 267.

20 Cf. Richard Ashley, 'Untying the Sovereign State: A Double Reading of the Anarchy Problématique', *Millennium*, vol. 17, 1988, no. 2.

21 It has been disputed whether we are entitled to talk of exemplars in political science. To Thomas Kuhn (*The Structure of Scientific Revolutions*, Chicago, 1962: Chicago University Press, pp. 10ff), the emergence of exemplars is a sign of scientific maturity within a field of knowledge, a condition which to some is lacking in political science. Be that as it may: an exemplar is a textbook – elementary or advanced – which both reflects and reproduces scientific consensus within a field, by (a) defining its ontology; (b) outlining criteria of validity and methods for verification; and (c) identifying research problems and techniques for their solution. In short, exemplars define what is problematic and what is unproblematic within a field of knowledge. See also Michel Foucault, *Archaeology of Knowledge* (New York, 1972: Pantheon) pp. 178ff.

22 Jacques Derrida, *Of Grammatology*, (Baltimore & London, 1974: Johns Hopkins) pp. 24–33; Jacques Derrida, 'Structure, Sign and Play in the Discourse of the Human Sciences' in *Writing and Difference* (London, 1978: Routledge) pp. 278ff; Jacques Derrida, *Positions* (Chicago, 1981: University of Chicago Press) p. 41. See also Jonathan Culler, *On Deconstruction: Theory and Criticism after Structuralism* (London, 1983: Routledge), pp. 85ff.

23 Derrida, *Positions*, p. 6.

24 Jacques Derrida, 'Signature, Event, Context' in *Margins of Philosophy* (Brighton, 1982: Harvester) p. 328.

25 Culler, *On Deconstruction*, p. 150.

26 When I speak of international political theory or the discourse on international politics, I speak of what I take to be its core assumptions, the unity behind the lack of overall theoretical coherence in the field. My sample of texts has been confined to the post-war period, a period crucial to the scientification and autonomy of international relations. Throughout, I have been guided by an eye to their sociological impact within the field, relying on textbook versions of intradisciplinary development (Hedley Bull, 'The Theory of International Politics 1919–1969'; W. Olson, 'The Growth of a Discipline', both in B. Porter, ed., *The Aberystwyth Papers* (London, 1972: Oxford University Press); W. Olson, & N. Onuf, 'The Growth of a Discipline: Reviewed', in S. Smith, ed., *International Relations: British and American Perspectives* (Oxford, 1985: Basil Blackwell)) as well as attempts to explain the production of knowledge within the field, as J. Vasquez, *The Power of*

Power Politics (London, 1983: Frances Pinter). From a genealogical perspective, most of these 'histories' appear as complacent hagiography: but this is precisely to the point, since what matters here is what the discipline thinks of itself.

Much can be said about the representativeness of the texts chosen. They are not intended to be representative of the entire field of knowledge, but of 'the big ones', and thus of the changing consensus within the field. Not surprisingly, the sociological basis of choice tends to favour 'political realists'. I have consistently avoided this label, since I partly agree with Kjell Goldmann, 'The Concept of Realism as a Source of Confusion', *Cooperation and Conflict*, vol. 23, 1988. However, the fact that traditions cannot be tested should not exclude the concept from historical analysis: as I argue in chapter 6 below, the birth of international relations is epistemically inseparable from what we loosely call 'realism'.

When it comes to texts on macrosociology, sampling skates on thin ice but is not altogether arbitrary. First, my concern has been with texts that are explicitly concerned with state formation in general, leaving out empirical studies of particular states. Second, I have focused on the conflict tradition in macrosociology, which seems to be dominant: the theoretical influence of Marx, Weber and Hintze is still pervasive. Thus, the 'cooperative' tradition has been neglected in my choice of examples, partly due to its small influence, partly because it does not matter logically to my deconstructive argument whether the state is seen as the result of human conflict or human cooperation, since in either case an 'outside' must be invoked, albeit with different rules of transformation. For an example of 'cooperative' theories of the state, see E.R. Service, *Origins of State and Civilization* (New York, 1975: Norton).

27 Derrida, *Of Grammatology*, p. 158.
28 B. Andrews, 'Social Rules and the State as a Political Actor', *World Politics*, vol. 27, 1975, no. 4; M. Wright, 'Central but Ambiguous: States and International Theory', *Review of International Studies*, vol. 10, 1984; Fred Halliday, 'State and Society in International Relations: A Second Agenda', in H.C. Dyer, & L. Mangasarian, eds., *The Study of International Relations* (London, 1989: Macmillan).
29 Raymond Aron, *Peace and War: A Theory of International Relations* (London, 1966: Weidenfeld & Nicolson), p. 8.
30 Aron, *Peace and War*, p. 51.
31 See for example Robert O. Keohane, & Joseph. S. Nye, *Power and Interdependence: World Politics in Transition* (Boston & Toronto, 1977: Little, Brown).
32 This view is also held by some historians and sociologists, see for example J. R. Strayer, *On the Medieval Origins of the Modern State* (Princeton, 1970: Princeton University Press), p. 108; Gianfranco Poggi, *The Development of the Modern State: A Sociological Introduction* (London, 1978: Hutchinson).
33 Martin Wight, *Power Politics*, ed. H. Bull & C. Holbraad (Leicester, 1978: Leicester University Press), p. 25.

34 Hans Morgenthau, *Politics Among Nations* (New York, 1985: Knopf) pp. 328–9.
35 Aron, *Peace and War*, p. 738.
36 Hedley Bull, *The Anarchical Society: A Study of Order in World Politics* (London, 1977: Macmillan), p. 8.
37 Kenneth N. Waltz, 'Reductionist and Systemic Theories' in Keohane, *Neorealism and Its Critics*, p. 53.
38 Waltz, 'Political Structures', p. 83, in Keohane, *Neorealism*.
39 Ibid., p. 90.
40 Ibid., p. 87.
41 Kenneth N. Waltz, *Man, the State, and War: A Theoretical Analysis* (New York, 1959: University of Columbia Press), pp. 227–8.
42 Aron, *Peace and War*, p. 755.
43 Stanley Hoffmann, *The State of War: Essays on the Theory and Practice of International Relations* (New York, 1965: Praeger), p. 13.
44 Aron, *War and Peace*, p. 6.
45 Morgenthau, *Politics Among Nations*, p. 38.
46 John Herz, *Political Realism and Political Idealism: A Study in Theories and Realities* (Chicago, 1951: University of Chicago Press), pp. 2–16; Waltz, *Man, the State, and War*, p. 238.
47 Waltz, 'Anarchic Orders and Balances of Power', p. 110.
48 Morgenthau, *Politics Among Nations*, p. 335.
49 Ibid., p. 342.
50 Ibid.
51 Cf. Alfons Söllner, 'German Conservatism in America: Morgenthau's Political Realism', Telos, no. 72, 1987.
52 Morgenthau, *Politics Among Nations*, p. 344.
53 Waltz, *Man, the State, and War*, p. 73.
54 Ibid., p. 178.
55 Ibid.
56 Aron, *Peace and War*, p. 751.
57 Ibid., p. 750.
58 Bull, *The Anarchical Society*, p. 35.
59 Waltz, 'Political Structures', p. 73; Waltz, 'Anarchic Orders and Balances of Power', pp. 111, 130 n2.
60 Cf. K.H.F. Dyson, *The State Tradition in Western Europe* (Oxford, 1980: Martin Robertson), pp. 137f; Andrew Vincent, *Theories of the State* (Oxford, 1987: Basil Blackwell), pp. 47ff, 181ff.
61 Bull, *The Anarchical Society*, p. 8.
62 Aron, *Peace and War*, p. 395.
63 John Herz, *International Relations in the Atomic Age* (New York, 1959) p. 58.
64 Morgenthau, *Politics Among Nations*, p. 355; Herz, *International Relations in the Atomic Age*, p. 40.
65 Waltz, 'Political Structures', p. 90; Waltz, 'Anarchic Orders and Balances of Power', p. 100; James, *Sovereign Statehood*, pp. 171ff, 196ff.
66 Aron, *Peace and War*, pp. 182ff.
67 Wight, *Power Politics*, p. 25.

68 Morgenthau, *Politics Among Nations*, p. 345.
69 Waltz, *Man, the State, and War*, p. 177.
70 Aron, *Peace and War*, p. 299.
71 Ibid., p. 295.
72 Waltz, 'Political Structures', pp. 91ff.
73 Waltz, 'Anarchic Orders and Balances of Power', pp. 112–15.
74 Ibid., pp. 110–11.
75 Robert Cox, 'Social Forces, States, and World Orders' in Keohane, *Neorealism and Its Critics*, pp. 219ff; Ruggie, 'Continuity and Transformation', p. 142; Barry Buzan, 'Rethinking System and Structure', in B. Buzan, C. Jones, & R. Little, *The Logic of Anarchy: From Neorealism to Structural Realism* (New York, 1993: Columbia University Press), pp. 38–43; Morgenthau, *Politics Among Nations*, p. 5.
76 Morgenthau, *Politics Among Nations*, p. 5.
77 Ibid., p. 10.
78 Cf. Randall Collins, *Sociology Since Mid-Century: Essays in Theory Cumulation* (New York, 1981: Academic Press), p. 4; Theda Skocpol, 'Bringing the State Back In: Strategies of Analysis in Current Research' in P. Evans, et al., *Bringing the State Back In* (Cambridge, 1985), pp. 3ff; see also, M. Carnoy, *The State and Political Theory* (Princeton, 1984: Princeton University Press).
79 Cf. Randall Collins, *Three Sociological Traditions* (New York, 1980: Oxford University Press).
80 Friedrich Engels, *The Origin of the Family, Private Property, and the State* (London, 1972: Lawrence and Wishart) p. 229.
81 Max Weber, *Economy and Society: An Outline of Interpretive Sociology*, ed. G. Roth & C. Wittich (New York, 1968: Bedminster Press), vol. 2, pp. 904–5.
82 Weber, *Economy and Society*, vol. 2, pp. 901–2.
83 Ibid., p. 905.
84 Norbert Elias, *Power and Civility: The Civilizing Process*, vol. 2 (New York, 1982: Pantheon), p. 99.
85 Otto Hintze, 'The State in Historical Perspective', in R. Bendix, ed., *State and Society* (Berkeley, 1968: University of California Press), p. 156.
86 Charles Tilly, 'Reflections on the History of European State-Making' in C. Tilly, ed., *The Formation of National States in Western Europe* (Princeton, 1975: Princeton University Press), p. 28.
87 Collins, *Sociology since Mid-Century*, p. 4.
88 Skocpol, 'Bringing the State Back In', p. 8.
89 Charles Tilly, 'Western State-Making and Theories of Political Transformation' in Tilly, *The Formation of National States*, p. 635.
90 Elias, *Power and Civility*, passim.
91 See for example Theda Skocpol, *States and Social Revolutions: A Comparative Analysis of France, Russia, and China* (Cambridge, 1979: Cambridge University Press); Immanuel Wallerstein, 'The Rise and the Future Demise of the World Capitalist System: Concepts for Comparative Analysis', *Comparative Studies in Society and History*, vol. 16, 1974.

92 Tilly, 'Reflections', p. 27; Collins, *Sociology Since Mid-Century*, p. 71; H.J.M. Claessen, & P. Skalnik, 'The Early State: Theories and Hypotheses' in H.J.M. Claessen & P. Skalnik, eds., *The Early State* (The Hague, 1978: Mouton), p. 17.

93 Tilly, 'Reflections', p. 27; Collins, *Sociology Since Mid-Century*, p. 71; Claessen, & Skalnik, 'The Early State', p. 17.

94 Claessen & Skalnik, 'The Early State', p. 18.

95 Tilly, 'Reflections', p. 19.

96 See for example Perry Anderson, *Lineages of the Absolutist State* (London, 1974: New Left Books), *passim*; Perry Anderson, *Passages from Antiquity to Feudalism* (London, 1974: New Left Books), *passim*.

97 Elias, *Power and Civility*, p. 95.

98 Tilly, 'Reflections', p. 78; Poggi, *The Development of the Modern State*, p. 93; R. Cohen, 'State Origins: A Reappraisal' in Claessen & Skalnik, *The Early State*, pp. 60–7; Collins, *Sociology Since Mid-Century*, p. 77; Cordelia Navari, 'The Origins of the Nation-State' in L. Tivey, ed., *The Nation-State: The Formation of Modern Politics* (Oxford, 1981: Martin Robertson), pp. 31ff.

99 Wendt, 'The Agent-Structure Problem'; Dessler, 'What's at Stake'; A. Wendt, & R. Duvall, 'Institutions and International Order' in C.O. Czempiel & J.N. Rosenau, eds., *Global Changes and Theoretical Challenges* (Lexington, 1989: Lexington Books).

100 Wendt, 'The Agent-Structure Problem', pp. 355ff.

101 Ibid.; Dessler, 'What's at Stake'; A. Wendt, & R. Duvall, 'Institutions and International Order', in C.O. Czempiel & J.N. Rosenau, eds., *Global Changes and Theoretical Challenges* (Lexington, 1989: Lexington Books); cf. also Giddens, *The Constitution of Society*; Roy Bhaskar, *Scientific Realism and Human Emancipation* (London, 1986: Verso).

102 Giddens, *The Nation-State and Violence*, p. 263.

103 Ibid., pp. 263–4.

104 Ibid., p. 289.

105 Ibid., p. 170.

106 Ibid., pp. 100–3.

107 Ibid., pp. 281–2.

108 Cf. Kjell Goldmann, 'The Line in Water: Domestic and International Politics: A Discussion Paper', *Cooperation and Conflict*, vol. 24, 1989.

109 Aron, *Peace and War*, p. 579.

110 Martin Wight, 'Why is there no International Theory?' in M. Wight & H. Butterfield, eds., *Diplomatic Investigations* (London, 1966: Allen & Unwin).

111 Immanuel Kant, *The Critique of Judgment*, (New York, 1951: Hafner) p. 61.

112 Cf. Jacques Derrida, *La vérité en peinture* (Paris, 1978: Flammarion) p. 93.

113 Ibid., p. 74.

114 Ibid., p. 71.

115 This also has been attempted, albeit from a different perspective, by R.B.J. Walker, *Inside/Outside*, pp. 1–25.

3 Beyond subject and structure: towards a genealogy of sovereignty

1 I owe this example to Richard Rorty, *Essays on Heidegger and Others*, Philosophical Papers vol. 2 (Cambridge, 1991: Cambridge University Press) p. 38.

2 F. Nietzsche, 'On the Uses and Disadvantages of History for Life', *Untimely Meditations* (Cambridge, 1983: Cambridge University Press).

3 For an interesting study in historiography, see H. White, *Metahistory: The Historical Imagination in Nineteenth-Century Europe* (London & Baltimore, 1973: Johns Hopkins).

4 Cf. J. Dunn, 'The Identity of the History of Ideas' in P. Laslett, ed., *Philosophy, Politics and Society* (Oxford, 1962: Basil Blackwell).

5 Cf. J.G.A. Pocock, 'The Concept of a Language and the Métier d'Historien: Some Considerations on Practice', Anthony Pagden, ed., *The Languages of Political Theory in Early Modern Europe* (Cambridge, 1987: Cambridge University Press).

6 Cf. Q. Skinner, 'Meaning and Understanding in the History of Ideas' in James Tully, ed., *Meaning and Context: Quentin Skinner and His Critics* (Cambridge,1988: Polity Press). For a sympathetic criticism of Skinner and Pocock, see P.L. Janssen, 'Political Thought as Traditionary Action: A Critical Response to Skinner and Pocock, *History and Theory*, vol. 24, 1985, no. 1.

7 See for example D. Bloor, *Knowledge and Social Imagery* (London, 1973: Routledge); B. Barnes, *Scientific Knowledge and Sociological Theory* (London, 1974: Routledge); *Interests and the Growth of Knowledge* (London, 1977: Routledge); P.T. Manicas, & A. Rosenberg, 'Naturalism, Epistemological Individualism and "The Strong Programme" in The Sociology of Knowledge' and 'The Sociology of Scientific Knowledge: Can We Ever Get It Straight?', both in *Journal for the Theory of Social Behaviour*, vol. 15, 1985, no. 1; vol. 18, 1988, no. 1.

8 A line of criticism similar to my own has been pursued by S. Seidman, 'Beyond Presentism and Historicism: Understanding the History of Social Science', *Sociological Inquiry*, vol. 53, 1983, no. 1. However, I disagree completely with his dismissal of Skinner as an historicist, and find his criticism of him partly misguided.

9 Cf. the discussion by Paul Veyne, *Did the Greeks Believe in their Myths? An Essay on the Constitutive Imagination* (Chicago, 1988: University of Chicago Press), chs. 2–3.

10 G.W.F. Hegel, *Elements of the Philosophy of Right* (Cambridge, 1991: Cambridge University Press), Preface, p. 23.

11 For an interesting analysis of different answers to the question of why history is rewritten, see Erik Ringmar, 'Historical Writing and Rewriting: Gustav II Adolf, the French Revolution, and the Historians', *Scandinavian Journal of History*, forthcoming.

12 See Karl R. Popper, *The Open Society and Its Enemies*, vol. 2 (London, 1966: Routledge) and Karl R. Popper, *The Poverty of Historicism* (London, 1974: Routledge). In the latter book, Popper defines historicism as 'an approach to the social sciences which assumes that *historical prediction* is their principal aim', thus, and ironically, flogging not only the finalist horse but also the objectivist one.

13 Just to take the worst example: Francis Fukuyama, *Have We Reached the End of History?* (Santa Monica, 1989: The RAND Corporation).

14 Although I here give it a wider and perhaps even more pejorative sense, the term 'whiggish' is Butterfield's. H. Butterfield, *The Whig Interpretation of History* (Hammondsworth, 1973: Penguin).

15 I am here indebted to R. Rorty, 'The Historiography of Philosophy: Four Genres' in R. Rorty, J.B. Schneewind & Q. Skinner, eds., *Philosophy in History: Essays on the Historiography of Philosophy* (Cambridge, 1984: Cambridge University Press).

16 Ringmar, 'Historical Writing and Rewriting', pp. 10–12.

17 For an excellent overview of the criticism directed against finalist history, see Michael S. Roth, *Knowing and History: Appropriations of Hegel in Twentieth-Century France* (Ithaca, 1988: Cornell University Press), esp. pp. 189–224.

18 The consequences of anti-foundationalism for historiography have been debated in *History and Theory*, by F.R. Ankersmit, 'Historiography and Postmodernism', vol. 28, 1989, no. 2, and P. Zagorin, 'Historiography and Postmodernism: Reconsiderations', vol. 29, 1990 no. 1. See also Robert Young, *White Mythologies* (London, 1990: Routledge) and his analysis of Said and Spivak. The problem of history versus fiction is analogous to that of philosophy versus literature; see Richard Rorty, 'Deconstruction and Circumvention' in R. Rorty, *Essays on Heidegger and Others*, pp. 85–106.

19 On the impact of behaviouralism and the reorientation in historiography, see J.G. Gunnell, *Political Theory: Tradition and Interpretation* (Cambridge, 1979: Cambridge University Press), pp. 5ff.

20 The main target of Skinner's criticism is of course Leo Strauss. By describing Skinner's position, I do not imply that his criticism of Strauss is altogether fair. In order to understand the sophistication of Strauss's position, see for example, Leo Strauss, 'Political Philosophy and History', 'What is Political Philosophy?' in *What is Political Philosophy? and Other Studies* (Glencoe, 1959: The Free Press).

21 Skinner, 'Meaning and Understanding', p. 30.

22 I have borrowed the term 'hermeneutics of conflict' from Charles Taylor, 'The Hermeneutics of Conflict' in Tully, ed., *Meaning and Context*.

23 Skinner, 'Meaning and Understanding', p. 31.

24 Ibid., p. 32.

25 Ibid., p. 35.

26 Ibid., p. 44.

27 Ibid., p. 37.

28 Ibid., p. 41.
29 F.H. Hinsley, *Sovereignty* (Cambridge, 1986: Cambridge University Press), p. 26, *passim*.
30 Nicolas Greenwood Onuf, 'Sovereignty: Outline of a Conceptual History', *Alternatives*, vol. 16, 1991.
31 Cf. Michael Donelan, 'Introduction' in M. Donelan, ed., *The Reason of States: A Study in International Political Theory* (London, 1977: Allen & Unwin); Torbjörn L. Knutsen, *A History of International Relations Theory* (Manchester, 1992: Manchester University Press), p. 1.
32 Howard Williams, *International Relations in Political Theory* (Milton Keynes, 1989: Open University Press).
33 Knutsen, *A History of International Relations Theory*, p. 6.
34 Ibid., p. 6.
35 J.L. Holzgrefe, 'The Origins of Modern International Relations Theory', *Review of International Studies*, vol. 15, 1989, p. 13.
36 Ibid., p. 22.
37 Skinner, 'Meaning and Understanding', p. 55.
38 Q. Skinner, '"Social Meaning" and the Explanation of Social Action' in J. Tully, ed., *Meaning and Context*.
39 Jacques Maritain, 'The Concept of Sovereignty' in Stankiewicz, ed., *In Defence of Sovereignty* (London, 1969: Oxford University Press), pp. 41–64.
40 Christopher Brewin, 'Sovereignty' in James Mayall, ed., *The Community of States: A Study in International Political Theory* (London, 1982: Allen & Unwin), pp. 39ff.
41 Harold Laski, *Reflections on the Revolution in our Time* (London, 1943: Allen & Unwin), p. 206.
42 'It may well be strenuously doubted, however, whether a knowledge of the causes of an action is really equivalent to an understanding of the action itself. For as well as – and quite apart from – the fact that such an understanding does presuppose a grasp of the antecedent causal conditions of the action taking place, it might equally be said to presuppose a grasp of the point of the action for the agent who performed it' (Skinner, 'Meaning and Understanding', p. 59).
43 Q. Skinner, 'A Reply to my Critics' in Tully, ed., *Meaning and Context*. Skinner's hermeneutic approach should be carefully distinguished from the kind of hermeneutics advocated by Husserl and Gadamer, and the kind of primordial identity between subject and object that they are based on. For a discussion, see A.T. Nuyen, 'Truth, Method, and Objectivity: Husserl and Gadamer on Scientific Method', *Philosophy of the Social Sciences*, vol. 20, 1990, no. 4.
44 J. Tully, 'The Pen is a Mighty Sword: Quentin Skinner's Analysis of Politics' in Tully, ed., *Meaning and Context*.
45 Skinner, 'Meaning and Understanding', p. 48. A similar position has been advanced by J.J.E. Gracia, 'Texts and Their Interpretation', *Review of Metaphysics*, vol. 43, 1990.

46 'Any particular belief in which an historian is interested will therefore be likely to present itself holistically as part of a network of beliefs, a network within which the various individual items supply each other with mutual support' (Skinner, 'Reply', p. 248).

47 Skinner, 'Reply', p. 239.

48 Ibid., p. 244.

49 Manicas & Rosenberg, 'Naturalism, Epistemological Individualism', 'The Sociology of Scientific Knowledge', *passim*.

50 Skinner, 'Reply' pp. 240–1.

51 Ibid., p. 246.

52 Ibid., p. 247.

53 Ibid., p. 286.

54 Ibid., p. 287.

55 Skinner, 'Meaning and Understanding', p. 66.

56 Skinner, 'Reply', p. 287. A similar point was made by Nietzsche: 'For since we are the outcome of earlier generations, we are also the outcome of their aberrations, passions and errors, and indeed of their crimes; it is not possible to free oneself from this chain. If we condemn these aberrations ... this does not alter the fact that we originate in them' (Nietzsche, 'On the Uses and Disadvantages', p. 76).

57 Skinner, 'Reply,' p. 256.

58 Skinner, 'Meaning and Understanding', p. 49.

59 At least Skinner said as much at a seminar at the Swedish Collegium for Advanced Study in the Social Sciences, held in Uppsala, Sweden in the Fall of 1990, when forced to comment on the possibility of settling interpretative disputes rationally.

60 Skinner, 'Reply', pp. 236–8.

61 See Herbert Dreyfus & Paul Rabinow, *Michel Foucault: Beyond Structuralism and Hermeneutics* (Chicago, 1982: The University of Chicago Press) pp. 180–2.

62 Skinner, 'Reply', p. 266.

63 See J.L. Austin, *How to do Things with Words* (Oxford, 1962: Oxford University Press). The demand that speech-acts must be serious in intention has been subjected to damaging criticism by J. Derrida, 'Signature, Event, Context' in *Margins of Philosophy* (Sussex, 1982: Harvester), which in turn provoked an angry exchange between Searle and Derrida in *Glyph*, vols. 1 & 2, 1977.

64 Cf. John Searle, 'Minds, Brains, and Programs', *Behavioral and Brain Sciences*, vol. 3, 1980, no. 3, pp. 417–24.

65 Quentin Skinner, 'The State' in T. Ball, J. Farr & R.L. Hanson, eds., *Political Innovation and Conceptual Change* (Cambridge, 1989: Cambridge University Press), pp. 112, 116, 120, 126.

66 Cf. Michel Foucault, *Archaeology of Knowledge* (New York, 1972: Pantheon), pp. 49, 55, 80f, 104; cf. also Dreyfus & Rabinow, *Beyond Structuralism*, p. 45; Gilles Deleuze, *Foucault* (Minneapolis, 1988: University of Minnesota Press) p. 7.

67 Foucault, *Archaeology of Knowledge*, p. 84.
68 Ibid., p. 111.
69 Ibid., p. 87.
70 I shall consistently use the term discourse to cover the meaning of both discourse and discursive formation, which would amount to quite an oversimplification if my aim was to convey an interpretation of Foucault's use of these terms.
71 Foucault, *Archaeology of Knowledge*, p. 27.
72 Ibid., p. 109.
73 Ibid., p. 98; cf. Dreyfus & Rabinow, *Beyond Structuralism*, pp. 57–8; Deleuze, *Foucault*, p. 11.
74 Jonathan Culler, *On Deconstruction: Theory and Criticism After Structuralism* (London, 1983: Routledge), p. 121.
75 Deleuze, *Foucault*, p. 9.
76 Foucault, *Archaeology of Knowledge*, pp. 32, 46.
77 This renders the question of the author problematic, and opens it to investigation, but does not mean that we have to dispense with the concept of the author, only that we have to treat it as a category susceptible to historical change. See Michel Foucault, 'What is an Author?' in Donald F. Bouchard, ed., *Language, Counter-Memory, Practice: Selected Essays and Interviews with Michel Foucault* (Ithaca, 1977: Cornell) pp. 113ff; Jacques Derrida, *Of Grammatology* (Baltimore & London, 1974: Johns Hopkins), pp. 158f.
78 Cf. Thomas R. Flynn, 'Foucault and the Spaces of History', *The Monist*, vol. 74, 1991, no. 2.
79 Foucault, *Archaeology of Knowledge*, pp. 46, 53–4; Dreyfus & Rabinow, *Beyond Structuralism*, pp. 64–7.
80 Dreyfus & Rabinow, *Beyond Structuralism*, pp. 79f.
81 Ibid., pp. 73–5.
82 It has been debated whether the archaeological approach of the early Foucault of which the assumptions of autonomy and primacy are integral parts is compatible with the genealogical approach articulated by the later Foucault. It seems to me that archaeology and genealogy are different enterprises, the former dealing with the question of *how* a system of statements hangs together, the latter with the question of *why* such systems are transformed over time, but no one has hitherto produced reasons to the effect that they should be logically incompatible, see Deleuze, *Foucault*, *passim*, Dreyfus & Rabinow, *Beyond Structuralism*, pp. 104f, Flynn, 'Foucault and the Spaces of History', pp. 174f, who all, albeit for different reasons, stress the continuity between the analysis of discourse and genealogy.
83 Much interpretative energy has been devoted to the ethical implications of genealogy. To take a few examples: N. Fraser, 'Foucault on Modern Power: Empirical Insights and Normative Confusions', *Praxis International*, vol. 1, 1981 no. 3; D.R. Hiley, 'Foucault and the Analysis of Power: Political Engagement Without Liberal Hope or Comfort', *Praxis International*, vol. 4, 1984, no. 2; S.D. Ross, 'Foucault's Radical Politics', *Praxis International*, vol. 5, 1985, no. 2; D. Ingram, 'Foucault and The Frankfurter School: A Discourse

on Nietzsche, Power and Knowledge', *Praxis International*, vol. 6, 1986, no. 3;
A. Megill, *Prophets of Extremity* (Berkeley, 1985: University of California
Press), pp. 181ff; M. Walzer, 'The Lonely Politics of Michel Foucault', *The
Company of Critics* (New York, 1988: Basic Books) For an interesting com-
parison of Nietzsche and Foucault, see L.P. Thiele, 'The Agony of Politics:
The Nietzschean Roots of Foucault's Political Thought', *American Political
Science Review*, vol. 84, 1991, no. 3.

84 Michel Foucault, *Discipline and Punish: The Birth of the Prison*, trans. A.
Sheridan (Harmondsworth, 1979: Penguin), p. 31, For an analysis, see M.S.
Roth, 'Foucault's "History of the Present"', *History and Theory*, vol. 20, 1981,
no. 1.

85 Michel Foucault, *The Order of Things: An Archaeology of the Human Sciences*
(London, 1991: Routledge), p. 275.

86 Michel Foucault, 'Truth and Power' in C. Gordon, ed., *Power/ Knowledge:
Selected Interviews and Other Writings 1972–1977 by Michel Foucault* (New
York, 1980: Pantheon), p. 117.

87 Michel Foucault, 'The Discourse on Language' in Foucault, *Archaeology of
Knowledge*, p. 234.

88 Michel de Montaigne, 'De l'Expérience', *Essais*, Book 3, 13 (Paris, 1922: Felix
Alcan).

89 Nietzsche, '"Guilt", "Bad Conscience", and the Like', in *The Genealogy of
Morals*, p. 77.

90 M. Foucault, 'Nietzsche, Genealogy, History' in D.F.Bouchard, ed., *Language, Counter-Memory, Practice* (Ithaca, 1977: Cornell), p. 146.

91 Foucault, 'Nietzsche, Genealogy', pp. 151–2.

92 Ibid., p. 142.

93 Aristotle, *Rhetorics* (London, 1947: Heinemann), book II, xxv. 8.

94 Ibid., book II, xxv. 11.

95 Michel Foucault, 'The History of Sexuality', interview by Lucette Finas, in
Gordon, ed., *Power/ Knowledge*, p. 193.

96 Michel Foucault, 'Truth and Power' in Gordon, ed., *Power/ Knowledge*, p. 131.

97 Although the textbook story of the concept of power is a long one, suffice it
here to note that the concept of power with few exceptions is tied to an idea
of agency and intentionality – whether individual or collective – and that it
implies some notion of causality, whether empiricist or scientific realist. See
D. Wrong, *Power: Its Forms, Bases and Uses* (Oxford, 1979: Basil Blackwell);
W. Connolly, *The Terms of Political Discourse* (Oxford, 1983: Robertson), pp.
85ff; S. Lukes, *Power: A Radical View* (London, 1974: Macmillan). Even if the
relation between agency and power has been increasingly problematized
(by, for example Hannah Arendt, 'What is Authority?' in *Between Past and
Future* (Harmondsworth, 1977: Penguin), pp. 91–143) even Giddens retains
a rather vague notion of unstructured subjectivity at the core of his account
of power. *The Constitution of Society* (Cambridge, 1984: Polity Press), pp. 1–34.

98 Cf. T. Ball, 'The Changing Face of Power' in *Transforming Political Discourse*
(Oxford, 1988: Basil Blackwell).

99 Deleuze, *Foucault*, p. 29.

100 Foucault, 'Truth and Power' in Gordon, ed., *Power/Knowledge*, p. 119.
101 Foucault, *Discipline and Punish*, p. 27.
102 The precise nature of this relationship has been analysed by T. Keenan, 'The "Paradox" of Knowledge and Power: Reading Foucault on a Bias', *Political Theory*, vol. 15, 1987, no. 1. Its historiographical implications have been discussed by L. Shiner, 'Reading Foucault: Anti-method and the Genealogy of Power/Knowledge', *History and Theory*, vol. 20, 1982, no. 3.
103 Deleuze, *Foucault*, pp. 81–2.
104 Keenan, 'The Paradox of Knowledge and Power', pp. 14–15.
105 Hilary Putnam, *Reason, Truth, and History* (Cambridge, 1981: Cambridge University Press), pp. 155–62; Megill, *Prophets of Extremity*, p. 251.
106 Walzer, 'The Lonely Politics of Michel Foucault' in *The Company of Critics*, pp. 205f.
107 See John Keane, 'More Theses on the Philosophy of History', in Tully, ed., *Meaning and Context*, p. 214.
108 Dreyfus & Rabinow, *Beyond Structuralism*, pp. 194, 196.
109 Ibid., p. 185; Deleuze, *Foucault*, p. 25.
110 Michel Foucault, 'Subject and Power' in Dreyfus & Rabinow, *Beyond Structuralism*, p. 220.
111 Michel Foucault, *The History of Sexuality*, vol. 1 (New York, 1978: Vintage), p. 93.
112 Foucault, Michel: 'Two Lectures' in Gordon, ed., *Power/ Knowledge*, p. 95.
113 Foucault, 'Truth and Power' in Gordon, ed., *Power/Knowledge*, p. 121.
114 This tension between analysis and criticism has been discussed by Rudi Visker, 'Can Genealogy be Critical? A Somewhat Unromantic Look at Nietzsche and Foucault', *Man and World*, vol. 23, 1990.
115 Cf. R. Ashley, 'The Geopolitics of Geopolitical Space: Toward a Critical Social Theory of International Politics', *Alternatives*, vol. 12, 1987.
116 Donald R. Kelley, *Foundations of Modern Historical Scholarship* (New York, 1970) p. 21 and *passim*; Walter Ullmann, *Medieval Foundations of Renaissance Humanism* (London, 1977: Paul Elek) p. 104; H. Weisinger, 'The Renaissance Theory of the Reaction against the Middle Ages as a Cause of the Renaissance', *Speculum*, vol. 20, 1945, and by the same author 'Ideas of History During the Renaissance', *Journal of the History of Ideas*, vol. 6, 1945.
117 Reinhart Koselleck, '"Neuzeit"': Remarks on the Semantics of the Modern Concepts of Movement' in Reinhart Koselleck, *Futures Past: On the Semantics of Historical Time* (Boston, 1985: MIT Press); John D. Lyons, *Exemplum: The Rhetoric of Example in Early Modern France and Italy* (Princeton, 1989: Princeton University Press), pp. 154ff.
118 The classical example of reinvention and reappropriation is of course Jacob Burkhardt, *The Civilization of the Renaissance in Italy* (London, 1951: Phaidon). On the ontology of nineteenth-century historiography, see Foucault, *The Order of Things*, pp. 217ff.
119 Martin Wight, *The Systems of States* (Leicester, 1977: Leicester University Press), pp. 110ff.

120 Hedley Bull, *The Anarchical Society: A Study of Order in World Politics* (London, 1977: Macmillan), p. 10.
121 F. H. Hinsley, *Nationalism and the International System* (London, 1973: Hodder and Stoughton), pp. 69–83.

4 Inventing outsides: proto-sovereignty, exempla and the general theory of the state in the Renaissance

1 Carl Schmitt, *Political Theology: Four Chapters on the Concept of Sovereignty* (Boston, 1985: MIT Press), p. 36.
2 Walter Ullmann, *A History of Political Thought: The Middle Ages* (Harmondsworth, 1965: Penguin), p. 156.
3 Cf. Michel Foucault, *The Archaeology of Knowledge* (New York, 1972: Pantheon), p. 186.
4 Cf. Quentin Skinner, 'The State' in T. Ball, J. Farr & R.L. Hanson, eds. *Political Innovation and Conceptual Change* (Cambridge, 1989: Cambridge University Press), pp. 93f.
5 Among the conceptual antecedents to sovereignty, we find an array of concepts with overlapping and sometimes contradictory connotations, such as *potesta, potentia, majestas, gubernaculum, regnum, imperium, dominium, status, republicae* etc.
6 A similar strategy has been pursued by James DerDerian, in his study *On Diplomacy: A Genealogy of Western Estrangement* (Oxford, 1987: Basil Blackwell), chs. 3, 4.
7 Martin Wight, *The Systems of States* (Leicester, 1977: Leicester University Press), pp. 110ff.
8 A case in point is war, which is organized and conducted without any firm distinctions between inside and outside, see J.R. Hale, *War and Society in Renaissance Europe 1450–1620* (London, 1985: Fontana), p. 13; Michael Howard, *War in European History* (Oxford, 1976: Oxford University Press), p. 6.
9 Friedrich Meinecke, *Machiavellism: The Doctrine of Raison d'Etat and its Place in Modern History* tr. by D. Scott (Boulder & London, 1984: Westview), chs. 1–3, p. 146.
10 Otto Gierke, *Natural Law and the Theory of Society, 1500–1800* (Boston, 1957: Beacon Press), p. 40, my emphasis. However, this statement must be qualified, since it seems to be restricted to continental theories of the state only. In Tudor England, it is hard to say that the state was explained by itself, thus being both subject and object simultaneously. Here the prevalent fiction was that of the 'king's two bodies', where the king himself, understood as a corporation sole, was embodying an analogous split. See above all, Ernst H. Kantorowicz, *The King's Two Bodies: A Study in Medieval Political Theology* (Princeton, 1957: Princeton University Press), p. 20 and also F.W. Maitland's introduction to O. Gierke, *Political Theories of the Middle Ages* (Boston, 1958: Beacon Press), passim, and compare with W.F. Church, *Constitutional Thought in Sixteenth Century France* (Cambridge, Mass. 1941: Harvard University Press), esp. pp. 22–41.

11 E.g in Purgatory, see Kantorowicz, *The King's Two Bodies*, pp. 485–95.
12 Michael Wilks, *The Problem of Sovereignty in the Later Middle Ages: The Papal Monarchy with Augustinus Triumphus and the Publicists* (Cambridge, 1963: Cambridge University Press), pp. 20f; Walter Ullmann, *Medieval Foundations of Renaissance Humanism* (London, 1977: Paul Elek), pp. 18–19; Gierke, *Political Theories of the Middle Ages*, pp. 7f, 22f.
13 Wilks, *The Problem of Sovereignty*, pp. 24f; Ullmann, *Medieval Foundations*, p. 20; Gierke, *Political Theories of the Middle Ages*, pp. 22f.
14 *Matthew*, XVI, 18–19.
15 Wilks, *The Problem of Sovereignty*, pp. 61–70.
16 Cf. Kantorowicz, *The King's Two Bodies*, p. 193.
17 Ullmann, *A History of Political Thought*, pp. 71–5, 85–7.
18 Kantorowicz, *The King's Two Bodies*, pp. 105ff. As Ullmann has pointed out (Ullmann, *A History of Political Thought*, p. 102n) this conception of 'living law' was alien to the earlier Middle Ages, and was derived from the Greek conception of a *nomos empsychos*.
19 Quoted in Kantorowicz, *The King's Two Bodies*, p. 134.
20 Wilks, *The Problem of Sovereignty*, p. 17.
21 Ullmann, *A History of Political Thought*, pp. 131–2.
22 Sheila Delany, 'Undoing the Substantial Connection: The Late Medieval Attack on Analogical Thought' in *Medieval Literary Politics: Shapes of Ideology* (Manchester 1990: Manchester University Press), pp. 20–3.
23 John of Salisbury, *Policraticus*, ed. C. Nederman (Cambridge, 1990: Cambridge University Press).
24 Roy Strong, *Art and Power: Renaissance Festivals 1450–1650* (Woodbridge, 1984: Boydell), pp. 8f.
25 See Marianne Shapiro, '"Mirror and Portrait": The Structure of *Il Libro del Cortegiano*', *Journal of Medieval and Renaissance Studies*, vol. 5, 1975, no. 1.
26 Strong, *Art and Power: Renaissance Festivals 1450–1650*, pp. 22–43.
27 Paul Ricoeur, *Time and Narrative*, vol. 1, (Chicago, 1984: University of Chicago Press), p. 7.
28 Augustine, *Confessions* (New York, 1943: Liveright), book 11, ch. 14:17.
29 Augustine, *Confessions*, book 11, ch. 20:26, my emphasis; cf. also ch. 28:37–8.
30 Ibid., book 11, ch. 13:15.
31 Ibid., book 11, chs. 10:12, 11:13, 12:14.
32 I owe much in this regard to Kantorowicz, *The King's Two Bodies*, p. 273 and to Ricoeur, *Time and Narrative*, pp. 25–30.
33 Ricoeur, *Time and Narrative*, p. 25.
34 See Stanislas Boros, 'Les catégories de la temporalité chez Saint Augustin', *Archives de Philosophie*, vol. 21, 1958.
35 Kantorowicz, *The King's Two Bodies*, pp. 274f. On the reception of Aristotle's ethical and political texts, see Cary J. Nederman, 'Aristotelianism and the Origins of "Political Science" in the Twelfth Century', *Journal of the History of Ideas*, vol. 52, 1991, no. 2, who unfortunately does not discuss the impact of Aristotle's physics and its transmission through Arab sources.
36 Aristotle, *Physics* (Oxford, 1953: Clarendon), 218a–b.

37 Augustine, *Confessions*, book 11, ch. 24:31.
38 On the impact of this transvaluation in literary art, see R. Quionones, *The Renaissance Discovery of Time* (Cambridge, Mass., 1975: Harvard University Press), esp. ch 1.
39 Augustine, *Confessions*, book 11, ch. 30:40.
40 Kantorowicz, *The King's Two Bodies*, pp. 275–7.
41 For an analysis of this important development, see Peter N. Riesenberg, *Inalienability of Sovereignty in Medieval Political Thought* (New York, 1956: Columbia University Press), pp. 81ff, 145ff.
42 Kantorowicz, *The King's Two Bodies*, pp. 164f and Ernst Kantorowicz, 'Mysteries of State: An Absolutist Concept and its Late Medieval Origins', *Harvard Theological Review*, vol. 48, 1955, pp. 83f.
43 Kantorowicz, *The King's Two Bodies*, pp. 232f and by the same author, 'Pro Patria Mori in Medieval Political Thought', *American Historical Review*, vol. 56, 1951. See also Gaines Post, 'Two Notes on Nationalism in the Middle Ages', *Traditio*, vol. 9, 1953; Jerrold E. Seigel, *Rhetoric and Philosophy in Renaissance Humanism: The Union of Eloquence and Wisdom. Petrarch to Valla* (Princeton, 1968: Princeton University Press), pp. 63f, 99f.
44 Kantorowicz, *The King's Two Bodies*, pp. 166f, 232f.
45 This had been recognized earlier by Innocent III's decretal Per Venerabilem (1202) in which it was laid down that the French king had no superior in temporal affairs; see Joseph R. Strayer, *On the Medieval Origins of the Modern State* (Princeton, 1970: Princeton University Press), pp. 53f.
46 For a detailed analysis of this episode, see Walter Ullmann, 'The Development of the Medieval Idea of Sovereignty', *English Historical Review*, vol. 64, 1949, no. 250.
47 Kantorowicz, *The King's Two Bodies*, p. 299.
48 Quoted in ibid., p. 299.
49 Aristotle, *Physics*, 220a: 'It is clear, then, that time is "number of movement in respect to before and after", and is continuous since it is an attribute of what is continuous', from which it follows in 220b: 'Not only do we measure movement by the time, but also the time by the movement, because they define each other', and in 222b: 'it is evident that every change and everything that moves is in time', from which is derived, somewhat spuriously, the assertion of 223b, that 'human affairs form a circle'.
50 Cf. Reinhart Koselleck, 'Historical Criteria of the Modern Concept of Revolution' in Koselleck, *Futures Past: On the Semantics of Historical Time* (Boston, 1985: MIT Press), pp. 42–5.
51 L. Valla, *The Treatise on the Donation of Constantine* (New Haven, 1922: Yale University Press).
52 Cf. Reinhart Koselleck, 'Historia Magistra Vitae: The Dissolution of the Topos into the Perspective of a Modernized Historical Process' in Koselleck, *Futures Past*, pp. 23f.
53 Aristotle, *Rhetorics* (London, 1947: Heinemann), I, book 2, section 8.
54 John D. Lyons, *Exemplum: The Rhetoric of Example in Early Modern France and Italy* (Princeton, 1990: Princeton University Press), pp. 6, 11.

55 Ullmann, *A History of Political Thought*, p. 12.
56 Wilks, *The Problem of Sovereignty*, p. 84; Walter Ullmann, *Principles of Government and Politics in the Middle Ages* (London, 1961: Methuen & Co.), pp. 231–43.
57 Nederman, 'Aristotelianism', *passim*.
58 Ullmann, *A History of Political Thought*, pp. 15–17.
59 See Nicolai Rubinstein, 'The History of the Word *Politicus* in Early-Modern Europe' in A. Pagden, ed., *The Languages of Political Theory in Early-Modern Europe* (Cambridge, 1987: Cambridge University Press); Quentin Skinner, *The Foundations of Modern Political Thought*, vol. 1 (Cambridge, 1978: Cambridge University Press), p. 50.
60 Aristotle, *The Politics*, ed. S. Everson (Cambridge, 1988: Cambridge University Press), book 2, ch. 6, book 4, ch. 14–15.
61 Ibid.
62 Ibid., book 3, chs. 1–5.
63 See Wilks, *The Problem of Sovereignty*, pp. 118ff.
64 As Wilks has noted: 'One of the tragedies of medieval history is to watch the undermining of a system by the very men who believed that they were doing everything in their power to build it up', *The Problem of Sovereignty*, p. 10.
65 This is analysed by Wilks, *The Problem of Sovereignty*, pp. 118–42.
66 Quoted in Wilks, *The Problem of Sovereignty*, pp. 94–5n.
67 Marsilius of Padua: *The Defender of Peace*, vol. 2: *The Defensor Pacis*, tr. by A. Gewirth (New York, 1956: Columbia University Press). For a contextual analysis, see Nicolai Rubinstein, 'Marsilius of Padua and Italian Political Thought of his Time', in J.R. Hale, J.R.L. Highfield & B. Smalley, eds., *Europe in the Late Middle Ages* (London, 1965: Faber and Faber), pp. 44–75.
68 Marsilius of Padua, *Defensor Pacis*, Discourse 1, Section 4.
69 Ibid., Discourse 1, Section 1, no. 8.
70 Ibid., Discourse 1, Section 17, no. 11. As Gewirth has pointed out (p. 85 n16), this passage is adopted more or less wholesale from Aquinas' *In Decem libros Ethicorum Aristotelis ad Nichomachum expositio*, lib. 1.
71 Dante, *The Monarchy and Three Letters* (New York, 1954), book 1, ch. 5: 'For, if it is agreed that mankind as a whole has a goal (and this we have shown to be so), then it needs one person to govern or rule over it, and the title appropriate to this person is Monarch or Emperor. Thus it has been demonstrated that a Monarch or Emperor is necessary for the well-being of the world.' For a comparison between Dante and Marsiglio, see Marjorie Reeves, 'Dante Aligheri and Marsiglio of Padua' in Beryl Smalley, ed., *Trends in Medieval Political Thought* (Oxford, 1965: Basil Blackwell).
72 Marsilius of Padua, *Defensor Pacis*, Discourse 1, Section 17, no. 3.
73 Ibid., Discourse 1, Section 17, no. 4.
74 The notion of an outside, an undefined logical externality, recurs also in the discussion of the function of the ruler, *Defensor Pacis*, Discourse 1, Section 4, no. 4 and the military, Discourse 1, Section 14, no. 8.
75 Marsilius of Padua, *Defensor Pacis*, Discourse 1, Section 17, no. 10.
76 Ibid., Discourse 2, Section 28, no. 15.

77 On Bartolus of Saxoferrato, see M.H. Keen, 'The Political Thought of the Fourteenth-Century Civilians' in Smalley, *Trends in Medieval Political Thought* pp. 105–24 and C.N.S. Woolf, *Bartolus of Sassoferrato* (Cambridge, 1913: Cambridge University Press).

78 J.H. Parry, *The Establishment of the European Hegemony, 1415–1715* (New York, 1961: Harper & Row), p. 13.

79 Dante, *Monarchia*, I:xi.

80 See Frederic Cheyette, 'The Sovereign and the Pirates, 1332', *Speculum*, vol. 45, pp. 44–50.

81 Ibid., pp. 54–68.

82 A similar interpretation of the problems caused by time has been provided by J.G.A. Pocock, *The Machiavellian Moment: Florentine Political Thought and the Atlantic Republican Tradition* (Princeton, 1975: Princeton University Press), p. 31.

83 Cf. Michel Foucault, *The Order of Things: An Archaeology of the Human Sciences* (London, 1991: Routledge), p. 40. For a comprehensive study on Renaissance knowledge, see Frances A. Yates, *Giordano Bruno and the Hermetic Tradition* (London, 1964: Routledge).

84 Cf. Paul Oskar Kristeller, *Renaissance Thought* vol. 1, *The Classic, Scholastic and Humanistic Strains* (New York, 1961: Harper & Row), pp. 55f.

85 Marsilio, Ficino, 'Five Questions Concerning the Mind' (1495) in E. Cassirer, et al., eds., *The Renaissance Philosophy of Man* (Chicago, 1948: University of Chicago Press), p. 194.

86 Ibid., p. 195.

87 Ibid., p. 196.

88 Giovanni Pico della Mirandola, 'Oration on the Dignity of Man' (1486) in Cassirer, et al., eds., *The Renaissance Philosophy of Man*, pp. 248–9.

89 Shapiro, 'Mirror and Portrait', *passim*; Hardin Craig, *The Enchanted Glass: The Elizabethan Mind in Literature* (Westport, Conn., 1975: Greenwood), *passim*. On the influence of optics on the Renaissance world-view, see Crombie, *Science, Optics and Music in Medieval and Early Modern Thought* (London, 1987: Hambledon Press), pp. 175–284. The problem of deciding between projection and reality could sometimes be very real; for how is it possible to draw such a distinction without tacitly presupposing prior access to it through a notion of representation? An interesting episode in this respect occurred when Charles V obtained a map of Provence in 1536, and immediately became convinced that he owned Provence in the very same sense as he owned the map of it; it would have taken a Descartes to persuade him to the contrary. See Martin Du Bellay, *Mémoirs*, ed. J.A.C. Bouchon (Paris, 1936), p. 582, quoted in Hale, *War and Society*, p. 45.

90 Marsilio, Ficino, 'Five Questions Concerning the Mind' (1495), p. 195.

91 Foucault, *The Order of Things*, pp. 25f.

92 The classical example in this respect is of course Niccòlo Machiavelli, *The Art of War* (1521), tr. by E. Farneworth (Indianapolis, 1965: Bobbs-Merrill), but which was followed by a great number of treatises on tactics, siege-craft, artillery etc., see Hale, *War and Society*, p. 56.

93 Cf. Robert Adams, *The Better Part of Valor: More, Erasmus, Colet, and Vives on Humanism, War and Peace, 1496–1535* (Seattle, 1962: University of Washington Press), pp. 4–10. On fate, providence and the human condition, see Antonio Poppio, 'Fate, Fortune, Providence and Human Freedom' in Charles B. Schmitt, et al., eds. *The Cambridge History of Renaissance Philosophy* (Cambridge, 1988: Cambridge University Press), pp. 641–67.

94 Valla, *Treatise on the Donation of Constantine*, p. 167 is a case in point. For a good overview, see J.R. Hale, 'Sixteenth-Century Explanations of War and Violence', *Past and Present*, no. 2, 1971.

95 Adams, *The Better Part of Valor*, pp. 82, 101, 117, 125f, *passim*.

96 Augustine, *Soliloquia*, II, vi, PLXXXII, 903, quoted in Shapiro, 'Mirror and Portrait', p. 42.

97 Niccòlo Machiavelli, *The Prince*, tr. by R. Price (Cambridge, 1988: Cambridge University Press), ch. 15, p. 54.

98 Cf. Michael McCanles, *The Discourse of Il Principe* (Malibu, 1983: Undena Publications), pp. 12ff, who stresses the rhetorical and strategic dimensions of the text of *Il Principe*.

99 Felix Gilbert, *Machiavelli and Guiccardini: Politics and History in Sixteenth Century Florence* (Princeton, 1965: Princeton University Press), p. 170.

100 Sometimes the concept of stato is used to denote 'power' or 'government', but also 'people' and 'territory'. On this point see J.H. Hexter, *The Vision of Politics on the Eve of the Reformation: More, Machiavelli, and Seyssel* (London, 1973: Allen Lane), pp. 150ff and Gilbert, *Machiavelli and Guicciardini*, pp. 177–8, Skinner, 'The State', p. 103.

101 Skinner, 'The State', pp. 98–100.

102 Hexter, *The Vision of Politics*, p. 161.

103 Machiavelli, *The Prince*, ch. 1, p. 5.

104 Ibid., ch. 2, p. 6.

105 Ibid., ch. 3, p. 6.

106 Ibid., ch. 5, p. 17.

107 Ibid., ch. 6, p. 21.

108 Ibid., ch. 25, p. 85.

109 Ibid., ch. 7, p. 22.

110 Ibid., ch. 6, p. 19.

111 Ibid., ch. 6, p. 21.

112 A similar interpretation has been proposed by Lyons, *Exemplum*, p. 38.

113 Cf. Machiavelli, *The Prince*, ch. 6, pp. 20–1.

114 Machiavelli, *The Discourses* (London, 1950: Routledge), book 1, Preface, p. 205.

115 For a survey of the enormous debate, see Eric W. Cochrane, 'Machiavelli: 1940–1960', *Journal of Modern History*, vol. 33, 1961, and John Geerken, 'Machiavelli Studies since 1969', *Journal of the History of Ideas*, vol. 37, 1976. On the meaning of *virtù*, see Neal Wood, 'Machiavelli's Concept of *Virtù* Reconsidered', *Political Studies*, vol. 15, 1972; Gilbert, *Machiavelli and Guicciardini*, p. 179; I. Hannaford, 'Machiavelli's Concept of *Virtù* in *The Prince* and *The Discourses* Reconsidered', *Political Studies*, vol. 20, 1972; Russell

Price, 'The Senses of *Virtù* in Machiavelli', *European Studies Review*, vol. 3, 1973, no. 4.

116 Cochrane, 'Machiavelli: 1940–1960', pp. 115f; Geerken, 'Machiavelli Studies since 1969', pp. 364f.

117 See Peter S. Donaldson, *Machiavelli and Mystery of State* (Cambridge, 1988: Cambridge University Press), ch. 1; Skinner, *Foundations of Modern Political Thought*, vol. 2, pp. 308–9; Leo Strauss, *Thoughts on Machiavelli* (Glencoe, Ill., 1958: The Free Press), p. 175.

118 Ernst Cassirer, *The Myth of the State* (New Haven, 1946: Yale University Press), pp. 117f, 140–1.

119 Bendetto Croce, *Politics and Morals* (New York, 1945), p. 59. For a similar view, see also Frederic Chabod, *Machiavelli and the Renaissance* (London, 1958: Bowes & Bowes), p. 142.

120 Isaiah Berlin, 'The Originality of Machiavelli', in Myron Gilmore, ed., *Studies on Machiavelli* (Florence, 1972: Sansoni), p. 193.

121 Berlin, 'The Originality of Machiavelli', pp. 195f.

122 Skinner, *Foundations of Modern Political Thought*, vol. 1, p. 138.

123 Pocock, *The Machiavellian Moment*, p. 177, my emphasis.

124 McCanles, *The Discourse of Il Principe*, p. 28.

125 Cf. ibid., p. 12.

126 Machiavelli, *The Prince*, ch. 15, p. 54.

127 Ibid., ch. 15, p. 55.

128 Ibid., ch. 18, p. 62, my emphasis.

129 Cf. Pocock, *The Machiavellian Moment*, p. 165, who stresses this tension but misses the supplementarity between traditional legitimacy and innovation.

130 Machiavelli, *The Prince*, ch. 17, p. 61.

131 Ibid., ch. 17, p. 61.

132 I owe this observation to Donaldson, *Machiavelli and the Mystery of State*, p. viii. What Donaldson partly neglects, however, is the full significance of the reference to Pindar. Pindar is held to be responsible for the reversal of the *nomos-physis* antithesis among the sophists, making *nomos* (law or convention) a force superior to that of the Gods, and simultaneously assimilate it to the order of the *physis* (nature). (W.K.C. Guthrie, *The Sophists* (Cambridge, 1971: Cambridge University Press) pp. 131–4). Later, this reversal was caricatured by Plato, *Gorgias*, 484b, when making Callicles a supporter of the doctrine that might is right, when the latter speaks about innovation: 'But if there arises a man sufficiently empowered by nature, he will ... tred underfoot our texts and spells and incantations and unnatural laws, and by an act of revolt reveal himself our master instead of our slave, in the full blaze of natural justice.'

133 Cf. Gilbert, *Machiavelli and Guicciardini*, p. 168 who discusses the use of allegory in Machiavelli's work.

134 Donaldson, *Machiavelli and Mystery of State*, p. viii.

135 Machiavelli, *The Prince*, ch. 18, p. 62.

136 On the problem of dating *Discorsi*, see Skinner, *Foundations of Modern*

Political Thought, vol. I, p. 154 and Hans Baron, 'Machiavelli: Republican Citizen and Author of "The Prince"', *English Historical Review*, vol. 76, 1961.

137 See Skinner, *Foundations of Modern Political Thought*, vol. I, p. 156.

138 Machiavelli, *The Prince*, ch. 5, p. 19.

139 Pocock, *The Machiavellian Moment*, p. 184.

140 Machiavelli, *The Discourses*, book 2, ch. 1, no. 2.

141 Ibid., book 1, ch. 2, no. 1.

142 Ibid., book 1, ch. 58.

143 Ibid., book 2, ch. 3.

144 Machiavelli, *The Art of War*, passim.

145 Machiavelli, *The Discourses*, book 2, ch. 1.

146 Ibid., book 1, ch. 2, p. 214.

147 Lyons, *Exemplum*, p. 46.

148 Machiavelli, *The Discourses*, book 1, ch. 3, pp. 218–19.

149 Ibid., book 2, ch. 20, p. 420.

150 Edward Surtz, 'Utopia as a Work of Literary Art', in E. Surtz & J.H. Hexter, eds., *The Complete Works of St. Thomas More*, vol. 4 (New Haven, 1964: Yale University Press), p. cxxxvi.

151 Stephen Greenblatt, *Renaissance Self-Fashioning. From More to Shakespeare* (Chicago, 1980: University of Chicago Press), p. 57.

152 For a similar mode of writing and constructing truth through re-reporting, see for example, Joseph Conrad's *Heart of Darkness* or Jorge Luis Borges' *Doctor Brodie's Report*. See also Paul Veyne, *Did the Greeks Believe in Their Myths? An Essay on the Constitutive Imagination* (Chicago, 1988: University of Chicago Press) for a discussion of the importance of trustworthiness in the construction of truth.

153 Thomas More, *Utopia: The Best State of a Commonwealth and the New Island of Utopia* in E. Surtz & J.H. Hexter, eds'. *The Complete Works of St. Thomas More*, vol. 4, (New Haven, 1964: Yale University Press), p. 101.

154 More, *Utopia*, p. 103.

155 Ibid., p. 101.

156 Ibid., p. 99.

157 Thomas More, *Letter to Peter Giles*, in Surtz & Hexter, *Complete Works*, vol. 4, p. 249.

158 More, *Letter to Peter Giles*, p. 251.

159 More, *Utopia*, pp. 63f.

160 Ibid., pp. 61, 89–93.

161 Ibid., pp. 103.

162 Robert P. Adams, *The Better Part of Valor*, pp. 145f.

163 Quentin Skinner, 'Sir Thomas More's Utopia and the Language of Renaissance Humanism', in Anthony Pagden, ed., *The Languages of Political Theory in Early Modern Europe* (Cambridge, 1988: Cambridge University Press); Hexter, *The Vision of Politics*, pp. 52–3.

164 More, *Utopia*, p. 111.

165 Ibid., pp. 121, 147.

166 Ibid., p. 125.

167 Ibid., pp. 153, 155, 157, 231.
168 Utopia had the benefit of evolving in relative isolation for 1760 years before Hythlodaeus' arrival: ibid., p. 121.
169 A similar point is made by Hexter, *The Vision of Politics*, pp. 76–8.
170 More, *Utopia*, p. 19.
171 Thomas More, *Selected Letters* (New Haven, 1961: Yale University Press), p. 85.
172 More, *Utopia*, p. 113.
173 Ibid., p. 111.
174 Ibid., pp. 199, 201.
175 Ibid., pp. 207, 209.
176 Ibid., p. 137.
177 Ibid., p. 137.
178 This is one consequence of what Avineri has called the paradox of perfection. 'If one starts with the assumption that a certain group is perfect, because it commits no crime or sin, the circle tends to close very soon by saying that it does not commit sin because it is perfect'; Shlomo Avineri, 'War and Slavery in More's Utopia', *International Review of Social History*, vol. 7, 1962, p. 289.
179 Machiavelli, *Discourses*, book I, Preface.
180 For a background to Vitoria's thought, see James Brown Scott, *The Spanish Origin of International Law: Francisco de Vitoria and his Law of Nations*, Carnegie Endowment for International Peace (Oxford, 1934: Clarendon), ch. 1, and B. Hamilton, *Political Thought in Sixteenth-Century Spain* (Oxford, 1963). See also the more recent J.A. Fernandez-Santamaria, *The State, War and Peace: Spanish Political Thought in the Renaissance 1516–1559* (Cambridge, 1977: Cambridge University Press), pp. 1–7, 58–63.
181 On the epistemic, moral and legal problems posed by the discoveries, see Tzvetan Todorov, *The Conquest of America: The Question of the Other* (New York, 1992: Harper & Row), esp. pp. 109, 156–8, 181, 185ff.
182 David Kennedy: 'Primitive Legal Scholarship', *Harvard International Law Journal*, vol. 27, 1986, no. 4, pp. 13ff. I am grateful to Pål Wrange for having drawn my attention to this excellent article.
183 Francisco de Vitoria, *De Potestate Civili* (1527/8) in Scott, *Spanish Origin of International Law*, p. lxxii.
184 Vitoria, *De Potestate Civili*, p. lxxv.
185 Ibid., p. lxxvi.
186 Ibid.
187 Ibid., p. lxxvii. Vitoria had no clear preference between monarchy and aristocracy; see ibid., p. lxxviii.
188 Ibid., p. lxxxi.
189 Vitoria, *De Potestate Ecclesiae I* (1530/1), in Scott, *The Spanish Origin of International Law*, p. xcvii.
190 Fernandez-Santamaria, *The State, War and Peace*, p. 77.
191 Vitoria, *De Potestate Civili*, p. lxxxv.
192 Vitoria, De Indis Recenter Inventis: *De Iure Bello*, in James Brown Scott,

ed., *The Classics of International Law* (Washington, 1917: Carnegie), p. 169.
193 Vitoria, *De Potestate Civili*, p. xc.
194 Cf. Todorov, *The Conquest of America*, pp. 185ff.
195 On this debate, see Anthony Pagden, 'Dispossessing the Barbarian: The Language of Spanish Thomism and the Debate over the Property Rights of the American Indians', in Pagden, ed., *The Languages of Political Theory in Early Modern Europe*.
196 Vitoria, *De Indis II* in Scott, *The Spanish Origin of International Law*, p. xxxi.
197 Vitoria, *De Indis I*, pp. vi–vii.
198 Ibid., p. ix.
199 Ibid., p. xi.
200 Ibid., p. xiii.
201 Vitoria, *De Jure Gentium et Naturali* in Scott, *The Spanish Origin of International Law*, p. cxii.
202 Ibid., p. cxiii.
203 Augustine, *Reply to Faustus the Manichean*, XXII. For an analysis of Augustine's idea of just war, see H. Deane, *The Social and Political Ideas of Saint Augustine* (New York, 1963).
204 Vitoria, *De Bello*, p. cxvii, in Scott, *The Spanish Origin of International Law*.

5 How policy became foreign: sovereignty, mathesis and interest in the Classical Age

1 See for example Hedley Bull, *The Anarchical Society: A Study of Order in World Politics* (London, 1977: Macmillan), p. 10.
2 Bull, *The Anarchical Society*, p. 10.
3 Samuel Pufendorf, *De Systematibus Civitatum* (1675), in Martin Wight, *The Systems of States* (Leicester, 1977: Leicester University Press), p. 21; Hugo Grotius, *De Jure Belli ac Pacis Libri Tres* ed. by James Brown Scott, *The Classics of International Law* (Oxford, 1925: Clarendon), p. 213; see also J.L. Holzgrefe, 'The Origins of Modern International Relations Theory', *Review of International Studies*, vol. 15, 1989, pp. 19f.
4 Samuel von Pufendorf, (*Elementorum Jurisprudentiae Universalis Libri Duo*, ed. James Brown Scott in *The Classics of International Law* (Oxford, 1931: Clarendon), vol. 2, p. 165), sometimes identified as one of the founding fathers of the international system by presentist writers, in fact found it difficult to speak of an independent law of nations, 'which, in the eyes of some men, is nothing other than the law of nature, insofar as different nations, not united with another by a supreme command, observe it, who must render one another the same duties in their fashion, as are prescribed for individuals by the law of nature. On this point there is no reason for our conducting any special discussion here, since what we recount on the subject of the law of nature and of the duties of individuals, can be readily applied to whole states and nations which have also coalesced into one moral person. Aside from this law, we are of the opinion that there is no law of nations, at least none which can properly be designated by such a name.' I am grateful to Jan Sellberg for drawing my attention to this passage.

5 Jean Bodin, *The Six Books of a Commonweale*, facsimile reprint of the Knolles edition of 1606, ed. by K.D. MacRae (Cambridge, Mass., 1962: Harvard University Press), book 2, ch. 1, p. 185.

6 Ibid., xxx.

7 Ibid., book 2, ch. 2, p. 199.

8 For an analysis of this problem, see Heinz Eulau, 'The Depersonalization of the Concept of Sovereignty', *Journal of Politics*, vol. 4, 1942 and Nannerl O. Keohane, *Philosophy and the State in France: The Renaissance to the Enlightenment* (Princeton, 1980: Princeton University Press), p. 17.

9 There is a number of excellent studies dealing with this development, most notably W.J. Stankiewicz, *Politics and Religion in Seventeenth-Century France* (Berkeley, 1960: University of California Press); Michael Walzer, *The Revolution of the Saints* (London, 1965: Weidenfeld & Nicolson); William F. Church, *Richelieu and the Reason of State* (Princeton, 1972: Princeton University Press); Quentin Skinner, *Foundations of Modern Political Thought*, vol. 2 (Cambridge, 1978: Cambridge University Press).

10 Thomas Hobbes, *Leviathan*, ed. by R. Tuck (Cambridge, 1991: Cambridge University Press), book 2, ch. 21, p. 149.

11 Ibid., book 2, ch. 13, p. 90.

12 Grotius, *De Jure Belli ac Pacis Libri Tres*, Prolegomena, pp. 15–17; For a recent analysis of 'The Grotian Tradition', see B. Kingsbury & A. Robert, 'Introduction: Grotian Thought in International Relations', in H. Bull, et al. eds., *Hugo Grotius and International Relations* (Oxford, 1990: Clarendon), pp. 1–65. In international relations theory, Hobbes and Grotius are sometimes placed in opposition to each other and treated as originators of two distinct traditions of thought. In the present context, no systematic attempt is made to evaluate this claim. Suffice it here to note that recent research suggests that this view is oversimplified, see for example R. Tuck, *Natural Rights Theories: Their Origin and Development* (Cambridge, 1979: Cambridge University Press).

13 Michel Foucault, *The Order of Things: An Archaeology of the Human Sciences* (London, 1991: Routledge), pp. 56–7.

14 Bodin, *The Six Books of a Commonweale*, book 1, ch. 8, p. 84.

15 Ibid. book 1, ch. 1, p. 1.

16 Ibid., book 6, ch. 6, p. 794.

17 J.U. Lewis, 'Jean Bodin's "Logic of Sovereignty"', *Political Studies*, vol. 16, 1968, pp. 212–17.

18 Julian H. Franklin, *Jean Bodin and the Sixteenth-Century Revolution in the Methodology of Law and History* (New York, 1963: Columbia University Press), pp. 137f; Kenneth D. McRae, 'Bodin and the Development of Empirical Political Science', in Horst Denzer, ed., *Jean Bodin: Proceedings* (Munich, 1973: Beck), pp. 333–43.

19 Bodin, *The Six Books of a Commonweale*, book 4, p. 450.

20 Bodin's influence on later absolutist theory has been discussed in numerous studies, the most comprehensive being: William F. Church, *Constitutional Thought in Sixteenth-Century France* (Cambridge, Mass., 1941: Harvard

University Press), pp. 303f; Julian H. Franklin, *Jean Bodin and the Rise of Absolutist Theory* (Cambridge, 1973: Cambridge University Press), *passim*.

21 René Descartes, *Rules for the Direction of our Native Intelligence*, in Descartes, *Selected Philosophical Writings* (Cambridge, 1988: Cambridge University Press), Rule 14, p. 18.

22 Ibid., Rule 13, p. 18.

23 Ibid., Rule 2, p. 1.

24 Ibid., Rule 6, p. 6.

25 Ibid., Rule 5, p. 6.

26 Ibid., Rule 7, p. 7.

27 Ibid., Rule 6–7, p. 7.

28 Foucault, *The Order of Things*, p. 53.

29 David R. Lachterman, *The Ethics of Geometry: A Genealogy of Modernity* (New York, 1989: Routledge), pp. 175, 178.

30 Reinhart Koselleck has argued ('Historia Magistra Vitae: The Dissolution of the Topos into the Perspective of a Modernized Historical Process' in Koselleck, *Futures Past: On the Semantics of Historical Time* (Boston, 1985: MIT Press)) that this shift arrives much later, and then as a result of the totalizing historiography of the Enlightenment. To my mind, however, the coming of the *mathesis* is the crucial event in this respect, since it delegitimizes exemplary history while legitimizing a nomothetic outlook. Bacon, for example, is scornful of exemplary history, and tells us that it applies to 'Exemplary States' only. (*Of the Advancement of Learning* (1605), ed. J.M. Robertson, in *The Philosophical Works of Francis Bacon* (London, 1905: Routledge), p. 83). If exemplary history and rhetoric based on example survives as late as in Montesquieu's *L'Esprit des Lois*, this is probably because the delegitimization is slow and piecemeal and because the emergent totalizing historiography also reopens a space of exemplary knowledge, but now with an altogether different purpose. Montesquieu is a case in point; he uses exempla to recover a republican tradition which itself is justified by means of exempla, to the effect that the republic can be understood as a container of tradition rather than as a container of virtue; it has a future because it has a continuous past.

31 Descartes, *Rules*, Rule 3, p. 3.

32 Foucault, *The Order of Things*, pp. 34f.

33 Bacon, *Of the Advancement of Learning*, p. 54.

34 Ibid., p. 56.

35 Ibid., p.118.

36 Ibid., p. 122.

37 On the relationship between representation and the mind-body distinction, see Richard Rorty, *Philosophy and the Mirror of Nature* (Oxford, 1980: Basil Blackwell), ch. 1.

38 Hobbes, *Leviathan*, Book 1, Ch. 4, p. 25.

39 Ibid., p. 26.

40 Foucault, *The Order of Things*, pp. 64–5.

41 Hobbes, *Leviathan*, book 1, ch. 4, p. 28.
42 Samuel von Pufendorf, *On the Duty of Man and Citizen According to Natural Law*, ed. by J. Tully (Cambridge, 1991: Cambridge University Press), ch. 10, p. 79.
43 Samuel von Pufendorf, *Of the Law of Nature and of Nations* (Oxford, 1703), book 4, ch. 1, p. 274.
44 Hobbes, *Leviathan*, book 1, ch. 4, p. 25.
45 John Locke, *An Essay Concerning Human Understanding* (London, 1990: Everyman's), book 3, ch. 2, no. 2.
46 Hobbes, *Leviathan*, book 1, ch. 4, p. 31.
47 Pufendorf, *On the Duty of Man*, ch. 10, p. 77.
48 Ibid., ch. 10, p. 77.
49 Pufendorf, *Of the Law of Nature*, ch. 1, p. 273.
50 Hobbes, *Leviathan*, book 1, ch. 4, p. 25.
51 Ibid., book 1, ch. 13, p. 89.
52 Pufendorf, *Of the Law of Nature*, book 4, ch. 1, pp. 273–4.
53 Jean-Jacques Rousseau, *Discours sur l'origine de l'inégalité* in *The Social Contract and Discourses*, G.D.H. Cole, ed. (London, 1990: Everyman's), pp. 65–70; Etienne Bonnot de Condillac, *Essai sur l'origine des connoissances humaines* (Amsterdam, 1746), vol. 2, pp. 4–15, 19–24.
54 Foucault, *The Order of Things*, pp. 107f. Cf. Condillac, *Essai sur l'origine des connoissances humaines*, vol. 2, pp. 4f.
55 Hobbes, *Leviathan*, book 1, ch. 5, p. 32.
56 Ibid., book 1, ch. 5, pp. 32–3.
57 Ibid., book 2, ch. 18, p. 125.
58 Ibid., book 2, ch. 17, p. 121f.
59 Ibid., book 2, ch. 31, p. 245.
60 Ibid., book 1, pp. 25–6, book 1, p. 58, see also W. Mathie, 'Reason and Rhetoric in Hobbes' Leviathan', *Interpretations*, vol. 14, 1986, no. 2.
61 Locke, *An Essay Concerning Human Understanding*, book 3, chs. 10–11, pp. 252–7.
62 'The History of Royal Society' in Springarn, ed., *Critical Essays of the Seventeenth Century*, vol. 2, quoted in Isaiah Berlin, *Vico and Herder: Two Studies in the History of Ideas* (London, 1976: The Hogarth Press), p. 104.
63 On this point, cf. Cornelia Navari, 'Knowledge, the State and the State of Nature', in Michael Donelan, ed., *The Reason of States: A Study in International Political Theory* (London, 1978: Allen & Unwin).
64 Cardin Le Bret, *De la souverainetée*, p. 19, quoted in Church, *Richelieu and the Reason of State*, p. 270.
65 A similar line of argument has been developed by William E. Connolly, *Political Theory & Modernity* (Oxford, 1988: Basil Blackwell), pp. 33–40.
66 Cf. Deborah Baumgold, *Hobbes's Political Theory* (Cambridge, 1988: Cambridge University Press), p. 45.
67 Hobbes, *Leviathan*, book 2, ch. 26, p. 184.
68 Ibid., book 2, ch. 16, p. 112.
69 Carl Schmitt, *Political Theology: Four Chapters on the Concept of Sovereignty*, (Boston, 1985: MIT Press), pp. 45–8.

70 Louis XIV, *Mémoires for the Instruction of the Dauphin*, ed. P. Sonnino (New York, 1970), p. 127.
71 Daniel de Priézac, *De la majesté*, in *Discours Politiques* (Paris, 1652), p. 142, tr. Church, *Richelieu and the Reason of State*, p. 452.
72 Cf. Reinhart Koselleck, *Critique and Crisis: Enlightenment and the Pathogenesis of Modern Society* (Oxford, 1988: Berg), pp. 15ff, 98ff.
73 Schmitt, *Political Theology*, p. 55.
74 Maurizio Viroli, *From Politics to Reason of State: The Acquisition and Transformation of the Language of Politics 1250–1600* (Cambridge, 1992: Cambridge University Press). In the present context, I am not in a position to do full justice to Viroli's study, which clearly improves on the conventional account in many respects.
75 Cf. Felix Raab, *The English Face of Machiavelli: A Changing Interpretation 1500–1700* (London, 1965: Routledge) and J. Ferrari, *Histoire de la Raison d'État* (Paris, 1860: Levy).
76 Hence Church omits treatises of Descartes in his seminal Richelieu and the Reason of State, 'since their influence lies outside the currents of thought that are examined in this book' (p. 7), while Meinecke throughout his *Machiavellism: The Doctrine of Raison d'État and its Place in Modern History* (1924) (Boulder and London, 1984: Westview) is content to connect *Raison d'État* with loose references to different *Weltanschauungen*.
77 Meinecke, *Machiavellism*, p. 53.
78 On the problematic reception of Machiavellian ideas, see for example, Meinecke, *Machiavellism*, chs. 2–4; Donald R. Kelley, 'Murd'rous Machiavel in France: A Post Mortem', *Political Science Quarterly*, vol. 85, 1970, no. 4; Donald W. Bleznick, 'Spanish Reaction to Machiavelli in the Sixteenth and Seventeenth Centuries', *Journal of the History of Ideas*, vol. 19, 1958; Adrianna E. Bakos, '"*Qui nescit dissimulare, nescit regnare*': Louis XI and Raison d'État during the Reign of Louis XIII', *Journal of the History of Ideas*, vol. 52, 1991, no. 3; F.E. Sutcliffe, 'La notion de Raison d'État dans la pensée française et espagnole au XVIIe siècle', in Roman Schnur, ed., *Staatsräson: Studien zur Geschichte eines politischen Begriffs* (Berlin, 1975: Duncker & Humblot).
79 Peter S. Donaldson, *Machiavelli and Mystery of State* (Cambridge, 1988: Cambridge University Press), pp. x–xiii, *passim*.
80 The books and manuscripts have been selected according to several criteria. First, since my primary target has been the analysis of state interests, rather than discussions of interest with reference to domestic contexts, manuscripts dealing solely with the latter have been left out. Second, since imitations are in abundance (especially of Rohan), they have been left out also, except in the case of the anonymous *Discours* of 1666, which furnishes evidence contrary to earlier interpretations of it. Third, I have omitted mere compilations of court gossip, even if they sometimes are informed by the notion of interest, such as the *Recueil de diverses relations remarquables des principales cours* (Cologne, 1681). As the reader may note, most examples of the analysis of interest are French. This French bias should not come as a surprise, however, since it was in France – which was gradually estab-

lishing itself as the great power during the seventeenth century – that the analysis of interest first developed in connection with foreign policy.

81 William E. Connolly, *The Terms of Political Discourse* (Oxford, 1983: Martin Robertson), pp. 45–84.

82 J.A.W. Gunn, *Politics and the Public Interest in the Seventeenth Century* (London, 1969: Routledge), p. 3.

83 Raab, *The English Face of Machiavelli*, pp. 157–68.

84 Gunn, *Politics and the Public Interest*, pp. 1–54, 322–30.

85 Albert O. Hirschmann, *The Passions and the Interests: Political Arguments for Capitalism before Its Triumph* (Princeton, 1977: Princeton University Press), pp. 33ff; Keohane, *Philosophy and the State in France*, pp. 151f.

86 Gunn, *Politics and the Public Interest*, p. 42.

87 Michel de Montaigne, 'L'utile et l'honorable', *Essais*, Book III, ch. I (Paris, 1922: Felix Alcan); Justus Lipsius, *Sixe bookes of Politickes or Civil Doctrine* (London, 1594), book 4, ch. 14; Pierre Charron, *De la sagesse* (Paris, 1820), book 3, ch. 2; René Descartes, *Correspondence*, ed. by C. Adam & G. Milhaud, (Paris, 1936–63) vol. 7, no. 548 (letter to Queen Elisabeth of Bavaria); Gabriel Naudé, *Considérations politiques sur les coups d'estat* (Amsterdam, 1679), pp. 55f, 297f.

88 Gunn, *Politics and the Public Interest*, pp. 29, 41; Hirschman, *The Passions and the Interests*, pp. 32–3.

89 Cf. Gigliola Rossini, 'The Criticism of Rhetorical Historiography and the Ideal of Scientific Method: History, Nature and Science in the Political Language of Thomas Hobbes', in A. Pagden, ed., *The Languages of Political Theory in Early Modern Europe* (Cambridge, 1988: Cambridge University Press); Connolly, *Political Theory & Modernity*, pp. 27–30; Preston King, *The Ideology of Order: A Comparative Analysis of Jean Bodin and Thomas Hobbes* (London, 1974: Allen & Unwin), pp. 161–77; Quentin Skinner, '"Scientia Civilis" in Classical Rhetoric and in the Early Hobbes', in N. Phillipson & Q. Skinner, *Political Discourse in Early Modern Britain* (Cambridge, 1993: Cambridge University Press).

90 This act of reinvention of the self and of knowledge is especially evident in Descartes' *Discours sur la methode*, *Selected Philosophical Writings*, pp. 20–56; see also Lachterman, *The Ethics of Geometry*, pp. 126–40.

91 Robert P. Adams, *The Better Part of Valor: More, Erasmus, Colet, and Vives on Humanism, War and Peace 1496–1535* (Seattle, 1962: University of Washington Press), pp. 82, 101, 224–6.

92 Thomas Hobbes, *Human Nature*, in *English Works*, ed. W. Molesworth (London, 1839–45), vol. 4, dedicatory epistle.

93 Gatien Courtilz de Sandras, *Nouveaux interets des Princes de l'Europe* (Cologne/the Hague [the exact place of publication is contested]: 1686), Preface: 'nous avons si peu de connoisance de l'antiquité, ils ont travesti les hommes à leur guise, & leur passion a été le pinceau avec lequel ils nous les ont peints'.

94 Henri duc de Rohan, *De l'interest des princes et estats de la Chrestienté* (Paris, 1643: Augustin Courbé), dedicatory epistle to Richelieu: 'La raison vient, de

ce qu'on ne peut establir une regle immuable dans le gouvernement des Estats. Ce qui cause la Revolution des affairs de ce monde, cause aussi le changement des maximes fondamentales pour bien regner.'

95 Joan-Pau Rubiés, 'Hugo Grotius's Dissertation on the Origin of the American Peoples and the Use of Comparative Methods', *Journal of the History of Ideas*, vol. 52: no. 2, 1991 and also Tzvetan Todorov, *The Conquest of America* (New York. 1992: Harper), pp. 185ff.

96 La Mothe le Vayer, *Discours de la contrariété d'humeurs qui se trouve entre certaines nationes, et singulièrement entre la françoise et l'espagnole*, in *Œuvres* (Paris, 1662), vol. 1, 157–91. Discussed in Church, *Richelieu and the Reason of State*, p. 390.

97 Rohan, *De l'interest des princes*, p. 1: 'Les Princes commandent aux peuples & l'interest commande aux Princes.'

98 Anon., *Discours des princes et états de la chrestienté plus considérables à la France, selon les diverses qualitez et conditions*, published in *Mercure Français*, vol. 10, 1625.

99 Rohan, *De l'interest des princes*, p. 1: 'La connoisance de cet interest, est d'autant plus relevée par dessus celle des actions des Princes, qu'eux mesmes le sont par dessus les peuples.'

100 La Rochefoucauld, François duc de: *réflexions ou sentences et maximes morales*, ed. P. Morand (Paris, 1965), no. 171 quoted by Keohane, *Philosophy and the State in France*, p. 291.

101 Jean Silhon, *De la certitude des connoissances humaines* (Paris, 1661), book II, ch. 2, pp. 101–3 quoted by Keohane, *Philosophy and the State in France*, p. 288.

102 Paul Gondi Cardinal de Retz, *Œuvres*, ed. A. Feillet (Paris, 1880), vol. 5, p. 307, quoted by Keohane, *Philosophy and the State in France*, p. 226.

103 Gunn, *Politics and the Public Interest*, p. 43, see also J.A.W. Gunn, '"Interest Will Not Lie"': A Seventeenth-Century Political Maxim', *Journal of the History of Ideas*, vol. 29, 1968.

104 Courtilz de Sandras, *Nouveaux interets des Princes de l'Europe*, p. 92; Samuel von Pufendorf, *An Introduction to the History of the Principal Kingdoms and States of Europe* (London: 1711), Preface; Paul Ardier, *Mémoire sur les affaires générales de la chrétienté au mois d'avril 1633*, in Mathieu Molé, *Mémoires*, vol. 4, pp. 166–223 (Paris, 1855–7: Jules Renouard), p. 166.

105 Jacob Viner, 'Power versus Plenty as Objectives of Foreign Policy in the Seventeenth and Eighteenth Centuries', *World Politics*, vol. 1, 1948 no. 1; Foucault, *The Order of Things*, pp. 186–9; Keohane, *Philosophy and the State in France*, pp. 158–60.

106 Cf. Terence Ball, 'The Changing Face of Power', in T. Ball, *Transforming Political Discourse*, (Oxford, 1988: Basil Blackwell), ch. 3; Keohane, *Philosophy and the State in France*, pp. 267–70.

107 Thomas Hobbes, *De Corpore*, in English Works, ed. Molesworth, ch. 10.

108 I say 'resemble', since even if the vocabulary of game theory was not accessible to the classics, decision theory was; see Ian Hacking, 'The Logic of Pascal's Wager', *American Philosophical Quarterly*, vol. 9, 1972, no. 2.

109 See G.M. Dillon, 'The Alliance of Security and Subjectivity', *Current Research on Peace and Violence*, vol. 13, 1990, no. 3.
110 Hobbes, *Leviathan*, book 1, ch. 17, pp. 118–19, my emphasis.
111 Baruch de Spinoza, *A Treatise partly Theological and Partly Political* (London, 1737), ch. 16, pp. 334–5.
112 As, for example, Thomas Schelling does, in his *The Strategy of Conflict* (Cambridge, Mass., 1960: Harvard University Press), pp. 14, 29–30, 36–7.
113 Armand-Jean du Plessis, cardinal de Richelieu, *Testament politique*, ed. Louis André (Paris, 1947: Lafont), p. 373; *Richelieu and Reason of State*, p. 500.
114 Foucault, *The Order of Things*, pp. 134ff.
115 Rohan, *De l'interest*, pp. 3–8.
116 Samuel von Pufendorf, *An Introduction to the History of Principal Kingdoms and States of Europe* (London, 1711), Preface.
117 Pufendorf, *An Introduction*, p. 3.
118 Ardier, *Mémoire*, pp. 166–7.
119 Ibid., p. 188.
120 Ibid., p. 216.
121 Courtilz de Sandras, *Nouveaux interets*, pp. 14, 26, 40.
122 Ibid., p. 125.
123 Ibid., p. 3.
124 Ibid., p. 40.
125 Ibid., p. 40.
126 Ibid., Preface.
127 A.L.C. Destutt de Tracy, *Élémens d'Idéologie*, vol. 1; (1801) (Paris, 1970: J. Vrin) pp. 1–19.
128 Bacon, *Of the Advancement of Learning*, p. 162.
129 Anon., *Discours des princes*, this passage quoted in Friedrich Meinecke, *Machiavellism*, p. 155 Since the only copy which I had access to was severely damaged by worms, I have been unable to check this translation.
130 Rohan, *De l'interest*, dedicatory epistle to Richelieu.
131 Pufendorf, *An Introduction*, Preface.
132 Ardier, *Mémoire*, p. 167.
133 Courtilz de Sandras, *Nouveaux interets*, pp. 3, 57, 119.
134 *De Rebus Sueciis ab Expeditione Gustavi Adolphi in Germaniam ad Abdicationem usque Christianae*, 1677–88, Preface, translated in Meinecke, *Machiavellism*, p. 236.
135 Courtilz de Sandras, *Nouveaux interets*, p. 3: 'nous sommes nés dans un Etat, qui n'est sujet d'aucune de ces deux couronnes, mais nous faisons profession de dire la verité'.
136 Rohan, *De l'interest*, p. 1: 'Le Prince se peut tromper, son conseil peut estre corrompu; mais l'interest seul ne peut iamais manquer, selon qu'il est bien ou mal entendu, il fait vivre ou mourir les Estats.'
137 Gunn, 'Interest Will not Lie', pp. 555f.
138 Charles Herle, *Interest Will not Lie or a View of England's True Interest* (London, 1659), p. 3, quoted in Gunn, 'Interest Will not Lie', p. 557.
139 Rohan, *De l'interest*, p. 26: 'qu'en matiere d'Estat on doit se laisser conduire

aux desirs de regles qui nous emportent souvent à entreprendre des choses au delà de nos forces, ny aux passions violentes qui nous agitent diversement selon qu'elles nous possedent ... [m]ais à notre propre intersest, guidé par la seule raison, qui doit estre la regle de nos actions.'

140 Rohan, *De l'interest*, p. 48: 'les Venetiens suivent exactement ce qui estoit de leur interest', p. 43: '[les Papes] poussez d'un zele inconsideré, ou enflammez du desir de se signaler à la posterité, ou emportez par la violence de leur passions'.

141 Courtilz de Sandras, *Nouveaux interets*, pp. 32, 36.

142 Pufendorf, *An Introduction*, Preface.

143 René Descartes, *Fourth Meditation, Selected Philosophical Writings*, p. 100.

144 René Descartes, *Sixth Meditation, Selected Philosophical Writings*, pp. 116f.

145 See, for example, Richard Popkin, *A History of Scepticism from Erasmus to Spinoza* (Berkeley, 1979: University of California Press).

146 Descartes, *Sixth Meditation*, p. 116.

147 Niccolò Machiavelli, *The Prince* (Cambridge, 1989: Cambridge University Press), dedicatory letter to Lorenzo de Medici, p. 4.

148 Gunn, 'Interest Will not Lie', p. 559.

149 Richelieu, *Testament politique*, book 2, ch. 9, no. 3, p. 375.

150 David Parker, *The Making of French Absolutism* (London, 1983: Edward Arnold), p. 32 and *passim*.

151 Rohan, *De l'interest*, p. 8; Courtilz de Sandras, *Nouveaux Interets*, pp. 159, 230.

152 R.A. Klein, *Sovereign Equality Among States: The History of an Idea* (Toronto, 1974: University of Toronto Press).

153 Baruch de Spinoza, *Ethics*, part 4, Prop. 33 (London, 1959: Dent).

154 Charles Herle, *Interest Will not Lie or a View of England's True Interest*, p. 3, quoted in Gunn, 'Interest Will not Lie', p. 557.

155 Anthony Giddens, *The Nation-State and Violence* (Oxford, 1985: Polity Press), pp. 87, 256; John B. Wolf, *Toward a European Balance of Power 1620–1715* (Chicago, 1970: Rand McNally), *passim*.

156 Rohan, *De l'interest*, pp. 2, 12.

157 Courtilz de Sandras, *Nouveaux interets*, p. 92: 'Mais y a-t-il d'alliance à l'épreuve de l'interet, & quand l'interet parle, tout le reste ne se taît-il-pas'.

158 Anon., *Interets et maximes des princes et des états souverains* (Cologne, 1666), p. 5: 'Si deux Princes Souverains, yssus d'un même tige, & ayans leurs Etats voisins, sont inferieurs l'un à l'autre en dignité & en puissance, on les verra de bonne intelligence entr'eux'.

159 Abraham de Wicquefort, *L'Ambassadeur et ses fonctions* (Cologne, 1690), book 1, p. 1: 'une science qui ait ses principes mathématiques, où qui son fondés sur des raisons demonstratives, sur lesquelles on puisse faire des règles certaines and infaillibles'.

160 Abraham de Wicquefort, *L'Ambassadeur et ses fonctions*, book 2, p. 72: 'Les principes de raisonement dans la politique sont aussy incertaines, que ceux de la Mathematique sont infaillibles'.

161 Anon., *Mémoire*: 'De remasser généralement toutes les depesches, toutes

les négociations, tous les traités, qu'on pourra trouver depuis deux cents ans ou environ, de les mettre par ordre, par pays et par année.' Quoted in Armand Baschet, *Histoire du Dépôt des Archives des Affaires Étrangères* (Paris, 1875), p. 111 and quoted and discussed in Maurice Keens-Soper, 'The French Political Academy', 1712: A School for Ambassadors', *European Studies Review*, vol. 2, 1972, no. 4, p. 336.

162 Baschet, *Histoire du Dépôt*, p. 121; Keens-Soper, 'The French Political Academy, 1712' p. 333.

163 Baschet, *Histoire du Dépôt*, p. 120; Keens-Soper, 'The French Political Academy, 1712', p. 339.

164 Keens-Soper, 'The French Political Academy, 1712', p. 345.

165 Maurice Keens-Soper, 'François de Callières and Diplomatic Theory', *The Historical Journal*, vol. 16, 1973, no. 3, p. 498.

166 Wicquefort, *L'Ambassadeur et ses fonctions*, book 1, p. 53.

167 François de Callières, *De la manière de negocier avec les souverains* (London, 1750: Jean Nourse), vol. 1, book 1, pp. 61–71; Wicquefort, *L'Ambassadeur et ses fonctions*, book 2, pp. 7, 12–3.

168 Callières, *De la manière de negocier*, vol. 1, book 1, p. 37; Wicquefort, *L'Ambassadeur et ses fonctions*, book 2, p. 99.

169 Callières, *De la manière de negocier*, vol. 1, book 1, pp. 41–7, 201.

170. Wicquefort, *L'Ambassadeur et ses fonctions*, book 2, pp. 72, 91; Callières, *De la manière de negocier*, vol. 2, pp. 27, 80, 82–84.

171 Wicquefort, *L'Ambassadeur et ses fonctions*, book 2, pp. 32–4, 114; Callières, *De la manière de negocier*, vol. 1, p. 282.

172 Wicquefort, *L'Ambassadeur et ses fonctions*, book 1, ch. 27, p. 383: 'La Necessité des Ambassades fait la seureté des Ambassadeurs, du consentement universel de toutes les nations de la terre; & c'est ce consentement qui fait qu'on apelle le Droit des Gens. Il tient le milieu entre le Droit naturel & le Droit civil, & est d'autant plus considerable que le dernier, qu'il ne peut estre changé n'y alteré, sinon du mesme consentement unanime de tous les peuples. Il n'y a point de Souverain, qui se puisse donner l'autorité d'expliquer les loix, dont ce Droit est composé, & il n'y point de juge, qui puisse estendre sa jurisdiction sur les personnes, que ce Droit protege; parce qu'il troubleroit un commerce, dont la liberté est fondée sur une necessité indispensable, & il osteroit de celuy des hommes le moyen de conserver la societé, qui ne pourroit pas subsister sans ce principe, qui est plus que Mathematique.'

173 Callières, *De la manière de negocier*, vol. 1, ch. 1, p. 9: 'i'l faut considerer que tous les Estats dont l'Europe est composée, ont entr'eux des liaisons & des commerces nécessaires qui font qu'on peut les regarder comme des membres d'une même République, & qu'il ne peut presque point arriver de changement considérable en quelques-uns de ses membres qui ne soit capable de troubler le repos de tous les autres.'

174 See for example Claire A. Cutler, 'The "Grotian Tradition" in International Relations', *Review of International Studies*, vol. 17, 1991, pp. 44–9, 63–5; Bull, *The Anarchical Society*, pp. 24f. For a criticism of this tendency to read into

Grotius doctrines he never could have advocated, see David Kennedy, 'Primitive Legal Scholarship', *Harvard International Law Journal*, vol. 27, 1986, no. 1, pp. 78ff. See also Hidemi Suganami, 'A Note on the Origin of the Word "International"', *British Journal of International Studies*, vol. 4, 1978, for a criticism of the widespread habit of equating older legal concepts with the modern notions of international system and society.

175 Grotius, *De Juri Belli ac Pacis Libri Tres*, vol. 1, p. 121.
176 Ibid.
177 Wicquefort, *L'Ambassadeur et ses fonctions*, book 1, pp. 255f, book 2, pp. 3–4, 49, 58–72, 91–4; Callières, *De la manière de negocier*, vol. 1, pp. 32–47, 229, 308, 313–14, vol. 2, pp. 33, 42, 61, 78, 82–84, 204f, 229, 231.

6 Reorganizing reality: sovereignty, modernity and the international

1 Jeremy Bentham, *An Introduction to the Principles of Morals and Legislation* (New York, 1963: Hafner), p. 326.
2 Cf. F.H. Hinsley, *Nationalism and the International System* (London, 1973: Hodder and Stoughton), pp. 69–83; F.H. Hinsley, *Sovereignty*, 2d ed. (Cambridge, 1986: Cambridge University Press), pp. 204ff. H. Bull (*The Anarchical Society: A Study of Order in World Politics* (London, 1977: Macmillan), p. 13) who dates the rise of the international system earlier, sees this as a phase of transition to what he calls a society of states, which 'exists when a group of states, conscious of certain common interests and common values, form a society in the sense that they conceive themselves to be bound by a common set of rules in their relations with one another, and share in the working of common institutions.' This distinction between 'system' and 'society' is arguably ontologically and methodologically void, see Geoffrey Berridge, 'The Political and Institutional History of States-Systems', *British Journal of International Studies*, vol. 6, 1980.
3 See David R. Lachtermann, *The Ethics of Geometry: A Genealogy of Modernity* (New York, 1989: Routledge), pp. 1–24 for a similar argument.
4 Cf. note 2 above.
5 Cf. Michel Foucault, *The Order of Things* (London, 1991: Routledge), pp. 218–230.
6 A similar interpretation has been proposed by Richard Ashley, 'Living on Border Lines: Man, Poststructuralism, and War', in J. DerDerian & M. Shapiro, eds., *International/Intertextual Relations* (Lexington, Mass., 1989: Lexington books), pp. 259–323, but then without the slightest sensitivity to the historicity of the problem itself.
7 For an analysis of the problems with Hobbes's theory of contract, see Jean Hampton, *Hobbes and the Social Contract Tradition* (Cambridge, 1986: Cambridge University Press), pp. 189ff, also Alessandro Pizzorno, 'On the Individualistic Theory of Social Order' in P. Bourdieu, & J.S. Coleman, eds., *Social Theory for a Changing Society* (Boulder, 1991: Westview).
8 For examples of retrospective readings, see Sylvester John Hemleben, *Plans for Peace through Six Centuries* (Chicago, 1943: Chicago University Press),

pp. 70ff; F.H. Hinsley, *Power and the Pursuit of Peace* (Cambridge, 1967: Cambridge University Press). For a criticism of 'the myth of tradition' in international relations theory, see Robert B.J. Walker, 'The Prince and "The Pauper": Tradition, Modernity and Practice in the Theory of International Relations' in James DerDerian & Michael J. Shapiro, eds., *International/ Intertextual Relations: Postmodern Readings of World Politics* (Lexington, 1989: Lexington books), pp. 26–32.

9 See for example Michael Doyle, 'Liberalism and World Politics', *American Political Science Review*, vol. 80, 1986, no. 4; Richard Rosencrance, *The Rise of the Trading State* (New York, 1986: Basic Books).

10 Jean Rousset, *Les interêts presens des puissances de l'Europe*, vols. 1–3 (La Haye, 1733), vol. 1, Preface, f. 3: 'Mais il est arrivé dans la situation des affaires de l'Europe, depuis ce tems-là, des revolutions si extraordinaires qu'on ne trouve plus une seule maxime dans ces Auteurs [Rohan & Courtilz] qui puisse être d'usage aujourd'hui; outre qu'on peut dire que le Duc, écrivant en grand seigneur, étoit trop concis, & que l'autre écrivant en Auteur, étoit trop prolixe & se jettoit souvent dans des disgressions ennuïeuses.'

11 Jean Rousset, *Les interêts*, Preface, f. 8.

12 Gabriel Bonnot de Mably, *Des principes des négociations pour servir d'introduction au droit public de l'Europe, fondé sur les traités* (Amsterdam, 1758), chs. 2, 3, 4, 5.

13 This separation of morals and politics has been thoroughly analysed by Reinhart Koselleck, *Critique and Crisis: Enlightenment and the Pathogenesis of Modern Society* (Oxford, 1988: Berg), pp. 23–48, 145–83.

14 This point seems to have been overlooked by Ian M. Wilson, *The Influence of Hobbes and Locke in the shaping of the Concept of Sovereignty in Eighteenth-century France: Studies on Voltaire and the Eighteenth Century* (Banbury, 1973).

15 Charles Louis de Secondat Montesquieu, *The Spirit of the Laws* (Cambridge, 1989: Cambridge University Press), book 10.

16 Jean-Jacques Rousseau, *A Discourse on the Origin of Inequality* in Jean-Jacques Rousseau, *The Social Contract and Discourses*, ed. G.D.H. Cole (London, 1990: Everyman's), p. 50. Cf. also Jean-Jacques Rousseau, *L'État de Guerre* in C.E. Vaughan, ed., *The Political Writings of Jean-Jacques Rousseau*, vol. 1 (Cambridge, 1915: Cambridge University Press), p. 306.

17 Cf. Montesquieu, *The Spirit of the Laws*, book 1, ch. 3: 'Each particular society comes to feel its strength, producing a state of war among nations. The individuals within each society begin to feel their strength; they seek to turn their favour the principal advantages of this society, which brings about a state of war among them.'

18 Jean-Jacques Rousseau, *A Discourse on the Origin of Inequality*, in Rousseau, *The Social Contract*, p. 100.

19 Jean-Jacques Rousseau, *Extrait du projet de paix perpétuelle de M. l'Abbé de Saint Pierre* in C.E. Vaughan, *The Political Writings of Jean-Jacques Rousseau*, vol. 1, p. 365. For an analysis of Rousseau's theory of war, see Stanley Hoffmann, 'Rousseau on War and Peace', in Stanley Hoffmann, *The State of War* (New York, 1965: Praeger), pp. 54–87.

20 Jean-Jacques Rousseau, *L'État de guerre*, in C.E. Vaughan, ed., *Political Writings*, vol. 1 p. 304: 'D'homme à homme, nous vivons dans l'état civil et soumis aux lois; de peuple à peuple, chacun jouit de la liberté naturelle: ce qui rend au fond notre situation pire que si ses distinctions étaient inconnues. Car vivant à la fois dans l'ordre social et dans l'état de nature, nous sommes assujettis aux inconvénients de l'un et de l'autre, sans trouver la sûreté dans aucun des deux.'

21 Jean-Jacques Rousseau, *L'État de guerre*, in C.E. Vaughan, ed., *Political Writings*, vol. 1, p. 304.

22 Jean-Jacques Rousseau, *A Discourse on the Origin of Inequality*, in Cole, ed., *The Social Contract*, p. 112.

23 Butler, who misses the critical upshot of the text, sees Vattel's significance in his having encapsulated 'agreements about identities and moral priorities that characterised eighteenth-century Europe', a statement which merely begs the question of what this agreement would consist in, 'Legitimacy in a States-System: Vattel's Law of Nations' in M. Donelan, ed., *The Reason of States: A Study in International Political Theory* (London, 1978: Allen & Unwin) p. 56.

24 Emerich de Vattel, *The Law of Nations or the Principles of Natural Law, Applied to the Conduct and to the Affairs of Nations and Sovereigns* in James Brown Scott, ed., *The Classics of International Law* (Washington, 1916: The Carnegie Institution), vol. 3, p. 4.

25 Vattel, *The Law of Nations*, p. 5.

26 Ibid., p. 6.

27 Ibid., p. 6.

28 Ibid., p. 7.

29 Ibid., p. 251.

30 Ibid., p. 8.

31 Ibid., p. 11.

32 Ibid., pp. 13, 20–2.

33 Ibid., p. 243.

34 Koselleck, *Critique and Crisis*, p. 160n6.

35 Reinhart Koselleck, 'Historical Criteria of the Modern Concept of Revolution' in *Futures Past: On the Semantics of Historical Time* (Boston, 1985: MIT Press), pp. 42–3.

36 Montesquieu, *The Spirit of the Laws*, book 5, ch. 11.

37 Koselleck, 'Historical Criteria', p. 43.

38 Ibid., pp. 46f.

39 M. le Marquis d'Argenson, *Considérations sur le gouvernement ancien et présent de la France, comparé avec celui des autres états*, 2nd edn (Liege, 1787), p. 12: 'Tout est revolution dans ce Monde; les Etats ont leur temps de progrès & de decadence.'

40 Guillaume Thomas Raynal, *Histoire philosophique et politique des établissemens et du commerce de Européens dans les Deux Indes* (Neuchatel & Genève, 1783), vol. I, p. 2: 'Tout est changé & doit changer encore. Mais les révolutions

passés & celles qui doivent suivre ont-elles été, seront-elles utiles à la nature humaine? L'homme decra-t-il un jour plus de tranquillité, de bonheur & de plaisir? Son état sera-t-il meilleur, ou ne sera-t-il que changer?' Subsequent notes to Raynal's text will be redered thus: volume: chapter: page.

41 Raynal, *Histoire Philosophique et Politique*, IX:II:38: 'ces énormes machines qu'on appelle societés, où, bandés les un contre les autres, ils agissent & réagissent avec toute la violence de leur énergie particuliere, on créa artificiellement un véritable état de guerre, & d'une guerre variée par une multitude innombrable d'intérêts & d'opinions'.

42 Ibid., IX:II:40–1.

43 Ibid., IX:II:53.

44 Ibid., IX:II:42.

45 Ibid., IX:III:128: 'Les bassins de la balance politique ne seront jamais dans un parfait équilibre, i assez juste pour determiner le degés de puissance avec une exacte precision. Peut-être même ce systême d'égalité n'est-il qu'un chimere. La balance ne peut s'établir que par des traités, & les traités n'ont aucune solidité qu'entre des souverains absolus, & non entre des nations. Ces actes doivent subsister entre des peuples, parce qu'ils ont pour objet la paix & la sûreté qui sont leurs plus grands biens: mais un despote sacrifie toujours ses sujets à son inequitude, & ses engagemens à son ambition.'

46 Koselleck, *Critique and Crisis*, p. 183.

47 Raynal, *Histoire Philosophique et Politique*, IX:III:129.

48 Thomas Paine, *The Rights of Man* (Harmondsworth, 1971: Penguin) p. 233.

49 Ibid., p. 234.

50 Ibid., p. 239.

51 Jean-Jacques Ròusseau, *A Discourse on the Origin of Inequality*, in Cole, ed., *The Social Contract and Discourses*, p. 51.

52 Foucault, *The Order of Things*, pp. 242ff.

53 Ibid., p. 236.

54 Precisely this mixture, when becoming folklore later in the nineteenth century, provoked Nietzsche's furious attack on History; see his 'On the Uses and Disadvantages of History for Life' (1874) in *Untimely Meditations* (Cambridge, 1989: Cambridge University Press), pp. 57–124.

55 Giambattista Vico, *The New Science* (Ithaca, 1968: Cornell University Press), §. 34, p. 21.

56 Ibid., § 51, p. 33.

57 Ibid., § 354, p. 106.

58 Ibid., § 145, p. 64.

59 Ibid., § 238, p. 78.

60 Ibid., § 146, p. 64.

61 Ibid., § 163, p. 67.

62 Ibid., § 161, p. 67.

63 Lachtermann, *The Ethics of Geometry*, pp. 7f. Cf. also P. Verene, *Vico's Science of Imagination* (Ithaca, 1981: Cornell University Press), ch. 2.

64 Vico, *De Antiquissima*, p. 150, quoted in Isaiah Berlin, *Vico and Herder: Two Studies in the History of Ideas* (London, 1976: Hogarth), p. 17.

65 Vico, *The New Science*, § 331, p. 96.

66 Ibid., § 320–1, p. 93.

67 Ibid., § 332, p. 97.

68 Ibid., § 347, p. 104.

69 Ibid., § 349, p. 104.

70 The influence – whether direct or indirect – of Vico upon Rousseau has been debated, and it is still disputed whether Rousseau ever read the *Scienza Nuova*; see, for example, Ernst Cassirer, *The Philosophy of Symbolic Forms* (New Haven, 1953: Yale University Press), vol. 1, ch. 1. The main difference, however, is that Vico sees divine providence as the source of language (Berlin, *Vico and Herder*, part 1, *passim*), and speech and writing as contemporaneous forms (*The New Science*, § 3), while Rousseau, however unsuccessfully, tries to place the origin of language on a wholly secular footing while insisting on the separation of writing and speech, thus prefiguring de Saussure; Jacques Derrida, 'The Linguistic Circle of Geneva', in *Margins of Philosophy* (Brighton, 1982: Harvester Press), pp. 137–54.

71 Rousseau, *A Discourse on the Origin of Inequality*, p. 44.

72 Ibid., pp. 64–6.

73 Ibid., pp. 67–8.

74 Ibid., p. 102.

75 Jean-Jacques Rousseau, *An Essay on the Origin of Languages*, pp. 38–9, quoted and discussed extensively in Jacques Derrida, *Of Grammatology* (Baltimore & London, 1976: Johns Hopkins), pp. 256ff.

76 Derrida, *Of Grammatology*, pp. 257–9.

77 Cf. the opening phrases in Jean-Jacques Rousseau, *The Social Contract*, in Cole, ed., *The Social Contract and Discourses*, p. 181.

78 Jean-Jacques Rousseau, *Émile* (Paris, 1929: Garnier), pp. 73, 105, discussed further in Derrida, *Of Grammatology*, pp. 170f.

79 Derrida, *Of Grammatology*, pp. 170f.

80 Johann Gottfried Herder, *Essay on the Origin of Language* in F.M. Barnard, ed., *J.G. Herder on Social and Political Culture* (Cambridge, 1969: Cambridge University Press), p. 137.

81 Ibid., p. 163.

82 Ibid., p. 135.

83 Ibid., pp. 141–2.

84 Ibid., p. 143.

85 Ibid., p. 147.

86 Ibid., p. 169.

87 Cf. Berlin, *Vico and Herder*, p. 153.

88 Herder, *Essay on the Origin of Language*, pp. 170, 174.

89 Immanuel Kant, *The Critique of Pure Reason* (London, 1985: Macmillan), Preface to the first edition, p. 7.

90 Ibid., Preface to the second edition, p. 24.

91 Ibid., p. 18.
92 Ibid., p.19.
93 Ibid., p. 27, text pp. 577–8.
94 Foucault, *The Order of Things*, pp. 244–50.
95 For a study of the formative moments of modernity and social science within the state, see John F. Rundell, *Origins of Modernity: The Origins of Modern Social Theory From Kant to Hegel to Marx* (Cambridge, 1987: Polity Press), esp. pp. 14–77.
96 See, for example, Benedict Anderson, *Imagined Communities: Reflections on the Origin and Spread of Nationalism* (London, 1991: Verso).
97 See Hinsley, *Nationalism and the International System*, pp. 35–63.
98 To my knowledge, Rousseau is the first in modernity to use the concept 'body politic' to denote the union of state and nation; see especially *The Social Contract*, ch. 4 and *A Discourse on Political Economy*, in Cole, ed., *The Social Contract and Discourses*, p. 132–3.
99 Argenson, *Considérations*, pp. 22–4: For an discussion of d'Argenson, see Nannerl O. Keohane, *Philosophy and the State in France: The Renaissance to the Enlightenment* (Princeton, 1980: Princeton University Press), pp. 376f.
100 Rousseau, *The Social Contract*, p. 191. Except for Hoffmann, 'Rousseau on War and Peace', pp. 65–67, the subdued dialectic between internal order and external and generalized war in Rousseau has not – as far as I know – attracted much attention.
101 Ibid., p. 205.
102 Ibid., pp. 200–2.
103 Ibid., p. 200.
104 Ibid., p. 216.
105 This problem is further discussed by William Connolly, *Political Theory and Modernity* (Oxford, 1988: Basil Blackwell), pp. 53f, but he fails to notice the external aspect of the general will, and instead settles for the doctrine of civil religion as the solution to the problem.
106 Rousseau, *The Social Contract*, p. 216.
107 Ibid., p. 211.
108 Rousseau's influence on Kant was pervasive. See for example Ernst Cassirer, *Rousseau, Goethe, Kant: Two Essays* (Princeton, 1970: Princeton University Press); Hans Saner, *Kant's Political Thought: Its Origins and Developments* (Chicago, 1973: Chicago University Press); Ernst Cassirer, *Kant's Life and Thought* (New Haven, 1981: Yale University Press).
109 Immanuel Kant, *Perpetual Peace* in H. Reiss, ed., *Kant: Political Writings* (Cambridge, 1991: Cambridge University Press), p. 94.
110 Immanuel Kant, *The Metaphysics of Morals* in Reiss, ed., *Kant: Political Writings*, p. 140.
111 Immanuel Kant, *On the Common Saying: 'This May be True in Theory, but it does not Apply in Practice'* in Reiss, ed., *Kant: Political Writings*, p. 79.
112 Immanuel Kant, *Idea for a Universal History*, in Reiss, ed., *Kant: Political Writings*, p. 44.

113 Kant, *Perpetual Peace*, p. 112.
114 Kant, *Idea for a Universal History*, p. 47; Kant, *The Metaphysics of Morals*, p. 165.
115 While the internal determinations of the Hegelian state have been thoroughly analysed and discussed, this cannot be said about the external determinations. See, for example, Z.A. Pelczynski, 'The Hegelian Conception of the State' in Pelczynski, ed., *Hegel's Political Philosophy: Problems and Perspectives* (Cambridge, 1971: Cambridge University Press), pp. 1–29: Charles Taylor, *Hegel* (Cambridge, 1975: Cambridge University Press), ch. 16; Peter J. Steinberger, *Logic and Politics: Hegel's Philosophy of Right* (New Haven, 1988: Yale University Press), *passim*. Even in a recent study such as Dallamayr's, the external aspects of the Hegelian state are somewhat neglected, see Fred R. Dallamayr, *G. W. F. Hegel: Modernity and Politics* (Newbury Park, 1993: SAGE), esp. pp. 155–64. A notable exception is, however, Shlomo Avineri, *Hegel's Theory of the Modern State* (Cambridge, 1974: Cambridge University Press), who in chapter 10 briefly discusses the external determinations of the state in the context of Hegel's theory of war.
116 Georg Wilhelm Friedrich Hegel, *The German Constitution,* in *Hegel's Political Writings* (Oxford, 1964: Clarendon), p. 153.
117 Ibid., p. 158.
118 Ibid., p. 159.
119 Ibid., p. 158.
120 Ibid., p. 227.
121 Georg Wilhelm Friedrich Hegel, *Elements of the Philosophy of Right*, H. B. Nisbet, trans., A.W. Wood, ed. (Cambridge, 1991: Cambridge University Press), § 274, p. 213.
122 Ibid., § 257–8: pp. 275–6.
123 Ibid., § 259, 271.
124 Ibid., § 270 addition p. 302.
125 Ibid., § 260, p. 282.
126 Ibid., 321, p. 359.
127 Ibid., § 322, p. 360.
128 Ibid., § 323, p. 360.
129 Ibid., § 324, p. 362.
130 Ibid., § 278, 279, pp. 316–18.
131 Cf. Avineri, *Hegel's Theory of the Modern State*, pp. 185–9.
132 Hegel, *Elements of the Philosophy of Right*, § 279, p. 319.
133 To my knowledge, no one has hitherto bothered to compare Hegel's theory of the sovereign with Carl Schmitt's decisionism, see Carl Schmitt, *Political Theology: Four Chapters on the Concept of Sovereignty* (1922) (Boston, 1985: MIT Press), ch. 1.
134 Hegel, *Elements of the Philosophy of Right*, § 278, p. 316.
135 Ibid., no. 330–1, pp. 366–7.
136 Ibid., no. 330, p. 366, see also G.W.F. Hegel, 'The Philosophical History of the World', second draft (1830) in G.W.F. Hegel, *Lectures on the Philosophy of World History* (Cambridge,1975: Cambridge University Press), p. 124.

137 Hegel, *Philosophical History of the World*, p. 28.
138 Hegel, *Elements of the Philosophy of Right*, § 340, p. 371.
139 Hegel, *Philosophical History of the World*, pp. 40f, 50f, *Elements of the Philosophy of Right*, no. 342, p. 372.
140 Hegel, *Philosophical History of the World*, pp. 51f, 63.
141 Hegel, *Elements of the Philosophy of Right*, § 344, p. 373.
142 Hegel, *Philosophical History of the World*, pp. 93f.
143 Cf. Reinhart Koselleck, 'Historia Magistra Vitae: The Dissolution of the Topos into the Perspective of a Modernized Historical Process', in *Futures Past*, pp. 31–5.
144 Savigny, *Zeitschrift für geschichtliche Wissenschaft*, vol. 1, 1815, no. 4, quoted in Koselleck, 'Historia Magistra Vitae', p. 38.
145 Theodore Mommsen, *Römische Geschichte* (Berlin, 1882), vol. 3, p. 477, quoted in Koselleck, 'Historia Magistra Vitae', p. 38.
146 Hegel, *Philosophical History of the World*, p. 25.
147 See Hayden White, *Metahistory: The Historical Imagination in Nineteenth-Century Europe* (Baltimore & London, 1973: Johns Hopkins), pp. 141ff.
148 Fréderic Ancillon, *Considérations générales sur l'histoire* (Berlin, 1801), pp. 62–3.
149 Wilhelm von Humboldt, *On the Historian's Task* (1821), *History and Theory*, vol. 6, 1967, no. 1, p. 59.
150 Ibid., p. 58.
151 Ibid., p. 58.
152 Ibid., p. 58.
153 Ibid., p. 61.
154 Ibid., p. 64.
155 Ibid., p. 65.
156 Ibid., p. 65 my emphasis.
157 Leopold Ranke, *History of the Latin and Teutonic Nations, 1494–1514*, tr. by P.A. Ashworth (London, 1887), Preface, reprinted in Fritz Stern, ed., *The Varieties of History: From Voltaire to the Present* (New York, 1956: Meridian books), p. 62.
158 Humboldt, *On the Historian's Task*, p. 60.
159 Ibid., p. 69.
160 Leopold Ranke, *The Great Powers* in Theodore H. von Laue, *Leopold Ranke: The Formative Years*, Princeton Studies in History, vol. 4 (Princeton, 1950: Princeton University Press), p. 181.
161 Ibid., p. 182.
162 Leopold Ranke, *A Dialogue on Politics*, in Theodore H. von Laue, *Leopold Ranke: The Formative Years*, p. 180.
163 Ranke, *The Great Powers*, pp. 182–3.
164 Ibid., p. 217.
165 Ibid., p. 217.
166 See Richard Little, 'Deconstructing the balance of power: two traditions of thought', *Review of International Studies*, vol. 15, 1989, pp. 87–100. Little,

however, fails to discern both the epistemic foundations of the various concepts of balance of power, and their historical consequences.

167 Mably, *Des principes des négociations*, ch. 6, p. 79–81.

168 I. Kant, *On the Common Saying: 'This May be True in Theory, but it does not Apply in Practice'*, in H. Reiss, ed., *Kant: Political Writing* (Cambridge, 1991: Cambridge University Press), p. 92.

169 Ancillon, *Considérations générales*, pp. 94f, Friedrich von Gentz, *Fragments upon the Balance of Power in Europe* (London, 1806: Pettier), *passim*; Carl von Clausewitz, *On War*, book 6, ch. 6: I have here relied on Aron's interpretation of Clausewitz; see Aron Raymond, *Penser la guerre, Clausewitz*, vol. 1, *L'Âge Européen* (Paris, 1976: Gallimard), p. 173.

170 Ranke, *The Great Powers*, p. 189.

171 Edmund Burke, *Letters on a Regicide Peace*, vol. 2, p. 345–6, vol. 3, pp. 441–3, in Edmund Burke, *Works*, (London, 1899).

172 A.H.L. Heeren, *Handbuch der Geschichte des Europäischen Staatensystems und seiner Kolonien, Historische Werke*, vol. 9–10 (Göttingen, 1822), vol. 9, p. 6: 'Die Geschichte des Europäischen Staaten-Systems ist keineswegs die Geschichte der einzelnen Staaten. Sie ist vielmehr die Geschichte iherer Behältnisse gegen einander; besonders der Hauptstaaten, insofern sie sich aus dem Wesen der einzelnen; der Personlichkeit der Gewalthaber; und den herrschenden Ideen der Zeit entwickelten. Allgemeine Bedingung des Wechsels dieser Berhältnisse, und das her allgemeiner Charakter dieses Staatensystems, war aber seiner innere Freiheit, d.i. die Selbständigheit und wechselseitige Unabhängigkeit seiner Glieder. Zu zeigen wie dieser gebildet, gefährdet, erhalten wurde, – bleibt also die Hauptausgabe für den Geschichtschreiber; sie aber nur durch die Entwicklung der ganzen Reihe der innern Berhältnisse des Systems, und der Ursachen die sie erzeugten, gelöst werden kann.'

173 Carl von Clausewitz, *On War* (Harmondsworth, 1984: Penguin), book 5, addition b, p. 378. Cf. also Aron, *Penser La Guerre, Clausewitz*, vol. 1, pp. 325–7.

174 For an analysis of utopianism and state practices in the classical age, see James DerDerian, *On Diplomacy: a Genealogy of Western Estrangement* (Oxford, 1987: Basil Blackwell), pp. 141–52, also, from another perspective, Krishnan Kumar, *Utopia and Anti-Utopia in Modern Times* (Oxford, 1986: Basil Blackwell).

175 Cf. Henri duc de Rohan, *De l'interest des Princes et Estats de la Chrestienté* (Paris, 1643: Augustin Courbé).

176 Cf. Gatien Courtilz de Sandras, *Nouveaux interets des Princes de l'Europe* (Cologne/the Hague (the exact place remains contested) 1686), table.

177 René Descartes, *A Discourse on Method*, tr by J. Cottingham, R. Stootthoff and D. Murdoch in Descartes, *Selected Philosophical Writings* (Cambridge, 1988: Cambridge University Press), pp. 32–3.

178 Hegel, *Philosophical History of the World*, p. 124.

179 Ibid., pp. 152–208.

180 Heeren, *Handbuch*, vol. 10, p. 408.
181 Ranke, *The Great Powers*, p. 187.
182 Cf. Hemleben, *Plans for Peace through Six Centuries*, pp. 42ff. This perhaps helps to explain the alleged 'realism' of Crucé's *Nouveaux Cyneas* (DerDerian, *On Diplomacy*, pp. 146–7).
183 Rousseau, *Extrait Du Projet*, in Vaughan, *Political Writings*, vol. 1, pp. 374–9.
184 Clausewitz, *On War*, p. 120, my emphasis.
185 Rousseau, *Extrait Du Projet*, p. 387: 'ce n'est donc pas qu'il soit chimerique; c'est que les hommes sont insensés, et que c'est une sorte de folie d'être sage au milieu des fous'. Cf. also Jugement sur la Paix Perpétuelle, in Vaughan, *Political Writings*, p. 396.
186 Hidemi Suganami, *The Domestic Analogy and World Order Proposals* (Cambridge, 1989: Cambridge University Press).
187 Hegel, *Elements of the Philosophy of Right*, no. 324 addition, p. 362.
188 Kant, *Idea*, pp. 41–2, and Immanuel Kant, *The Contest of the Faculties* in H. Reiss, ed., *Kant: Political Writings*. This aspect has been more fully elaborated by Y. Yovel, *Kant and the Philosophy of History* (Princeton, 1980: Princeton University Press).
189 Kant, *Idea for a Universal History*, p. 41.
190 Cf. Jean-François Lyotard, *The Differend: Phrases in Dispute* (Manchester, 1988: Manchester University Press), pp. 161–71. For a comment on Lyotard's quite idiosyncratic interpretation of Kant, see David Ingram, 'The Postmodern Kantianism of Arendt and Lyotard', *Review of Metaphysics*, vol. 42, 1988.
191 Waltz, in his *Man, the State, and War: a Theoretical Analysis* (New York, 1959: Columbia University Press), pp. 162f and in 'Kant, Liberalism and War', *American Political Science Review*, vol. 56, 1962, pp. 337–40, interprets the Kantian theory of international relations wholly in the context of his moral philosophy and regards the internal moral perfection of states as the ultimate condition of perpetual peace, which in turn is assimilated to purely moral ends. To Hinsley, Kantian peace is propelled by the collaboration of natural and moral forces, but concludes his interpretation with a tilt in favour of the latter; F.H. Hinsley, *Power and the Pursuit of Peace* (Cambridge, 1967: Cambridge University Press), pp. 69–80. Gallie, perhaps more sensitive to the conflict between moral reason and natural necessity which animates Kant's later philosophy, nevertheless holds that 'the requirements of practical (moral) reason impose and define the task of peace between nations'. W.B. Gallie, *Philosophers of Peace and War* (Cambridge, 1978: Cambridge University Press), p. 34.
　　Apart from these authors, who as a result of their emphasis of the moral dimension of the project of peace end up in an all but optimistic view of the possibility of its realization, there are authors who have focused on the alleged inevitability of peace. Read from this vantage point, perpetual peace becomes not so much dependent on voluntary agency, but rather the result of the benevolent workings of an invisible – that is, systemic –

hand in international politics, which in the long run is said to produce cooperation out of conflict. Thus, the inner logic of anarchy and conflict constitutes the main force of peace: as Doyle has argued, 'our guarantee of perpetual peace does not rest on ethical conduct ... [but on] how ... free and intelligent devils could be motivated by fear, force, and calculated advantage to undertake a course of action whose outcome we could reasonably anticipate to be perpetual peace'. Michael Doyle, 'Liberalism and World Politics', *American Political Science Review*, vol. 80, 1986, no. 4, p. 1159. Modelski, assimilating Kant to his theory of evolutionary learning in world politics, similarly argues that Kant's project of perpetual peace is 'a study in self-organization because it asserts the possibility of morphogenetic change in the world system ... tending to bring about a condition of lasting peace'. George Modelski, 'Is World Politics Evolutionary Learning?', *International Organization*, vol. 44, 1990, no. 1, pp. 4–6. Finally, Kriele, although an industrious reader of Kantian texts, somewhat naively celebrates the spirit of capitalist democracy as an autonomous force in world politics that will render perpetual peace inevitable. Martin Kriele, *Die demokratische Weltrevolution* (Munich, 1987: Piper), *passim.*

192 Immanuel Kant, *The Critique of Judgment* (New York, 1951: Hafner), p. 12.

193 Cassirer fails to see any clear continuity between Kant's political philosophy and the *Critique of Judgment* (Cassirer, *Kant's Life and Thought*, pp. 271ff), while Saner misses the antagonistic and unresolved play of the faculties in the *Third Critique* (Saner, *Kant's Political Thought*, pp. 280ff). The importance of the *Third Critique* remains disputed: see Patrick Riley, 'The "Elements" of Kant's Practical Philosophy', *Political Theory*, vol. 14, 1986, no. 4, pp. 564f.

194 Kant, *The Critique of Judgment*, p. 13.

195 Kant, *Perpetual Peace*, pp. 108–9.

196 Kant, *The Critique of Judgment*, p. 244.

197 Ibid., pp. 256–8.

198 Kant, *The Contest of the Faculties*, p. 177.

199 Ibid., pp. 180–1.

200 Ibid., p. 180.

201 Kant, *Critique of Judgment*, p. 112.

202 Ibid., pp. 105–6; Kant, *The Contest of the Faculties*, p. 182.

203 Cf. Jean-François Lyotard, *L'Enthousiasme. La critique Kantienne de l'histoire* (Paris, 1986: Galilée), pp. 45ff.

7 Conclusion: the end of sovereignty

1 Cf. James N. Rosenau, 'Sovereignty in a Turbulent World', paper presented at the Conference on Sovereignty and Collective Intervention, Hanover, NH (18–20 May 1992).

Bibliography

Adams, R.P., *The Better Part of Valor: More, Erasmus, Colet and Vives on Human-ism, War and Peace, 1496–1535* (Seattle, 1962: University of Washington Press)

Ancillon, F., *Considérations générales sur l' histoire* (Berlin, 1801)

Anderson, B., *Imagined Communities: Reflections on the Origin and Spread of Nationalism* (London, 1991: Verso)

Anderson, P., *Lineages of the Absolutist State* (London, 1974: New Left Books)

Passages from Antiquity to Feudalism (London, 1974: New Left Books)

Andrews, B., 'Social Rules and the State as a Political Actor', *World Politics*, vol. 27, 1975, no. 4

Ankersmit, F.R., 'Historiography and Postmodernism', *History and Theory*, vol. 28, 1989, no. 2

Anon., *Discours des Princes et États de la Chrestienté plus considérables à la France, selon les diverses qualitez et conditions*, Mercure Français, vol. 10 (Paris, 1625)

Anon., *Interets et maximes des Princes et des états souverains* (Cologne, 1666)

Ardier, P., 'Mémoire sur les affaires générales de la chréienté au mois d'Avril 1633', in Molé, M., *Mémoires*, vol. 4 (Paris, 1855–7: Jules Renouard)

Arendt, H., *Between Past and Future* (Harmondsworth, 1977: Penguin)

Argenson, M., *Considérations sur le gouvernement ancien et présent de la france, comparé avec celui des autres états*, 2nd edn (Liege, 1787: Plompteux)

Aristotle, *Rhetorics*, trans. J.H. Freese (London, 1947: Heinemann)

Physics tr. R.P. Hardie & R.K. Gaye (Oxford, 1953: Clarendon)

The Politics (Cambridge, 1988: Cambridge University Press)

Aron, R., *Peace and War: A Theory of International Relations*, trans. R. Howard & A. Baker Fox (London, 1966: Weidenfeld and Nicolson)

Penser la guerre, Clauswitz, vol. 1, *L'Age Européen* (Paris, 1976: Gallimard)

Ashley, R.K., 'The Geopolitics of Geopolitical Space: Toward a Critical Social Theory of International Politics', *Alternatives*, vol. 23, 1987

'Untying the Sovereign State: A Double Reading of the Anarchy Problémati-que', *Millenium*, vol. 17, 1988, no. 2

'Living on Border Lines: Man, Poststructuralism, and War' in DerDerian, J. &

Shapiro, M., eds., *International /Intertextual Relations: Postmodern Readings of World Politics* (Lexington, Mass., 1989: Lexington Books)

Ashley, R.K. & Walker, R.B.J., 'Speaking the Language of Exile: Dissident Thought in International Relations', *International Studies Quarterly*, vol. 34, 1990

Augustine, *Confessions*, trans. J.G. Pilkington (New York, 1943: Liveright)

Austin, J.L., *How to do Things with Words* (Oxford, 1962: Oxford University Press)

Avineri, S., 'War and Slavery in More's Utopia', *International Review of Social History*, vol. 7, 1962

Hegel's Theory of the Modern State (Cambridge, 1979: Cambridge University Press)

Bachelard, G., *The Psychoanalysis of Fire* (London, 1987: Quartet Books)

Bacon, F., 'Of The Advancement of Learning', in Robertson, J.M., ed., *The Philosophical Works of Francis Bacon* (London, 1905: Routledge)

Bakos, A.E., '"*Qui nescit dissimulare, nescit regnare*": Louis XI and Raison d'État during the reign of Louis XIII', *Journal of the History of Ideas*, vol. 52, 1991, no. 3

Ball, T., *Transforming Political Discourse* (Oxford, 1988: Basil Blackwell)

Ball, T. et al., eds., *Political Innovation and Conceptual Change* (Cambridge, 1989: Cambridge University Press)

Barnard, F.M., ed., *J.G. Herder on Social and Political Culture* (Cambridge, 1969: Cambridge University Press)

Barnes, B., *Scientific Knowledge and Sociological Theory* (London, 1974: Routledge)

Interests and the Growth of Knowledge (London, 1977: Routledge)

Baron, H., *Humanistic and Political Literature in Florence and Venice at the Beginning of the Quatrocento* (Cambridge, Mass., 1955: Harvard University Press)

'Machiavelli: Republican Citizen and Author of The Prince', *English Historical Review*, vol. 76, 1961

The Crisis of the Early Italian Renaissance (Princeton, 1966: Princeton University Press)

Baschet, A., *Histoire du Dépôt des Archives des Affaires Étrangères* (Paris, 1875)

Baumann, Z., 'Modernity and Ambivalence', *Theory, Culture and Society*, vol. 7, 1990 (SAGE Publications, London)

Baumgold, D., *Hobbes's Political Theory* (Cambridge, 1988: Cambridge University Press)

Becker, M., 'The Florentine Territorial State and Civic Humanism in the Early Renaissance' in Rubinstein, N. ed., *Florentine Studies: Politics and Society in Renaissance Florence* (London, 1968: Faber & Faber)

Bendix, R., *Kings or People: Power and the Mandate to Rule* (Berkeley, 1971: University of California Press)

Bendix, R., ed., *State and Society* (Berkeley, 1968: University of California Press)

Benn, S.I., 'The Uses of Sovereignty', *Political Studies*, vol. 3, 1955, no. 2

Bentham, J., *An Introduction to the Principles of Morals and Legislation* (New York, 1963: Hafner)

Berlin, I., 'The Originality of Machiavelli' in Gilmore, M. ed., *Studies on Machiavelli* (Florence, 1972: Sansoni)

Vico and Herder: Two Studies in the History of Ideas (London, 1976: The Hogarth Press)

Berridge, G., 'The Political and Institutional History of States-Systems', *British Journal of International Studies*, vol. 6, 1980

Bhaskar, R., *Scientific Realism and Human Emancipation* (London, 1986: Verso)

Black, M., *The Importance of Language* (Englewood Cliffs, NJ, 1962: Prentice-Hall)

Bleznick, D.W., 'Spanish Reaction to Machiavelli in the Sixteenth and Seventeenth Centuries', *Journal of the History of Ideas*, vol. 19, 1958

Bloor, D., *Knowledge and Social Imagery* (London, 1973: Routledge)

Bodin, J., *Six Books of a Commonweale*, ed. K.D. McRae (Cambridge, Mass., 1962: Harvard University Press)

Boros, S., 'Les catégories de la temporalité chez Saint Augustin', *Archives de Philosophie*, vol. 21, 1958

Bouchard, D.F., ed., *Language, Counter-Memory, Practice: Selected Essays and Interviews by Michel Foucault* (Ithaca, 1977: Cornell University Press)

Bourdieu, P. & Coleman, J.S., eds., *Social Theory for a Changing Society* (Boulder, 1991: Westview)

Brewin, C., 'Sovereignty' in Mayall, J. ed., *The Community of States: A Study in International Political Theory* (London, 1982: Allen & Unwin)

Bull, H. 'The Theory of International Politics, 1919–1969' in Porter, B., ed., *The Aberystwyth Papers* (London, 1972: Oxford University Press)

The Anarchical Society: A Study of Order in World Politics (London, 1977: Macmillan)

'The Emergence of a Universal International Society' in Bull, H. & Watson, A., eds., *The Expansion of International Society* (Oxford, 1984: Clarendon)

Bull, H. & Watson, A., eds., *The Expansion of International Society* (Oxford, 1984: Clarendon)

Bull, H. et al., eds., *Hugo Grotius and International Relations* (Oxford, 1990: Clarendon)

Burke, E., *Works* (London, 1899)

Burkhardt, J., *The Civilization of the Renaissance in Italy* (London, 1951: Phaidon)

Butler, P.F., 'Legitimacy in a States-System: Vattel's law of Nations' in Donelan, M., ed., *The Reason of States: A Study in international political theory* (London, 1978: Allen & Unwin)

Butterfield, H., *The Whig Interpretation of History* (Harmondsworth, 1973: Penguin)

Buzan, B., *Peoples, States, and Fear: The National Security Problem in International Relations* (Brighton, 1983: Wheatsheaf)

'Rethinking System and Structure' in Buzan, B., Jones, C. & Little, R., *The Logic of Anarchy: From Neorealism to Structural Realism* (New York, 1993: Columbia University Press)

Buzan, B., Jones, C. & Little, R., *The Logic of Anarchy: From Neorealism to Structural Realism* (New York, 1993: Columbia University Press)

Bibliography

Callières, F., *De la Manière de negocier avec les souverains*, vol. 1–2 (London, 1750: Jean Nourse)
Carnoy, M., *The State and Political Theory* (Princeton, 1984 :Princeton University Press)
Carr, E.H., *The Twenty Years Crisis 1919–1939: An Introduction to the Study of International Relations* (London, 1978: Macmillan)
Cassirer, E., *The Myth of the State* (New Haven, 1946: Yale University Press)
   The Philosophy of Symbolic Forms (New Haven, 1953: Yale University Press)
   Rousseau, Goethe, Kant: Two Essays, trans. J. Gutman (Princeton, 1970: Princeton University Press)
   Kant's Life and Thought (New Haven, 1981: Yale University Press)
Cassirer, E., ed., *The Renaissance Philosophy of Man* (Chicago, 1948: University of Chicago Press)
Chabod, F., *Machiavelli and the Renaissance* (London, 1958: Bowes & Bowes)
Charron, P., *De la sagesse* (Paris, 1820)
Cheyette, F.L., 'The Sovereign and the Pirates, 1332', *Speculum*, vol. 45
Church, W.F., *Constitutional Thought in Sixteenth Century France* (Cambridge, Mass., 1941: Harvard University Press)
   Richelieu and the Reason of State (Princeton, 1972: Princeton University Press)
Claessen, H.J.M. & Skalnik, P., 'The Early State: Theories and Hypotheses' in Claessen, H.J.M. & Skalnik, P., eds., *The Early State* (The Hague, 1978: Mouton)
Clausewitz, C., *On War* (Harmondsworth, 1984: Penguin)
Cochrane, E.W., 'Machiavelli: 1940–1960', *Journal of Modern History*, vol. 33, 1961, no. 2
Cohen, R., 'State Origins: A Reappraisal' in Claessen, H.J.M. & Skalnik, P., eds., *The Early State* (The Hague, 1978: Mouton)
Cole, G.D.H., ed., *The Social Contract and Discourses* (London, 1990: Everyman's)
Collins, R., *Three Sociological Traditions* (New York: 1980: Oxford University Press)
   Sociology Since Mid-century: Essays in Theory Cumulation (New York, 1981: Academic Press)
Condillac, E.B., *Essai sur l'origine des connoissances humaines* (Amsterdam, 1746)
Connolly, W., *The Terms of Political Discourse* (Oxford, 1983: Martin Robertson)
   Political Theory and Modernity (Oxford, 1988: Basil Blackwell)
Cottingham, J., et al. eds., *Descartes: Selected Philosophical Writings* (Cambridge, 1988: Cambridge University Press)
Courtilz de Sandras, G., *Nouveaux interets des Princes de l'Europe* (Cologne/the Hague, 1686)
Cox, R., 'Social Forces, States and World Orders' in Keohane, R., ed., *Neorealism and its Critics* (New York, 1986: Columbia)
Craig, H., *The Enchanted Glass: The Elisabethan Mind in Literature* (Westport, Conn., 1975: Greenwood)
Croce, B., *Politics and Morals* (New York, 1945)

Crombie, A.C. *Science, Optics and Music in Medieval and Early Modern Thought* (London, 1987: Hambledon Press)

Culler, J., *On Deconstruction: Theory and Criticism After Structuralism* (London, 1983: Routledge)

Cutler, C.A., 'The "Grotian Tradition" in International Relations', *Review of International Studies*, vol. 17, 1991

Czempiel, E.O. & Rosenau, J.N., eds., *Global Changes and Theoretical Challenges* (Lexington, 1989: Lexington Books)

Dallamayr, F.R., *G.W.F. Hegel: Modernity and Politics* (Newbury Park, 1993: SAGE)

Dante Alighieri, *The Monarchy and Three Letters*, tr. D. Nicholl & C. Hardie (New York, 1954)

Deane, H., *The Social and Political Ideas of Saint Augustine* (New York, 1963)

Delany, S., *Medieval Literary Politics: Shapes of Ideology* (Manchester, 1990: Manchester University Press)

Deleuze, G., *Foucault*, trans. S. Hand (Minneapolis 1988: University of Minnesota Press)

Denzer, H., ed., *Jean Bodin: Proceedings* (Munich, 1973: Beck)

DerDerian, J., *On Diplomacy: A Genealogy of Western Estrangement* (Oxford, 1987: Basil Blackwell)

DerDerian, J. & Shapiro, M.J., eds., *International/Intertextual Relations: Postmodern Readings of World Politics* (Lexington, 1989: Lexington Books)

Derrida, J., *Of Grammatology*, trans. G.C. Spivak (Baltimore & London, 1974: Johns Hopkins)

La verité en peinture (Paris, 1978: Flammarion)

Writing and Difference, trans. A. Bass (London, 1978: Routledge)

Positions, trans. A. Bass (Chicago, 1981: University of Chicago Press)

Margins of Philosophy, trans. A. Bass (Sussex, 1982: Harvester Press)

Descartes, R., *Correspondence*, ed. Adam C. & Milhaud, G., (Paris, 1936–63)

'A Discourse on Method' in Cottingham, J., ed., *Descartes: Selected Philosophical Writings* (Cambridge, 1988: Cambridge University Press)

'Fourth Meditation"in Cottingham, J., ed., *Descartes: Selected Philosophical Writings* (Cambridge, 1988: Cambridge University Press)

Rules for the Direction of our Native Intelligence Cottingham, J. et al., eds., and tr. *Descartes: Selected Philosophical Writings* (Cambridge, 1988: Cambridge University Press)

'Sixth Meditation' in Cottingham, J., ed., *Descartes: Selected Philosophical Writings* (Cambridge, 1988: Cambridge University Press)

Dessler, D., 'What's at Stake in the Agent-Structure Debate?', *International Organization*, vol. 43, 1989, no. 3

Destutt de Tracy, A.L.C., *Eleméns d'Ideologie*, vol. 1 (Paris, 1970: J. Vrin)

Dillon, G.M., 'The Alliance of Security and Subjectivity', *Current Research on Peace and Violence*, vol. 13, 1990, no. 3

Donaldson, P.S., *Machiavelli and Mystery of State* (Cambridge, 1988: Cambridge University Press)

Bibliography

Donelan, M., 'Introduction' in Donelan, M., ed., *The Reason of States: A Study in International Political Theory* (London, 1978: Allen & Unwin)

Donelan, M. ed., *The Reason of States: A Study in International Political Theory* (London, 1978: Allen & Unwin)

Doyle, M., 'Liberalism and World Politics', *American Political Science Review*, vol. 80, 1986, no. 4

Dreyfus, H. & Rabinow, P., *Michel Foucault: Beyond Structuralism and Hermeneutics* (Chicago, 1982: University of Chicago Press)

Dunn, J., 'The Identity of the History of Ideas' in Laslett, P., ed., *Philosophy, Politics and Society* (Oxford, 1962: Basil Blackwell)

Dyer, H.C. & Mangasarian, L., eds., *The Study of International Relations* (London, 1989: Macmillan)

Dyson, K.H.F., *The State Tradition in Western Europe* (Oxford, 1980: Martin Robertson)

Elias, N., *Power and Civility: The Civilizing Process*, vol. 2, trans. by E. Jephcott (New York, 1982: Pantheon)

Engels, F., *The Origin of the Family, Private Property, and the State* (London, 1972: Lawrence & Wishart)

Eulau, H., 'The Depersonalization of the Concept of Sovereignty', *Journal of Politics*, vol. 4, 1942

Evans, P. et al., eds., *Bringing the State Back In* (Cambridge, 1985: Cambridge University Press)

Ferguson, W.K., *The Renaissance in Historical Thought: Five Centuries of Interpretation* (New York, 1948: Houghton Mifflin Company)

Fernández-Santamaria, J.A., *State, War, and Peace: Spanish Political Thought in the Renaissance 1516–1559* (Cambridge, 1977: Cambridge University Press)

Ferrari, J., *Histoire de la Raison d'Etat* (Paris, 1860: Levy)

Ficino, M., 'Five Questions Concerning the Mind' in Cassirer, E., et. al., eds., *The Renaissance Philosophy of Man* (Chicago, 1948: University of Chicago Press)

Flynn, T., 'Foucault and the Spaces of History', *The Monist*, vol. 74, 1991, no. 2

Foucault, M., *The Archaeology of Knowledge*, trans. A.M. Sheridan (New York, 1972: Pantheon Books)

　'The Discourse on Language' in *Archaeology of Knowledge* (New York, 1972: Pantheon Books)

　'Nietzsche, Genealogy, History' in Bouchard, D.F., ed., *Language, Counter-Memory, Practice* (Ithaca, 1977: Cornell University Press)

　'What is an Author?' in Bouchard, D.F., ed., *Language, Counter-Memory, Practice* (Ithaca, 1977: Cornell University Press)

　The History of Sexuality, vol. 1 (New York, 1978: Vintage Books)

　Discipline and Punish: The Birth of the Prison, trans. A. Sheridan (Harmondsworth, 1979: Penguin)

　'Truth and Power' in Gordon, C. ed., *Power/Knowledge: Selected Interviews and Other Writings 1972–1977 by Michel Foucault* (New York, 1980: Pantheon Books)

'The History of Sexuality' interview by Lucette Finas in Gordon, C., ed., *Power/Knowledge: Selected Interviews and Other Writings 1972–1977 by Michel Foucault* (New York, 1980: Pantheon Books)

'The Subject and Power' postscript to Dreyfus, H. & Rabinow, P., *Michel Foucault: Beyond Structuralism and Hermeneutics* (Berkeley, 1982: University of California Press)

The Order of Things: An Archaeology of the Human Sciences (London, 1991: Routledge)

Franklin, J.H., *Jean Bodin and the 16th Century Revolution in the Methodology of Law and History* (New York, 1963: Columbia University Press)

Jean Bodin and the Rise of Absolutist Theory (Cambridge, 1973: Cambridge University Press)

Fraser, N., 'Foucault on Modern Power: Empirical Insights and Normative Confusions', *Praxis International*, vol. 4, 1981, no. 2

Fukuyama, F., *Have We Reached the End of History?* (Santa Monica, 1989: The RAND Corporation)

Gallie, W.B., 'Essentially Contested Concepts' in Black, M., ed., *The Importance of Language* (Englewood Cliffs, NJ, 1962: Prentice-Hall)

Geerken, J.H., 'Machiavelli Studies since 1969', *Journal of the History of Ideas*, vol. 37, 1976

Gentz, F., *Fragments upon the Balance of Power in Europe* (London, 1806: Pettier)

Gewirth, A., *Marsilius of Padua: The Defender of Peace* (New York, 1956: Columbia University Press)

Giddens, A., *The Constitution of Society: Outline of the Theory of Sructuration* (Cambridge, 1984: Polity Press)

The Nation-State and Violence: Volume Two of a Contemporary Critique of Historical Materialism (Cambridge, 1985: Polity Press)

Gierke, O., *Natural Law and the Theory of Society 1500–1800*, trans. E. Barker (Boston, 1957: Beacon Press)

Political Theories of the Middle Age, trans F.W. Maitland (Boston, 1958: Beacon Press)

Gilbert, F., *Machiavelli and Guicciardini: Politics and History in Sixteenth-Century Florence* (Princeton, 1965: Princeton University Press)

Gilmore, M.P., 'Freedom and Determinism in Renaissance Historians', *Studies in the Renaissance*, vol. 3, 1956

Studies on Machiavelli (Florence, 1972: G.C. Sansoni)

Goldmann, K., 'The Concept of "Realism" as a Source of Confusion', *Cooperation and Conflict*, vol. 23, 1988

'The Line in Water: Domestic and International Politics: A Discussion Paper', *Cooperation and Conflict*, vol. 24, 1989

Gordon, C., ed., *Power/Knowledge: Selected Interviews and Other Writings 1972–1977 by Michel Foucault* (New York, 1980: Pantheon Books)

Gracia, J.J.E., 'Texts and Their Interpretation', *Review of Metaphysics*, vol. 43, 1990

Greenblatt, S., *Renaissance Self-Fashioning. From More to Shakespeare* (Chicago, 1980: University of Chicago Press)

Bibliography

Grotius, H., *De Jure Belli ac Pacis Libri Tres* tr. F.W. Kelsey in Scott, J. Brown, *The Classics of International Law* (Oxford, 1925: Clarendon)

Gunn, J.A.W., '"Interest Will Not Lie": A Seventeenth-Century Political Maxim', *Journal of the History of Ideas*, vol. 29, 1968
Politics and the Public Interest in the 17th Century (London, 1969: Routledge)

Gunnell, J.G., *Political Theory: Tradition and Interpretation* (Cambridge, 1979: Cambridge University Press)

Guthrie, W.K.C., *The Sophists* (Cambridge, 1971: Cambridge University Press)

Hacking, I., 'The Logic of Pascal's Wager', *American Philosophical Quarterly*, vol. 9, 1972, no. 2

Hale, J.R., 'Sixteenth-Century Explanations of War and Violence', *Past and Present*, no. 2, 1971
War and Society in Renaissance Europe, 1450–1620 (London, 1985: Fontana)

Hale, J.R., Highfield, J.R.L. & Smalley, B., eds., *Europe in the Late Middle Ages* (London, 1965: Faber & Faber)

Halliday, F., 'State and Society in International Relations: A Second Agenda' in Dyer, H.C. & Mangasarian, L., eds., *The Study of International Relations* (London, 1989: Macmillan)

Hamilton, B., *Political Thought in Sixteenth-Century Spain* (Oxford, 1963: Oxford University Press)

Hampton, J., *Hobbes and the Social Contract Tradition* (Cambridge, 1986: Cambridge University Press)

Hannaford, I., 'Machiavelli's Concept of Virtù in the Prince and the Discourses Reconsidered', *Political Studies*, vol. 20, 1972, no. 2

Heeren, A.H.L., *Handbuch der Geschichte des Europäischen Staatensystems und seiner Kolonien, Historische Werke*, vol. 9–10 (Göttingen, 1822)

Hegel, G.W.F., *The German Constitution* tr. T.M. Knox, *Hegel's Political Writings* (Oxford, 1964: Clarendon)
Lectures on the Philosophy of World History, trans. H.B. Nisbet (Cambridge, 1975: Cambridge University Press)
Elements of the Philosophy of Right, trans. H.B. Nisbet, A.W. Wood, ed. (Cambridge, 1991: Cambridge University Press)

Hemleben, S.J., *Plans for Peace through Six Centuries* (Chicago, 1943: University of Chicago Press)

Herder, J.G., *Essay on the Origin of Language* in Barnard, F. M., ed. and tr., *J.G. Herder on Social and Political Culture* (Cambridge, 1969: Cambridge University Press)

Herz, J., *Political Realism and Political Idealism: A Study in Theories and Realities* (Chicago, 1951: University of Chicago Press)
International Relations in the Atomic Age (New York, 1959)

Hexter, J.H., *The Vision of Politics on the Eve of Reformation: More, Machiavelli, and Seyssel* (London, 1973: Allen & Unwin)

Hiley, D.R., 'Foucault and the Analysis of Power: Political Engagement Without Liberal Hope or Comfort', *Praxis International*, vol. 4, 1984, no. 2

Hinsley, F.H., *Power and the Pursuit of Peace* (Cambridge, 1967: Cambridge University Press)
Nationalism and the International System (London, 1973: Hodder & Stoughton)
Sovereignty (Cambridge, 1986: Cambridge University Press)
Hintze, O., 'The State in Historical Perspective' in Bendix, R., ed., *State and Society* (Berkeley, 1968: University of California Press)
Hirschmann, A.O., *The Passions and the Interests: Political Arguments for Capitalism before Its Triumph* (Princeton, 1977: Princeton University Press)
Hobbes, T., 'De Corpore' in Molesworth, W., ed., *English Works* (London, 1839–45: Bohn)
'Human Nature' in Molesworth, W., ed., *English Works* (London, 1839–45: Bohn)
Leviathan (Cambridge, 1991: Cambridge University Press)
Hoffmann, S., *The State of War: Essays on the Theory and Practice of International Relations* (New York, 1965: Praeger)
Holsti, K.J., *The Dividing Discipline: Hegemony and Diversity* (Boston, 1985: Allen & Unwin)
Holzgrefe, J.L., 'The Origins of Modern International Relations Theory', *Review of International Studies*, no. 15, 1989
Howard, M., *War in European History* (Oxford, 1976: Oxford University Press)
Humboldt, W., *On the Historian's Task, History and Theory* , vol. 6, 1967
Ingram, D., 'Foucault and the Frankfurter School: A Discourse on Nietzsche, Power and Knowledge', *Praxis International*, vol. 6, 1986, no. 3
'The Postmodern Kantianism of Arendt and Lyotard', *Review of Metaphysics*, vol. 42, 1988
Jackson, R.H., 'Quasi-States, Dual Regimes, and Neoclassical Theory: International Jurisprudence and the Thirld World', *International Organization*, vol. 41, 1987
James, A., *Sovereign Statehood* (London, 1986: Allen & Unwin)
Janssen, P.L., 'Political Thought as Traditionary Action: A Critical Response to Skinner and Pocock', *History and Theory*, vol. 24, 1985, no. 1
John of Salisbury, *Policraticus* (Cambridge, 1990: Cambridge University Press)
Kant, I., *The Critique of Judgment*, trans. J.H. Bernard (New York, 1951: Hafner)
The Critique of Pure Reason, trans. N. Kemp-Smith (London, 1985: Macmillan)
Perpetual Peace, tr. H.B. Nisbet in H. Reiss, ed., *Kant: Political Writings* (Cambridge, 1991: Cambridge University Press)
'The Metaphysics of Morals' in H. Reiss, ed., *Kant: Political Writings* (Cambridge, 1991: Cambridge University Press)
On the Common Saying: "This May be True in Theory, but it does not Apply in Practice" in H. Reiss, ed., *Kant: Political Writings* (Cambridge, 1991: Cambridge University Press)
'Idea for a Universal History with a Cosmopolitan Purpose' in H. Reiss, ed., *Kant: Political Writings* (Cambridge, 1991: Cambridge University Press)
'The Contest of the Faculties' in H. Reiss, ed., *Kant: Political Writings* (Cambridge, 1991: Cambridge University Press)

Kantorowicz, E.H., 'Pro Patria Mori in Medieval Political Thought', *American Historical Review*, vol. 56, 1951
  'Mysteries of State: An Absolutist Concept and its Late Medieval Origins', *Harvard Theological Review*, vol. 48, 1955
  The King's Two Bodies: A Study in Medieval Political Theology (Princeton, 1957: Princeton University Press)
Keane, J., 'More Theses on the Philosophy of History' in J. Tully, ed., *Meaning and Context: Quentin Skinner and his Critics* (Cambridge, 1988: Polity Press)
Keen, M.H., 'The Political Thought of the Fourteenth-Century Civilians' in Smalley, B., ed., *Trends in Medieval Political Thought* (Oxford, 1965: Basil Blackwell)
Keenan, T., 'The "Paradox" of Knowledge and Power: Reading Foucault on a Bias', *Political Theory*, vol. 15, 1987, no. 1
Keens-Soper, M., 'The French Political Academy, 1712: A School for Ambassadors', *European Studies Review*, vol. 2, 1972, no. 4
  'François de Callières and Diplomatic Theory', *Historical Journal*, vol. 16, 1973, no. 3
Kelley, D.R., 'Legal Humanism and the Sense of History', *Studies in the Renaissance*, vol. 13, 1966
  'Murd'rous Machiavel in France: a Post-Mortem', *Political Science Quarterly*, vol. 85, 1970
  Foundations of Modern Historical Scholarship (New York, 1970)
Kelley, D.R., 'Civil Science in the Renaissance: the Problem of Interpretation' in Pagden, A., ed., *The Languages of Political Theory in Early Modern Europe* (Cambridge, 1987: Cambridge University Press)
Kelsen, H., 'Sovereignty and International Law' in Stankiewicz, W. J., ed., *In Defense of Sovereignty* (London, 1969: Oxford University Press)
Kennedy, D., 'Primitive Legal Scholarship', *Harvard International Law Journal*, vol. 27, 1986, no. 1
Keohane, N.O., *Philosophy and the State in France: The Renaissance to the Enlightenment* (Princeton, 1980: Princeton University Press)
Keohane, R.O., ed., *Neorealism and Its Critics* (New York, 1986: Columbia University Press)
Keohane, R.O. & Nye, J.S., *Power and Interdependence: World Politics in Transition* (Boston & Toronto, 1977: Little, Brown & Co)
King, P., *The Ideology of Order: A Comparative Analysis of Jean Bodin and Thomas Hobbes* (London, 1974: Allen & Unwin)
Kingsbury, B. & Robert, A., 'Introduction: Grotian Thought in International Relations' in Bull, H. et al., eds., *Hugo Grotius and International Relations* (Oxford, 1990: Clarendon)
Klein, R.A., *Sovereign Equality Among States: The History of an Idea* (Toronto, 1974: University of Toronto Press)
Knox, T.M., *Hegel's Political Writings*, trans. T.M. Knox (Oxford, 1964: Clarendon)

Knutsen, T.L., *A History of International Relations Theory* (Manchester, 1992: Manchester University Press)

Koselleck, R., *Futures Past: On the Semantics of Historical Time*, tr. K. Tribe (Boston, 1985: MIT Press)

Critique and Crisis: Enlightenment and Pathogenesis of Modern Society (Oxford, 1988: Berg)

Krailsheimer, A.J., *Studies in Self-Interest from Descartes to la Bruyere* (Oxford, 1962)

Kratochwil, F., 'Of Systems, Boundaries, and Territoriality: An Inquiry into the Formation of the State System', *World Politics*, vol. 39, 1986, no. 1

Kriele, M., *Die Demokratische Weltrevolution* (Munich, 1987: Piper)

Kristeller, P.O., *Renaissance Thought*, vol. 1, *The Classic, Scholastic, and Humanistic Strains* (New York, 1961: Harper & Row)

Kuhn, T.S., *The Structure of Scientific Revolutions* (Chicago, 1962: University of Chicago Press)

Kumar, K., *Utopia and Anti-Utopia in Modern Times* (Oxford, 1986: Basil Blackwell)

La Mothe le Vayer, *Œuvres* (Paris, 1662)

Lachterman, D.R., *The Ethics of Geometry: A Genealogy of Modernity* (London, 1989: Routledge)

Laski, H., *Reflections on the Revolution in our Time* (London, 1943: Allen & Unwin)

Laslett, P., ed., *Philosophy, Politics and Society* (Oxford, 1962: Basil Blackwell)

Laue, T.H., *Leopold Ranke: The Formative Years, Princeton Studies in History*, vol. 4, tr. H. Hunt-von Laue (Princeton, 1950: Princeton University Press)

Lewis, J.U., 'Jean Bodin's "Logic of Sovereignty"', *Political Studies*, vol. 16, 1968

Lipsius, J., *Sixe Bookes of Politickes or Civil Doctrine* (London, 1594)

Little, R., 'Deconstructing the Balance of Power: Two Traditions of Thought', *Review of International Studies*, vol. 15, 1989

Locke, J., *An Essay Concerning Human Understanding* (London, 1990: Everyman's)

Louis XIV, *Mémoires for the Instruction of the Dauphin* (New York, 1970)

Lukes, S., *Power: A Radical View* (London, 1974: Macmillan)

Lyons, J.D., *Exemplum: The Rhetoric of Example in Early Modern France and Italy* (Princeton, 1990: Princeton University Press)

Lyotard, J.-F., *L'Enthousiasme: La critique Kantienne de l'histoire* (Paris, 1986: Galilée)

The Differend: Phrases in Dispute (Manchester, 1988: Manchester University Press)

Mably, G.B. de, *Des principes des négociations pour servir d'introduction au droit public de l'Europe, fondé sur les traités* (Amsterdam, 1758)

Machiavelli, N., *The Discourses*, vol. 1, trans. L. Walker (London, 1950: Routledge)

The Art of War, trans. E. Farneworth (Indianapolis, 1965: Bobbs-Merrill)

The Prince, trans. R. Price (Cambridge, 1988: Cambridge University Press)

Bibliography

McCanles, M., *The Discourse of Il Principe* (Malibu, 1983: Undena Publications)

McRae, K.D., *Introduction to Jean Bodin's Six Books* (Cambridge, Mass., 1962: Harvard University Press)

'Bodin and the Development of Empirical Political Science' in Denzer, H., ed., *Jean Bodin: Proceedings* (Munich, 1973: Beck)

Manicas, P.T. & Rosenberg, A., 'Naturalism, Epistemological Individualism and The Strong Programme in the Sociology of Knowledge', *Journal for the Theory of Social Behaviour*, vol. 15, 1985, no. 1

'The Sociology of Scientific Knowledge: Can We Ever Get it Straight?', *Journal for the Theory of Social Behaviour*, vol. 18, 1988, no. 1

Manuel, F., ed., *Reflections on the Philosophy of History of Mankind* (Chicago, 1968: University of Chicago Press)

Maritain, J., 'The Concept of Sovereignty' in Stankiewicz, W.J., ed., *In Defense of Sovereignty* (London, 1969: Oxford University Press)

Marsilius of Padua, *The Defender of Peace*, vol. 2, trans. A. Gewirth (New York, 1956: Columbia University Press)

Mathie, W., 'Reason and Rhetoric in Hobbes Leviathan', *Interpretations*, vol. 14, 1986, no. 2

Mattingly, G., *Renaissance Diplomacy* (London, 1955: Jonathan Cape)

Mayall, J., ed., *The Community of States: A Study in International Political Theory* (London, 1982: Allen & Unwin)

Megill, A., *Prophets of Extremity: Nietzsche, Heidegger, Foucault and Derrida* (Berkeley, 1985: University of California Press)

Meinecke, F., *Machiavellism: The Doctrine of Raison d'Etat and its Place in Modern History* tr. D. Scott (Boulder & London, 1984: Westview)

Merriam, C.E., *History of the Theory of Sovereignty since Rousseau* (New York, 1900: Columbia University Press)

Modelski, G., 'Is World Politics Evolutionary Learning?', *International Organization*, vol. 44, 1990, no. 1

Molé, M., *Mémoirs*, vol. 4 (Paris, 1855–7)

Molesworth, W., ed., *Thomas Hobbes: English Works* (London, 1839–45: Bohn)

Montaigne, M., *Essais* (Paris, 1922: Felix Alcan)

Montesquieu, C.L., *The Spirit of the Laws*, tr. A.M. Cohler et al. (Cambridge, 1989: Cambridge University Press)

More, T., *Selected Letters* (New Haven, 1961: Yale University Press)

'Letter to Peter Giles' in Surtz, E. & Hexter, J.H., eds., *The Complete Works of St. Thomas More*, vol. 4 (New Haven, 1964: Yale University Press)

'Utopia: The Best State of a Commonwealth and the New Island of Utopia' in Surtz, E. & Hexter, J.H., eds., *The Complete Works of St. Thomas More*, vol. 4 (New Haven, 1964: Yale University Press)

Morgenthau, H.J., *Politics Among Nations*, 6th edn (New York, 1985: Knopf)

Naudé, G., *Considerations Politiques sur les Coups d'État* (Amsterdam, 1667)

Navari, C., 'The Origins of The Nation-State' in Tivey, L., ed., *The Nation-State: The Formation of Modern Politics* (Oxford, 1981: Martin Robertson)

Nederman, C.J., 'Aristotelianism and the Origins of "Political Science" in the Twelfth Century', *Journal of the History of Ideas*, vol. 52, 1991, no. 2

Nietzsche, F., *On the Genealogy of Morals*, trans. W. Kaufmann & R.J. Hollingdale (New York, 1969: Vintage Books)
Untimely Meditations, trans. R.J. Hollingdale (Cambridge, 1983: Cambridge University Press)

Nuyen, A.T. 'Truth, Method, and Objectivity: Husserl and Gadamer on Scientific Method', *Philosophy of the Social Sciences*, vol. 20, 1990, no. 4

Olson, W., 'The Growth of a Discipline', in Porter, B. ed., *The Aberystwyth Papers* (London, 1972: Oxford University Press)

Olson, W. & Onuf, N., 'The Growth of a Discipline: Reviewed' in Smith, S. ed., *International Relations: British and American Perspectives* (Oxford, 1985: Basil Blackwell)

Onuf, N., 'Sovereignty: Outline of a Conceptual History', *Alternatives*, vol. 16, 1991

Pagden, A., 'Dispossessing the Barbarian: the Language of Spanish Thomism and the Debate over the Property Rights of the American Indians', in A. Pagden ed., *The Languages of Political Theory in Early Modern Europe* (Cambridge, 1987: Cambridge University Press)

Pagden, A., ed., *The Languages of Political Theory in Early Modern Europe* (Cambridge, 1987: Cambridge University Press)

Paine, T., *The Rights of Man* (Harmondsworth, 1971: Penguin)

Parker, D., *The Making of French Absolutism* (London, 1983: Edward Arnold)

Parry, J.H., *The Establishment of the European Hegemony 1415–1715* (New York, 1961: Harper & Row)

Pelczynski, Z.A., 'The Hegelian Conception of the State' in Z.A. Pelczynski, ed., *Hegel's Political Philosophy: Problems and Perspectives* (Cambridge, 1971: Cambridge University Press)

Pelczynski, Z.A. ed., *Hegel's Political Philosophy: Problems and Perspectives* (Cambridge, 1971: Cambridge University Press)

Phillipson, N. & Skinner, Q., eds., *Political Discourse in Early Modern Britain*, (Cambridge, 1993: Cambridge University Press)

Pico della Mirandola, G., 'Oration on the Dignity of Man' in Cassirer, E., ed., *The Renaissance Philosophy of Man* (Chicago, 1948: University of Chicago Press)

Pizzorno, A., 'On the Individualistic Theory of Social Order' in Bourdieu, P. & Coleman, J.S. eds., *Social Theory for a Changing Society*, (Boulder, 1991: Westview)

Plato, *Gorgias* (Harmondsworth, 1971: Penguin)

Pocock, J.G.A., *The Machiavellian Moment: Florentine Political Thought and the Atlantic Republican Tradition* (Princeton, 1975: Princeton University Press)
'The Concept of Language and the *Métier d'historien*: Some Considerations on Practice' in Pagden, A., ed., *The Languages of Political Theory in Early Modern Europe* (Cambridge, 1987: Cambridge University Press)

Poggi, G., *The Development of the Modern State: A Sociological Introduction* (London, 1978: Hutchinson)

Popkin, R., *History of Scepticism from Erasmus to Spinoza* (Berkeley, 1979: University of California Press)

Popper, K.R., *The Open Society and its Enemies*, vol. 2 (London, 1966: Routledge)
   The Poverty of Historicism (London, 1974: Routledge)
Poppio, A., 'Fate, Fortune, Providence and Human Freedom' in Schmitt C.B.,
   et al., eds., *The Cambridge History of Renaissance Philosophy* (Cambridge,
   1988: Cambridge University Press)
Porter, B., ed., *The Aberytswyth Papers* (London, 1972: Oxford University Press)
Post, G., 'Two Notes on Nationalism in the Middle Ages', *Traditio*, vol. 9, 1953
Price, R., 'The Senses of *Virtù* in Machiavelli', *European Studies Review*, vol. 3,
   1973, no. 4
Priézac, D., *Discours politiques* (Paris, 1652)
Pufendorf, S. von *Of the Law of Nature and of Nations* (Oxford, 1703)
   An Introduction to the History of Principal Kingdoms and States of Europe
   (London, 1711)
   Elementorum Jurisprudentiæ Universalis Libri Duo, tr. W.A. Oldfather in Scott,
   J. Brown, *The Classics of International Law* (Oxford, 1931: Clarendon)
   On the Duty of Man and Citizen According to Natural Law, trans. M. Sil-
   verthorne, ed. J. Tully (Cambridge, 1991: Cambridge University Press)
Putnam, H., *Reason, Truth, and History* (Cambridge, 1981: Cambridge University
   Press)
Quinones, R., *The Renaissance Discovery of Time* (Cambridge, Mass., 1975:
   Harvard University Press)
Raab, F., *The English Face of Machiavelli: A Changing Interpretation 1500–1700*
   (London, 1965: Routledge)
Ranke, L. von, 'A Dialogue on Politics', trans. H. Hunt-von Laue, in Laue, T.H.,
   Leopold Ranke: The Formative Years, Princeton Studies in History, vol. 4
   (Princeton, 1950: Princeton University Press)
   The Great Powers, trans. H. Hunt-von Laue, in Laue, T.H., *Leopold Ranke: The
   Formative Years, Princeton Studies in History*, vol. 4 (Princeton, 1950: Prince-
   ton University Press)
Raynal, G.T., *Histoire philosophique et politique des établissemens et du commerce de
   Européens dans les deux Indes* (Neuchâtel & Geneva, 1783)
Reeves, M., 'Dante Alighieri and Marsiglio of Padua' in Smalley, B., ed., *Trends
   in Medieval Political Thought* (Oxford, 1965: Basil Blackwell)
Richelieu, A.-J., *Testament politique* (Paris, 1947: Lafont)
Ricoeur, P., *Time and Narrative*, vol. 1, trans. K. McLaughlin & D. Pellauer, vol. 3
   tr. K. Blamey & D. Pallauer (Chicago, 1988: Chicago University Press)
Riesenberg, P., *The Inalienability of Sovereignty in Medieval Political Thought* (New
   York, 1956: Columbia University Press)
Riley, P., 'The "Elements" of Kant's Practical Philosophy', *Political Theory*, vol.
   14, 1986, no. 4
Ringmar, E., 'Historical Writing and Rewriting: Gustav II Adolf, the French
   Revolution, and the Historians', *Scandinavian Journal of History*, forth-
   coming
Robertson, J.M., ed., *The Philosophical Works of Francis Bacon* (London, 1905:
   Routledge)

Rohan, H., *De l'interest des Princes et Estats de la Chrestienté* (Paris, 1643: Augustin Courbé)

Rokkan, S., 'Dimensions of State Formation and Nation-Building: A Possible Paradigm for Research on Variations within Europe' in Tilly, C., ed., *The Formation of Nation State in Western Europe* (Princeton, 1975: Princeton University Press)

Rorty, R., *Philosophy and the Mirror of Nature* (Oxford, 1980: Basil Blackwell)

'The Historiography of Philosophy: Four Genres' in Rorty, R., Schneewind, J.B. & Skinner, Q., eds., *Philosophy in History: Essays on the Historiography of Philosophy* (Cambridge, 1984: Cambridge University Press)

Essays on Heidegger and Others, Philosophical Papers, vol. 2 (Cambridge, 1991: Cambridge University Press)

Rorty, R. et al. eds., *Philosophy in History: Essays on the Historiography of Philosophy* (Cambridge, 1984: Cambridge University Press)

Rosenau, J.N., *Sovereignty in a Turbulent World*, Paper presented at the Conference on Sovereignty and Collective Intervention, Hanover, NH, (18–20 May 1992)

Rosencrance, R., *The Rise of the Trading State* (New York, 1986: Basic Books)

Ross, S.D., 'Foucault's Radical Politics', *Praxis International*, vol. 5, 1985, no. 2

Rossini, G., 'The Criticism of Rhetorical Historiography and the Ideal of Scientific Method: History, Nature and Science in the Political Language of Thomas Hobbes' in Pagden, A., ed., *The Languages of Political Theory in Early Modern Europe* (Cambridge, 1988: Cambridge University Press)

Roth, M.S., 'Foucault's "History of the Present"', *History and Theory*, vol. 20, 1981, no. 1

Knowing and History: Appropriations of Hegel in Twentieth-Century France (Ithaca, 1988: Cornell University Press)

Rousseau, J.-J., *A Discourse on the Origin of Inequality* in Cole, G.D.H., ed., *The Social Contract and Discourses* (London, 1990: Everyman's)

L'État de Guerre in Vaughan, C.E., ed., *The Political Writings of Jean-Jacques Rousseau*, vol. 1 (Cambridge, 1915: Cambridge University Press)

Extrait du Projet de Paix Perpetuelle de M. l'Abbé de Saint Pierre in Vaughan, C.E., ed., *The Political Writings of Jean-Jacques Rousseau*, vol. 1 (Cambridge, 1915: Cambridge University Press)

'Jugement sur la paix perpétuelle' in Vaughan, C.E., ed., *The Political Writings of Jean-Jacques Rousseau*, vol. 1 (Cambridge, 1915: Cambridge University Press)

Émile (Paris, 1929: Garnier)

A Discourse on Political Economy in Cole, G.D.H., ed. and tr., *The Social Contract and Discourses* (London, 1990: Everyman's)

The Social Contract in Cole, G.D.H., ed. and tr., *The Social Contract and Discourses*, (London, 1990: Everyman's)

Rousset, J., *Les interêts presens des Puissances de l'Europe*, vols. 1–3 (The Hague, 1733)

Rubiés, J.-P., 'Hugo Grotius's Dissertation on the Origin of the American

Peoples and the Use of Comparative Methods', *Journal of the History of Ideas*, vol. 52, 1991, no. 2

Rubinstein, N., 'Marsilius of Padua and Italian Political Thought of his Time' in Hale, J.R., Highfield, J.R.L. & Smalley, B., eds., *Europe in the Late Middle Ages* (London, 1965: Faber & Faber)

'The History of the Word *Politicus* in Early-Modern Europe' in Pagden, A., ed., *The Languages of Political Theory in Early Modern Europe* (Cambridge, 1987: Cambridge University Press)

Rubinstein, N., ed., *Florentine Studies: Politics and Society in Renaissance Florence* (London, 1968: Faber & Faber)

Ruggie, J.G., 'Continuity and Transformation in the World Polity' in Keohane, R., ed., *Neorealism and Its Critics* (New York, 1986: Columbia University Press).

'International Structure and International Transformation: Space, Time and Method' in Czempiel, E.O. & Rosenau, J.N., eds., *Global Changes and Theoretical Challenges* (Lexington, 1989: Lexington Books)

Rundell, J.F., *Origins of Modernity: The Origins of Modern Social Theory From Kant to Hegel to Marx* (Cambridge, 1987: Polity Press)

Saner, H., *Kant's Political Thought: Its Origins and Developments* trans. E.B. Ashton (Chicago, 1973: University of Chicago Press)

Schelling, T., *The Strategy of Conflict* (Cambridge, Mass., 1960: Harvard University Press)

Schmitt, C., *Political Theology: Four Chapters on the Concept of Sovereignty*, tr. G. Schwab (Boston, 1985: MIT Press)

Schnur, R. ed., *Staatsräson: Studien zur Geschichte eines politischen Begriffs* (Berlin, 1975: Duncker & Humblot)

Scott, J. Brown, *The Classics of International Law* (Washington, 1911–50: Carnegie)

The Spanish Origin of International Law: Francisco de Vitoria and his Law of Nations, *Carnegie Endowment for International Peace* (Oxford, 1934: Clarendon)

Searle, J., 'Minds, Brains, and Programs', *Behavioral and Brain Sciences*, vol. 3, 1980, no. 3

Intentionality: An Essay in the Philosophy of Mind (Cambridge, 1983: Cambridge University Press)

Seidman, S., 'Beyond Presentism and Historicism: Understanding the History of Social Science', *Sociological Inquiry*, vol. 53, 1983, no. 1

Seigel, J.E., *Rhetoric and Philosophy in Renaissance Humanism: The Union of Eloquence and Wisdom. Petrach to Valla* (Princeton, 1968: Princeton University Press)

Service, E.R., *Origins of State and Civilization* (New York, 1975: Norton)

Shapiro, M., 'Mirror and Portrait: The Structure of *Il Libro del Cortegiano*', *Journal of Medieval and Renaissance Studies*, vol. 5, 1975, no. 1

Shiner, L., 'Reading Focault: Anti-Method and the Genealogy of Power/Knowledge', *History and Theory*, vol. 20, 1982, no. 3

Skinner, Q., *Foundations of Modern Political Thought*, vol. 1, *The Renaissance*, vol. 2, *The Reformation* (Cambridge, 1978: Cambridge University Press)

'Sir Thomas More's Utopia and the Language of Renaissance Humanism' in Pagden, A., ed., *The Languages of Political Theory in Early Modern Europe* (Cambridge, 1988: Cambridge University Press)

'Meaning and Understanding in the History of Ideas', in Tully, J. ed. *Meaning and Context: Quentin Skinner and His Critics* (Cambridge, 1988: Polity Press)

'A Reply to my Critics' in J. Tully ed. *Meaning and Context: Quentin Skinner and his Critics* (Cambridge, 1988: Polity Press)

'Social Meaning and the Explanation of Social Action', in J. Tully ed. *Meaning and Context: Quentin Skinner and his Critics* (Cambridge, 1988: Polity Press)

'The State' in Ball, T. et al., eds., *Political Innovation and Conceptual Change* (Cambridge 1989: Cambridge University Press)

'"Scientia Civilis" in Classical Rhetoric and in the Early Hobbes', in Phillipson, N. & Skinner, Q., eds., *Political Discourse in Early Modern Britain* (Cambridge, 1993: Cambridge University Press)

Skinner, Q. & Schmitt, C.B., eds., *The Cambridge History of Renaissance Philosophy* (Cambridge, 1987: Cambridge University Press)

Skocpol, T., *States and Social Revolutions: A Comparative Analysis of France, Russia and China* (Cambridge, 1979: Cambridge University Press)

'Bringing the State Back in: Strategies of Analysis in Current Research' in Evans, P. et al., eds., *Bringing the State Back In* (Cambridge, 1985: Cambridge University Press)

Smalley, B., ed., *Trends in Medieval Political Thought* (Oxford, 1965: Oxford University Press)

Smith, S., ed., *International Relations: British and American Perspectives* (Oxford, 1985: Basil Blackwell)

Söllner, Alfons, 'German Conservatism in America: Morgenthau's Political Realism', *Telos*, no. 72, 1987

Spinoza, B., *A Treatise partly Theological and partly Political* (London, 1737)

Ethics (London, 1959: Dent)

Stankiewicz, W.J., *Politics and Religion in Seventeenth Century France* (Berkeley, 1960: University of California Press)

'In Defense of Sovereignty: A Critique and an Interpretation' in Stankiewicz, W.J., ed., *In Defense of Sovereignty*, (Oxford, 1969: Oxford University Press)

Stankiewich, W.J., ed., *In Defense of Sovereignty* (Oxford, 1969: Oxford University Press)

Steinberger, P.J., *Logic and Politics: Hegel's Philosophy of Right* (New Haven, 1988: Yale University Press)

Stern, F., ed., *The Varieties of History: From Voltaire to the Present* (New York, 1956: Meridian Books)

Strauss, L., *Thoughts on Machiavelli* (Glencoe, Ill., 1958: The Free Press)

What is Political Philosophy? and Other Studies (Glencoe, Ill., 1959: The Free Press)

Strayer, J., *On the Medieval Origins of the Modern State* (Princeton, 1970: Princeton University Press)

Strong, R., *Art and Power: Renaissance Festivals 1450–1650* (Woodbridge, 1984: Boydell)

Suganami, H., 'A Note on the Origin of the Word "International"', *British Journal of International Studies*, vol. 4, 1978

    The Domestic Analogy and World Order Proposals (Cambridge, 1989: Cambridge University Press)

Surtz, E., 'Utopia as a Work of Literary Art' in Surtz, E. & Hexter, J.H., eds., *The Complete Works of St. Thomas More*, vol. 4 (New Haven, 1964: Yale University Press)

Sutcliffe, F.E., 'La notion de Raison d'État dans la pensée française et espagnole au XVIIe siècle' in Schnur, R., ed., *Staatsräson: Studien zur Geschichte eines politischen Begriffs* (Berlin, 1975: Dunker & Humblot)

Taylor, C., *Hegel* (Cambridge, 1975: Cambridge University Press)

    'The Hermeneutics of Conflict' in J. Tully, ed., *Meaning and Context: Quentin Skinner and His Critics* (Cambridge, 1988: Polity Press)

Thiele, L.P., 'The Agony of Politics: The Nietzschean Roots of Foucault's Political Thought', *American Political Science Review*, vol. 84, 1991, no. 3

Tilly, C., 'Reflections on the History of European State-Making' in Tilly, C., ed., *The Formation of National States in Western Europe* (Princeton, 1975: Princeton University Press)

    'Western State-Making and Theories of Political Transformation, in Tilly, C., ed., *The Formation of National States in Western Europe* (Princeton, 1975: Princeton University Press)

Tivey, L., ed., *The Nation-State: The Formation of Modern Politics* (Oxford, 1981: Martin Robertson)

Todorov, T., *The Conquest of America: The Question of the Other*, tr. R. Howard (New York, 1992: Harper & Row)

Tuck, R., *Natural Rights Theories: Their Origin and Development*, (Cambridge, 1979: Cambridge University Press)

Tully, J., 'The Pen is a Mighty Sword: Quentin Skinner's Analysis of Politics' in J. Tully, ed., *Meaning and Context: Quentin Skinner and his Critics* (Cambridge, 1988: Polity Press)

Ullmann, W., *A History of Political Thought: The Middle Ages* (Harmondsworth, 1975: Penguin)

    'The Development of the Medieval Idea of Sovereignty', *English Historical Review*, vol. 64, 1949, no. 250

    Principles of Government in the Middle Ages (London, 1961)

    Law and Politics in the Middle Ages: An Introduction to the Sources of Medieval Political Ideas (Ithaca, 1975: Cornell University Press)

    Medieval Foundations of Renaissance Humanism (London, 1977: Paul Elek)

Valla, L., *The Treatise on the Donation of Constantine*, tr. C.B. Coleman (New Haven, 1922: Yale University Press)

Vasquez, J., *The Power of Power Politics* (London, 1983: Frances Pinter)

Vattel, E. de, *The Law of Nations or the Principles of Natural Law, Applied to the Conduct and to the Affairs of Nations and Sovereigns*, tr. C.G. Fenwick in Scott, J. Brown, ed., *The Classics of International Law* (Washington, 1916: Carnegie)

Vaughan, C.E., ed., *The Political Writings of Jean-Jacques Rousseau*, vol. 1–2 (Cambridge, 1915: Cambridge University Press)

Verene, P., *Vico's Science of Imagination* (Ithaca, 1981: Cornell University Press)

Veyne, P., *Did the Greeks Believe in Their Myths? An Essay on the Constitutive Imagination*, trans. P. Wissig (Chicago, 1988: University of Chicago Press)

Vico, G., *The New Science*, trans. T.G. Bergin & M.H. Fisch (Ithaca, 1968: Cornell University Press)

Vincent, A., *Theories of the State* (Oxford, 1987: Basil Blackwell)

Viner, J., 'Power versus Plenty as Objectives of Foreign Policy in the Seventeenth and Eighteenth Centuries', *World Politics*, vol. 1, 1948, no. 1

Viroli, M., *From Politics to Reason of State: The Acquisition and Transformation of Language of Politics 1250–1600* (Cambridge, 1992: Cambridge University Press)

Visker, R., 'Can Genealogy be Critical? A Somewhat Unromantic Look at Nietzsche and Foucault', *Man and World*, vol. 23, 1990

Vitoria, F., 'De Indis Recenter Inventis: De Iure Bello' in Scott, J. Brown, ed., *The Classics of International Law* (Washington, 1917: Carnegie)

'De Indis I-II' in Scott, J. Brown, ed., *The Spanish Origin of International Law* (Oxford, 1934: Clarendon)

'De Jure Gentium et Naturali' in Scott, J. Brown, ed., *The Spanish Origin of International Law* (Oxford, 1934: Clarendon)

'De Potestate Civili' in Scott, J. Brown, ed., *The Spanish Origin of International Law* (Oxford, 1934: Clarendon)

'De Potestate Ecclesiae I' in Scott, J. Brown, ed., *The Spanish Origin of International Law* (Oxford, 1934: Clarendon)

Walker, R.B.J., 'The Prince and "the Pauper": Tradition, Modernity and Practice in the Theory of International Relations' in DerDerian, J. & Shapiro, M.J., eds., *International/Intertextual Relations* (Lexington, 1989: Lexington Books)

'Security, Sovereignty, and the Challenge of World Politics', *Alternatives*, vol. 15, 1990

'Sovereignty, Identity, Community: Reflections on the Horizons of Contemporary Political Practice' in Walker, R.B.J. & Mendlovitz, S., eds., *Contending Sovereignties: Redefining Political Community* (Boulder, 1990: Lynne)

Inside/Outside: International Relations as Political Theory (Cambridge, 1993: Cambridge University Press)

Walker, R.B.J. & Mendlovitz, S., eds., *Contending Sovereignties: Redefining Political Community* (Boulder, 1990: Lynne)

Wallerstein, I., 'The Rise and the Future Demise of the World Capitalist System: Concepts for Comparative Analysis', *Comparative Studies in Society and History*, vol. 16, 1974

Bibliography

Waltz, K.N., *Man, the State, and War: A Theoretical Analysis* (New York, 1959: Columbia University Press)
   'Kant, Liberalism, and War', *American Political Science Review*, vol. 56, 1962
   'Laws and Theories' in Keohane, R., ed., *Neorealism and its Critics* (New York, 1986: Columbia University Press)
   'Reductionist and Systemic Theories' in Keohane, R., ed., *Neorealism and Its Critics* (New York, 1986: Columbia University Press)
   'Political Structure' in Keohane, R., ed., *Neorealism and its Critics* (New York, 1986: Columbia University Press)
   'Anarchic Orders and Balances of Power' in Keohane, R., ed., *Neorealism and Its Critics* (New York, 1986: Columbia University Press)
   'A Response to My Critics' in Keohane, R., ed., *Neorealism and Its Critics*, (New York, 1986: Columbia University Press)
Walzer, M., *The Revolution of the Saints* (London, 1966: Weidenfeld & Nicolson)
   The Company of Critics (New York, 1988: Basic Books)
Watson, A., 'European International Society and Its Expansion' in Bull, H. & Watson, A., eds., *The Expansion of International Society* (Oxford, 1984: Clarendon)
Weber, C., 'Reconsidering Statehood: Examining the Sovereignty/Intervention Boundary', *Review of International Studies*, vol. 18, 1992
Weber, M., *Economy and Society: An Outline of Interpretive Sociology*, ed. G. Roth and C. Wittich (New York, 1968: Bedminster Press)
Weisinger, H., 'Ideas of History during the Renaissance', *Journal of the History of Ideas*, vol. 6, 1945
   'Renaissance Theory of the Reaction against Middle Ages as Cause of the Renaissance', *Speculum*, vol. 20, 1945
Wendt, A., 'The Agent-Structure Problem in International Relations Theory', *International Organization*, vol. 41, 1987, no. 3
Wendt, A. & Duvall, R., 'Institutions and International Order' in Czempiel, C.O. & Rosenau, J.N., eds., *Global Changes and Theoretical Challenges* (Lexington, 1989: Lexington Books)
White, H., *Metahistory: The Historical Imagination in Nineteenth-Century Europe* (London and Baltimore, 1973: Johns Hopkins)
Wicquefort, A., *L'Ambassadeur et ses fonctions* (Cologne, 1690)
Wight, M., *Systems of States* (Leicester, 1977: Leicester University Press)
   Power Politics, ed. by H. Bull & C. Holbraad (Leicester, 1978: Leicester University Press)
Wight, M. & Butterfield, H. eds., *Diplomatic Investigations* (London, 1966: Allen & Unwin)
Wilks, M., *The Problem of Sovereignty in the Later Middle Ages: The Papal Monarchy with Augustinus Triumphus and the Publicists* (Cambridge, 1963: Cambridge University Press)
Williams, H., *International Relations in Political Theory* (Milton Keynes, 1989: Open University Press)

Wilson, I.M., *The Influence of Hobbes and Locke in the Shaping of the Concept of Sovereignty in Eighteenth-Century France* (Banbury, 1973)

Wolf, J.B., *Toward a European Balance of Power, 1620–1715* (Chicago, 1970: Chicago University Press)

Wood, N., 'Machiavelli's Concept of *Virtú* Reconsidered', *Political Studies*, vol. 15, 1967, no. 2

Wright, M., 'Central but Ambiguous: States and International Theory', *Review of International Studies*, vol. 10, 1984

Wrong, D., *Power: Its Forms, Bases and Uses* (Oxford, 1979: Basil Blackwell)

Yates, F.A., *Giordano Bruno and the Hermetic Tradition* (London, 1964: Routledge)

Young, R., *White Mythologies* (London, 1990: Routledge)

Yovel, Y., *Kant and the Philosophy of History* (Princeton, 1980: Princeton University Press)

Zagorin, P., 'Historiography and Postmodernism: Reconsiderations', *History and Theory*, vol. 24, 1990, no. 1

Index

CAMBRIDGE STUDIES IN INTERNATIONAL RELATIONS

For EU product safety concerns, contact us at Calle de José Abascal, 56–1°,
28003 Madrid, Spain or eugpsr@cambridge.org.

www.ingramcontent.com/pod-product-compliance
Ingram Content Group UK Ltd.
Pitfield, Milton Keynes, MK11 3LW, UK
UKHW042149130625
459647UK00011B/1251